EX LIBRIS

VINTAGE CLASSICS

PARADISE LOST

John Milton was born on 9 December 1608. He studied at St Paul's School and then at Christ's College, Cambridge. He wrote poetry in Latin and Italian as well as English and travelled in Italy between 1638 and 1639. He married Mary Powell in 1642 but their relationship quickly broke down and they lived apart until 1645, when Mary returned to him. They had four children, three daughters and a son who died in infancy. During the Interregnum after the execution of Charles I, Milton worked for the civil service and wrote pamphlets in support of the new republic as well as beginning work on his masterpiece, *Paradise Lost*. His first wife died in 1652 and he married again in 1656, although his second wife died not long afterwards in 1658. When the monarchy was restored in 1660 Milton was arrested but was released with a fine. In 1663 he married his third wife and he is thought to have finished *Paradise Lost* in this same year. He published the companion poem, *Paradise Regained*, in 1671.

John Milton died on 8 November 1674.

OTHER POETICAL WORKS BY JOHN MILTON

Comus

Lycidas

Samson Agonistes

Poems

JOHN MILTON

Paradise Lost

AND

Paradise Regained

EDITED BY
Gordon Campbell

VINTAGE BOOKS
London

Published by Vintage 2008

2 4 6 8 10 9 7 5 3 1

Paradise Lost was first published in 1667
Paradise Regained was first published in 1671

Vintage
Random House, 20 Vauxhall Bridge Road,
London SW1V 2SA

www.vintage-classics.info

Addresses for companies within The Random House Group Limited
can be found at: www.randomhouse.co.uk/offices.htm

The Random House Group Limited Reg. No. 954009

A CIP catalogue record for this book
is available from the British Library

ISBN 9780099529460

The Random House Group Limited supports The Forest
Stewardship Council (FSC), the leading international forest
certification organisation. All our titles that are printed on
Greenpeace approved FSC certified paper carry the FSC logo.
Our paper procurement policy can be found at:
www.rbooks.co.uk/environment

Printed and bound in Great Britain by
CPI Cox & Wyman, Reading RG1 8EX

ParadiseLost.

A

POEM

IN

TWELVE BOOKS

The Author
John Milton.

COMMENDATORY POEMS

IN *PARADISUM AMISSAM*
SUMMI POETÆ
JOHANNIS MILTONI

Qui Legis *Amissam Paradisum*, grandia magni
    Carmina Miltoni, quid nisi cuncta legis?
Res cunctas, et cunctarum primordia rerum
    Et fata, et fines, continet iste liber.
Intima panduntur magni penetralia mundi,
    Scribitur et toto quicquid in orbe latet;
Terræque, tractusque maris, cœlumque profundum,
    Sulphureumque Erebi flammivomumque specus;
Quæque colunt terras, pontumque, et Tartara cæca,
    Quæque colunt summi lucida regna poli;
Et quodcunque ullis conclusum est finibus usquam;
    Et sine fine chaos, et sine fine Deus;
Et sine fine magis, si quid magis est sine fine,
    In Christo erga homines conciliatus amor.
Hæc qui speraret quis crederet esse futurum?
    Et tamen hæc hodie terra Britanna legit.
O quantos in bella duces, quæ protulit arma!
    Quæ canit, et quantâ prælia dira tubâ!
Cœlestes acies, atque in certamine coelum!
    Et quæ cœlestes pugna deceret agros!
Quantus in ætheriis tollis se Lucifer armis,
    Atque ipso graditur vix Michæle minor!
Quantis et quam funestis concurritur iris,
    Dum ferus hic stellas protegit, ille rapit!
Dum vulsos montes ceu tela reciproca torquent,
    Et non mortali desuper igne pluunt,
Stat dubius cui se parti concedat Olympus,
    Et metuit pugnæ non superesse suæ.
At simul in cœlis Messiæ insignis fulgent,
    Et currus animes, armaque digna Deo,
Horrendumque rotæ strident, et sæva rotarum
    Erumpunt torvis fulgura luminibus,
Et flammæ vibrant, et vera tonitrua rauco
    Admistis flammis insonuere polo,
Excidit attonitis mens omnis, et impetus omnis,

Et cassis dextris irrita tela cadunt;
Ad pœnas fugiunt, et, ceu foret Orcus asylum,
   Infernis certant condere se tenebris.
Cedite, Romani scriptores; cedite, Graii;
   Et quos fama recens vel celebravit anus:
Hæc quicunque leget tantum cecinisse putabit
   Mæonidem ranas, Virgilium culices.

                                              S.B., M.D.

In Paradisum Amissam
On Paradise Lost, by John Milton, the Greatest Poet.

You who read Paradise Lost, the sublime poem of the great Milton, what do you read except the whole poem? That book contains all things, the first beginnings of all things, their destinies and their final ends. The innermost chambers of the great world are thrown open and whatever in the world lies hidden is described: the lands and the stretches of sea, the depths of the heavens, and the sulphurous, flame-vomiting den of Erebus; all that dwell on earth, in the sea, and in dark Tartarus and in the bright kingdom of highest heaven; whatever is confined anywhere by any bounds, and also boundless chaos and boundless God, and more that is boundless, if anything be more without limits, love among men united in Christ. Who that had hoped for this would believe that it would ever be written? And yet the land of Britain reads these things today. O, what leaders in war, what arms, appear! What fearful battles he sings on the war-trumpet! Celestial armies and heaven in conflict! What a battle, fit for the celestial fields! What a Lucifer, bearing ethereal armour, and as he walks, hardly inferior to Michael himself! With what great and deadly anger do they join battle. While the latter fiercely defends the stars the former assaults. While they fling uprooted mountains at each other as darts, rain falls from above with immortal fire. Olympus stands doubtful to which side it will submit, and fears that it may not survive its own battle. But as soon as the standards of the Messiah glisten in the heavens with living chariots and armour worthy of God, the wheels creak horribly and fierce flashes burst forth from savage eyes, the flames threaten and real thunder mixed with flames resounds hoarsely in the heavens. All the boldness and fury of the amazed foe fails, and useless weapons fall from hands that have lost all strength. They flee to their punishments as if Orcus were a refuge and they struggle to hide themselves in the infernal darkness. Yield writers of Rome, yield writers of Greece and those whom fame, recent or ancient, has celebrated. Who reads this poem will think Maeonides sang of frogs, Virgil of gnats.

[The author of the poem was probably Milton's physician friend, Dr Samuel Barrow. The last line refers to the pseudo-Homeric *Batrachomyomachia* ('Battle of the Frogs and Mice') and to Virgil's *Culex* ('Gnat').]

ON PARADISE LOST

When I beheld the poet blind, yet bold,
In slender book his vast design unfold –
Messiah crowned, God's reconciled decree,
Rebelling angels, the forbidden tree,
Heaven, hell, earth, chaos, all – the argument   5
Held me a while misdoubting his intent,
That he would ruin (for I saw him strong)
The sacred truths to fable and old song
(So Samson groped the temple's posts in spite),
The world o'erwhelming to revenge his sight.   10
    Yet, as I read, soon growing less severe,
I liked his project, the success did fear –
Through that wide field how he his way should find
O'er which lame faith leads understanding blind;
Lest he perplexed the things he would explain,   15
And what was easy he should render vain.
    Or, if a work so infinite he spanned,
Jealous I was that some less skilful hand
(Such as disquiet always what is well,
And by ill-imitating would excel)   20
Might hence presume the whole creation's day
To change in scenes, and show it in a play.
    Pardon me, mighty poet; nor despise
My causeless, yet not impious, surmise.
But I am now convinced, and none will dare   25
Within thy labours to pretend a share.
Thou hast not missed one thought that could be fit,
And all that was improper dost omit;
So that no room is here for writers left,
But to detect their ignorance or theft.   30
    That majesty which through thy work doth reign
Draws the devout, deterring the profane.
And things divine thou treat'st of in such state
As them preserves, and thee, inviolate.
At once delight and horror on us seize;   35
Thou sing'st with so much gravity and ease,

9] Milton had published *SA* in 1671.
18–22] The lines allude to Dryden, to whom (according to John Aubrey) Milton
    had granted permission to 'putt his Paradise Lost into a drama in rhymne'.

And above human flight dost soar aloft
With plume so strong, so equal, and so soft.
The bird named from the paradise you sing
So never flags, but always keeps on wing.   40
   Where could'st thou words of such a compass find?
Whence furnish such a vast expense of mind?
Just heaven, thee like Tiresias to requite,
Rewards with prophecy thy loss of sight.
   Well might'st thou scorn thy readers to allure   45
With tinkling rhyme, of thy own sense secure;
While the Town-Bayes writes all the while and spells,
And, like a pack-horse, tires without his bells.
Their fancies like our bushy points appear;
The poets tag them, we for fashion wear.   50
I too, transported by the mode, offend,
And, while I meant to praise thee, must commend.
Thy verse, created, like thy theme sublime,
In number, weight, and measure, needs not rhyme.

                                                 A.M.

39–40] Birds of Paradise were popularly believed to have no feet, and therefore
    to be perpetually in flight.
43 Tiresias] See *PL* III 36n.
47 Bayes] a popular nickname for Dryden, originating in the satire on Dryden
    in Buckingham's *The Rehearsal* (1672).
45–54] Rhyme was a much-debated subject at the time. Marvell alludes
    specifically to Milton's remarks on the subject in his note on 'The Verse'
    (p. 148).
49 bushy points] tasselled hose-fasteners.
    A.M.] Andrew Marvell.

THE PRINTER TO THE READER

Courteous reader, there was no argument at first intended to the book, but for the satisfaction of many that have desired it, I have procured it, and withal a reason of that which stumbled many others: why the poem rhymes not.

S. Simmons

THE VERSE

The measure is English heroic verse without rhyme, as that of Homer in Greek, and of Virgil in Latin – rhyme being no necessary adjunct or true ornament of poem or good verse, in longer works especially, but the invention of a barbarous age, to set off wretched matter and lame metre; graced indeed since by the use of some famous modern poets, carried away by custom, but much to their own vexation, hindrance, and constraint to express many things otherwise, and for the most part worse, than else they would have expressed them. Not without cause therefore some both Italian and Spanish poets[1] of prime note have rejected rhyme both in longer and shorter works, as have also long since our best English tragedies, as a thing of itself, to all judicious ears, trivial and of no true musical delight; which consists only in apt numbers, fit quantity of syllables, and the sense variously drawn out from one verse into another, not in the jingling sound of like endings – a fault avoided by the learned ancients both in poetry and all good oratory. This neglect then of rhyme so little is to be taken for a defect, though it may seem so perhaps to vulgar readers, that it rather is to be esteemed an example set, the first in English, of ancient liberty recovered to heroic poem from the troublesome and modern bondage of rhyming.

[1]Spanish poets] Spanish poetry was normally rhymed, but blank verse (*versos sueltos*) was introduced into Spain (at the invitation of the Venetian ambassador) by Joan Boscà Almugaver in *Leandro* (1543), and was subsequently used by Boscà's friend Garcilaso de la Vega; it was later popularised by Cervantes' friend Francisco de Figueroa. The form was never acclimatised, and was always seen as a conscious imitation of the Italian *versi sciolti*.

PARADISE LOST

BOOK I

THE ARGUMENT

This first book proposes, first in brief, the whole subject – man's disobedience, and the loss thereupon of Paradise, wherein he was placed: then touches the prime cause of his fall – the serpent, or rather Satan in the serpent; who, revolting from God, and drawing to his side many legions of angels, was, by the command of God, driven out of heaven, with all his crew, into the great deep. Which action passed over, the poem hastens into the midst of things; presenting Satan, with his angels, now fallen into hell – described here not in the centre (for heaven and earth may be supposed as yet not made, certainly not yet accursed) but in a place of utter darkness, fitliest called Chaos. Here Satan, with his angels lying on the burning lake, thunderstruck and astonished, after a certain space recovers, as from confusion; calls up him who, next in order and dignity, lay by him; they confer of their miserable fall. Satan awakens all his legions, who lay till then in the same manner confounded; they rise: their numbers; array of battle; their chief leaders named, according to the idols known afterwards in Canaan and the countries adjoining. To these Satan directs his speech; comforts them with hope yet of regaining heaven; but tells them, lastly, of a new world and new kind of creature to be created, according to an ancient prophecy, or report, in heaven – for that angels were long before this visible creation was the opinion of many ancient fathers. To find out the truth of this prophecy, and what to determine thereon, he refers to a full council. What his associates thence attempt. Pandemonium, the palace of Satan, rises, suddenly built out of the deep: the infernal peers there sit in council.

Of man's first disobedience, and the fruit
Of that forbidden tree whose mortal taste
Brought death into the world, and all our woe,
With loss of Eden, till one greater man
Restore us, and regain the blissful seat, 5
Sing, heavenly Muse, that, on the secret top
Of Oreb, or of Sinai, didst inspire

---

1 fruit] means 'fruit' and 'result'.
4 greater man] Jesus. See Rom. v. 12, 19.
6 heavenly Muse] Urania. See *PL* VII 1n.
7-8] Moses saw the burning bush on Mount Horeb (Exod. iii). There is some confusion in the Pentateuch about the mountain on which Moses received the tablets of the law, for the names Sinai and Horeb seem to be interchangeable. See Exod. xix. 16-25 and Deut. iv. 10-13. The 'chosen seed' is Israel, whom Moses taught about the creation in Genesis.

That shepherd who first taught the chosen seed
In the beginning how the heavens and earth
Rose out of chaos: or, if Zion hill   10
Delight thee more, and Siloa's brook that flowed
Fast by the oracle of God, I thence
Invoke thy aid to my adventurous song,
That with no middle flight intends to soar
Above the Aonian mount, while it pursues   15
Things unattempted yet in prose or rhyme.
And chiefly thou, O Spirit, that dost prefer
Before all temples the upright heart and pure,
Instruct me, for thou know'st; thou from the first
Wast present, and, with mighty wings outspread   20
Dove-like sat'st brooding on the vast abyss,
And mad'st it pregnant: what in me is dark
Illumine, what is low raise and support:
That, to the height of this great argument,
I may assert eternal providence,   25
And justify the ways of God to men.
    Say first – for heaven hides nothing from thy view,
Nor the deep tract of hell – say first what cause
Moved our grand parents, in that happy state,
Favoured of heaven so highly, to fall off   30
From their creator, and transgress his will
For one restraint, lords of the world besides.
Who first seduced them to that foul revolt?
    The infernal serpent; he it was whose guile,
Stirred up with envy and revenge, deceived   35
The mother of mankind, what time his pride
Had cast him out from heaven, with all his host
Of rebel angels, by whose aid, aspiring
To set himself in glory above his peers,
He trusted to have equalled the most high,   40
If he opposed, and, with ambitious aim
Against the throne and monarchy of God,
Raised impious war in heaven and battle proud,

10 Zion hill] one of the hills of Jerusalem, and the site of the temple.
11 Siloa] a pool near the temple in Jerusalem. See Isa. viii. 6, John ix. 7, 11.
15 Aonian mount] Helicon, home of the muses.
16] An ironic translation of a line in the second octave of Ariosto's *Orlando Furioso*: 'Cosa non detta in prosa mai, né in rima'.
21] Gen. i. 2; Luke iii. 22.
34 infernal serpent] Satan. See Rev. xii. 9.
38-48] a tissue of Biblical phrases (e.g. Isa. xiv. 13-15, Luke x. 18, Rev. xvii. 8, II Pet. ii. 4, Jude 6).

With vain attempt. Him the almighty power
Hurled headlong flaming from the ethereal sky,   45
With hideous ruin and combustion, down
To bottomless perdition, there to dwell
In adamantine chains and penal fire,
Who durst defy the omnipotent to arms.
   Nine times the space that measures day and night   50
To mortal men, he with his horrid crew
Lay vanquished, rolling in the fiery gulf,
Confounded, though immortal: but his doom
Reserved him to more wrath; for now the thought
Both of lost happiness and lasting pain   55
Torments him; round he throws his baleful eyes,
That witnessed huge affliction and dismay,
Mixed with obdurate pride and steadfast hate;
At once, as far as angels ken, he views
The dismal situation waste and wild: 60
A dungeon horrible, on all sides round,
As one great furnace flamed, yet from those flames
No light, but rather darkness visible
Served only to discover sights of woe,
Regions of sorrow, doleful shades, where peace   65
And rest can never dwell, hope never comes
That comes to all, but torture without end
Still urges, and a fiery deluge, fed
With ever-burning sulphur unconsumed:
Such place eternal justice had prepared   70
For those rebellious; here their prison ordained
In utter darkness, and their portion set,
As far removed from God and light of heaven
As from the centre thrice to the utmost pole.
O how unlike the place from whence they fell!   75
There the companions of his fall, o'erwhelmed
With floods and whirlwinds of tempestuous fire,
He soon discerns; and weltering by his side,
One next himself in power, and next in crime,
Long after known in Palestine, and named   80

50] Recalls the fall of the Titans, who according to Hesiod fell nine days and
    nights into Tartarus (*Theogony* 664–735).
57 witnessed] bore witness to.
59 angels] May be a possessive, in the which case 'ken' would be a noun.
66] Alludes to the inscription over the gate of Hell in Dante's *Inferno* iii. 9,
    Lasciate ogni speranza voi ch'entrate ('Abandon all hope, you who enter
    here').
72 utter] outer.

Beëlzebub. To whom the arch-enemy,
And thence in heaven called Satan, with bold words
Breaking the horrid silence, thus began:
   'If thou beest he – but O how fallen! How changed
From him, who in the happy realms of light,   85
Clothed with transcendent brightness, didst outshine
Myriads, though bright – if he whom mutual league,
United thoughts and counsels, equal hope
And hazard in the glorious enterprise,
Joined with me once, now misery hath joined   90
In equal ruin; into what pit thou seest
From what height fallen: so much the stronger proved
He with his thunder: and till then who knew
The force of those dire arms? Yet not for those,
Nor what the potent victor in his rage   95
Can else inflict, do I repent, or change,
Though changed in outward lustre, that fixed mind,
And high disdain from sense of injured merit,
That with the mightiest raised me to contend,
And to the fierce contentions brought along   100
Innumerable force of spirits armed,
That durst dislike his reign, and, me preferring,
His utmost power with adverse power opposed
In dubious battle on the plains of heaven,
And shook his throne. What though the field be lost?   105
All is not lost – the unconquerable will,
And study of revenge, immortal hate,
And courage never to submit or yield:
And what is else not to be overcome?
That glory never shall his wrath or might   110
Extort from me. To bow and sue for grace
With suppliant knee, and deify his power
Who, from the terror of this arm, so late
Doubted his empire – that were low indeed;
That were an ignominy and shame beneath   115
This downfall; since, by fate, the strength of gods,
And this empyreal substance, cannot fail;
Since, through experience of this great event,

---

81 Beëlzebub] 'prince of devils' (Matt. xii. 24), and in the O.T. a Philistine god
   (see *SA* 1231 and II Kings i. 2) whose name means 'Lord of the Flies' in
   Hebrew.
82 Satan] the name means 'adversary', or 'one who plots against another' in
   Hebrew. See the A.V. marginal note to Job i. 6.
84–5] Isa. xiv. 12, *Aeneid* ii. 274–5.
114 Doubted] feared for.

In arms not worse, in foresight much advanced,
We may with more successful hope resolve   120
To wage by force or guile eternal war,
Irreconcilable to our grand foe,
Who now triumphs, and in the excess of joy
Sole reigning holds the tyranny of heaven.'
        So spake the apostate angel, though in pain,   125
Vaunting aloud, but racked with deep despair;
And him thus answered soon his bold compeer:
        'O Prince, O chief of many thronèd powers
That led the embattled seraphim to war
Under thy conduct, and in dreadful deeds   130
Fearless, endangered heaven's perpetual king,
And put to proof his high supremacy,
Whether upheld by strength, or chance, or fate,
Too well I see and rue the dire event
That, with sad overthrow and foul defeat,   135
Hath lost us heaven, and all this mighty host
In horrible destruction laid thus low,
As far as gods and heavenly essences
Can perish: for the mind and spirit remains
Invincible, and vigour soon returns,   140
Though all our glory extinct, and happy state
Here swallowed up in endless misery.
But what if he our conqueror (whom I now
Of force believe almighty, since no less
Than such could have o'erpowered such force as ours)   145
Have left us this our spirit and strength entire,
Strongly to suffer and support our pains,
That we may so suffice his vengeful ire,
Or do him mightier service as his thralls
By right of war, whate'er his business be,   150
Here in the heart of hell to work in fire,
Or do his errands in the gloomy deep?
What can it then avail though yet we feel
Strength undiminished, or eternal being
To undergo eternal punishment?'   155
        Whereto with speedy words the arch-fiend replied:
'Fallen cherub, to be weak is miserable,
Doing or suffering: but of this be sure –
To do aught good never will be our task,
But ever to do ill our sole delight,   160

128 powers] one of the orders of angels; seraphim (l.129) and cherubim (l. 157)
   are other orders.

As being the contrary to his high will
Whom we resist. If then his providence
Out of our evil seek to bring forth good,
Our labour must be to pervert that end,
And out of good still to find means of evil;   165
Which ofttimes may succeed so as perhaps
Shall grieve him, if I fail not, and disturb
His inmost counsels from their destined aim.
But see, the angry victor hath recalled
His ministers of vengeance and pursuit   170
Back to the gates of heaven: the sulphurous hail,
Shot after us in storm, o'erblown hath laid
The fiery surge that from the precipice
Of heaven received us falling; and the thunder,
Winged with red lightning and impetuous rage,   175
Perhaps hath spent his shafts, and ceases now
To bellow through the vast and boundless deep.
Let us not slip the occasion, whether scorn
Or satiate fury yield it from our foe.
Seest thou yon dreary plain, forlorn and wild,   180
The seat of desolation, void of light,
Save what the glimmering of these livid flames
Casts pale and dreadful? Thither let us tend
From off the tossing of these fiery waves;
There rest, if any rest can harbour there;   185
And, re-assembling our afflicted powers,
Consult how we may henceforth most offend
Our enemy, our own loss how repair,
How overcome this dire calamity,
What reinforcement we may gain from hope,   190
If not, what resolution from despair.'
    Thus Satan, talking to his nearest mate,
With head uplift above the wave, and eyes
That sparkling blazed; his other parts besides
Prone on the flood, extended long and large,   195
Lay floating many a rood, in bulk as huge
As whom the fables name of monstrous size,
Titanian or Earth-born, that warred on Jove,
Briareos or Typhon, whom the den

---

167 fail] err.
187 offend] injure.
197-200] Briareos was a Titan, Typhon, a Giant; both were sons of Gaea
    (Mother Earth). The Titans and the Giants (the two races were sometimes
    confused in antiquity) rebelled against Zeus. A later Christian tradition
    established the parallel between these rebellions and the rebellion of Satan.

By ancient Tarsus held, or that sea-beast   200
Leviathan, which God of all his works
Created hugest that swim the ocean stream;
Him, haply slumbering on the Norway foam,
The pilot of some small night-foundered skiff,
Deeming some island, oft, as seamen tell,   205
With fixèd anchor in his scaly rind,
Moors by his side under the lee, while night
Invests the sea, and wishèd morn delays;
So stretched out huge in length the arch-fiend lay,
Chained on the burning lake; nor ever thence   210
Had risen, or heaved his head, but that the will
And high permission of all-ruling heaven
Left him at large to his own dark designs,
That with reiterated crimes he might
Heap on himself damnation, while he sought   215
Evil to others, and enraged might see
How all his malice served but to bring forth
Infinite goodness, grace and mercy, shown
On man by him seduced, but on himself
Treble confusion, wrath, and vengeance poured.   220
    Forthwith upright he rears from off the pool
His mighty stature; on each hand the flames
Driven backward slope their pointing spires, and, rolled
In billows, leave i' the midst a horrid vale.
Then with expanded wings he steers his flight   225
Aloft, incumbent on the dusky air,
That felt unusual weight; till on dry land
He lights – if it were land that ever burned
With solid, as the lake with liquid fire,
And such appeared in hue as when the force   230

200-8] Leviathan, the sea-monster of Job xli, was often thought to be a whale.
    The story of the illusory island occurs in *Physiologus* ('The Naturalist'), the
    moralizing anecdotes of which were translated into the main languages of
    Europe and the Near East. Many versions of the story exist in medieval
    and Renaissance art and literature.
202 ocean stream] See *Comus* 97n.
208 Invests] covers, envelops.
224 horrid] The primary sense is 'bristling' (with 'pointing spires'), but the
    word probably carries the secondary sense of 'abominable'. The image
    ironically echoes Exod. xiv. 21-2.
230-7] The lines conflate Virgil's and Ovid's descriptions of Etna (*Aeneid* iii.
    570-7, *Metamorphoses* xv. 298-306). In antiquity and in the Renaissance
    volcanoes and earthquakes were attributed to the periodic escape of winds
    trapped in the earth. Pelorus is the promontory at the north-eastern corner
    of Sicily, near Etna. 'Sublimed' is an alchemical term meaning 'vaporized'.

Of subterranean wind transports a hill
Torn from Pelorus, or the shattered side
Of thundering Etna, whose combustible
And fuelled entrails, thence conceiving fire,
Sublimed with mineral fury, aid the winds,   235
And leave a singèd bottom all involved
With stench and smoke: such resting found the sole
Of unblessed feet. Him followed his next mate,
Both glorying to have scaped the Stygian flood
As gods, and by their own recovered strength,   240
Not by the sufferance of supernal power.
  'Is this the region, this the soil, the clime,'
Said then the lost archangel, 'this the seat
That we must change for heaven, this mournful
      gloom
For that celestial light? Be it so, since he   245
Who now is sovereign can dispose and bid
What shall be right: farthest from him is best,
Whom reason hath equalled, force hath made supreme
Above his equals. Farewell, happy fields,
Where joy for ever dwells; hail, horrors, hail,   250
Infernal world; and thou, profoundest hell,
Receive thy new possessor – one who brings
A mind not to be changed by place or time.
The mind is its own place, and in itself
Can make a heaven of hell, a hell of heaven.   255
What matter where, if I be still the same,
And what I should be, all, but less than he
Whom thunder hath made greater? Here at least
We shall be free; the almighty hath not built
Here for his envy, will not drive us hence: 260
Here we may reign secure; and, in my choice,
To reign is worth ambition, though in hell:
Better to reign in hell than serve in heaven.
But wherefore let we then our faithful friends,
The associates and co-partners of our loss,   265

239 Stygian] here means 'dark'. Cf. *Comus* l.132.
254-5] The heresy that heaven and hell are merely states of mind was devised
    by Amalric of Bena (near Chartres), a scholastic philosopher whose
    doctrines were condemned in 1204, and probably has its ultimate origins in
    Stoic doctrine.
263] Cf. Milton's translation of Psalm lxxxiv. 10 (ll 37-40). The sentiment is
    virtually proverbial in antiquity and the Renaissance.

Lie thus astonished on the oblivious pool,
And call them not to share with us their part
In this unhappy mansion, or once more
With rallied arms to try what may be yet
Regained in heaven, or what more lost in hell?'　　　　270
　　So Satan spake, and him Beëlzebub
Thus answered: 'Leader of those armies bright
Which, but the omnipotent, none could have foiled;
If once they hear that voice, their liveliest pledge
Of hope in fears and dangers – heard so oft　　　　275
In worst extremes, and on the perilous edge
Of battle, when it raged, in all assaults
Their surest signal – they will soon resume
New courage and revive, though now they lie
Grovelling and prostrate on yon lake of fire,　　　　280
As we erewhile, astounded and amazed;
No wonder, fallen such a pernicious height.'
　　He scarce had ceased when the superior fiend
Was moving toward the shore; his ponderous shield,
Ethereal temper, massy, large, and round,　　　　285
Behind him cast; the broad circumference
Hung on his shoulders like the moon, whose orb
Through optic glass the Tuscan artist views
At evening, from the top of Fesolè,
Or in Valdarno, to descry new lands,　　　　290
Rivers, or mountains, in her spotty globe.
His spear – to equal which the tallest pine
Hewn on Norwegian hills, to be the mast
Of some great ammiral, were but a wand –
He walked with, to support uneasy steps　　　　295
Over the burning marl, not like those steps
On heaven's azure; and the torrid clime
Smote on him sore besides, vaulted with fire;
Nathless he so endured, till on the beach

266 oblivious pool] Milton's 'forgetful lake' (II 74) is an adaptation of the river
　　Lethe of the classical underworld, for the devil's loss of memory is
　　temporary. Cf. the classic version of Lethe in *PL* II 582-6, 604-14.
276 edge] carries the Latin sense of 'front line'.
285 Ethereal temper] tempered by celestial fire.
288-91] The 'Tuscan artist' (i.e. scientist) is Galileo, whom Milton visited in
　　1638 or 1639. Fiesole (Fesolè) overlooks the valley of Arno (Valdarno).
　　Cf. III 588-90, V 261-3.
294 ammiral] flagship.
296 marl] a kind of soil.
299 Nathless] nevertheless.

Of that inflamèd sea he stood, and called   300
His legions – angel forms, who lay entranced
Thick as autumnal leaves that strew the brooks
In Vallombrosa, where the Etrurian shades
High over-arched embower; or scattered sedge
Afloat, when with fierce winds Orion armed   305
Hath vexed the Red Sea coast, whose waves o'erthrew
Busiris and his Memphian chivalry,
While with perfidious hatred they pursued
The sojourners of Goshen, who beheld
From the safe shore their floating carcasses   310
And broken chariot-wheels: so thick bestrewn,
Abject and lost, lay these, covering the flood,
Under amazement of their hideous change.
He called so loud that all the hollow deep
Of hell resounded: 'Princes, potentates,   315
Warriors, the flower of heaven – once yours; now lost,
If such astonishment as this can seize
Eternal spirits; or have ye chosen this place
After the toil of battle to repose
Your wearied virtue, for the ease you find   320
To slumber here, as in the vales of heaven?
Or in this abject posture have ye sworn
To adore the conqueror, who now beholds
Cherub and seraph rolling in the flood
With scattered arms and ensigns, till anon   325
His swift pursuers from heaven-gates discern
The advantage, and, descending, tread us down
Thus drooping, or with linkèd thunderbolts
Transfix us to the bottom of this gulf?
Awake, arise, or be for ever fallen.'   330
    They heard, and were abashed, and up they sprung
Upon the wing, as when men wont to watch,
On duty sleeping found by whom they dread,
Rouse and bestir themselves ere well awake.
Nor did they not perceive the evil plight   335
In which they were, or the fierce pains not feel;

303] Vallombrosa is a wooded valley in Tuscany (ancient Etruria); on the leaf
    simile cf. *Iliad* vi 146, *Aeneid* vi 309.
305] The late rising of Orion was anciently thought to portend stormy weather.
306-11] The Pharaoh of Exod. xiv was sometimes identified with the mythical
    king Busiris. Memphis was the ancient capital of Egypt; Goshen was the
    area east of the Nile where the Israelites lived. The connection between the
    destruction of Pharaoh's cavalry and Orion may have been suggested by
    Amos v. 8.

Yet to their general's voice they soon obeyed
Innumerable. As when the potent rod
Of Amram's son, in Egypt's evil day,
Waved round the coast, up called a pitchy cloud   340
Of locusts, warping on the eastern wind,
That o'er the realm of impious Pharaoh hung
Like night, and darkened all the land of Nile;
So numberless were those bad angels seen
Hovering on wing under the cope of hell,   345
'Twixt upper, nether, and surrounding fires;
Till, as a signal given, the uplifted spear
Of their great sultan waving to direct
Their course, in even balance down they light
On the firm brimstone, and fill all the plain: 350
A multitude like which the populous North
Poured never from her frozen loins to pass
Rhene or the Danaw, when her barbarous sons
Came like a deluge on the South, and spread
Beneath Gibraltar to the Libyan sands.   355
Forthwith, from every squadron and each band,
The heads and leaders thither haste where stood
Their great commander – godlike shapes, and forms
Excelling human, princely dignities,
And powers that erst in heaven sat on thrones;   360
Though of their names in heavenly records now
Be no memorial, blotted out and razed
By their rebellion from the Books of Life.
Nor had they yet among the sons of Eve
Got them new names, till wandering o'er the earth,   365
Through God's high sufferance for the trial of man,
By falsities and lies the greatest part
Of mankind they corrupted to forsake
God their creator, and the invisible
Glory of him that made them, to transform   370
Oft to the image of a brute, adorned
With gay religions full of pomp and gold,

338-43] Moses was the son of Amram. See Exod. x. 12-15, and cf. *PL* XII
    184-8.
351-5] refers to the barbarian invasions of late antiquity. Rhene is the Rhine,
    Danaw the Danube.
363 Books of Life] Rev. iii. 5, xx. 15, xxi. 27; Exod. xxxii. 32-3.
365 new names] an ironic contrast to Rev. iii. 12, for the new names of the fallen
    angels are those of the idols of l.375.
368-71] Rom. i. 23.
372 religions] religious rites.

And devils to adore for deities:
Then were they known to men by various names,
And various idols through the heathen world.   375
    Say, Muse, their names then known, who first, who
        last,
Roused from the slumber on that fiery couch,
At their great emperor's call, as next in worth
Came singly where he stood on the bare strand,
While the promiscuous crowd stood yet aloof.   380
    The chief were those who, from the pit of hell
Roaming to seek their prey on earth, durst fix
Their seats, long after, next the seat of God,
Their altars by his altar, gods adored
Among the nations round, and durst abide   385
Jehovah thundering out of Zion, throned
Between the cherubim; yea, often placed
Within his sanctuary itself their shrines,
Abominations; and with cursed things
His holy rites and solemn feasts profaned,   390
And with their darkness durst affront his light.
First, Moloch, horrid king, besmeared with blood
Of human sacrifice, and parents' tears;
Though for the noise of drums and timbrels loud,
Their children's cries unheard that passed through fire   395
To his grim idol. Him the Ammonite
Worshipped in Rabba and her watery plain,
In Argob and in Basan, to the stream
Of utmost Arnon. Nor content with such
Audacious neighbourhood, the wisest heart   400
Of Solomon he led by fraud to build
His temple right against the temple of God
On that opprobrious hill, and made his grove

376] The Homeric and Virgilian catalogues which Milton is about to imitate
    begin with appeals to the muse (*Iliad* ii 484, *Aeneid* vii 641).
386 Jehovah] see *Areopagitica*, p. 590, n.6.
387 Between the cherubim] Cf. Milton's translation of Psalm lxxx. 1.
392] Moloch means 'king' in Hebrew. See *Nativity* 205-12 and 205n.
396-7] Rabba, the royal city of the Ammonites, was conquered by David (II
    Sam. xii. 26-31).
398-9] The Israelites conquered the Ammonites of Argob and Basan, parts of
    the kingdom of Og, as far as the border with the Moabites, the stream of
    Arnon (Deut. iii. 1-13).
400-3] I Kings xi. 7. The 'opprobrious hill' is the Mount of Olives, the 'hill of
    scandal' of l.416, the 'offensive mountain' of 1.443, and the 'mount of
    corruption' of II Kings xxiii. 13.

The pleasant valley of Hinnom, Tophet thence
And black Gehenna called, the type of hell.   405
Next Chemos, the obscene dread of Moab's sons,
From Aroer to Nebo and the wild
Of southmost Abarim; in Hesebon
And Horonaim, Seon's realm, beyond
The flowery dale of Sibma clad with vines,   410
And Elealè to the Asphaltic Pool:
Peor his other name, when he enticed
Israel in Sittim, on their march from Nile,
To do him wanton rites, which cost them woe.
Yet thence his lustful orgies he enlarged   415
Even to that hill of scandal, by the grove
Of Moloch homicide, lust hard by hate,
Till good Josiah drove them thence to hell.
With these came they who, from the bordering flood
Of old Euphrates to the brook that parts   420
Egypt from Syrian ground, had general names
Of Baälim and Ashtaroth – those male,
These feminine. For spirits, when they please,
Can either sex assume, or both; so oft
And uncompounded is their essence pure,   425
Not tied or manacled with joint or limb,
Nor founded on the brittle strength of bones,
Like cumbrous flesh; but in what shape they choose,
Dilated or condensed, bright or obscure,
Can execute their airy purposes,   430
And works of love or enmity fulfil.
For those the race of Israel oft forsook

404–5] II Kings xxiii. 10. The Greek word *Gehenna* (Matt. v. 29) derives from
    the Hebrew phrase which means 'valley of the son of Hinnom'.
406] I Kings xi. 7.
407–8] I Chron. v. 8. On Aroer see Deut. ii. 36 and Jer. xlviii. 19. Milton's Nebo
    may be the town in Moab, or the mountain from which Moses viewed the
    promised land; the city was near the Abarim mountains.
408–11] Isa. xv. 4–5, xvi. 8–9. Seon was an Amorite king: see Numbers xxi.
    21–30. The 'Asphaltic Pool' is the Dead Sea, called *Asphaltites* by Josephus
    because of its deposits of bitumen.
412 Peor] See *Nativity* 197n.
412–14] Numbers xxv. 1–9. On the 'woe' see also I Cor. x. 8.
418] On Josiah see II Kings xxii–xxiii.
420 brook] Besor. I Sam. xxx. 9, 10, 21.
422–3] See *Nativity* 197n., 200n.; 'im' is normally a masculine plural inflection,
    'oth' a feminine plural inflection.
432–3] I Sam. xv. 29.

Their living strength, and unfrequented left
His righteous altar, bowing lowly down
To bestial gods; for which their heads, as low   435
Bowed down in battle, sunk before the spear
Of despicable foes. With these in troop
Came Ashtoreth, whom the Phoenicians called
Astarte, queen of heaven, with crescent horns;
To whose bright image nightly by the moon   440
Sidonian virgins paid their vows and songs;
In Zion also not unsung, where stood
Her temple on the offensive mountain, built
By that uxorious king whose heart, though large,
Beguiled by fair idolatresses, fell   445
To idols foul. Thammuz came next behind,
Whose annual wound in Lebanon allured
The Syrian damsels to lament his fate
In amorous ditties all a summer's day,
While smooth Adonis from his native rock   450
Ran purple to the sea, supposed with blood
Of Thammuz yearly wounded: the love-tale
Infected Zion's daughters with like heat,
Whose wanton passions in the sacred porch
Ezekiel saw, when by the vision led   455
His eye surveyed the dark idolatries
Of alienated Judah. Next came one
Who mourned in earnest, when the captive ark
Maimed his brute image, head and hands lopped off,
In his own temple, on the groundsel edge,   460
Where he fell flat and shamed his worshippers:
Dagon his name, sea-monster, upward man
And downward fish; yet had his temple high
Reared in Azotus, dreaded through the coast
Of Palestine, in Gath and Ascalon,   465
And Accaron and Gaza's frontier bounds.

438–9] See *Nativity* 200n.
441 Sidonian] of Sidon, the Phoenician city.
444 king] Solomon, whose wives 'turned away his heart after other gods' (I
     Kings xi. 1–8).
446–57] See *Nativity* 204n. and Ezek. viii. 14. It is appropriate for Thammuz to
     follow Ashtoreth because Adonis (Thammuz) was the lover of
     Astarte-Aphrodite.
457–66] See *Nativity* 199n. 'Groundsel' (460) means 'threshold'.
464–6] The five cities of Philistia were Azotus (or Asdod), Gath, Ascalon,
     Accaron (or Ecron) and Gaza (or Azza). The forms in parentheses appear in
     SA.

Him followed Rimmon, whose delightful seat
Was fair Damascus, on the fertile banks
Of Abbana and Pharphar, lucid streams.
He also against the house of God was bold: 470
A leper once he lost, and gained a king –
Ahaz, his sottish conqueror, whom he drew
God's altar to disparage and displace
For one of Syrian mode, whereon to burn
His odious offerings, and adore the gods   475
Whom he had vanquished. After these appeared
A crew who, under names of old renown –
Osiris, Isis, Orus, and their train –
With monstrous shapes and sorceries abused
Fanatic Egypt and her priests to seek   480
Their wandering gods disguised in brutish forms
Rather than human. Nor did Israel scape
The infection, when their borrowed gold composed
The calf in Oreb; and the rebel king
Doubled that sin in Bethel and in Dan,   485
Likening his maker to the grazèd ox –
Jehovah, who, in one night, when he passed
From Egypt marching, equalled with one stroke
Both her first-born and all her bleating gods.
Belial came last; than whom a spirit more lewd   490
Fell not from heaven, or more gross to love
Vice for itself: to him no temple stood
Or altar smoked; yet who more oft than he
In temples and at altars, when the priest

467 Rimmon] a Syrian god.
468–71] In II Kings v Elisha tells the Syrian leper Naaman to wash in the
    Jordan, and Naaman replies (v. 12) 'Are not Abbana and Pharpar ['Phar-
    phar' in LXX and Vulgate] rivers of Damascus, better than all the waters
    of Israel?'
471–6] The king is Ahaz; see II Kings xvi.
478] See *Nativity* 212 13n.
482–4] Exod. xxxii; Psalm cvi. 19. The connection with Egypt is the traditional
    identification of the golden calf with the Egyptian Apis. On the gold having
    been 'borrowed' see Exod. xii. 35.
484–5] The 'rebel king' is Jereboam, who 'doubled that sin' by making two
    calves of gold, one for Bethel and one for Dan (I Kings xii. 28–9).
486] Psalm cvi. 19–20.
487–9] Exod. xii. 12–30.
490 Belial] The word *Belial* in Hebrew is not a proper name, but an abstraction,
    and can mean either 'worthlessness' or 'destruction'; it is usually rendered
    in the Vulgate as a proper name. In II Cor. vi. 15 the word appears as a
    proper name.
494–6] I Sam. ii. 12–25; 'the sons of Eli were sons of Belial' (v. 12).

Turns atheist, as did Eli's sons, who filled   495
With lust and violence the house of God?
In courts and palaces he also reigns,
And in luxurious cities, where the noise
Of riot ascends above their loftiest towers,
And injury and outrage; and when night   500
Darkens the streets, then wander forth the sons
Of Belial, flown with insolence and wine.
Witness the streets of Sodom, and that night
In Gibeah, when the hospitable door
Exposed a matron, to avoid worse rape.   505
   These were the prime in order and in might:
The rest were long to tell, though far renowned,
The Ionian gods – of Javan's issue held
Gods, yet confessed later than heaven and earth,
Their boasted parents – Titan, heaven's first-born,   510
With his enormous brood, and birthright seized
By younger Saturn: he from mightier Jove,
His own and Rhea's son, like measure found;
So Jove usurping reigned; these, first in Crete
And Ida known, thence on the snowy top   515
Of cold Olympus ruled the middle air,
Their highest heaven; or on the Delphian cliff,
Or in Dodona, and through all the bounds
Of Doric land; or who with Saturn old
Fled over Adria to the Hesperian fields,   520
And o'er the Celtic roamed the utmost isles.

   All these and more came flocking; but with looks
Downcast and damp; yet such wherein appeared
Obscure some glimpse of joy to have found their chief

---

502 flown] This archaic past-participle of 'flow' (not 'fly') literally means
   'swollen' or 'in flood'.
503-5] Gen. xix. 4-11; Judges xix. 12-30.
508] Javan, the grandson of Noah (Gen. x. 1-5) was thought to be the
   progenitor of the Ionians.
509-21] Uranus and Gaea ('heaven and earth') were the parents of the twelve
   Titans, two of whom were Saturn and Rhea, who became the parents of
   Jove. Jove, who was born in a cave on Mount Ida in Crete, overthrew his
   father. Jove lived on Mt Olympus (on 'middle air' see *Fair Infant* 16n.), and
   was venerated at Dodona (in northern Greece), and throughout Greece
   ('Doric land'); his son Apollo revealed the will of the gods at Delphi. Saturn
   was eventually banished by Jove, and fled across the Adriatic (Adria) to
   Italy ('Hesperian fields'). Later he fled to France ('Celtic' fields) and finally
   to the 'utmost isles', the *ultima Thule* of classical antiquity. The story of
   Titan to which Milton alludes (1.510) exists only in a late tradition
   transmitted by Lactantius.

Not in despair, to have found themselves not lost   525
In loss itself; which on his countenance cast
Like doubtful hue; but he, his wonted pride
Soon recollecting, with high words, that bore
Semblance of worth, not substance, gently raised
Their fainting courage, and dispelled their fears.   530
Then straight commands that, at the warlike sound
Of trumpets loud and clarions, be upreared
His mighty standard; that proud honour claimed
Azazel as his right, a cherub tall:
Who forthwith from the glittering staff unfurled   535
The imperial ensign, which, full high advanced,
Shone like a meteor streaming to the wind,
With gems and golden lustre rich emblazed,
Seraphic arms and trophies; all the while
Sonorous metal blowing martial sounds: 540
At which the universal host upsent
A shout that tore hell's concave, and beyond
Frighted the reign of Chaos and old Night.
All in a moment through the gloom were seen
Ten thousand banners rise into the air,   545
With orient colours waving: with them rose
A forest huge of spears; and thronging helms
Appeared, and serried shields in thick array
Of depth immeasurable; anon they move
In perfect phalanx to the Dorian mood   550
Of flutes and soft recorders – such as raised
To height of noblest temper heroes old
Arming to battle, and instead of rage
Deliberate valour breathed, firm and unmoved
With dread of death to flight or foul retreat;   555
Nor wanting power to mitigate and swage
With solemn touches troubled thoughts, and chase
Anguish and doubt and fear and sorrow and pain

533-4] The word translated as 'scapegoat' in Lev. xvi refers in Hebrew to the
    goat 'for Azazel', Azazel being the name of the spirit living in the wilderness
    to whom the goat was sent. In a cabbalistic tradition with which Milton
    was familiar the spirit Azazel is represented as an angel who serves in
    Satan's army as a standard-bearer.
543 reign] realm.
550 Dorian mood] one of the musical modes of ancient Greece, characterized by
    simplicity and solemnity.
551] The Spartan army went into battle to the music of the flute (whereas the
    Romans used trumpets).
556 swage] assuage.

From mortal or immortal minds. Thus they,
Breathing united force with fixèd thought,   560
Moved on in silence to soft pipes that charmed
Their painful steps o'er the burnt soil; and now
Advanced in view they stand – a horrid front
Of dreadful length and dazzling arms, in guise
Of warriors old, with ordered spear and shield,   565
Awaiting what command their mighty chief
Had to impose: he through the armèd files
Darts his experienced eye, and soon traverse
The whole battalion views – their order due,
Their visages and stature as of gods;   570
Their number last he sums. And now his heart
Distends with pride, and, hardening in his strength,
Glories: for never, since created man,
Met such embodied force as, named with these,
Could merit more than that small infantry   575
Warred on by cranes – though all the giant brood
Of Phlegra with the heroic race were joined
That fought at Thebes and Ilium, on each side
Mixed with auxiliar gods; and what resounds
In fable or romance of Uther's son,   580
Begirt with British and Armoric knights;
And all who since, baptized or infidel,
Jousted in Aspramont, or Montalban,
Damasco, or Marocco, or Trebizond,
Or whom Bizerta sent from Afric shore   585

---

563 horrid] means both 'bristling' (with spears) and 'abominable'.
571-3] Dan. v. 20; 'since created man' is a Latin construction meaning 'since man was created'.
575 small infantry] pygmies. On the attack on the pygmies by cranes see *Iliad* iii 3-6; 'infantry' may be a pun.
577 Phlegra] The war of the giants and the gods took place on the Phlegraean plains in Macedonia, and on the Phlegraean Fields near Naples.
578] The fates of the Theban princes and the tale of Troy ('Ilium') were the central themes of Greek tragedy and epic.
580-1] Uther's son is King Arthur, some of whose knights were Breton ('Armoric').
583-4] Aspramont, a mountain range in Calabria, was celebrated in romances as the site of one of Charlemagne's victories over the Saracens. Montalban, in Languedoc, was the home of Rinaldo, whose story was a popular romance subject; Damascus ('Damasco') is the scene of a tournament in one of these romances, *Orlando Furioso* (xvii); Marocco is Marrakesh, a sultanate in what is now Morocco; Trebizond (now Trabzon), the Byzantine city on the Black Sea, was associated with the romance tradition.
585 Bizerta] a Tunisian port at which, according to Boiardo, the Saracens assembled for their invasion of Spain (*Orlando Innamorato* ii).

When Charlemagne with all his peerage fell
By Fontarabbia. Thus far these beyond
Compare of mortal prowess, yet observed
Their dread commander; he above the rest
In shape and gesture proudly eminent,   590
Stood like a tower; his form had yet not lost
All her original brightness, nor appeared
Less than archangel ruined, and the excess
Of glory obscured: as when the sun new risen
Looks through the horizontal misty air   595
Shorn of his beams, or from behind the moon
In dim eclipse, disastrous twilight sheds
On half the nations, and with fear of change
Perplexes monarchs. Darkened so, yet shone
Above them all the archangel: but his face   600
Deep scars of thunder had intrenched, and care
Sat on his faded cheek, but under brows
Of dauntless courage, and considerate pride
Waiting revenge; cruel his eye, but cast
Signs of remorse and passion, to behold   605
The fellows of his crime, the followers rather
(Far other once beheld in bliss), condemned
For ever now to have their lot in pain –
Millions of spirits for his fault amerced
Of heaven, and from eternal splendours flung   610
For his revolt – yet faithful how they stood,
Their glory withered; as, when heaven's fire
Hath scathed the forest oaks or mountain pines,
With singèd top their stately growth, though bare,
Stands on the blasted heath. He now prepared   615
To speak; whereat their doubled ranks they bend
From wing to wing, and half enclose him round
With all his peers: attention held them mute.
Thrice he assayed, and thrice, in spite of scorn,
Tears, such as angels weep, burst forth: at last   620

586–7] No extant version of the Charlemagne legend records the death of
   Charlemagne and his peers (see *PR* III 337–43n.) at 'Fontarabbia' (Fuen-
   terrabia, on the coast of Spain by the French border), though several late
   versions record the massacre of Roland (Orlando) and his rearguard at
   Roncesvalles, about 40 miles inland. Milton may be alluding to the abortive
   visit of Charles II to Fuenterrabia after the failure of the Royalist uprising
   in August 1659.
597 disastrous] foreboding disaster.
603 considerate] considered, deliberate.
609 amerced] deprived.

Words interwove with sighs found out their way:
  'O myriads of immortal spirits, O powers
Matchless, but with the Almighty – and that strife
Was not inglorious, though the event was dire,
As this place testifies, and this dire change,   625
Hateful to utter; but what power of mind,
Foreseeing or presaging, from the depth
Of knowledge past or present, could have feared
How such united force of gods, how such
As stood like these, could ever know repulse?   630
For who can yet believe, though after loss,
That all these puissant legions, whose exile
Hath emptied heaven, shall fail to re-ascend,
Self-raised, and repossess their native seat?
For me be witness all the host of heaven   635
If counsels different, or danger shunned
By me, have lost our hopes. But he who reigns
Monarch in heaven, till then as one secure
Sat on his throne, upheld by old repute,
Consent or custom, and his regal state   640
Put forth at full, but still his strength concealed –
Which tempted our attempt, and wrought our fall.
Henceforth his might we know, and know our own,
So as not either to provoke, or dread
New war provoked: our better part remains   645
To work in close design, by fraud or guile,
What force effected not; that he no less
At length from us may find, who overcomes
By force hath overcome but half his foe.
Space may produce new worlds; whereof so rife   650
There went a flame in heaven that he ere long
Intended to create, and therein plant
A generation whom his choice regard
Should favour equal to the sons of heaven.
Thither, if but to pry, shall be perhaps   655
Our first eruption – thither, or elsewhere;
For this infernal pit shall never hold
Celestial spirits in bondage, nor the abyss
Long under darkness cover. But these thoughts
Full counsel must mature; peace is despaired,   660
For who can think submission? War, then, war
Open or understood, must be resolved.'
  He spake; and to confirm his words, outflew

636 different] may mean 'differing' or 'procrastinating'.

Millions of flaming swords, drawn from the thighs
Of mighty cherubim; the sudden blaze   665
Far round illumined hell; highly they raged
Against the highest, and fierce with graspèd arms
Clashed on their sounding shields the din of war,
Hurling defiance toward the vault of heaven.
    There stood a hill not far, whose grisly top   670
Belched fire and rolling smoke; the rest entire
Shone with a glossy scurf – undoubted sign
That in his womb was hid metallic ore,
The work of sulphur. Thither, winged with speed,
A numerous brigade hastened: as when bands   675
Of pioneers with spade and pickaxe armed,
Forerun the royal camp, to trench a field,
Or cast a rampart. Mammon led them on –
Mammon, the least erected spirit that fell   679
From heaven; for even in heaven his looks and thoughts
Were always downward bent, admiring more
The riches of heaven's pavement, trodden gold,
Than aught divine or holy else enjoyed
In vision beatific; by him first
Men also, and by his suggestion taught,   685
Ransacked the centre, and with impious hands
Rifled the bowels of their mother earth
For treasures better hid. Soon had his crew
Opened into the hill a spacious wound,
And digged out ribs of gold. Let none admire   690
That riches grow in hell; that soil may best
Deserve the precious bane. And here let those
Who boast in mortal things, and wondering tell
Of Babel, and the works of Memphian kings,
Learn how their greatest monuments of fame   695
And strength, and art, are easily outdone

678] *Mammon*, the Aramaic word for 'riches', is personified in Matt. vi. 24 and
    Luke xvi. 13. In late traditions this personification became identified with
    Plutus, the Greek god of wealth, and with Pluto, the god of the under-
    world. Burton made him prince of the ninth order of devils (*Anatomy of
    Melancholy* I ii I 2).
679] erected] exalted.
682] Rev. xxi. 21.
684 vision beatific] the scholastic term for the 'sight of God' promised in Matt.
    v. 8. Cf. 'On Time' 18, *PL* V 613, and *Areopagitica* p. 607.
684–92] See *Metamorphoses* i 137–42.
694] Alludes to the tower of Babel (cf. *PL* XII 38–62) and the pyramids of
    Egypt.

By spirits reprobate, and in an hour
What in an age they, with incessant toil
And hands innumerable, scarce perform.
Nigh on the plain, in many cells prepared,   700
That underneath had veins of liquid fire
Sluiced from the lake, a second multitude
With wondrous art founded the massy ore,
Severing each kind, and scummed the bullion-dross.
A third as soon had formed within the ground   705
A various mould, and from the boiling cells
By strange conveyance filled each hollow nook;
As in an organ, from one blast of wind,
To many a row of pipes the sound-board breathes.
Anon out of the earth a fabric huge   710
Rose like an exhalation, with the sound
Of dulcet symphonies and voices sweet –
Built like a temple, where pilasters round
Were set, and Doric pillars overlaid
With golden architrave; nor did there want   715
Cornice or frieze, with bossy sculptures graven;
The roof was fretted gold. Not Babylon
Nor great Alcairo such magnificence
Equalled in all their glories, to enshrine
Belus or Serapis their gods, or seat   720
Their kings, when Egypt with Assyria strove
In wealth and luxury. The ascending pile
Stood fixed her stately height; and straight the doors,
Opening their brazen folds discover, wide
Within, her ample spaces o'er the smooth   725
And level pavement: from the archèd roof,
Pendent by subtle magic, many a row
Of starry lamps and blazing cressets, fed
With naphtha and asphaltus, yielded light
As from a sky. The hasty multitude   730
Admiring entered; and the work some praise,
And some the architect: his hand was known
In heaven by many a towered structure high,
Where sceptred angels held their residence,
And sat as princes, whom the supreme king   735
Exalted to such power, and gave to rule,
Each in his hierarchy, the orders bright.

718 Alcairo] Memphis, the ancient city near modern Cairo.
720 Belus] Babylonian Baal.
    Serapis] The state god of Ptolemaic Egypt, a combination of Apsis and
    Osiris.

Nor was his name unheard or unadored
In ancient Greece; and in Ausonian land
Men called him Mulciber; and how he fell   740
From heaven they fabled, thrown by angry Jove
Sheer o'er the crystal battlements: from morn
To noon he fell, from noon to dewy eve,
A summer's day, and with the setting sun
Dropped from the zenith, like a falling star,   745
On Lemnos, the Aegean isle: thus they relate,
Erring; for he with his rebellious rout
Fell long before; nor aught availed him now
To have built in heaven high towers; nor did he scape
By all his engines, but was headlong sent,   750
With his industrious crew, to build in hell.
    Meanwhile the wingèd heralds, by command
Of sovereign power, with awful ceremony
And trumpet's sound, throughout the host proclaim
A solemn council forthwith to be held   755
At Pandemonium, the high capital
Of Satan and his peers; their summons called
From every band and squarèd regiment
By place or choice the worthiest; they anon
With hundreds and with thousands trooping came   760
Attended; all access was thronged; the gates
And porches wide, but chief the spacious hall
(Though like a covered field, where champions bold
Wont ride in armed, and at the soldan's chair
Defied the best of paynim chivalry   765
To mortal combat, or career with lance),
Thick swarmed, both on the ground and in the air,
Brushed with the hiss of rustling wings. As bees
In spring-time, when the sun with Taurus rides,
Pour forth their populous youth about the hive   770
In clusters; they among fresh dews and flowers

738-46] Mulciber (Vulcan), the god of fire and of arts for which fire is needed,
    was known in Greece as Hephaestus; see *Iliad*, i 588-95. In Augustan
    poetry 'Ausonia' is a synonym for Italy.
756 Pandemonium] Milton's coinage, probably formed from πάν (all) + δαίμον
    ('demon, evil spirit', especially in New Testament Greek) + ιον, a suffix
    which here suggests 'place'.
765 paynim] pagan.
766 career] a charge or encounter at a tournament.
768-75] A common metaphor in antiquity. See *Iliad* ii 87-90. *Aeneid* i 430-6,
    and especially Virgil's *Georgics* iv 149-227.
769] The sun enters the zodiacal sign of Taurus in April.

Fly to and fro, or on the smoothèd plank,
The suburb of their straw-built citadel,
New rubbed with balm, expatiate, and confer
Their state-affairs: so thick the airy crowd   775
Swarmed and were straitened; till, the signal given
Behold a wonder! They but now who seemed
In bigness to surpass Earth's giant sons,
Now less than smallest dwarfs, in narrow room
Throng numberless – like that pygmean race   780
Beyond the Indian mount, or fairy elves,
Whose midnight revels, by a forest side
Or fountain, some belated peasant sees,
Or dreams he sees, while overhead the moon
Sits arbitress, and nearer to the earth   785
Wheels her pale course: they, on their mirth and dance
Intent, with jocund music charm his ear;
At once with joy and fear his heart rebounds.
Thus incorporeal spirits to smallest forms
Reduced their shapes immense, and were at large,   790
Though without number still amidst the hall
Of that infernal court. But far within,
And in their own dimensions like themselves,
The great seraphic lords and cherubim
In close recess and secret conclave sat,   795
A thousand demi-gods on golden seats,
Frequent and full. After short silence then,
And summons read, the great consult began.

THE END OF THE FIRST BOOK

774 expatiate] to walk about at large.
780-1] Since antiquity the land of the pygmies was thought to be in eastern
Asia. See l.575n.
783-4] See *Aeneid* vi 451-4.
795 close recess] secret meeting-place.
conclave] here used to refer to an assembly of cardinals who have met to
elect a pope.
797 Frequent] crowded.

BOOK II

THE ARGUMENT

The consultation begun, Satan debates whether another battle be
to be hazarded for the recovery of heaven: some advise it, others
dissuade; a third proposal is preferred, mentioned before by Satan
– to search the truth of that prophecy or tradition in heaven
concerning another world, and another kind of creature, equal, or
not much inferior, to themselves, about this time to be created;
their doubt who shall be sent on this difficult search: Satan, their
chief, undertakes alone the voyage; is honoured and applauded.
The council thus ended, the rest betake them several ways and to
several employments, as their inclinations lead them, to entertain
the time till Satan return. He passes on his journey to hell gates,
finds them shut, and who sat there to guard them; by whom at
length they are opened, and discover to him the great gulf between
hell and heaven. With what difficulty he passes through, directed
by Chaos, the power of that place, to the sight of this new world
which he sought.

High on a throne of royal state, which far
Outshone the wealth of Ormus and of Ind,
Or where the gorgeous East with richest hand
Showers on her kings barbaric pearl and gold,
Satan exalted sat, by merit raised   5
To that bad eminence; and, from despair
Thus high uplifted beyond hope, aspires
Beyond thus high, insatiate to pursue
Vain war with heaven; and, by success untaught,
His proud imaginations thus displayed: 10
   'Powers and dominions, deities of heaven –
For since no deep within her gulf can hold
Immortal vigour, though oppressed and fallen,
I give not heaven for lost. From this descent
Celestial virtues rising will appear   15
More glorious and more dread than from no fall,
And trust themselves to fear no second fate –
Me though just right, and the fixed laws of heaven,

---

2 Ormus] Hormuz, a Portuguese trading city on an island at the mouth of the
    Persian Gulf; it had been attacked by an English expedition in 1622, and
    some of the booty had been paid to King James and the Duke of
    Buckingham: it was thus associated with corruption.
9 success] result.
11-15 powers, dominions, virtues] three of the orders of angels.

Did first create your leader – next, free choice,
With what besides in council or in fight   20
Hath been achieved of merit – yet this loss,
Thus far at least recovered, hath much more
Established in a safe unenvied throne,
Yielded with full consent. The happier state
In heaven, which follows dignity, might draw   25
Envy from each inferior; but who here
Will envy whom the highest place exposes
Foremost to stand against the thunderer's aim
Your bulwark, and condemns to greatest share
Of endless pain? Where there is, then, no good   30
For which to strive, no strife can grow up there
From faction: for none sure will claim in hell
Precedence; none whose portion is so small
Of present pain that with ambitious mind
Will covet more. With this advantage, then,   35
To union, and firm faith, and firm accord,
More than can be in heaven, we now return
To claim our just inheritance of old,
Surer to prosper than prosperity
Could have assured us; and by what best way,   40
Whether of open war or covert guile,
We now debate: who can advise may speak.'
    He ceased; and next him Moloch, sceptred king,
Stood up – the strongest and the fiercest spirit
That fought in heaven, now fiercer by despair   45
His trust was with the eternal to be deemed
Equal in strength, and rather than be less
Cared not to be at all; with that care lost
Went all his fear: of God, or hell, or worse,
He recked not, and these words thereafter spake: 50
    'My sentence is for open war; of wiles,
More unexpert, I boast not: them let those
Contrive who need, or when they need; not now.
For while they sit contriving, shall the rest –
Millions that stand in arms, and longing wait   55
The signal to ascend – sit lingering here,
Heaven's fugitives, and for their dwelling place
Accept this dark opprobrious den of shame,
The prison of his tyranny who reigns
By our delay? No, let us rather choose,   60
Armed with hell flames and fury all at once

---

28 thunderer] classical epithet for Jove.
51 sentence] judgement, opinion.

O'er heaven's high towers to force resistless way,
Turning our tortures into horrid arms
Against the torturer; when to meet the noise
Of his almighty engine, he shall hear   65
Infernal thunder, and for lightning see
Black fire and horror shot with equal rage
Among his angels, and his throne itself
Mixed with Tartarean sulphur and strange fire,
His own invented torments. But perhaps   70
The way seems difficult, and steep to scale
With upright wing against a higher foe.
Let such bethink them, if the sleepy drench
Of that forgetful lake benumb not still,
That in our proper motion we ascend   75
Up to our native seat; descent and fall
To us is adverse. Who but felt of late,
When the fierce foe hung on our broken rear
Insulting, and pursued us through the deep,
With what compulsion and laborious flight   80
We sunk thus low? The ascent is easy, then;
The event is feared; should we again provoke
Our stronger, some worse way his wrath may find
To our destruction, if there be in hell
Fear to be worse destroyed; what can be worse   85
Than to dwell here, driven out from bliss, condemned
In this abhorrèd deep to utter woe;
Where pain of unextinguishable fire
Must exercise us without hope of end
The vassals of his anger, when the scourge   90
Inexorably, and the torturing hour,
Calls us to penance? More destroyed than thus,
We should be quite abolished, and expire.
What fear we then? What doubt we to incense
His utmost ire? Which, to the height enraged,   95
Will either quite consume us, and reduce
To nothing this essential – happier far
Than miserable to have eternal being –
Or, if our substance be indeed divine,
And cannot cease to be, we are at worst   100

69] Tartarus was the place of the damned in the classical underworld.
73-4] See I 266n.
79 Insulting] means both 'contemptuously abusing' and 'assaulting'.
81] Milton asserts the falseness of the boast by the allusion to *Aeneid* vi 126-9.
87 utter] acts as both verb and adjective.
89 exercise] afflict.
97 essential] essence.

On this side nothing; and by proof we feel
Our power sufficient to disturb his heaven,
And with perpetual inroads to alarm,
Though inaccessible, his fatal throne:
Which, if not victory, is yet revenge.'   105
   He ended frowning, and his look denounced
Desperate revenge, and battle dangerous
To less than gods. On the other side up rose
Belial, in act more graceful and humane;
A fairer person lost not heaven; he seemed   110
For dignity composed, and high exploit:
But all was false and hollow; though his tongue
Dropped manna, and could make the worse appear
The better reason, to perplex and dash
Maturest counsels: for his thoughts were low –   115
To vice industrious, but to nobler deeds
Timorous and slothful; yet he pleased the ear,
And with persuasive accent thus began:
   'I should be much for open war, O peers,
As not behind in hate, if what was urged   120
Main reason to persuade immediate war
Did not dissuade me most, and seem to cast
Ominous conjecture on the whole success;
When he who most excels in fact of arms,
In what he counsels and in what excels   125
Mistrustful, grounds his courage on despair
And utter dissolution, as the scope
Of all his aim, after some dire revenge.
First, what revenge? The towers of heaven are filled
With armèd watch, that render all access   130
Impregnable: oft on the bordering deep
Encamp their legions, or with obscure wing
Scout far and wide into the realm of night,
Scorning surprise. Or could we break our way
By force, and at our heels all hell should rise   135
With blackest insurrection to confound
Heaven's purest light, yet our great enemy,
All incorruptible, would on his throne
Sit unpolluted, and the ethereal mould,
Incapable of stain, would soon expel   140
Her mischief, and purge off the baser fire,
Victorious. Thus repulsed, our final hope

104 fatal] means both 'destined' and 'ruinous'.
106 denounced] portended.
124 fact] feat of valour or skill.

Is flat despair: we must exasperate
The almighty victor to spend all his rage,
And that must end us, that must be our cure –   145
To be no more; sad cure; for who would lose,
Though full of pain, this intellectual being,
Those thoughts that wander through eternity,
To perish rather, swallowed up and lost
In the wide womb of uncreated night,   150
Devoid of sense and motion? And who knows,
Let this be good, whether our angry foe
Can give it, or will ever? How he can
Is doubtful; that he never will is sure.
Will he, so wise, let loose at once his ire,   155
Belike through impotence or unaware,
To give his enemies their wish, and end
Them in his anger whom his anger saves
To punish endless? "Wherefore cease we, then?"
Say they who counsel war; "we are decreed,   160
Reserved, and destined to eternal woe;
Whatever doing, what can we suffer more,
What can we suffer worse?" Is this, then, worst –
Thus sitting, thus consulting, thus in arms?
What when we fled amain, pursued and struck   165
With heaven's afflicting thunder, and besought
The deep to shelter us? This hell then seemed
A refuge from those wounds; or when we lay
Chained on the burning lake? That sure was worse.
What if the breath that kindled those grim fires,   170
Awaked, should blow them into sevenfold rage,
And plunge us in the flames? Or from above
Should intermitted vengeance arm again
His red right hand to plague us? What if all
Her stores were opened, and this firmament   175
Of hell should spout her cataracts of fire,
Impendent horrors, threatening hideous fall
One day upon our heads; while we perhaps,
Designing or exhorting glorious war,
Caught in a fiery tempest, shall be hurled,   180
Each on his rock transfixed, the sport and prey

156 Belike] in all likelihood.
165 What] what about the occasion.
       amain] in haste.
170] Isa. xxx. 33.
174] Horace, *Odes* I. ii. 2-3.
180-82] Cf. the punishment of Ajax (*Aeneid* i 44-5).

Of racking whirlwinds, or for ever sunk
Under yon boiling ocean, wrapped in chains,
There to converse with everlasting groans,
Unrespited, unpitied, unreprieved,   185
Ages of hopeless end? This would be worse.
War, therefore, open or concealed, alike
My voice dissuades; for what can force or guile
With him, or who deceive his mind, whose eye
Views all things at one view? He from heaven's
          height   190
All these our motions vain sees and derides,
Not more almighty to resist our might
Than wise to frustrate all our plots and wiles.
Shall we, then, live thus vile – the race of heaven
Thus trampled, thus expelled, to suffer here   195
Chains and these torments? Better these than worse,
By my advice; since fate inevitable
Subdues us, and omnipotent decree,
The victor's will. To suffer, as to do,
Our strength is equal, nor the law unjust   200
That so ordains; this was at first resolved,
If we were wise, against so great a foe
Contending, and so doubtful what might fall.
I laugh when those who at the spear are bold
And venturous, if that fail them, shrink, and fear   205
What yet they know must follow – to endure
Exile, or ignominy, or bonds, or pain,
The sentence of their conqueror: this is now
Our doom; which if we can sustain and bear,
Our supreme foe in time may much remit   210
His anger, and perhaps, thus far removed,
Not mind us not offending, satisfied
With what is punished; whence these raging fires
Will slacken, if his breath stir not their flames.
Our purer essence then will overcome   215
Their noxious vapour, or, inured, not feel,
Or, changed at length, and to the place conformed
In temper and in nature, will receive
Familiar the fierce heat; and, void of pain,
This horror will grow mild, this darkness light;   220
Besides what hope the never-ending flight
Of future days may bring, what chance, what change

190-1] Cf. Milton's translation of Psalm II. 4 (ll. 8-9).
218 temper] temperament (the balance of humours; see *Education* p. 562).
220 light] means both 'brighter' and 'easier to bear'.

Worth waiting – since our present lot appears
For happy though but ill, for ill not worst,
If we procure not to ourselves more woe.'   225
    Thus Belial, with words clothed in reason's garb,
Counselled ignoble ease and peaceful sloth,
Not peace; and after him thus Mammon spake:
    'Either to disenthrone the king of heaven
We war, if war be best, or to regain   230
Our own right lost; him to unthrone we then
May hope, when everlasting Fate shall yield
To fickle Chance, and Chaos judge the strife:
The former, vain to hope, argues as vain
The latter; for what place can be for us   235
Within heaven's bound, unless heaven's lord supreme
We overpower? Suppose he should relent,
And publish grace to all, on promise made
Of new subjection; with what eyes could we
Stand in his presence humble, and receive   240
Strict laws imposed, to celebrate his throne
With warbled hymns, and to his Godhead sing
Forced halleluiahs, while he lordly sits
Our envied sovereign, and his altar breathes
Ambrosial odours and ambrosial flowers,   245
Our servile offerings? This must be our task
In heaven, this our delight; how wearisome
Eternity so spent in worship paid
To whom we hate. Let us not then pursue,
By force impossible, by leave obtained   250
Unacceptable, though in heaven, our state
Of splendid vassalage; but rather seek
Our own good from ourselves, and from our own
Live to ourselves, though in this vast recess,
Free and to none accountable, preferring   255
Hard liberty before the easy yoke
Of servile pomp. Our greatness will appear
Then most conspicuous when great things of small,
Useful of hurtful, prosperous of adverse,
We can create, and in what place so e'er   260

224 For happy] in terms of happiness.
238 publish] announce.
243 halleluiahs] refers to the heavenly songs of Rev. xix. 1-7, and also recalls
    the origin of the word as a transliteration of the Hebrew injunction 'praise
    Jah' (Yahweh).
245] Ambrosia is the food of the gods.
249-51] The object of 'pursue' is 'state'.
256 easy yoke] Matt. xi. 30.

Thrive under evil, and work ease out of pain
Through labour and endurance. This deep world
Of darkness do we dread? How oft amidst
Thick clouds and dark doth heaven's all-ruling sire
Choose to reside, his glory unobscured,   265
And with the majesty of darkness round
Covers his throne, from whence deep thunders roar,
Mustering their rage, and heaven resembles hell?
As he our darkness, cannot we his light
Imitate when we please? This desert soil   270
Wants not her hidden lustre, gems and gold;
Nor want we skill or art from whence to raise
Magnificence; and what can heaven show more?
Our torments also may, in length of time,
Become our elements, these piercing fires   275
As soft as now severe, our temper changed
Into their temper; which must needs remove
The sensible of pain. All things invite
To peaceful counsels, and the settled state
Of order, how in safety best we may   280
Compose our present evils, with regard
Of what we are and where, dismissing quite
All thoughts of war; ye have what I advise.'

    He scarce had finished, when such murmur filled
The assembly as when hollow rocks retain   285
The sound of blustering winds, which all night long
Had roused the sea, now with hoarse cadence lull
Seafaring men o'erwatched, whose bark by chance,
Or pinnace anchors in a craggy bay
After the tempest; such applause was heard   290
As Mammon ended, and his sentence pleased,
Advising peace: for such another field
They dreaded worse than hell; so much the fear
Of thunder and the sword of Michaël
Wrought still within them; and no less desire   295
To found this nether empire, which might rise,
By policy and long process of time,
In emulation opposite to heaven.
Which when Beëlzebub perceived – than whom,
Satan except, none higher sat – with grave   300
Aspect he rose, and in his rising seemed

263-7] Exod. xix. 16-29, II Chron. v. 13-vi. 1.
278 sensible] perception through the senses.
297 policy] statesmanship. The word was often used pejoratively to refer to
    political cunning.

A pillar of state; deep on his front engraven
Deliberation sat, and public care;
And princely counsel in his face yet shone,
Majestic, though in ruin; sage he stood,   305
With Atlantean shoulders, fit to bear
The weight of mightiest monarchies; his look
Drew audience and attention still as night
Or summer's noontide air, while thus he spake:
    'Thrones and imperial powers, offspring of heaven,   310
Ethereal virtues; or these titles now
Must we renounce, and, changing style, be called
Princes of hell? For so the popular vote
Inclines – here to continue, and build up here
A growing empire; doubtless; while we dream,   315
And know not that the king of heaven hath doomed
This place our dungeon – not our safe retreat
Beyond his potent arm, to live exempt
From heaven's high jurisdiction, in new league
Banded against his throne, but to remain   320
In strictest bondage, though thus far removed,
Under the inevitable curb, reserved
His captive multitude; for he, be sure,
In height or depth, still first and last will reign
Sole king, and of his kingdom lose no part   325
By our revolt, but over hell extend
His empire, and with iron sceptre rule
Us here, as with his golden those in heaven.
What sit we then projecting peace and war?
War hath determined us, and foiled with loss   330
Irreparable; terms of peace yet none
Vouchsafed or sought; for what peace will be given
To us enslaved, but custody severe,
And stripes and arbitrary punishment
Inflicted? And what peace can we return,   335
But, to our power, hostility and hate,
Untamed reluctance, and revenge, though slow,
Yet ever plotting how the conqueror least
May reap his conquest, and may least rejoice
In doing what we most in suffering feel?   340

302 front] forehead or face.
306 Atlantean] Atlas, one of the Titans, was condemned to carry the heavens
     on his shoulders as a punishment for his part in the invasion of the heavens.
312 style] ceremonial designation.
324 first and last] Rev. i. 11.
327 iron sceptre] See Milton's translation of Psalm II. 9 (l.20).
336 to] to the limit of.

Nor will occasion want, nor shall we need
With dangerous expedition to invade
Heaven, whose high walls fear no assault or siege,
Or ambush from the deep. What if we find
Some easier enterprise? There is a place   345
(If ancient and prophetic fame in heaven
Err not) – another world, the happy seat
Of some new race called Man, about this time
To be created like to us, though less
In power and excellence, but favoured more   350
Of him who rules above; so was his will
Pronounced among the gods, and by an oath
That shook heaven's whole circumference, confirmed.
Thither let us bend all our thoughts, to learn
What creatures there inhabit, of what mould   355
Or substance, how endued, and what their power
And where their weakness; how attempted best
By force or subtlety; though heaven be shut,
And heaven's high arbitrator sit secure
In his own strength, this place may lie exposed,   360
The utmost border of his kingdom, left
To their defence who hold it: here perhaps
Some advantageous acts may be achieved
By sudden onset – either with hell-fire
To waste his whole creation, or possess   365
All as our own, and drive, as we are driven,
The puny habitants; or if not drive,
Seduce them to our party, that their God
May prove their foe, and with repenting hand
Abolish his own works. This would surpass   370
Common revenge, and interrupt his joy
In our confusion, and our joy upraise
In his disturbance; when his darling sons,
Hurled headlong to partake with us, shall curse
Their frail original, and faded bliss –   375
Faded so soon. Advise if this be worth
Attempting, or to sit in darkness here
Hatching vain empires.' Thus Beëlzebub
Pleaded his devilish counsel – first devised

352] Isa. xiii. 12-13; Heb. vi. 17; *Iliad* i 530; *Aeneid* ix 106.
367 puny] means 'born later' (*puis né*), 'inferior in rank' (cf. ll. 349-50, Psalm
viii. 5) and 'weak'.
375 original] progenitor, i.e. Adam.
376 Advise] ponder.
377 sit in darkness] Psalm cvii. 10-11.

By Satan, and in part proposed: for whence,   380
But from the author of all ill, could spring
So deep a malice, to confound the race
Of mankind in one root, and earth with hell
To mingle and involve, done all to spite
The great creator? But their spite still serves   385
His glory to augment. The bold design
Pleased highly those infernal states, and joy
Sparkled in all their eyes; with full assent
They vote: whereat his speech he thus renews:
    'Well have ye judged, well ended long debate,   390
Synod of gods, and like to what ye are,
Great things resolved, which from the lowest deep
Will once more lift us up, in spite of fate,
Nearer our ancient seat – perhaps in view   394
Of those bright confines, whence, with neighbouring arms
And opportune excursion, we may chance
Re-enter heaven; or else in some mild zone
Dwell, not unvisited of heaven's fair light
Secure, and at the brightening orient beam
Purge off this gloom: the soft delicious air,   400
To heal the scar of these corrosive fires,
Shall breathe her balm. But, first, whom shall we send
In search of this new world, whom shall we find
Sufficient? Who shall tempt with wandering feet
The dark, unbottomed, infinite abyss,   405
And through the palpable obscure find out
His uncouth way, or spread his airy flight,
Upborne with indefatigable wings
Over the vast abrupt, ere he arrive
The happy isle? What strength, what art, can then   410
Suffice, or what evasion bear him safe,
Through the strict senteries and stations thick
Of angels watching round? Here he had need
All circumspection, and we now no less
Choice in our suffrage; for on whom we send   415
The weight of all, and our last hope, relies.'
    This said, he sat; and expectation held

387 states] the 'estates' of Parliament.
391 Synod] means 'assembly of clergy' and secondarily, 'conjunction of stars'.
402-4] Isa. vi. 8.
404 tempt] risk the perils of.
406 palpable obscure] See XII 184-8n.
407 uncouth] unknown.
409 abrupt] abyss.
412 senteries] sentries.

His look suspense, awaiting who appeared
To second, or oppose, or undertake
The perilous attempt; but all sat mute,   420
Pondering the danger with deep thoughts; and each
In other's countenance read his own dismay,
Astonished; none among the choice and prime
Of those heaven-warring champions could be found
So hardy as to proffer or accept,   425
Alone, the dreadful voyage; till at last
Satan, whom now transcendent glory raised
Above his fellows, with monarchal pride
Conscious of highest worth, unmoved thus spake:
      'O progeny of heaven, empyreal thrones;   430
With reason hath deep silence and demur
Seized us, though undismayed; long is the way
And hard, that out of hell leads up to light;
Our prison strong, this huge convex of fire,
Outrageous to devour, immures us round   435
Ninefold; and gates of burning adamant,
Barred over us, prohibit all egress.
These passed, if any pass, the void profound
Of unessential night receives him next,
Wide gaping, and with utter loss of being   440
Threatens him, plunged in that abortive gulf.
If thence he scape, into whatever world,
Or unknown region, what remains him less
Than unknown dangers, and as hard escape?
But I should ill become this throne, O peers,   445
And this imperial sovereignty, adorned
With splendour, armed with power, if aught proposed
And judged of public moment in the shape
Of difficulty or danger, could deter
Me from attempting. Wherefore do I assume   450
These royalties, and not refuse to reign,
Refusing to accept as great a share
Of hazard as of honour, due alike
To him who reigns, and so much to him due
Of hazard more as he above the rest   455
High honoured sits? Go therefore mighty powers,
Terror of heaven, though fallen; intend at home,

432-3] Cf.*Aeneid* vi 126-9, and Dante, *Inferno* xxxiv. 95.
434 convex] the vault of hell.
439 unessential] without being, uncreated (cf.l.150).
441 abortive] rendering fruitless.
452 Refusing] if I refuse.
457 intend] consider.

While here shall be our home, what best may ease
The present misery, and render hell
More tolerable; if there be cure or charm　　　　460
To respite or deceive, or slack the pain
Of this ill mansion: intermit no watch
Against a wakeful foe, while I abroad
Through all the coasts of dark destruction seek
Deliverance for us all; this enterprise　　　　465
None shall partake with me.' Thus saying, rose
The monarch, and prevented all reply;
Prudent lest, from his resolution raised,
Others among the chief might offer now
(Certain to be refused) what erst they feared,　　　　470
And so refused might in opinion stand
His rivals, winning cheap the high repute
Which he through hazard huge must earn. But they
Dreaded not more the adventure than his voice
Forbidding; and at once with him they rose;　　　　475
Their rising all at once was as the sound
Of thunder heard remote. Towards him they bend
With awful reverence prone, and as a god
Extol him equal to the highest in heaven.
Nor failed they to express how much they praised　　　　480
That for the general safety he despised
His own: for neither do the spirits damned
Lose all their virtue; lest bad men should boast
Their specious deeds on earth, which glory excites,
Or close ambition varnished o'er with zeal.　　　　485
　　Thus they their doubtful consultations dark
Ended, rejoicing in their matchless chief:
As, when from mountain tops the dusky clouds
Ascending, while the north wind sleeps, o'erspread
Heaven's cheerful face, the louring element　　　　490
Scowls o'er the darkened landscape snow or shower,
If chance the radiant sun, with farewell sweet,
Extend his evening beam, the fields revive,
The birds their notes renew, and bleating herds
Attest their joy, that hill and valley rings.　　　　495
O shame to men! Devil with devil damned
Firm concord holds; men only disagree
Of creatures rational, though under hope
Of heavenly grace, and, God proclaiming peace,

461 deceive] beguile.
468 raised] inspired with courage.
478 awful] full of awe.

Yet live in hatred, enmity, and strife   500
Among themselves, and levy cruel wars
Wasting the earth, each other to destroy:
As if (which might induce us to accord)
Man had not hellish foes enow besides,
That day and night for his destruction wait.   505
    The Stygian council thus dissolved; and forth
In order came the grand infernal peers:
Midst came their mighty paramount, and seemed
Alone the antagonist of heaven, nor less
Than hell's dread emperor, with pomp supreme   510
And god-like imitated state; him round
A globe of fiery seraphim enclosed
With bright emblazonry, and horrent arms.
Then of their session ended they bid cry
With trumpets' regal sound the great result: 515
Toward the four winds four speedy cherubim
Put to their mouths the sounding alchemy,
By herald's voice explained; the hollow abyss
Heard far and wide, and all the host of hell
With deafening shout returned them loud acclaim.   520
Thence more at ease their minds, and somewhat raised
By false presumptuous hope, the rangèd powers
Disband; and, wandering, each his several way
Pursues, as inclination or sad choice
Leads him perplexed, where he may likeliest find   525
Truce to his restless thoughts, and entertain
The irksome hours, till his great chief return.
Part on the plain, or in the air sublime,
Upon the wing or in swift race contend,
As at the Olympian games or Pythian fields;   530
Part curb their fiery steeds, or shun the goal
With rapid wheels, or fronted brigades form:
As when, to warn proud cities, war appears
Waged in the troubled sky, and armies rush
To battle in the clouds; before each van   535
Prick forth the airy knights, and couch their spears,
Till thickest legions close; with feats of arms

504 enow] enough.
512 globe] used in the Latin sense of 'a throng of people'.
513 emblazonry] heraldic devices.
        horrent] bristling.
517 alchemy] brass (i.e. trumpets).
521–69] *Iliad* xxiii 287–897, *Aeneid* v 104–603, vi 642–59.
522 powers] here means 'armies'.
530 Pythian] The Pythian games were held at Delphi.

From either end of heaven the welkin burns.
Others, with vast Typhoean rage, more fell,
Rend up both rocks and hills, and ride the air   540
In whirlwind; hell scarce holds the wild uproar:
As when Alcides, from Oechalia crowned
With conquest, felt the envenomed robe, and tore
Through pain up by the roots Thessalian pines,
And Lichas from the top of Oeta threw   545
Into the Euboic sea. Others, more mild,
Retreated in a silent valley, sing
With notes angelical to many a harp
Their own heroic deeds, and hapless fall
By doom of battle, and complain that fate   550
Free virtue should enthral to force or chance.
Their song was partial; but the harmony
(What could it less when spirits immortal sing?)
Suspended hell, and took with ravishment
The thronging audience. In discourse more sweet   555
(For eloquence the soul, song charms the sense)
Others apart sat on a hill retired,
In thoughts more elevate, and reasoned high
Of providence, foreknowledge, will, and fate —
Fixed fate, free will, foreknowledge absolute,   560
And found no end, in wandering mazes lost.
Of good and evil much they argued then,
Of happiness and final misery,
Passion and apathy, and glory and shame:
Vain wisdom all, and false philosophy —   565
Yet with a pleasing sorcery could charm
Pain for a while or anguish, and excite
Fallacious hope, or arm the obdurèd breast
With stubborn patience as with triple steel.
Another part, in squadrons and gross bands,   570

539 Typhoean] See I 197 200n. The word 'Typhon' also meant 'whirlwind' (see
  l. 541).
542–6] Hercules ('Alcides') mortally wounded the Centaur Nessus, who took his
  revenge by telling Deianira (Hercules' wife) that she should soak a garment
  in Nessus' blood in order to revive Hercules' love for her. Hercules,
  returning from a victory on Oechalia, put on the poisoned robe, which
  corroded his flesh. Distracted with pain, Hercules blamed his attendant
  Lichas (who had brought the robe) and threw him from the top of Oeta, a
  mountain in southern Thessaly, into the Euboean (Euboic) sea. See
  Metamorphoses ix 134 ff.
552 partial] biased.
564 apathy] refers to the Stoic ideal of calmness, dispassionateness (ἀπάθεια); cf.
  PR IV 300–9.

On bold adventure to discover wide
That dismal world, if any clime perhaps
Might yield them easier habitation, bend
Four ways their flying march, along the banks
Of four infernal rivers, that disgorge   575
Into the burning lake their baleful streams –
Abhorrèd Styx, the flood of deadly hate;
Sad Acheron of sorrow, black and deep;
Cocytus, named of lamentation loud
Heard on the rueful stream; fierce Phlegeton,   580
Whose waves of torrent fire inflame with rage.
Far off from these, a slow and silent stream,
Lethe, the river of oblivion, rolls
Her watery labyrinth, whereof who drinks
Forthwith his former state and being forgets –   585
Forgets both joy and grief, pleasure and pain.
Beyond this flood a frozen continent
Lies dark and wild, beat with perpetual storms
Of whirlwind and dire hail, which on firm land
Thaws not, but gathers heap, and ruin seems   590
Of ancient pile; all else deep snow and ice,
A gulf profound as that Serbonian bog
Betwixt Damiata and Mount Casius old,
Where armies whole have sunk: the parching air
Burns frore, and cold performs the effect of fire.   595
Thither, by harpy-footed Furies haled,
At certain revolutions all the damned
Are brought; and feel by turns the bitter change
Of fierce extremes, extremes by change more fierce,
From beds of raging fire to starve in ice   600
Their soft ethereal warmth, and there to pine
Immovable, infixed, and frozen round
Periods of time – thence hurried back to fire.
They ferry over this Lethean sound
Both to and fro, their sorrow to augment,   605
And wish and struggle, as they pass, to reach
The tempting stream, with one small drop to lose
In sweet forgetfulness all pain and woe,

575–81] The epithet which Milton applies to each of the four rivers of Hades is a
    translation of its Greek name.
592–4] According to an ancient tradition which survived into the Renaissance,
    Lake Serbonis (near the Egyptian coast) had swallowed whole armies.
    Damiata, modern Damietta, is a city at the eastern mouth of the Nile.
595 frore] cold, frosty.
596 Furies] The Roman name for the Erinyes, the avenging goddesses. On
    harpies see *Comus* 605n.

All in one moment, and so near the brink;
But fate withstands, and, to oppose the attempt,   610
Medusa with Gorgonian terror guards
The ford, and of itself the water flies
All taste of living wight, as once it fled
The lip of Tantalus. Thus roving on
In confused march forlorn, the adventurous bands   615
With shuddering horror pale, and eyes aghast,
Viewed first their lamentable lot, and found
No rest; through many a dark and dreary vale
They passed, and many a region dolorous,
O'er many a frozen, many a fiery alp,   620
Rocks, caves, lakes, fens, bogs, dens, and shades of death –
A universe of death, which God by curse
Created evil, for evil only good;
Where all life dies, death lives, and nature breeds,
Perverse, all monstrous, all prodigious things,   625
Abominable, inutterable, and worse
Than fables yet have feigned or fear conceived,
Gorgons, and Hydras, and Chimeras dire.
    Meanwhile the adversary of God and man,
Satan, with thoughts inflamed of highest design,   630
Puts on swift wings, and toward the gates of hell
Explores his solitary flight; sometimes
He scours the right hand coast, sometimes the left;
Now shaves with level wing the deep, then soars
Up to the fiery concave towering high.   635
As when far off at sea a fleet descried
Hangs in the clouds, by equinoctial winds
Close sailing from Bengala, or the isles
Of Ternate and Tidore, whence merchants bring
Their spicy drugs; they on the trading flood,   640
Through the wide Ethiopian to the Cape,
Ply stemming nightly toward the pole: so seemed
Far off the flying fiend; at last appear

---

611 Medusa] See *Comus* 447-52n.
614] Tantalus was condemned to stand in a pool in Tartarus; the water in the
    pool receded when he tried to drink. (*Odyssey* xi 582-92).
628] See *Comus* 447-52n., and 517n.; *Aeneid* vi 287-9. The Hydras are sea-
    serpents, not the Hydras of *Comus* 605.
632 Explores] used in the Latin sense of 'tests'.
639 Ternate, Tidore] Two tiny islands of the Moluccas.
641 Ethiopian] Indian Ocean.
    Cape] Cape of Good Hope.
642 Ply stemming] make headway against the wind.
    Pole] South Pole.

Hell-bounds, high reaching to the horrid roof,
And thrice threefold the gates; three folds were brass,   645
Three iron, three of adamantine rock,
Impenetrable, impaled with circling fire,
Yet unconsumed. Before the gates there sat
On either side a formidable shape;
The one seemed woman to the waist, and fair,   650
But ended foul in many a scaly fold,
Voluminous and vast – a serpent armed
With mortal sting; about her middle round
A cry of hell hounds never ceasing barked
With wide Cerberean mouths full loud, and rung   655
A hideous peal; yet, when they list, would creep,
If aught disturbed their noise, into her womb,
And kennel there; yet there still barked and howled
Within unseen. Far less abhorred than these
Vexed Scylla, bathing in the sea that parts   660
Calabria from the hoarse Trinacrian shore;
Nor uglier follow the night-hag, when, called
In secret, riding through the air she comes,
Lured with the smell of infant blood, to dance
With Lapland witches, while the labouring moon   665
Eclipses at their charms. The other shape –
If shape it might be called that shape had none
Distinguishable in member, joint, or limb;
Or substance might be called that shadow seemed,
For each seemed either – black it stood as night,   670
Fierce as ten Furies, terrible as hell,
And shook a dreadful dart: what seemed his head
The likeness of a kingly crown had on.
Satan was now at hand, and from his seat
The monster moving onward came as fast   675
With horrid strides; hell trembled as he strode.

647 impaled] surrounded, fenced in.
648–889] The allegory of Sin and Death is based on James i. 15, and examples of
   expansions of the allegory exist in patristic, medieval, and Renaissance
   literature.
652 Voluminous] consisting of many coils.
654 cry] pack.
655] On Cerberus see *Allegro* 1-2n.
660 Scylla] See *Comus* 257-9n. According to an ancient Christian tradition
   Scylla was a symbol of sin.
661 Trinacrian] Sicilian.
662 night-hag] Hecate, goddess of witchcraft.
665 labouring] suffering eclipse. Cf. *faticosa Luna* (*Sonnet* IV 12).
673] Rev. vi. 2.

The undaunted fiend what this might be admired,
Admired, not feared – God and his Son except,
Created thing nought valued he nor shunned –
And with disdainful look thus first began: 680
    'Whence and what art thou, execrable shape,
That dar'st, though grim and terrible, advance
Thy miscreated front athwart my way
To yonder gates? Through them I mean to pass,
That be assured, without leave asked of thee: 685
Retire, or taste thy folly, and learn by proof,
Hell-born, not to contend with spirits of heaven.'
    To whom the goblin, full of wrath, replied:
'Art thou that traitor angel, art thou he,
Who first broke peace in heaven and faith, till then   690
Unbroken, and in proud rebellious arms
Drew after him the third part of heaven's sons,
Conjured against the highest – for which both thou
And they outcast from God, are here condemned
To waste eternal days in woe and pain?   695
And reckon'st thou thyself with spirits of heaven,
Hell-doomed, and breath'st defiance here and scorn,
Where I reign king, and to enrage thee more,
Thy king and lord? Back to thy punishment,
False fugitive, and to thy speed add wings,   700
Lest with a whip of scorpions I pursue
Thy lingering, or with one stroke of this dart
Strange horror seize thee, and pangs unfelt before.'
    So spake the grisly terror, and in shape,
So speaking and so threatening, grew tenfold   705
More dreadful and deform; on the other side,
Incensed with indignation, Satan stood
Unterrified, and like a comet burned,
That fires the length of Ophiucus huge
In the arctic sky, and from his horrid hair   710
Shakes pestilence and war. Each at the head
Levelled his deadly aim; their fatal hands
No second stroke intend; and such a frown
Each cast at the other as when two black clouds,
With heaven's artillery fraught, come rattling on   715

677 admired] wondered.
692] Rev. xii. 4. Cf. *PL* I 633.
693 Conjured] sworn together in a conspiracy.
701] I Kings xii. 11.
708–11] Comets were traditionally an ominous sign; see *Aeneid* x 272–5. The 'hair' of l.710 alludes to the Greek phrase for a comet, 'long-haired (κομήτης) star'. Ophiucus is the constellation of the Serpent Bearer.

Over the Caspian – then stand front to front
Hovering a space, till winds the signal blow
To join their dark encounter in mid air;
So frowned the mighty combatants that hell
Grew darker at their frown; so matched they stood;   720
For never but once more was either like
To meet so great a foe; and now great deeds
Had been achieved, whereof all hell had rung,
Had not the snaky sorceress, that sat
Fast by hell gate and kept the fatal key,   725
Risen, and with hideous outcry rushed between.
　'O father, what intends thy hand,' she cried,
'Against thy only son? What fury, O son,
Possesses thee to bend that mortal dart
Against thy father's head? And know'st for whom?   730
For him who sits above, and laughs the while
At thee, ordained his drudge to execute
Whate'er his wrath, which he calls justice, bids –
His wrath, which one day will destroy ye both.'
　She spake, and at her words the hellish pest   735
Forbore; then these to her Satan returned;
　'So strange thy outcry, and thy words so strange
Thou interposest, that my sudden hand,
Prevented, spares to tell thee yet by deeds
What it intends, till first I know of thee   740
What thing thou art, thus double-formed, and why,
In this infernal vale first me, thou call'st
Me father, and that phantasm call'st my son.
I know thee not, nor ever saw till now
Sight more detestable than him and thee.'   745
　To whom thus the portress of hell gate replied:
'Hast thou forgot me, then; and do I seem
Now in thine eye so foul? – once deemed so fair
In heaven, when at the assembly, and in sight
Of all the seraphim with thee combined   750
In bold conspiracy against heaven's king,
All on a sudden miserable pain
Surprised thee, dim thine eyes and dizzy swum
In darkness, while thy head flames thick and fast
Threw forth, till on the left side opening wide,   755

---

718 mid air] see *Fair Infant* 16n.
752–9] The primary allusion is to the myth of Athena's birth from the head of
　　Zeus, but as that myth was seen in the Renaissance as a pagan counterpart
　　to the generation of God the Son, the passage can also be seen as a parody of
　　that event.

Likest to thee in shape and countenance bright,
Then shining heavenly fair, a goddess armed,
Out of thy head I sprung; amazement seized
All the host of heaven; back they recoiled afraid
At first, and called me Sin, and for a sign　　　760
Portentous held me; but, familiar grown,
I pleased, and with attractive graces won
The most averse – thee chiefly, who, full oft
Thyself in me thy perfect image viewing,
Becam'st enamoured; and such joy thou took'st　　　765
With me in secret that my womb conceived
A growing burden. Meanwhile war arose,
And fields were fought in heaven: wherein remained
(For what could else?) to our almighty foe
Clear victory; to our part loss and rout　　　770
Through all the empyrean; down they fell,
Driven headlong from the pitch of heaven, down
Into this deep, and in the general fall
I also: at which time this powerful key
Into my hand was given, with charge to keep　　　775
These gates for ever shut, which none can pass
Without my opening. Pensive here I sat
Alone; but long I sat not, till my womb,
Pregnant by thee, and now excessive grown,
Prodigious motion felt and rueful throes.　　　780
At last this odious offspring whom thou seest,
Thine own begotten, breaking violent way,
Tore through my entrails, that with fear and pain
Distorted, all my nether shape thus grew
Transformed: but he my inbred enemy　　　785
Forth issued, brandishing his fatal dart,
Made to destroy: I fled, and cried out "Death";
Hell trembled at the hideous name, and sighed
From all her caves, and back resounded "Death".
I fled, but he pursued (though more, it seems,　　　790
Inflamed with lust than rage) and swifter far,
Me overtook, his mother, all dismayed,
And, in embraces forcible and foul
Engendering with me, of that rape begot
These yelling monsters, that with ceaseless cry　　　795
Surround me, as thou saw'st – hourly conceived
And hourly born, with sorrow infinite
To me; for, when they list, into the womb
That bred them they return, and howl, and gnaw
My bowels, their repast; then, bursting forth　　　800
Afresh, with conscious terrors vex me round,

That rest or intermission none I find.
Before mine eyes in opposition sits
Grim Death, my son and foe, who sets them on,
And me, his parent, would full soon devour   805
For want of other prey, but that he knows
His end with mine involved, and knows that I
Should prove a bitter morsel, and his bane,
Whenever that shall be: so Fate pronounced.
But thou, O father, I forewarn thee, shun   810
His deadly arrow; neither vainly hope
To be invulnerable in those bright arms,
Though tempered heavenly; for that mortal dint,
Save he who reigns above, none can resist.'
     She finished, and the subtle fiend his lore   815
Soon learned, now milder, and thus answered smooth:
'Dear daughter – since thou claim'st me for thy sire,
And my fair son here show'st me, the dear pledge
Of dalliance had with thee in heaven, and joys
Then sweet, now sad to mention, through dire change   820
Befallen us unforeseen, unthought-of – know
I come no enemy, but to set free
From out this dark and dismal house of pain
Both him and thee, and all the heavenly host
Of spirits that, in our just pretences armed,   825
Fell with us from on high; from them I go
This uncouth errand sole, and one for all
Myself expose, with lonely steps to tread
The unfounded deep, and through the void immense
To search, with wandering quest, a place foretold   830
Should be – and, by concurring signs, ere now
Created vast and round – a place of bliss
In the purlieus of heaven; and therein placed
A race of upstart creatures, to supply
Perhaps our vacant room, though more removed,   835
Lest heaven, surcharged with potent multitude,
Might hap to move new broils; be this, or aught
Than this more secret, now designed, I haste
To know; and this once known, shall soon return,
And bring yet to the place where thou and Death   840
Shall dwell at ease, and up and down unseen
Wing silently the buxom air, embalmed

815 lore] lesson.
825 pretences] assertions of claims.
829 unfounded] bottomless.
842 buxom] unresisting.

With odours; there ye shall be fed and filled
Immeasurably: all things shall be your prey.'
   He ceased, for both seemed highly pleased, and
      Death   845
Grinned horrible a ghastly smile, to hear
His famine should be filled, and blessed his maw
Destined to that good hour; no less rejoiced
His mother bad, and thus bespake her sire:
   'The key of this infernal pit, by due   850
And by command of heaven's all-powerful king,
I keep, by him forbidden to unlock
These adamantine gates; against all force
Death ready stands to interpose his dart,
Fearless to be o'ermatched by living might.   855
But what owe I to his commands above,
Who hates me, and hath hither thrust me down
Into this gloom of Tartarus profound,
To sit in hateful office here confined,
Inhabitant of heaven and heavenly born –   860
Here in perpetual agony and pain,
With terrors and with clamours compassed round
Of mine own brood, that on my bowels feed?
Thou art my father, thou my author, thou
My being gav'st me; whom should I obey   865
But thee, whom follow? Thou wilt bring me soon
To that new world of light and bliss, among
The gods who live at ease, where I shall reign
At thy right hand voluptuous, as beseems
Thy daughter and thy darling, without end.'   870
   Thus saying, from her side the fatal key,
Sad instrument of all our woe, she took;
And, towards the gate rolling her bestial train,
Forthwith the huge portcullis high updrew,
Which, but herself, not all the Stygian powers   875
Could once have moved; then in the key-hole turns
The intricate wards, and every bolt and bar
Of massy iron or solid rock with ease
Unfastens; on a sudden open fly,
With impetuous recoil and jarring sound,   880
The infernal doors, and on their hinges grate
Harsh thunder, that the lowest bottom shook
Of Erebus. She opened, but to shut
Excelled her power: the gates wide open stood,
That with extended wings a bannered host,   885
Under spread ensigns marching, might pass through

883 Erebus] here refers to hell.

With horse and chariots ranked in loose array;
So wide they stood, and like a furnace-mouth
Cast forth redounding smoke and ruddy flame.
Before their eyes in sudden view appear   890
The secrets of the hoary deep – a dark
Illimitable ocean without bound,
Without dimension; where length, breadth, and height,
And time and place, are lost; where eldest Night
And Chaos, ancestors of Nature, hold   895
Eternal anarchy, amidst the noise
Of endless wars, and by confusion stand.
For Hot, Cold, Moist, and Dry, four champions fierce,
Strive here for mastery, and to battle bring
Their embryon atoms: they around the flag   900
Of each his faction, in their several clans,
Light-armed or heavy, sharp, smooth, swift, or slow,
Swarm populous, unnumbered as the sands
Of Barca or Cyrene's torrid soil,
Levied to side with warring winds, and poise   905
Their lighter wings. To whom these most adhere
He rules a moment: Chaos umpire sits,
And by decision more embroils the fray
By which he reigns: next him, high arbiter,
Chance governs all. Into this wild abyss,   910
The womb of Nature, and perhaps her grave,
Of neither sea, nor shore, nor air, nor fire,
But all these in their pregnant causes mixed
Confusedly, and which thus must ever fight,
Unless the almighty maker them ordain   915
His dark materials to create more worlds –
Into this wild abyss the wary fiend
Stood on the brink of hell and looked a while,
Pondering his voyage; for no narrow frith
He had to cross. Nor was his ear less pealed   920
With noises loud and ruinous (to compare
Great things with small) than when Bellona storms
With all her battering engines, bent to raze
Some capital city; or less than if this frame
Of heaven were falling, and these elements   925

891 hoary deep] Job xli. 32.
904] Barca and Cyrene were cities in Cyrenaica, a Roman province in the
    northeast of modern Libya.
905] The atoms are enlisted ('levied') to provide weight for ('poise') and thus
    stabilize the wings.
919 frith] firth.
922 Bellona] Roman goddess of war.

In mutiny had from her axle torn
The steadfast earth. At last his sail-broad vans
He spreads for flight, and, in the surging smoke
Uplifted, spurns the ground; thence many a league,
As in a cloudy chair, ascending rides   930
Audacious, but that seat soon failing, meets
A vast vacuity; all unawares,
Fluttering his pennons vain, plumb-down he drops
Ten thousand fathom deep, and to this hour
Down had been falling, had not by ill chance   935
The strong rebuff of some tumultuous cloud,
Instinct with fire and nitre, hurried him
As many miles aloft; that fury stayed –
Quenched in a boggy Syrtis, neither sea,
Nor good dry land – nigh foundered, on he fares,   940
Treading the crude consistence, half on foot,
Half flying; behoves him now both oar and sail.
As when a griffin through the wilderness
With wingèd course, o'er hill or moory dale,
Pursues the Arimaspian, who by stealth   945
Had from his wakeful custody purloined
The guarded gold; so eagerly the fiend
O'er bog or steep, through strait, rough, dense, or rare,
With head, hands, wings or feet, pursues his way,
And swims, or sinks, or wades, or creeps, or flies;   950
At length a universal hubbub wild
Of stunning sounds, and voices all confused,
Borne through the hollow dark, assaults his ear
With loudest vehemence; thither he plies
Undaunted, to meet there whatever power   955
Or spirit of the nethermost abyss
Might in that noise reside, of whom to ask
Which way the nearest coast of darkness lies
Bordering on light; when straight behold the throne
Of Chaos, and his dark pavilion spread   960
Wide on the wasteful deep; with him enthroned

927 vans] fans, i.e. wings.
933 pennons] used in the Latin sense of 'wings'.
937 Instinct] impelled, animated, inflamed.
939] The Syrtes were two sandbanks near Tripoli. Acts xxvii. 17 refers to
    quicksands (from σύρτιν), and in the R.V., Syrtis (from Σύρτιν).
943-7 Griffins were monsters who guarded the gold of Scythia against the one-
    eyed Arimaspians.
948 strait] may mean 'straight', which would contrast with 'rough', as 'dense'
    does with 'rare'.
959-67] Cf. Aeneid vi 273-81.

Sat sable-vested Night, eldest of things,
The consort of his reign; and by them stood
Orcus and Ades, and the dreaded name
Of Demogorgon; Rumour next, and Chance,   965
And Tumult and Confusion, all embroiled,
And Discord with a thousand various mouths.
    To whom Satan, turning boldly, thus: 'Ye powers
And spirits of this nethermost abyss,
Chaos and ancient Night, I come no spy   970
With purpose to explore or to disturb
The secrets of your realm, but by constraint
Wandering this darksome desert, as my way
Lies through your spacious empire up to light
Alone and without guide, half lost, I seek   975
What readiest path leads where your gloomy bounds
Confine with heaven; or if some other place,
From your dominion won, the ethereal king
Possesses lately, thither to arrive
I travel this profound; direct my course: 980
Directed, no mean recompense it brings
To your behoof, if I that region lost,
All usurpation thence expelled, reduce
To her original darkness and your sway
(Which is my present journey) and once more   985
Erect the standard there of ancient Night.
Yours be the advantage all, mine the revenge.'
    Thus Satan; and him thus the anarch old,
With faltering speech and visage incomposed,
Answered: 'I know thee, stranger, who thou art –   990
That mighty leading angel, who of late
Made head against heaven's king, though overthrown.
I saw and heard; for such a numerous host
Fled not in silence through the frighted deep,
With ruin upon ruin, rout on rout,   995
Confusion worse confounded; and heaven gates
Poured out by millions her victorious bands,
Pursuing. I upon my frontiers here
Keep residence; if all I can will serve
That little which is left so to defend,   1000

---

964 Orcus, Ades] Both are names for Pluto (Hades), god of the underworld.
965 Demogorgon] an infernal deity mentioned in a scholium on Statius, who
    refers to a mysterious 'name' dreaded by ghosts (*Thebais* iv 514).
988 anarch] Chaos.
989 incomposed] wanting in composure.
990] Mark i. 24.

Encroached on still through our intestine broils
Weakening the sceptre of old Night: first hell,
Your dungeon, stretching far and wide beneath;
Now lately heaven and earth, another world
Hung o'er my realm, linked in a golden chain   1005
To that side heaven from whence your legions fell;
If that way be your walk, you have not far;
So much the nearer danger; go, and speed;
Havoc and spoil and ruin are my gain.'
   He ceased; and Satan stayed not to reply,   1010
But glad that now his sea should find a shore,
With fresh alacrity and force renewed
Springs upward, like a pyramid of fire,
Into the wild expanse, and through the shock
Of fighting elements, on all sides round   1015
Environed, wins his way; harder beset
And more endangered than when Argo passed
Through Bosporus betwixt the jostling rocks,
Or when Ulysses on the larboard shunned
Charybdis, and by the other whirlpool steered.   1020
So he with difficulty and labour hard
Moved on, with difficulty and labour he;
But, he once passed, soon after, when man fell,
Strange alteration! Sin and Death amain,
Following his track – such was the will of heaven –   1025
Paved after him a broad and beaten way
Over the dark abyss, whose boiling gulf
Tamely endured a bridge of wondrous length,
From hell continued, reaching the utmost orb
Of this frail world; by which the spirits perverse   1030
With easy intercourse pass to and fro
To tempt or punish mortals, except whom
God and good angels guard by special grace.
   But now at last the sacred influence
Of light appears, and from the walls of heaven   1035
Shoots far into the bosom of dim Night
A glimmering dawn; here Nature first begins
Her farthest verge, and Chaos to retire,

1001 our] possibly a misprint for 'your'.
1004 heaven] the earth's sky (in 1006, God's heaven).
1005] Homer's golden chain (*Iliad* viii 18-27), a traditional symbol of the order
    and harmony of the universe.
1017-18] The Argo, with Jason and his Argonauts on board, passed through the
    Bosporus, narrowly missing the Symplegades ('jostling rocks').
1019-20] See *Comus* 257-9n., and *Odyssey* xii 234-59.
1026] Matt. vii. 13.

As from her outmost works, a broken foe,
With tumult less and with less hostile din;   1040
That Satan with less toil, and now with ease,
Wafts on the calmer wave by dubious light,
And, like a weather-beaten vessel, holds
Gladly the port, though shrouds and tackle torn;
Or in the emptier waste, resembling air,   1045
Weighs his spread wings, at leisure to behold
Far off the empyreal heaven, extended wide
In circuit, undetermined square or round,
With opal towers and battlements adorned
Of living sapphire, once his native seat;   1050
And, fast by, hanging in a golden chain,
This pendent world, in bigness as a star
Of smallest magnitude close by the moon.
Thither, full fraught with mischievous revenge,
Accursed, and in a cursed hour, he hies.   1055

THE END OF THE SECOND BOOK

1043 holds] remains in.
1048-50] Rev. xxi. 16, 19-21, Cf. *PL* X 381.
1052 pendent world] the created universe.

BOOK III

THE ARGUMENT

God, sitting on his throne, sees Satan flying towards this world, then newly created; shows him to the Son, who sat at his right hand; foretells the success of Satan in perverting mankind; clears his own justice and wisdom from all imputation, having created man free, and able enough to have withstood his tempter; yet declares his purpose of grace towards him, in regard he fell not of his own malice, as did Satan, but by him seduced. The Son of God renders praises to his Father for the manifestation of his gracious purpose towards man: but God again declares that grace cannot be extended towards man without the satisfaction of divine justice; man hath offended the majesty of God by aspiring to Godhead, and therefore, with all his progeny, devoted to death, must die, unless some one can be found sufficient to answer for his offence, and undergo his punishment. The Son of God freely offers himself a ransom for man: the Father accepts him, ordains his incarnation, pronounces his exaltation above all names in heaven and earth; commands all the angels to adore him; they obey, and hymning to their harps in full choir, celebrate the Father and the Son. Meanwhile Satan alights upon the bare convex of this world's outermost orb; where wandering he first finds a place since called the Limbo of Vanity; what persons and things fly up thither: thence comes to the gate of heaven, described ascending by stairs, and the waters above the firmament that flow about it; his passage thence to the orb of the sun: he finds there Uriel, the regent of that orb, but first changes himself into the shape of a meaner angel, and pretending a zealous desire to behold the new creation, and man whom God had placed here, enquires of him the place of his habitation, and is directed: alights first on Mount Niphates.

Hail, holy Light, offspring of heaven first-born
Or of the eternal coeternal beam
May I express thee unblamed? Since God is light,
And never but in unapproachèd light
Dwelt from eternity – dwelt then in thee, 5
Bright effluence of bright essence increate.
Or hear'st thou rather pure ethereal stream,
Whose fountain who shall tell? Before the sun,
Before the heavens thou wert, and at the voice

1 first-born] Col. i. 15.
3 God is light] I John i. 5.
4] I Tim. vi. 16.
6 effluence] emanation.
  increate] uncreated.
7 hear'st thou rather] a Latinism meaning 'would you prefer to be called'.

Of God, as with a mantle didst invest   10
The rising world of waters dark and deep,
Won from the void and formless infinite.
Thee I revisit now with bolder wing,
Escaped the Stygian pool, though long detained
In that obscure sojourn, while in my flight   15
Through utter and through middle darkness borne,
With other notes than to the Orphean lyre
I sung of Chaos and eternal Night,
Taught by the heavenly Muse to venture down
The dark descent, and up to re-ascend,   20
Though hard and rare; thee I revisit safe,
And feel thy sovereign vital lamp; but thou
Revisit'st not these eyes, that roll in vain
To find thy piercing ray, and find no dawn;
So thick a drop serene hath quenched their orbs,   25
Or dim suffusion veiled. Yet not the more
Cease I to wander where the Muses haunt
Clear spring, or shady grove, or sunny hill,
Smit with the love of sacred song; but chief
Thee, Zion, and the flowery brooks beneath,   30
That wash thy hallowed feet, and warbling flow,
Nightly I visit: nor sometimes forget
Those other two equalled with me in fate,
So were I equalled with them in renown,
Blind Thamyris and blind Maeonides,   35
And Tiresias and Phineus, prophets old:
Then feed on thoughts that voluntary move
Harmonious numbers; as the wakeful bird

10 invest] cover, surround.
12-16] The 'void and formless infinite' is chaos, as is 'middle darkness'; the
    'Stygian pool' is hell, as is 'utter' (i.e. outer) darkness.
17 Orphean] see *Allegro* 145-50n.
19 heavenly Muse] Urania. See VII 1-39.
25-6 drop serene, dim suffusion] translations of *gutta serena* and *suffusio nigra*,
    medical terms for diseases of the eye.
26-9] Virgil, *Georgics* ii 475-89.
30 Zion] here represents the Hebrew poetry of the Old Testament. Cf. *PR* IV
    347.
35 Thamyris] mythical Thracian bard blinded by the Muses (*Iliad* ii 594-600).
    Maeonides] Homer's surname.
36 Tiresias] Theban prophet whose blindness, according to Milton's Latin poem
    De Idea Platonica, gave him 'limitless light' *profundun lumen*). Cf. Marvell's
    'On *PL*' ll. 43-4 (p. 147).
    Phineus] mythical Thracian king who was blinded for revealing the
    counsels of Zeus to mortals (Hyginus, *Fabulae* xix).
38 numbers] metrical feet, hence 'lines, verses'.
    bird] nightingale.

Sings darkling, and, in shadiest covert hid,
Tunes her nocturnal note. Thus with the year   40
Seasons return; but not to me returns
Day, or the sweet approach of even or morn
Or sight of vernal bloom, or summer's rose,
Or flocks, or herds, or human face divine;
But cloud instead and ever-during dark   45
Surrounds me, from the cheerful ways of men
Cut off, and, for the book of knowledge fair,
Presented with a universal blank
Of nature's works, to me expunged and razed,
And wisdom at one entrance quite shut out.   50
So much the rather thou, celestial Light,
Shine inward, and the mind through all her powers
Irradiate; there plant eyes; all mist from thence
Purge and disperse, that I may see and tell
Of things invisible to mortal sight.   55
   Now had the almighty Father from above,
From the pure empyrean where he sits
High throned above all height, bent down his eye,
His own works and their works at once to view:
About him all the sanctities of heaven   60
Stood thick as stars, and from his sight received
Beatitude past utterance; on his right
The radiant image of his glory sat,
His only Son; on earth he first beheld
Our two first parents, yet the only two   65
Of mankind, in the happy garden placed,
Reaping immortal fruits of joy and love,
Uninterrupted joy, unrivalled love,
In blissful solitude; he then surveyed
Hell and the gulf between, and Satan there   70
Coasting the wall of heaven on this side night,
In the dun air sublime, and ready now
To stoop with wearied wings, and willing feet,
On the bare outside of this world, that seemed
Firm land imbosomed without firmament,   75
Uncertain which, in ocean or in air.
Him God beholding from his prospect high,

39 darkling] in the dark.
60 sanctities] a metonymy for 'angels'.
61 his sight] the sight of him.
72 sublime] means 'aloft', and refers to Satan's flight.
73 stoop] 'swoop down', a term from falconry.
74 bare outside] see ll.416-19n.

Wherein past, present, future, he beholds,
Thus to his only Son foreseeing spake:
   'Only-begotten Son, seest thou what rage   80
Transports our adversary, whom no bounds
Prescribed, no bars of hell, nor all the chains
Heaped on him there, nor yet the main abyss
Wide interrupt, can hold; so bent he seems
On desperate revenge, that shall redound   85
Upon his own rebellious head. And now
Through all restraint broke loose he wings his way
Not far off heaven, in the precincts of light,
Directly towards the new-created world,
And man there placed, with purpose to assay   90
If him by force he can destroy, or, worse,
By some false guile pervert: and shall pervert;
For man will hearken to his glozing lies,
And easily transgress the sole command,
Sole pledge of his obedience: so will fall   95
He and his faithless progeny: whose fault?
Whose but his own? Ingrate, he had of me
All he could have; I made him just and right,
Sufficient to have stood, though free to fall.
Such I created all the ethereal powers   100
And spirits, both them who stood and them who failed:
Freely they stood who stood, and fell who fell.
Not free, what proof could they have given sincere
Of true allegiance, constant faith, or love,
Where only what they needs must do appeared,   105
Not what they would? What praise could they receive,
What pleasure I, from such obedience paid,
When will and reason (reason also is choice),
Useless and vain, of freedom both despoiled,
Made passive both, had served necessity,   110
Not me? They therefore as to right belonged
So were created, nor can justly accuse
Their maker, or their making, or their fate,
As if predestination overruled
Their will, disposed by absolute decree   115
Or high foreknowledge; they themselves decreed
Their own revolt, not I: if I foreknew,
Foreknowledge had no influence on their fault,
Which had no less proved certain unforeknown.
So without least impulse or shadow of fate,   120
Or aught by me immutably foreseen,
They trespass, authors to themselves in all,
Both what they judge and what they choose; for so

I formed them free, and free they must remain
Till they enthral themselves: I else must change   125
Their nature, and revoke the high decree
Unchangeable, eternal, which ordained
Their freedom; they themselves ordained their fall.
The first sort by their own suggestion fell,
Self-tempted, self-depraved: man falls, deceived   130
By the other first: man, therefore, shall find grace,
The other, none; in mercy and justice both,
Through heaven and earth, so shall my glory excel;
But mercy, first and last, shall brightest shine.'
　　Thus while God spake ambrosial fragrance filled   135
All heaven, and in the blessed spirits elect
Sense of new joy ineffable diffused:
Beyond compare the Son of God was seen
Most glorious; in him all his Father shone
Substantially expressed, and in his face   140
Divine compassion visibly appeared,
Love without end, and without measure grace;
Which uttering, thus he to his Father spake:
　　'O Father, gracious was that word which closed
Thy sovereign sentence, that man should find grace;   145
For which both heaven and earth shall high extol
Thy praises, with the innumerable sound
Of hymns and sacred songs, wherewith thy throne
Encompassed shall resound thee ever blessed.
For, should man finally be lost – should man,   150
Thy creature late so loved, thy youngest son,
Fall circumvented thus by fraud, though joined
With his own folly? That be from thee far,
That far be from thee, Father, who art judge
Of all things made, and judgest only right.   155
Or shall the adversary thus obtain
His end, and frustrate thine? Shall he fulfil
His malice, and thy goodness bring to naught
Or proud return, though to his heavier doom
Yet with revenge accomplished, and to hell   160
Draw after him the whole race of mankind,
By him corrupted? Or wilt thou thyself

129 first sort] the rebellious angels.
136 spirits elect] the good angels. I Tim. v. 21.
139-40 Heb. 1. i. 3.
153-4] Gen. xviii. 25.
156 adversary] See I 82n.
158 naught] means both 'nothing' and 'evil' (cf. 'naughty').

Abolish thy creation, and unmake,
For him, what for thy glory thou hast made?
So should thy goodness and thy greatness both   165
Be questioned and blasphemed without defence.'
    To whom the great creator thus replied:
'O Son, in whom my soul hath chief delight,
Son of my bosom, Son who art alone
My word, my wisdom, and effectual might,   170
All hast thou spoken as my thoughts are, all
As my eternal purpose hath decreed:
Man shall not quite be lost, but saved who will,
Yet not of will in him, but grace in me
Freely vouchsafed; once more I will renew   175
His lapsèd powers, though forfeit, and enthralled
By sin to foul exorbitant desires:
Upheld by me, yet once more he shall stand
On even ground against his mortal foe –
By me upheld, that he may know how frail   180
His fallen condition is, and to me owe
All his deliverance, and to none but me.
Some I have chosen of peculiar grace,
Elect above the rest; so is my will:
The rest shall hear me call, and oft be warned   185
Their sinful state, and to appease betimes
The incensèd Deity, while offered grace
Invites; for I will clear their senses dark
What may suffice, and soften stony hearts
To pray, repent, and bring obedience due.   190
To prayer, repentance, and obedience due,
Though but endeavoured with sincere intent,
Mine ear shall not be slow, mine eye not shut.
And I will place within them as a guide
My umpire conscience; whom if they will hear,   195
Light after light well used they shall attain,
And to the end persisting safe arrive.
This my long sufferance, and my day of grace,
They who neglect and scorn shall never taste;
But hard be hardened, blind be blinded more,   200
That they may stumble on, and deeper fall;
And none but such from mercy I exclude.
But yet all is not done; man disobeying,

168-9] *Aeneid* i 664, Matt. iii. 17, John i. 18.
180-1] Psalm xxxix. 4.
183-5] Matt. xxii. 14.
189] Ezek. xxxvi. 26.

Disloyal, breaks his fealty, and sins
Against the high supremacy of heaven,   205
Affecting Godhead, and so losing all,
To expiate his treason hath naught left,
But to destruction sacred and devote,
He with his whole posterity must die –
Die he or justice must; unless for him   210
Some other, able, and as willing, pay
The rigid satisfaction, death for death.
Say heavenly powers, where shall we find such love?
Which of ye will be mortal, to redeem
Man's mortal crime, and just, the unjust to save?   215
Dwells in all heaven charity so dear?'
    He asked, but all the heavenly choir stood mute,
And silence was in heaven: on man's behalf
Patron or intercessor none appeared –
Much less that durst upon his own head draw   220
The deadly forfeiture, and ransom set.
And now without redemption all mankind
Must have been lost, adjudged to death and hell
By doom severe, had not the Son of God,
In whom the fullness dwells of love divine,   225
His dearest mediation thus renewed:
    'Father, thy word is passed, man shall find grace;
And shall Grace not find means, that finds her way,
The speediest of thy wingèd messengers,
To visit all thy creatures, and to all   230
Comes unprevented, unimplored, unsought?
Happy for man, so coming; he her aid
Can never seek, once dead in sins and lost –
Atonement for himself, or offering meet,
Indebted and undone, hath none to bring;   235
Behold me, then: me for him, life for life,
I offer; on me let thine anger fall;
Account me man: I for his sake will leave
Thy bosom, and this glory next to thee

---

206 Affecting] seeking.
208 sacred] primarily 'dedicated', but also 'accursed'.
    devote] doomed.
215] I Pet. iii. 18.
216 charity] the 'love' of Rom. v. 8 (ἀγάπη, translated into Latin as *caritas*).
218] Rev. viii. 1.
225] Col. ii. 9.
231 unprevented] unanticipated (i.e. not achieved by prayer). On grace preced-
    ing prayer see XI 3n. Contrast Milton's translation of Psalm lxxxviii. 13
    (ll.55–6).

Freely put off, and for him lastly die   240
Well pleased; on me let Death wreak all his rage;
Under his gloomy power I shall not long
Lie vanquished; thou hast given me to possess
Life in myself for ever; by thee I live;
Though now to Death I yield, and am his due,   245
All that of me can die, yet that debt paid,
Thou wilt not leave me in the loathsome grave
His prey, nor suffer my unspotted soul
For ever with corruption there to dwell;
But I shall rise victorious, and subdue   250
My vanquisher, spoiled of his vaunted spoil;
Death his death's wound shall then receive, and stoop
Inglorious, of his mortal sting disarmed.
I through the ample air in triumph high
Shall lead hell captive maugre hell, and show   255
The powers of darkness bound. Thou, at the sight
Pleased, out of heaven shall look down and smile,
While, by thee raised, I ruin all my foes —
Death last, and with his carcass glut the grave;
Then, with the multitude of my redeemed,   260
Shall enter heaven, long absent, and return,
Father, to see thy face, wherein no cloud
Of anger shall remain, but peace assured
And reconcilement; wrath shall be no more
Thenceforth, but in thy presence joy entire.'   265
　　His words here ended; but his meek aspéct
Silent yet spake, and breathed immortal love
To mortal men, above which only shone
Filial obedience: as a sacrifice
Glad to be offered, he attends the will   270
Of his great Father. Admiration seized
All heaven, what this might mean, and whither tend,
Wondering; but soon the almighty thus replied:
　　'O thou in heaven and earth the only peace
Found out for mankind under wrath, O thou   275
My sole complacence! Well thou know'st how dear
To me are all my works; nor man the least,
Though last created, that for him I spare
Thee from my bosom and right hand, to save,

247-9] Psalm xvi. 10.
252-3] I Cor. xv. 55-6.
255] Psalm lxviii. 18, Eph. iv. 8. 'Maugre' means 'notwithstanding the power
　　of'.
259] I Cor. xv. 26.
276 complacence] source of pleasure and satisfaction.

By losing thee a while, the whole race lost.   280
Thou, therefore, whom thou only canst redeem,
Their nature also to thy nature join;
And be thyself man among men on earth,
Made flesh, when time shall be, of virgin seed,
By wondrous birth; be thou in Adam's room   285
The head of all mankind, though Adam's son.
As in him perish all men, so in thee,
As from a second root, shall be restored
As many as are restored; without thee, none.
His crime makes guilty all his sons; thy merit   290
Imputed, shall absolve them who renounce
Their own both righteous and unrighteous deeds,
And live in thee transplanted, and from thee
Receive new life. So man, as is most just,
Shall satisfy for man, be judged and die,   295
And dying rise, and rising with him raise
His brethren, ransomed with his own dear life.
So heavenly love shall outdo hellish hate,
Giving to death, and dying to redeem,
So dearly to redeem what hellish hate   300
So easily destroyed, and still destroys
In those who, when they may, accept not grace.
Nor shalt thou, by descending to assume
Man's nature, lessen or degrade thine own.
Because thou hast, though throned in highest bliss 305
Equal to God, and equally enjoying
God-life fruition, quitted all to save
A world from utter loss, and hast been found
By merit more than birthright Son of God –
Found worthiest to be so by being good,   310
Far more than great or high; because in thee
Love hath abounded more than glory abounds;
Therefore thy humiliation shall exalt
With thee thy manhood also to this throne:
Here shalt thou sit incarnate, here shalt reign   315
Both God and man, Son both of God and man,
Anointed universal king; all power

287-9] I Cor. xv. 22.
290-1 merit/Imputed] refers to the theological doctrine whereby the sins of
    mankind are imputed to Christ, and his righteousness or merits are
    imputed to mankind. See Romans iv. 3-8, and cf. *PL* XII 294-5, 408-9.
293 transplanted] refers to the theological doctrine whereby God the Father is
    said to 'plant' or 'engraft' believers in Christ, thus rendering them fit for
    their eventual union with the body of Christ. Cf. XII 7n.
299 Giving] submitting.
317-18] Matt. xxviii. 18.

I give thee; reign for ever, and assume
Thy merits; under thee, as head supreme,
Thrones, princedoms, powers, dominions, I reduce: 320
All knees to thee shall bow of them that bide
In heaven, or earth, or under earth in hell;
When thou, attended gloriously from heaven,
Shalt in the sky appear, and from thee send
The summoning archangels to proclaim   325
Thy dread tribunal, forthwith from all winds
The living, and forthwith the cited dead
Of all past ages, to the general doom
Shall hasten; such a peal shall rouse their sleep.
Then all thy saints assembled, thou shalt judge   330
Bad men and angels; thy arraigned shall sink
Beneath thy sentence; hell, her numbers full,
Thenceforth shall be for ever shut. Meanwhile
The world shall burn, and from her ashes spring
New heaven and earth, wherein the just shall dwell,   335
And after all their tribulations long,
See golden days, fruitful of golden deeds,
With joy and love triumphing, and fair truth.
Then thou thy regal sceptre shalt lay by,
For regal sceptre then no more shall need;   340
God shall be all in all. But all ye gods,
Adore him who, to compass all this, dies;
Adore the Son, and honour him as me.'
   No sooner had the almighty ceased but – all
The multitude of angels, with a shout   345
Loud as from numbers without number, sweet
As from blessed voices, uttering joy – heaven rung
With jubilee, and loud hosannas filled
The eternal regions; lowly reverent
Towards either throne they bow, and to the ground   350
With solemn adoration down they cast
Their crowns, inwove with amarant and gold –
Immortal amarant, a flower which once

320] See Col. i. 16 (where Milton's 'princedoms' are called 'principalities').
321-2] Phil. ii. 10.
323-4] Matt. xxiv. 30-1.
327-9] I Cor. xv. 51-2.
334-5] II Pet. iii. 12-13.
343] John v. 23.
352-61] Amarant ('amaranthus' in *Lycidas* 149) is a flower that was an ancient
     symbol of immortality. In I Pet. i. 4 and v. 4 the crown of glory 'that fadeth
     not away' is said in the Greek to be ἀμαράντινον, i.e. unfading, imperishable
     (cf. l. 360).

In Paradise, fast by the tree of life,
Began to bloom, but soon for man's offence   355
To heaven removed where first it grew, there grows
And flowers aloft, shading the fount of life,
And where the river of bliss through midst of heaven
Rolls o'er Elysian flowers her amber stream;
With these, that never fade, the spirits elect   360
Bind their resplendent locks, inwreathed with beams;
Now in loose garlands thick thrown off, the bright
Pavement, that like a sea of jasper shone,
Impurpled with celestial roses smiled.
Then, crowned again, their golden harps they took –   365
Harps ever tuned, that glittering by their side
Like quivers hung; and with preamble sweet
Of charming symphony they introduce
Their sacred song, and waken raptures high:
No voice exempt, no voice but well could join   370
Melodious part; such concord is in heaven.
    'Thee, Father', first they sung, 'omnipotent,
Immutable, immortal, infinite,
Eternal king; thee, author of all being,
Fountain of light, thyself invisible   375
Amidst the glorious brightness where thou sitt'st
Throned inaccessible, but when thou shad'st
The full blaze of thy beams, and through a cloud
Drawn round about thee like a radiant shrine
Dark with excessive bright thy skirts appear,   380
Yet dazzle heaven, that brightest seraphim
Approach not, but with both wings veil their eyes.
Thee next they sang, of all creation first,
Begotten Son, divine similitude,
In whose conspicuous countenance, without cloud   385
Made visible, the almighty Father shines,
Whom else no creature can behold: on thee
Impressed the effulgence of his glory abides;
Transfused on thee his ample spirit rests.
He heaven of heavens, and all the powers therein,   390
By thee created, and by thee threw down
The aspiring dominations; thou that day
Thy Father's dreadful thunder didst not spare,
Nor stop thy flaming chariot-wheels, that shook

370 exempt] excluded from participation.
375-9] I Tim. vi. 16.
381-2] Isa. vi. 2.
383] Col. i. 15-17; Rev. iii. 14.

Heaven's everlasting frame, while o'er the necks   395
Thou drov'st of warring angels disarrayed.
Back from pursuit, thy powers with loud acclaim
Thee only extolled, Son of thy Father's might,
To execute fierce vengeance on his foes,
Not so on man: him, through their malice fallen,   400
Father of mercy and grace, thou didst not doom
So strictly, but much more to pity incline;
No sooner did thy dear and only Son
Perceive thee purposed not to doom frail man
So strictly, but much more to pity inclined   405
He to appease thy wrath, and end the strife
Of mercy and justice in thy face discerned,
Regardless of the bliss wherein he sat
Second to thee, offered himself to die
For man's offence. O unexampled love,   410
Love nowhere to be found less than divine!
Hail, Son of God, saviour of men; thy name
Shall be the copious matter of my song
Henceforth, and never shall my harp thy praise
Forget, nor from thy Father's praise disjoin.'   415
      Thus they in heaven, above the starry sphere,
Their happy hours in joy and hymning spent.
Meanwhile, upon the firm opacous globe
Of this round world, whose first convex divides
The luminous inferior orbs, enclosed   420
From Chaos and the inroad of darkness old,
Satan alighted walks; a globe far off
It seemed, now seems a boundless continent,
Dark, waste, and wild, under the frown of Night
Starless exposed, and ever-threatening storms   425
Of Chaos blustering round, inclement sky,
Save on that side which from the wall of heaven,
Though distant far, some small reflection gains
Of glimmering air less vexed with tempest loud;
Here walked the fiend at large in spacious field.   430
As when a vulture, on Imaus bred,
Whose snowy ridge the roving Tartar bounds,
Dislodging from a region scarce of prey,
To gorge the flesh of lambs or yeanling kids

416-19] The 'starry sphere' is the sphere of the fixed stars; the opaque
('opacous') globe is the created universe; the 'round world' is Earth; the
'first convex' (i.e. first sphere) is the *primum mobile*, the 'bare outside of
this world' of l. 74. Cf. ll. 481-3n.
431 Imaus] mountain range extending from the Himalayas to the Arctic Ocean.

On hills where flocks are fed, flies toward the springs   435
Of Ganges or Hydaspes, Indian streams,
But in his way lights on the barren plains
Of Sericana, where Chineses drive
With sails and wind their cany wagons light;
So, on this windy sea of land, the fiend   440
Walked up and down alone, bent on his prey:
Alone, for other creature in this place,
Living or lifeless, to be found was none,
None yet, but store hereafter from the earth
Up hither like aerial vapours flew   445
Of all things transitory and vain, when sin
With vanity had filled the works of men –
Both all things vain, and all who in vain things
Built their fond hopes of glory or lasting fame,
Or happiness in this or the other life.   450
All who have their reward on earth, the fruits
Of painful superstition and blind zeal,
Naught seeking but the praise of men, here find
Fit retribution, empty as their deeds;
All the unaccomplished works of nature's hand,   455
Abortive, monstrous, or unkindly mixed,
Dissolved on earth, fleet hither, and in vain,
Till final dissolution, wander here –
Not in the neighbouring moon, as some have dreamed;
Those argent fields more likely habitants,   460
Translated saints, or middle spirits hold,
Betwixt the angelical and human kind;
Hither of ill-joined sons and daughters born
First from the ancient world those Giants came,
With many a vain exploit, though then renowned;   465
The builders next of Babel on the plain
Of Sennaär, and still with vain design

436 Hydaspes] modern Jhelum, in Pakistan
438 Sericana] Cathay, here apparently not distinguished from China (but cf. XI
   388, 90).
452 painful] painstaking, laborious.
456 unkindly] contrary to the usual course of nature.
459 some] Ariosto. Milton's Paradise of Fools (ll.444-97) is loosely modelled on
   a lunar limbo described in *Orlando Furioso* xxxiv.
461 Translated saints] 'Translated' is the term used in Heb. xi. 5 for the
   conveyance of Enoch to heaven without death (Gen. v. 24); Elijah was
   similarly honoured (II Kings ii. 1-18).
463-5] Gen. vi. 2-4; cf. *PL* V 447-8, XI 621-2.
466-7] Gen. xi. 1-9. Sennaär is the LXX and Vulgate form of 'Shinar' (verse 2).
   Cf. XII 38-62.

New Babels, had they wherewithal, would build:
Others came single; he who to be deemed
A god, leaped fondly into Aetna flames,   470
Empedocles; and he who to enjoy
Plato's Elysium, leaped into the sea,
Cleombrotus; and many more, too long,
Embryos and idiots, eremites and friars,
White, black and grey, with all their trumpery.   475
Here pilgrims roam, that strayed so far to seek
In Golgotha him dead who lives in heaven;
And they who, to be sure of Paradise,
Dying put on the weeds of Dominic,
Or in Franciscan think to pass disguised.   480
They pass the planets seven, and pass the fixed,
And that crystalline sphere whose balance weighs
The trepidation talked, and that first moved;
And now Saint Peter at heaven's wicket seems
To wait them with his keys, and now at foot   485
Of heaven's ascent they lift their feet, when lo
A violent cross wind from either coast
Blows them transverse ten thousand leagues awry,
Into the devious air; then might ye see
Cowls, hoods and habits, with their wearers, tossed   490
And fluttered into rags; then relics, beads,
Indulgences, dispenses, pardons, bulls,
The sport of winds: all these, upwhirled aloft,

469-71] There are conflicting accounts of the death of the philosopher and
    statesman Empedocles; according to one tradition he committed suicide to
    hide his own mortality.
471-3] Cleombrotus was so eager to enjoy the immortality described by Plato
    in *Phaedo* that he drowned himself.
474] In Catholic theology a limbo is provided for those who die in original sin,
    but are guiltless of personal sin. 'Embryos and idiots' were consigned to
    this *limbus infantum*.
474-5] The satire is directed against four orders of mendicant friars: Augusti-
    nian Hermits ('eremites'), Carmelites (White Friars), Dominicans (Black
    Friars), and Franciscans (Grey Friars).
477 Golgotha] The Hebrew name for Calvary, where Jesus was crucified.
481-3] Medieval Ptolemaic astronomy assumed the existence of ten spheres;
    seven were planetary spheres (including the sun), the eighth was the sphere
    of the fixed stars (the 'starry sphere' of l. 416), the ninth was the
    'crystalline sphere', and the tenth was the *primum mobile* (see *Fair Infant*
    39n). The 'trepidation' (i.e. libration, oscillation) of the eighth and ninth
    spheres was held to be responsible for the precession of the equinoxes.
484-5] Matt. xvi. 19. Cf. *Lycidas* 108-31.
492 dispenses] dispensations.

Fly o'er the backside of the world far off
Into a limbo large and broad, since called   495
The Paradise of Fools, to few unknown
Long after, now unpeopled and untrod;
All this dark globe the fiend found as he passed,
And long he wandered, till at last a gleam
Of dawning light turned thitherward in haste   500
His travelled steps; far distant he descries,
Ascending by degrees magnificent
Up to the wall of heaven, a structure high;
At top whereof, but far more rich, appeared
The work as of a kingly palace gate,   505
With frontispiece of diamond and gold
Embellished; thick with sparkling orient gems
The portal shone, inimitable on earth
By model, or by shading pencil drawn.
The stairs were such as whereon Jacob saw   510
Angels ascending and descending, bands
Of guardians bright, when he from Esau fled
To Padan-Aram, in the field of Luz
Dreaming by night under the open sky,
And waking cried 'This is the gate of heaven.'   515
Each stair mysteriously was meant, nor stood
There always, but drawn up to heaven sometimes
Viewless; and underneath a bright sea flowed
Of jasper, or of liquid pearl, whereon
Who after came from earth sailing arrived   520
Wafted by angels, or flew o'er the lake
Rapt in a chariot drawn by fiery steeds.
The stairs were then let down, whether to dare
The fiend by easy ascent, or aggravate
His sad exclusion from the doors of bliss: 525
Direct against which opened from beneath,
Just o'er the blissful seat of Paradise,
A passage down to the earth – a passage wide,
Wider by far than that of after-times
Over Mount Zion, and, though that were large,   530

---

501 travelled] means both 'experienced in travel' and 'wearied'.
502 degrees] steps.
510–15] Gen. xxviii. John i. 51.
518 Viewless] invisible.
     sea] described in 'The Argument' (p. 201) as 'the waters above the
     firmament'.
521 Wafted by angels] refers to Lazarus (Luke xvi. 22).
522] describes Elijah (II Kings ii. 11). Cf. *PR* II 16–17. 'Rapt' means 'carried
     away'.

Over the Promised Land to God so dear,
By which, to visit oft those happy tribes,
On high behests his angels to and fro
Passed frequent, and his eye with choice regard
From Paneas, the fount of Jordan's flood,   535
To Beërsaba, where the Holy Land
Borders on Egypt and the Arabian shore;
So wide the opening seemed, where bounds were set
To darkness, such as bound the ocean wave.
Satan from hence, now on the lower stair,   540
That scaled by steps of gold to heaven gate,
Looks down with wonder at the sudden view
Of all this world at once. As when a scout,
Through dark and desert ways with peril gone
All night, at last by break of cheerful dawn   545
Obtains the brow of some high-climbing hill,
Which to his eye discovers unaware
The goodly prospect of some foreign land
First seen, or some renowned metropolis
With glistering spires and pinnacles adorned,   550
Which now the rising sun gilds with his beams;
Such wonder seized, though after heaven seen,
The spirit malign, but much more envy seized,
At sight of all this world beheld so fair.
Round he surveys – and well might, where he stood   555
So high above the circling canopy
Of night's extended shade – from eastern point
Of Libra to the fleecy star that bears
Andromeda far off Atlantic seas
Beyond the horizon; then from pole to pole   560
He views his breadth, and without longer pause,
Down right into the world's first region throws
His flight precipitant, and winds with ease
Through the pure marble air his oblique way
Amongst innumerable stars, that shone   565
Stars distant, but nigh-hand seemed other worlds;
Or other worlds they seemed, or happy isles,
Like those Hesperian gardens famed of old,

535-6] The fountain Leddan, the largest source of the Jordan, is on the western
side of the city of Dan, which in late Greek is called *Paneas* (modern
Baniyas, in Syria). The formula 'from Dan even to Beer-sheba' is common
in the O.T., and refers to the extreme northern and southern points of
Israel; Beërsaba is the Vulgate and LXX form.
558 fleecy star] Aries, the Ram.
564 marble] smooth as marble.
568] See *Comus* 393-5n.

Fortunate fields, and groves, and flowery vales;
Thrice happy isles – but who dwelt happy there   570
He stayed not to inquire: above them all
The golden sun, in splendour likest heaven,
Allured his eye; thither his course he bends,
Through the calm firmament – but up or down,
By centre or eccentric, hard to tell,   575
Or longitude – where the great luminary,
Aloof the vulgar constellations thick,
That from his lordly eye keep distance due,
Dispenses light from far; they, as they move
Their starry dance in numbers that compute   580
Days, months, and years, towards his all-cheering lamp
Turn swift their various motions, or are turned
By his magnetic beam, that gently warms
The universe, and to each inward part
With gentle penetration, though unseen,   585
Shoots invisible virtue even to the deep;
So wondrously was set his station bright.
There lands the fiend, a spot like which perhaps
Astronomer in the sun's lucent orb
Through his glazed optic tube yet never saw.   590
The place he found beyond expression bright,
Compared with aught on earth, metal or stone –
Not all parts like, but all alike informed
With radiant light, as glowing iron with fire.
If metal, part seemed gold, part silver clear;   595
If stone, carbuncle most or chrysolite,
Ruby or topaz, to the twelve that shone
In Aaron's breast-plate, and a stone besides,
Imagined rather oft than elsewhere seen –
That stone, or like to that, which here below   600

575 centre] centric (orbit). A centric orbit has the earth or sun at its centre; an
      eccentric orbit does not. In the Ptolemaic system eccentric orbits were used
      (along with epicycles; see VIII 84n.) to account for irregularities in
      planetary motion. Ll. 574-6 thus accommodate the possibility of either a
      Ptolemaic or a Copernican universe.
576 longitude] distance as measured by degrees of longitude along the ecliptic.
577 Aloof] apart from.
      vulgar] used for the calculation of distance.
588-90 Sun-spots had been observed by Galileo in 1610, and by Fabricius in
      1611.
596-8] Exod. xxviii. 17-20. Chrysolite appears as the first stone in the fourth
      row in the LXX and Vulgate.
600-1] The 'philosophers' stone' was supposed by alchemists to possess the
      property of changing other metals into gold or silver.

Philosophers in vain so long have sought;
In vain, though by their powerful art they bind
Volatile Hermes, and call up unbound
In various shapes old Proteus from the sea,
Drained through a limbeck to his native form.   605
What wonder then if fields and regions here
Breathe forth elixir pure, and rivers run
Potable gold, when with one virtuous touch
The arch-chemic sun, so far from us remote,
Produces, with terrestrial humour mixed,   610
Here in the dark so many precious things
Of colour glorious and effect so rare?
Here matter new to gaze the devil met
Undazzled; far and wide his eye commands;
For sight no obstacle found here, nor shade,   615
But all sunshine, as when his beams at noon
Culminate from the equator, as they now
Shot upward still direct, whence no way round
Shadow from body opaque can fall; and the air,
Nowhere so clear, sharpened his visual ray   620
To objects distant far, whereby he soon
Saw within ken a glorious angel stand,
The same whom John saw also in the sun;
His back was turned, but not his brightness hid;
Of beaming sunny rays a golden tiar   625
Circled his head, nor less his locks behind
Illustrious on his shoulders fledge with wings
Lay waving round: on some great charge employed
He seemed, or fixed in cogitation deep.

602-3 bind ... Hermes] solidify mercury.
604 Proteus] Greek sea-god who had the power to assume any form he wished,
    hence an appropriate metaphor for the alchemical transmutation of matter.
605 limbeck] alembic, an apparatus used to distil mercury.
606 here] in the sun.
607 elixir] a substance such as the philosophers' stone which would change
    metals into gold.
608 Potable] drinkable.
    virtuous] life-giving.
609 arch-chemic] chief of alchemists, so called because its rays were said to
    penetrate the surface of the earth and produce precious stones. Cf. *PL* V
    300-2, VI 477-81.
610 humour] moisture.
618 still direct] Before the fall occasioned the 'changes in the heavens'
    described in *PL* X 668-91, the sun's ecliptic coincided with the earth's
    equator, and 'direct' beams were therefore a daily occurrence.
623] Rev. xix. 17.
627 Illustrious] lustrous, shining.

Glad was the spirit impure, as now in hope   630
To find who might direct his wandering flight
To Paradise, the happy seat of man,
His journey's end, and our beginning woe.
But first he casts to change his proper shape,
Which else might work him danger or delay: 635
And now a stripling cherub he appears,
Not of the prime, yet such as in his face
Youth smiled celestial, and to every limb
Suitable grace diffused, so well he feigned;
Under a coronet his flowing hair   640
In curls on either cheek played; wings he wore
Of many a coloured plume sprinkled with gold,
His habit fit for speed succinct, and held
Before his decent steps a silver wand.
He drew not nigh unheard; the angel bright,   645
Ere he drew nigh, his radiant visage turned,
Admonished by his ear, and straight was known
The archangel Uriel – one of the seven
Who in God's presence, nearest to his throne,
Stand ready at command, and are his eyes   650
That run through all the heavens, or down to the earth
Bear his swift errands over moist and dry,
O'er sea and land; him Satan thus accosts:
     'Uriel, for thou of those seven spirits that stand
In sight of God's high throne, gloriously bright,   655
The first art wont his great authentic will
Interpreter through highest heaven to bring,
Where all his sons thy embassy attend,
And here art likeliest by supreme decree
Like honour to obtain, and as his eye   660
To visit oft this new Creation round –
Unspeakable desire to see and know
All these his wondrous works, but chiefly man,
His chief delight and favour, him for whom
All these his works so wondrous he ordained,   665
Hath brought me from the choirs of cherubim
Alone thus wandering. Brightest seraph, tell
In which of all these shining orbs hath man

---

634 casts] decides.
643 succinct] modifies 'habit', and means 'close-fitting, scant'.
648 Uriel] The name means in Hebrew 'flame (or light) of God', but in the O.T.
     it is never used of an angel. Milton probably had access to the tradition
     embodied in the pseudepigraphical Ethiopic Book of Enoch (xx. 2), where
     Uriel is described as 'the angel who is over the world and Tartarus'.
648-9] Rev. i. 4.

His fixèd seat – or fixèd seat hath none,
But all these shining orbs his choice to dwell –   670
That I may find him, and with secret gaze
Or open admiration him behold
On whom the great creator hath bestowed
Worlds, and on whom hath all these graces poured;
That both in him and all things, as is meet,   675
The universal maker we may praise;
Who justly hath driven out his rebel foes
To deepest hell, and, to repair that loss,
Created this new happy race of men
To serve him better: wise are all his ways.'   680
    So spake the false dissembler unperceived;
For neither man nor angel can discern
Hypocrisy – the only evil that walks
Invisible, except to God alone,
By his permissive will, through heaven and earth;   685
And oft, though wisdom wake, suspicion sleeps
At wisdom's gate, and to simplicity
Resigns her charge, while godness thinks no ill
Where no ill seems: which now for once beguiled
Uriel, though regent of the sun, and held   690
The sharpest-sighted spirit of all in heaven;
Who to the fraudulent impostor foul,
In his uprightness, answer thus returned:
    'Fair angel, thy desire, which tends to know
The works of God, thereby to glorify   695
The great work-master, leads to no excess
That reaches blame, but rather merits praise
The more it seems excess, that led thee hither
From thy empyreal mansion thus alone,
To witness with thine eyes what some perhaps,   700
Contented with report, hear only in heaven:
For wonderful indeed are all his works,
Pleasant to know, and worthiest to be all
Had in remembrance always with delight;
But what created mind can comprehend   705
Their number, or the wisdom infinite
That brought them forth, but hid their causes deep?
I saw when, at his word, the formless mass,
This world's material mould, came to a heap:
Confusion heard his voice, and wild uproar   710

671-2] Echoes Herod's words in Matt. ii. 8.
706-7] Prov. iii. 19.
709 mould] substance.

Stood ruled, stood vast infinitude confined;
Till, at his second bidding, darkness fled,
Light shone, and order from disorder sprung;
Swift to their several quarters hasted then
The cumbrous elements – earth, flood, air, fire;   715
And this ethereal quintessence of heaven
Flew upward, spirited with various forms,
That rolled orbicular, and turned to stars
Numberless, as thou seest, and how they move:
Each had his place appointed, each his course;   720
The rest in circuit walls this universe.
Look downward on that globe, whose hither side
With light from hence, though but reflected, shines:
That place is earth, the seat of man; that light
His day, which else, as the other hemisphere,   725
Night would invade; but there the neighbouring moon
(So call that opposite fair star) her aid
Timely interposes, and her monthly round
Still ending, still renewing, through mid-heaven,
With borrowed light her countenance triform   730
Hence fills and empties, to enlighten the earth,
And in her pale dominion checks the night.
That spot to which I point is Paradise,
Adam's abode; those lofty shades his bower.
Thy way thou canst not miss; me mine requires.'   735
    Thus said, he turned; and Satan, bowing low,
As to superior spirits is wont in heaven,
Where honour due and reverence none neglects,
Took leave, and toward the coast of earth beneath,
Down from the ecliptic, sped with hoped success,   740
Throws his steep flight in many an airy wheel,
Nor stayed till on Niphates' top he lights.

THE END OF THE THIRD BOOK

716 quintessence] the 'fifth essence', the substance of which heavenly bodies
     were composed, was 'ether'. Cf. *PL* VII 243-4.
730 triform] Diana was thought to be triform for several reasons, among which
     was conformity to the three phases of the moon.
742 Niphates] mountain on the border of Armenia and Assyria.

BOOK IV

Satan, now in prospect of Eden, and nigh the place where he must now attempt the bold enterprise which he undertook alone against God and man, falls into many doubts with himself and many passions – fear, envy, and despair; but at length confirms himself in evil; journeys on to Paradise, whose outward prospect and situation is described; overleaps the bounds; sits, in the shape of a cormorant, on the tree of life, as highest in the garden, to look about him. The garden described; Satan's first sight of Adam and Eve; his wonder at their excellent form and happy state, but with resolution to work their fall; overhears their discourse; thence gathers that the tree of knowledge was forbidden them to eat of under penalty of death, and thereon intends to found his temptation by seducing them to transgress; then leaves them a while, to know further of their state by some other means. Meanwhile Uriel, descending on a sunbeam, warns Gabriel, who had in charge the gate of Paradise, that some evil spirit had escaped the deep, and passed at noon by his sphere, in the shape of a good angel, down to Paradise, discovered after by his furious gestures in the mount. Gabriel promises to find him ere morning. Night coming on, Adam and Eve discourse of going to their rest: their bower described; their evening worship. Gabriel, drawing forth his bands of night-watch to walk the round of Paradise, appoints two strong angels to Adam's bower, lest the evil spirit should be there doing some harm to Adam or Eve sleeping: there they find him at the ear of Eve, tempting her in a dream, and bring him, though unwilling, to Gabriel; by whom questioned, he scornfully answers; prepares resistance; but hindered by a sign from heaven, flies out of Paradise.

O for that warning voice, which he who saw
The Apocalypse heard cry in heaven aloud,
Then when the dragon, put to second rout,
Came furious down to be revenged on men,
'Woe to the inhabitants on Earth!' that now,   5
While time was, our first parents had been warned
The coming of their secret foe, and scaped,
Haply so scaped, his mortal snare; for now
Satan, now first inflamed with rage, came down,
The tempter, ere the accuser, of mankind,   10
To wreak on innocent frail man his loss
Of that first battle, and his flight to hell;
Yet not rejoicing in his speed, though bold

1-12] On the 'warning voice' which John heard see Rev. xii. 3-12.

Far off and fearless, nor with cause to boast,
Begins his dire attempt; which, nigh the birth   15
Now rolling, boils in his tumultuous breast,
And like a devilish engine back recoils
Upon himself; horror and doubt distract
His troubled thoughts, and from the bottom stir
The hell within him; for within him hell   20
He brings, and round about him, nor from hell
One step, no more than from himself, can fly
By change of place; now conscience wakes despair
That slumbered, wakes the bitter memory
Of what he was, what is, and what must be   25
Worse; of worse deeds worse sufferings must ensue.
Sometimes towards Eden, which now in his view
Lay pleasant, his grieved look he fixes sad;
Sometimes towards heaven and the full-blazing sun, .
Which now sat high in his meridan tower: 30
Then, much revolving, thus in sighs began:
  'O thou that, with surpassing glory crowned,
Look'st from thy sole dominion like the God
Of this new world – at whose sight all the stars
Hide their diminished heads – to thee I call,   35
But with no friendly voice, and add thy name,
O sun, to tell thee how I hate thy beams
That bring to my remembrance from what state
I fell, how glorious once above thy sphere,
Till pride and worse ambition threw me down,   40
Warring in heaven against heaven's matchless king;
Ah, wherefore? He deserved no such return
From me, whom he created what I was
In that bright eminence, and with his good
Upbraided none; nor was his service hard.   45
What could be less than to afford him praise,
The easiest recompense, and pay him thanks,
How due! Yet all his good proved ill in me,
And wrought but malice; lifted up so high,
I sdeigned subjection, and thought one step higher   50
Would set me highest, and in a moment quit
The debt immense of endless gratitude,

---

17 engine] The primary meaning is 'cannon', and the secondary 'plot'.
2–8] 'Eden' means 'pleasure, delight' in Hebrew.
31 revolving] deliberating, meditating.
37] John iii. 20.
38–9] Rev. ii. 5.
50 sdeigned] disdained.

So burdensome, still paying, still to owe;
Forgetful what from him I still received,
And understood not that a grateful mind   55
By owing owes not, but still pays, at once
Indebted and discharged – what burden then?
Oh, had his powerful destiny ordained
Me some inferior angel, I had stood
Then happy; no unbounded hope had raised   60
Ambition. Yet why not? Some other power
As great might have aspired, and me, though mean,
Drawn to his part; but other powers as great
Fell not, but stand unshaken, from within
Or from without to all temptations armed.   65
Hadst thou the same free will and power to stand?
Thou hadst; whom hast thou then, or what, to accuse,
But heaven's free love dealt equally to all?
Be then his love accursed, since love or hate
To me alike it deals eternal woe.   70
Nay, cursed be thou; since against his thy will
Chose freely what it now so justly rues.
Me miserable! Which way shall I fly
Infinite wrath and infinite despair?
Which way I fly is hell; myself am hell;   75
And, in the lowest deep, a lower deep
Still threatening to devour me opens wide,
To which the hell I suffer seems a heaven.
O, then, at last relent; is there no place
Left for repentance, none for pardon left?   80
None left but by submission; and that word
Disdain forbids me, and my dread of shame
Among the spirits beneath, whom I seduced
With other promises and other vaunts
Than to submit, boasting I could subdue   85
The omnipotent. Ay me, they little know
How dearly I abide that boast so vain,
Under what torments inwardly I groan;
While they adore me on the throne of hell,
With diadem and sceptre high advanced,   90
The lower still I fall, only supreme
In misery: such joy ambition finds.
But say I could repent, and could obtain,
By act of grace my former state; how soon
Would height recall high thoughts, how soon unsay   95

53 still] continually.
66, 67, 71 thou] Satan addresses himself.
79–80] Heb. xii. 17.

What feigned submission swore; ease would recant
Vows made in pain, as violent and void;
For never can true reconcilement grow
Where wounds of deadly hate have pierced so deep;
Which would but lead me to a worse relapse　　　100
And heavier fall: so should I purchase dear
Short intermission, bought with double smart.
This knows my punisher; therefore as far
From granting he, as I from begging, peace;
All hope excluded thus, behold, instead　　　105
Of us, outcast, exiled, his new delight,
Mankind, created, and for him this world.
So farewell hope, and, with hope, farewell fear,
Farwell remorse; all good to me is lost;
Evil, be thou my good: by thee at least　　　110
Divided empire with heaven's king I hold,
By thee, and more than half perhaps will reign;
As man ere long, and this new world, shall know.'
　　Thus while he spake, each passion dimmed his face,
Thrice changed with pale – ire, envy, and despair,　　　115
Which marred his borrowed visage, and betrayed
Him counterfeit, if any eye beheld:
For heavenly minds from such distempers foul
Are ever clear. Whereof he soon aware
Each perturbation smoothed with outward calm,　　　120
Artificer of fraud; and was the first
That practised falsehood under saintly show,
Deep malice to conceal, couched with revenge:
Yet not enough had practised to deceive
Uriel, once warned; whose eye pursued him down　　　125
The way he went, and on the Assyrian mount
Saw him disfigured, more than could befall
Spirit of happy sort: his gestures fierce
He marked and mad demeanour, then alone,
As he supposed, all unobserved, unseen.　　　130
So on he fares, and to the border comes
Of Eden, where delicious Paradise,
Now nearer, crowns with her enclosure green,
As with a rural mound, the champaign head
Of a steep wilderness, whose hairy sides　　　135
With thicket overgrown, grotesque and wild,

110] Isa. v. 20.
115 pale] pallor.
123 couched] hidden.
126 Assyrian mount] Niphates (III 742).
134 champaign] free from woods and enclosures.

Access denied; and overhead up-grew
Insuperable height of loftiest shade,
Cedar, and pine, and fir, and branching palm,
A sylvan scene, and as the ranks ascend   140
Shade above shade, a woody theatre
Of stateliest view. Yet higher than their tops
The verderous wall of Paradise up-sprung;
Which to our general sire gave prospect large
Into his nether empire neighbouring round.   145
And higher than that wall a circling row
Of goodliest trees, loaded with fairest fruit,
Blossoms and fruits at once of golden hue,
Appeared, with gay enamelled colours mixed;
On which the sun more glad impressed his beams   150
Than in fair evening cloud, or humid bow,
When God hath showered the earth: so lovely seemed
That landscape; and of pure now purer air
Meets his approach, and to the heart inspires
Vernal delight and joy, able to drive   155
All sadness but despair; now gentle gales,
Fanning their odoriferous wings, dispense
Native perfumes, and whisper whence they stole
Those balmy spoils. As when to them who sail
Beyond the Cape of Hope, and now are past   160
Mozàmbique, off at sea north-east winds blow
Sabean odours from the spicy shore
Of Araby the Blest, with such delay
Well pleased they slack their course, and many a league
Cheered with the grateful smell old Ocean smiles;   165
So entertained those odorous sweets the fiend
Who came their bane, though with them better pleased
Than Asmodëus with the fishy fume
That drove him, though enamoured, from the spouse
Of Tobit's son, and with a vengeance sent   170
From Media post to Egypt, there fast bound.
    Now to the ascent of that steep savage hill

149 enamelled] beautified with various colours.
153 of] expresses transformation from one condition to another.
163 Araby the Blest] the *Arabia Felix* of classical antiquity: Saba (hence
    'Sabean'), i.e. Sheba, modern Yemen.
166-71] In the apocryphal Book of Tobit, Asmodeus (Asmadai in *PL* VI 365,
    and Asmodai in *PR* II 151) is the evil spirit who kills Sara's seven
    husbands, and is exorcized by Tobias ('Tobit's son'), who on the advice of
    the angel Raphael burns the heart and liver of a fish, the smell of which
    drives the spirit 'into the utmost parts of Egypt, and the angel bound him'
    (Tobit viii. 3). In the Greek version of Tobit Asmodeus is merely an evil
    spirit (τὸ πονηρὸν οἀιμόνιον), but Milton probably knew that in the Aramaic
    and Hebrew versions he is 'King of the Shedhim (i.e. demons)'.

Satan had journeyed on, pensive and slow;
But further way found none, so thick entwined,
As one continued brake, the undergrowth   175
Of shrubs and tangling bushes had perplexed
All path of man or beast that passed that way;
One gate there only was, and that looked east
On the other side: which when the arch-felon saw,
Due entrance he disdained, and, in contempt,   180
At one slight bound high overleaped all bound
Of hill or highest wall, and sheer within
Lights on his feet. As when a prowling wolf,
Whom hunger drives to seek new haunt for prey,
Watching where shepherds pen their flocks at eve,   185
In hurdled cotes amid the field secure,
Leaps o'er the fence with ease into the fold;
Or as a thief, bent to unhoard the cash
Of some rich burgher, whose substantial doors,
Cross-barred and bolted fast, fear no assault,   190
In at the window climbs, or o'er the tiles;
So clomb this first grand thief into God's fold:
So since into his church lewd hirelings climb.
Thence up he flew, and on the tree of life,
The middle tree and highest there that grew,   195
Sat like a cormorant; yet not true life
Thereby regained, but sat devising death
To them who lived; nor on the virtue thought
Of that life-giving plant, but only used
For prospect, what well used had been the pledge   200
Of immortality. So little knows
Any, but God alone, to value right
The good before him, but perverts best things
To worst abuse, or to their meanest use.
Beneath him, with new wonder, now he views,   205
To all delight of human sense exposed,
In narrow room nature's whole wealth; yea, more –
A heaven on earth: for blissful Paradise
Of God the garden was, by him in the east
Of Eden planted; Eden stretched her line   210
From Auran eastward to the royal towers
Of great Seleucia, built by Grecian kings,

176 had perplexed] would have entangled.
193 lewd] evil, unprincipled.
211 Auran] the Vulgate form of Hauran (Ezek. xlvii. 16, 18), a tract of land east
    of the Jordan.
212] Seleucus Nicator, Alexander's general, built nine cities called Seleucia, one
    of which, on the Tigris, was called 'The Great' to distinguish it from others
    of the same name. Cf. *PR* III 291.

Or where the sons of Eden long before
Dwelt in Telassar; in this pleasant soil
His far more pleasant garden God ordained;   215
Out of the fertile ground he caused to grow
All trees of noblest kind for sight, smell, taste;
And all amid them stood the tree of life,
High eminent, blooming ambrosial fruit
Of vegetable gold; and next to life,   220
Our death, the tree of knowledge, grew fast by –
Knowledge of good, bought dear by knowing ill.
Southward through Eden went a river large,
Nor changed his course, but through the shaggy hill
Passed underneath ingulfed; for God had thrown   225
That mountain, as his garden-mould, high raised
Upon the rapid current, which through veins
Of porous earth with kindly thirst up-drawn,
Rose a fresh fountain, and with many a rill
Watered the garden; thence united fell   230
Down the steep glade, and met the nether flood,
Which from his darksome passage now appears,
And now, divided into four main streams,
Runs diverse, wandering many a famous realm
And country whereof here needs no account;   235
But rather to tell how, if art could tell
How, from that sapphire fount the crispèd brooks,
Rolling on orient pearl and sands of gold,
With mazy error under pendant shades
Ran nectar, visiting each plant, and fed   240
Flowers worthy of Paradise, which not nice art
In beds and curious knots, but nature boon
Poured forth profuse on hill and dale and plain,
Both where the morning sun first warmly smote
The open field, and where the unpierced shade   245
Embrowned the noontide bowers; thus was this place,
A happy rural seat of various view:
Groves whose rich trees wept odorous gums and balm;
Others whose fruit, burnished with golden rind,

214 Telassar] II Kings xix. 12; Isa. xxxvii. 12.
219 blooming] causing to flourish.
223 river] identified as the Tigris in *PL* IX 71-3.
229 fountain] The Vulgate version of Gen. ii. 6 has a fountain instead of mist;
     Sed fons ascendebat e terra.
239 error] used in the Latin sense of 'wandering'.
242 knots] alludes to the dying fashion for formal geometrical garden designs.
     bon] bountiful.
246 Embrowned] darkened.

Hung amiable – Hesperian fables true,   250
If true, here only – and of delicious taste;
Betwixt them lawns, or level downs, and flocks
Grazing the tender herb, were interposed,
Or palmy hillock; or the flowery lap
Of some irriguous valley spread her store,   255
Flowers of all hue, and without thorn the rose.
Another side, umbrageous grots and caves
Of cool recess, o'er which the mantling vine
Lays forth her purple grape, and gently creeps
Luxuriant; meanwhile murmuring waters fall   260
Down the slope hills dispersed, or in a lake,
That to the fringèd bank with myrtle crowned
Her crystal mirror holds, unite their streams.
The birds their choir apply; airs, vernal airs,
Breathing the smell of field and grove, attune   265
The trembling leaves, while universal Pan,
Knit with the Graces and the Hours in dance,
Led on the eternal Spring. Not that fair field
Of Enna, where Prosperpine gathering flowers,
Herself a fairer flower, by gloomy Dis   270
Was gathered – which cost Ceres all that pain
To seek her through the world – nor that sweet grove
Of Daphne, by Orontes and the inspired
Castalian spring, might with this Paradise
Of Eden strive; nor that Nyseian isle,   275
Girt with the river Triton, where old Cham,

250-1] See *Comus* 393-5n.
255 irriguous] well-watered.
256 without thorn the rose] a common patristic inference from Gen. iii. 18.
266 universal Pan] here means universal nature, but cf. *Nativity* 89n.
267 Graces, Hours] See *Allegro* 12-16n. and *Comus* 986n.
268-72] Proserpina, daughter of Ceres, was carried off by Dis (Pluto) while
    gathering flowers (near Enna, according to *Metamorphoses* v 385-95).
    Proserpina was never allowed to leave the underworld permanently,
    because she had eaten six seeds from the pomegranate of Jove, which in the
    Renaissance was identified with the fruit which Eve ate.
272-4] Daphne is here a grove near Antioch, beside the river Orontes; in
    antiquity it had an oracle of Apollo (hence 'inspired') and a stream named
    Castalia after the spring on Parnassus. Here the nymph Daphne, daughter
    of the river-god Peneus, was turned into a laurel (see *Comus* 661-2) to
    protect her from the ravages of Apollo. Cf. *PR* II 187.
275-9] Cham is the Vulgate name for Ham, the son of Noah, who was
    commonly identified with Ammon, Libyan Jove (called Libyc Hammon in
    Nativity 203), the Egyptian god. According to Diodorus Siculus (*Library* iii.
    67-70) the Libyan King Ammon (who was identified with the god Ammon)
    became the lover of the nymph Amalthea, who gave birth to Bacchus.
    Ammon hid his lover and their child on Nysa, an island in the 'river Triton'
    near modern Tunis, in order to protect them from the wrath of his wife
    Rhea.

Whom Gentiles Ammon call and Libyan Jove,
Hid Amalthea and her florid son,
Young Bacchus, from his stepdame Rhea's eye;
Nor, where Abassin kings their issue guard,   280
Mount Amara – though this by some supposed
True Paradise – under the Ethiop line
By Nilus' head, enclosed with shining rock,
A whole day's journey high, but wide remote
From this Assyrian garden, where the fiend   285
Saw undelighted all delight, all kind
Of living creatures, new to sight and strange.
Two of far nobler shape, erect and tall,
God-like erect, with native honour clad
In naked majesty, seemed lords of all,   290
And worthy seemed; for in their looks divine
The image of their glorious maker shone,
Truth, wisdom, sanctitude severe and pure –
Severe, but in true filial freedom placed,
Whence true authority in men: though both   295
Not equal, as their sex not equal seemed;
For contemplation he and valour formed,
For softness she and sweet attractive grace;
He for God only, she for God in him;
His fair large front and eye sublime declared   300
Absolute rule; and hyacinthine locks
Round from his parted forelock manly hung
Clustering, but not beneath his shoulders broad:
She as a veil down to the slender waist,
Her unadornèd golden tresses wore   305
Dishevelled, but in wanton ringlets waved
As the vine curls her tendrils – which implied
Subjection, but required with gentle sway,
And by her yielded, by him best received
Yielded, with coy submission, modest pride,   310
And sweet reluctant amorous delay.
Nor those mysterious parts were then concealed;
Then was not guilty shame, dishonest shame

280–5] The sons ('issue') of Abyssinian ('Abassin') kings were raised in seclusion
    in palaces on 'Mount Amara', on the equator ('Ethiop line').
300 front] forehead.
    sublime] means both 'exalted, lofty' and 'raised up'.
301–5] See I Cor. xi. 7–15 (and A.V. marginal note to v. 10). Hyacinthine may
    allude to the hair of Odysseus (*Odyssey* vi. 230–1) or to Hyacinth, the boy
    whom Apollo loved (see *Fair Infant* 23–6n.).
310 coy] modest, shy, quiet.
313 dishonest] unchaste, lewd.

Of nature's works, honour dishonourable,
Sin-bred, how have ye troubled all mankind   315
With shows instead, mere shows of seeming pure,
And banished from man's life his happiest life,
Simplicity and spotless innocence.
So passed they naked on, nor shunned the sight
Of God or angel, for they thought no ill: 320
So hand in hand they passed, the liveliest pair
That ever since in love's embraces met –
Adam the goodliest man of men since born
His sons; the fairest of her daughters Eve.
Under a tuft of shade that on a green   325
Stood whispering soft, by a fresh fountain-side,
They sat them down, and after no more toil
Of their sweet gardening labour than sufficed
To recommend cool Zephyr, and made ease
More easy, wholesome thirst and appetite   330
More grateful, to their supper-fruits they fell –
Nectarine fruits, which the compliant boughs
Yielded them, sidelong as they sat recline
On the soft downy bank damasked with flowers:
The savoury pulp they chew, and in the rind,   335
Still as they thirsted, scoop the brimming stream;
Nor gentle purpose, nor endearing smiles
Wanted, nor youthful dalliance, as beseems
Fair couple linked in happy nuptial league,
Alone as they. About them frisking played   340
All beasts of the earth, since wild, and of all chase
In wood or wilderness, forest or den;
Sporting the lion ramped, and in his paw
Dandled the kid; bears, tigers, ounces, pards,
Gambolled before them; the unwieldy elephant,   345
To make them mirth, used all his might, and wreathed
His lithe proboscis; close the serpent sly,
Insinuating, wove with Gordian twine
His braided train, and of his fatal guile
Gave proof unheeded; others on the grass   350

321] The clasping of hands is a traditional symbol of the pledging of faith. Cf.
     IV 488-9, 689, 739, IX 385-6, 1037, XII 648.
329 Zephyr] the west wind.
332 Nectarine] as sweet as nectar, the drink of the gods.
337 purpose] conversation.
341 chase] habitat of wild animals.
344 ounces] See *Comus* 71n.
     pards] The name was used of both panthers and leopards.
348 Insinuating] penetrating by sinuous windings.

Couched, and, now filled with pasture, gazing sat,
Or bedward ruminating; for the sun,
Declined, was hasting now with prone career
To the Ocean Isles, and in the ascending scale
Of heaven the stars that usher evening rose: 355
When Satan, still in gaze as first he stood,
Scarce thus at length failed speech recovered sad:
    'O hell! What do mine eyes with grief behold?
Into our room of bliss thus high advanced
Creatures of other mould – earth-born perhaps,   360
Not spirits, yet to heavenly spirits bright
Little inferior – whom my thoughts pursue
With wonder, and could love; so lively shines
In them divine resemblance, and such grace   364
The hand that formed them on their shape hath poured.
Ah gentle pair, ye little think how nigh
Your change approaches, when all these delights
Will vanish, and deliver ye to woe –
More woe, the more your taste is now of joy:
Happy, but for so happy ill secured   370
Long to continue, and this high seat, your heaven,
Ill fenced for heaven to keep out such a foe
As now is entered; yet no purposed foe
To you, whom I could pity thus forlorn,
Though I unpitied; league with you I seek,   375
And mutual amity, so strait, so close,
That I with you must dwell, or you with me,
Henceforth; my dwelling haply may not please,
Like this fair Paradise, your sense; yet such
Accept your maker's work; he gave it me,   380
Which I as freely give; hell shall unfold,
To entertain you two, her widest gates,
And send forth all her kings; there will be room,
Not like these narrow limits, to receive
Your numerous offspring; if no better place,   385
Thank you who puts me loath to this revenge
On you, who wrong me not, for him who wronged.
And should I at your harmless innocence
Melt, as I do, yet public reason just –
Honour and empire with revenge enlarged   390
By conquering this new world – compels me now
To do what else, though damned, I should abhor.'

354 Ocean Isles] The Azores.
361-2] Psalm viii. 5; Heb. ii. 7.
380-1] Matt. x. 8.

So spake the fiend, and with necessity,
The tyrant's plea, excused his devilish deeds.
Then from his lofty stand on that high tree   395
Down he alights among the sportful herd
Of those four-footed kinds, himself now one,
Now other, as their shape served best his end
Nearer to view his prey, and unespied,
To mark what of their state he more might learn   400
By word or action marked; about them round
A lion now he stalks with fiery glare;
Then as a tiger, who by chance hath spied
In some purlieu two gentle fawns at play,
Straight couches close; then rising changes oft   405
His couchant watch, as one who chose his ground,
Whence rushing he might surest seize them both
Griped in each paw: when Adam, first of men,
To first of women, Eve, thus moving speech,
Turned him all ear to hear new utterance flow: 410
    'Sole partner and sole part of all these joys,
Dearer thyself than all, needs must the power
That made us, and for us this ample world,
Be infinitely good, and of his good
As liberal and free as infinite;   415
That raised us from the dust, and placed us here
In all this happiness, who at his hand
Have nothing merited, nor can perform
Aught whereof he hath need; he who requires
From us no other service than to keep   420
This one, this easy charge – of all the trees
In Paradise that bear delicious fruit
So various, not to taste that only tree
Of knowledge, planted by the tree of life;
So near grows death to life, whate'er death is –   425
Some dreadful thing no doubt; for well thou know'st
God hath pronounced it death to taste that tree:
The only sign of our obedience left
Among so many signs of power and rule
Conferred upon us, and dominion given   430
Over all other creatures that possess
Earth, air, and sea. Then let us not think hard
One easy prohibition, who enjoy

---

404 purlieu] tract of land on the edge of a forest.
418 him all ear] ambiguous: 'him' may be Adam or Satan, and 'all ear' can
    apply to Adam or Eve or Satan.
411] The first 'sole' means 'only', the second 'unique, unrivalled'.

Free leave so large to all things else, and choice
Unlimited of manifold delights;   435
But let us ever praise him, and extol
His bounty, following our delightful task,
To prune these growing plants, and tend these flowers;
Which, were it toilsome, yet with thee were sweet.'
   To whom thus Eve replied: 'O thou for whom   440
And from whom I was formed flesh of thy flesh,
And without whom am to no end, my guide
And head, what thou hast said is just and right.
For we to him indeed all praises owe,
And daily thanks – I chiefly, who enjoy   445
So far the happier lot, enjoying thee
Pre-eminent by so much odds, while thou
Like consort to thyself canst nowhere find.
That day I oft remember, when from sleep
I first awaked, and found myself reposed,   450
Under a shade on flowers, much wondering where
And what I was, whence thither brought, and how.
Not distant far from thence a murmuring sound
Of waters issued from a cave, and spread
Into a liquid plain, then stood unmoved,   455
Pure as the expanse of heaven; I thither went
With unexperienced thought, and laid me down
On the green bank, to look into the clear
Smooth lake, that to me seemed another sky.
As I bent down to look, just opposite   460
A shape within the watery gleam appeared,
Bending to look on me; I started back,
It started back, but pleased I soon returned,
Pleased it returned as soon with answering looks
Of sympathy and love; there I had fixed   465
Mine eyes till now, and pined with vain desire,
Had not a voice thus warned me: "What thou seest,
What there thou seest, fair creature, is thyself:
With thee it came and goes: but follow me,
And I will bring thee where no shadow stays   470
Thy coming, and thy soft embraces – he
Whose image thou art; him thou shalt enjoy
Inseparably thine; to him shalt bear

443 head] I Cor. xi. 3.
447 odds] construed as singular in the seventeenth century, and means 'the
amount by which one thing exceeds or excels another'.
460–6] Alludes to Ovid's story of Narcissus. See *Comus* 230n.
470 stays] waits for.

Multitudes like thyself, and thence be called
Mother of human race"; what could I do,   475
But follow straight, invisibly thus led?
Till I espied thee, fair indeed and tall,
Under a platan; yet methought less fair,
Less winning soft, less amiably mild,
Than that smooth watery image; back I turned;   480
Thou, following, cried'st aloud, "Return, fair Eve;
Whom fliest thou? Whom thou fliest, of him thou art,
His flesh, his bone; to give thee being I lent
Out of my side to thee, nearest my heart,
Substantial life, to have thee by my side   485
Henceforth an individual solace dear:
Part of my soul I seek thee, and thee claim
My other half"; with that thy gentle hand
Seized mine: I yielded, and from that time see
How beauty is excelled by manly grace   490
And wisdom, which alone is truly fair.'
     So spake our general mother, and with eyes
Of conjugal attraction unreproved,
And meek surrender, half-embracing leaned
On our first father; half her swelling breast   495
Naked met his under the flowing gold
Of her loose tresses hid; he in delight
Both of her beauty and submissive charms,
Smiled with superior love, as Jupiter
On Juno smiles when he impregns the clouds   500
That shed May flowers, and pressed her matron lip
With kisses pure; aside the devil turned
For envy, yet with jealous leer malign
Eyed them askance, and to himself thus plained: 504
     'Sight hateful, sight tormenting! Thus these two,
Imparadised in one another's arms,
The happier Eden, shall enjoy their fill
Of bliss on bliss, while I to hell am thrust,
Where neither joy nor love, but fierce desire,
Among our other torments not the least,   510
Still unfulfilled, with pain of longing pines;
Yet let me not forget what I have gained
From their own mouths; all is not theirs, it seems:
One fatal tree there stands, of knowledge called,
Forbidden them to taste: knowledge forbidden?   515

478 platan] plane tree.
486 individual] inseparable. Cf. *Time* 12.
499–501] *Iliad* xiv 246–51; Virgil, *Georgics* ii 325–7.

Suspicious, reasonless: Why should their Lord
Envy them that? Can it be sin to know,
Can it be death? And do they only stand
By ignorance, is that their happy state,
The proof of their obedience and their faith?   520
O fair foundation laid whereon to build
Their ruin! Hence I will excite their minds
With more desire to know, and to reject
Envious commands, invented with design
To keep them low, whom knowledge might exalt   525
Equal with gods; aspiring to be such,
They taste and die: what likelier can ensue?
But first with narrow search I must walk round
This garden, and no corner leave unspied;
A chance but chance may lead where I may meet   530
Some wandering spirit of heaven, by fountain-side,
Or in thick shade retired, from him to draw
What further would be learned. Live while ye may,
Yet happy pair; enjoy, till I return,
Short pleasures; for long woes are to succeed.'   535
    So saying, his proud step he scornful turned,
But with sly circumspection, and began
Through wood, through waste, o'er hill, o'er dale, his roam.
Meanwhile in utmost longitude, where heaven
With earth and ocean meets, the setting sun   540
Slowly descended, and with right aspect
Against the eastern gate of Paradise
Levelled his evening rays; it was a rock
Of alabaster, piled up to the clouds,
Conspicuous far, winding with one ascent   545
Accessible from earth, one entrance high;
The rest was craggy cliff, that overhung
Still as it rose, impossible to climb.
Betwixt these rocky pillars Gabriel sat,
Chief of the angelic guards, awaiting night;   550
About him exercised heroic games
The unarmed youth of heaven; but nigh at hand
Celestial armoury, shields, helms, and spears,
Hung high with diamond flaming and with gold.

539 utmost longitude] the extreme west.
541 with right aspect] directly.
549 Gabriel] means 'man of God' or 'strength of God' in Hebrew. Gabriel is an
    archangel, and his traditional function in Christian (and Muslim) thought is
    to reveal God. In Muslim and Cabbalistic traditions (though not in the
    Bible) he is a warrior (cf. l. 576). Milton seems to have had access to the
    tradition embodied in the Book of Enoch (xx. 7) that Gabriel was
    responsible for Paradise and the cherubim.

Thither came Uriel, gliding through the even   555
On a sunbeam, swift as a shooting star
In autumn thwarts the night, when vapours fired
Impress the air, and shows the mariner
From what point of his compass to beware
Impetuous winds; he thus began in haste: 560
    'Gabriel, to thee thy course by lot hath given
Charge and strict watch that to this happy place
No evil thing approach or enter in;
This day at height of noon came to my sphere
A spirit, zealous, as he seemed, to know   565
More of the almighty's works, and chiefly man,
God's latest image; I described his way
Bent all on speed, and marked his airy gait,
But in the mount that lies from Eden north,
Where he first lighted, soon discerned his looks   570
Alien from heaven, with passions foul obscured;
Mine eye pursued him still, but under shade
Lost sight of him; one of the banished crew,
I fear, hath ventured from the deep, to raise
New troubles; him thy care must be to find.'   575
    To whom the winged warrior thus returned:
'Uriel, no wonder if thy perfect sight,
Amid the sun's bright circle where thou sitt'st,
See far and wide; in at this gate none pass
The vigilance here placed, but such as come   580
Well known from heaven; and since meridian hour
No creature thence; if spirit of other sort,
So minded, have o'erleaped these earthy bounds
On purpose, hard thou know'st it to exclude
Spiritual substance with corporeal bar.   585
But if within the circuit of these walks,
In whatsoever shape, he lurk of whom
Thou tell'st, by morrow dawning I shall know.'
    So promised he; and Uriel to his charge
Returned on that bright beam, whose point now raised
Bore him slope downward to the sun, now fallen   591
Beneath the Azores; whether the prime orb,

557 thwarts] traverses.
561 by lot] like the porters of the temple. I Chron. xxvi. 13.
567 God's latest image] His first image was the Son (III 63).
    described] descried.
568 gait] journey.
580 vigilance] guard.
592-7] Ptolemaic and Copernican cosmologies are presented as alternatives;
    hence the 'prime orb' may be the sun of the first sphere. 'Voluble' means
    'capable of rotation on its axis'.

Incredible how swift, had thither rolled
Diurnal, or this less volúble earth,
By shorter flight to the east, had left him there   595
Arraying with reflected purple and gold
The clouds that on his western throne attend;
Now came still evening on, and twilight grey
Had in her sober livery all things clad;
Silence accompanied; for beast and bird,   600
They to their grassy couch, these to their nests
Were slunk, all but the wakeful nightingale:
She all night long her amorous descant sung;
Silence was pleased; now glowed the firmament
With living sapphires; Hesperus, that led   605
The starry host, rode brightest, till the moon,
Rising in clouded majesty, at length
Apparent queen, unveiled her peerless light,
And o'er the dark her silver mantle threw;
  When Adam thus to Eve: 'Fair consort, the hour   610
Of night, and all things now retired to rest,
Mind us of like repose; since God hath set
Labour and rest, as day and night, to men
Successive, and the timely dew of sleep,
Now falling with soft slumbrous weight, inclines   615
Our eye-lids; other creatures all day long
Rove idle, unemployed, and less need rest;
Man hath his daily work of body or mind
Appointed, which declares his dignity,
And the regard of heaven on all his ways;   620
While other animals unactive range,
And of their doings God takes no account.
To-morrow, ere fresh morning streak the east
With first approach of light, we must be risen,
And at our pleasant labour, to reform   625
Yon flowery arbours, yonder alleys green,
Our walk at noon, with branches overgrown,
That mock our scant manuring, and require
More hands than ours to lop their wanton growth;
Those blossoms also, and those dropping gums,   630
That lie bestrewn, unsightly and unsmooth,
Ask riddance, if we mean to tread with ease;
Meanwhile, as nature wills, night bids us rest.'
  To whom thus Eve, with perfect beauty adorned:
'My author and disposer, what thou bidd'st   635

608 Apparent] manifest.
628 manuring] cultivating.

Unargued I obey: so God ordains:
God is thy law, thou mine: to know no more
Is woman's happiest knowledge, and her praise.
With thee conversing, I forget all time,
All seasons, and their change; all please alike.   640
Sweet is the breath of morn, her rising sweet,
With charm of earliest birds; pleasant the sun,
When first on this delightful land he spreads
His orient beams, on herb, tree, fruit, and flower,
Glistering with dew; fragrant the fertile earth   645
After soft showers; and sweet the coming-on
Of grateful evening mild; then silent night,
With this her solemn bird, and this fair moon,
And these the gems of heaven, her starry train:
But neither breath of morn, when she ascends   650
With charm of earliest birds, nor rising sun
On this delightful land, nor herb, fruit, flower,
Glistering with dew, nor fragrance after showers,
Nor grateful evening mild, nor silent night,
With this her solemn bird, nor walk by moon,   655
Or glittering starlight, without thee is sweet.
But wherefore all night long shine these, for whom
This glorious sight, when sleep hath shut all eyes?'
     To whom our general ancestor replied:
'Daughter of God and man, accomplished Eve,   660
Those have their course to finish round the earth
By morrow evening, and from land to land
In order, though to nations yet unborn,
Ministering light prepared, they set and rise;
Lest total darkness should by night regain   665
Her old possession, and extinguish life
In nature and all things; which these soft fires
Not only enlighten, but with kindly heat
Of various influence foment and warm,
Temper or nourish, or in part shed down   670
Their stellar virtue on all kinds that grow
On earth, made hereby apter to receive
Perfection from the sun's more potent ray.
These, then, though unbeheld in deep of night,   674
Shine not in vain; nor think, though men were none,
That heaven would want spectators, God want praise;
Millions of spiritual creatures walk the earth

639 conversing] consorting.
640 seasons] times of day.
642 charm] song.

Unseen, both when we wake, and when we sleep:
All these with ceaseless praise his works behold
Both day and night; how often from the steep   680
Of echoing hill or thicket, have we heard
Celestial voices to the midnight air,
Sole, or responsive each to other's note,
Singing their great creator; oft in bands
While they keep watch, or nightly rounding walk,   685
With heavenly touch of instrumental sounds
In full harmonic number joined, their songs
Divide the night, and lift our thoughts to heaven.'
        Thus talking, hand in hand alone they passed
On to their blissful bower; it was a place   690
Chosen by the sovereign planter, when he framed
All things to man's delightful use; the roof
Of thickest covert was inwoven shade,
Laurel and myrtle, and what higher grew
Of firm and fragrant leaf; on either side   695
Acanthus, and each odorous bushy shrub,
Fenced up the verdant wall; each beauteous flower,
Iris all hues, roses, and jessamine,
Reared high their flourished heads between, and wrought
Mosaic; under foot the violet,   700
Crocus, and hyacinth, with rich inlay
Broidered the ground, more coloured than with stone
Of costliest emblem; other creature here,
Beast, bird, insect, or worm, durst enter none;
Such was their awe of man. In shadier bower   705
More sacred and sequestered, though but feigned,
Pan or Sylvanus never slept, nor nymph
Nor Faunus haunted. Here, in close recess,
With flowers, garlands, and sweet-smelling herbs,
Espousèd Eve decked her first nuptial bed.   710
And heavenly choirs the hymenean sung,
What day the genial angel to our sire

---

688 Divide] means both 'divide into watches' and 'execute florid variations' (cf.
    Passion 4n.).
691 planter] 'God planted a garden' (Gen. ii. 8); God is also a planter in the
    sense of the founder of a colony.
699 flourished] adorned with flowers.
703 emblem] inlay.
707-8] Pan, Sylvanus, and Faunus are often not clearly distinguished from one
    another, but are commonly mentioned together. Cf. *Comus* 268, *PR* II
    190-1.
711 hymenean] wedding hymn; Hymen was the god of marriage. Cf. *PL* XI
    590-1.
712 genial] presiding over marriage and generation.

Brought her, in naked beauty more adorned,
More lovely than Pandora, whom the gods
Endowed with all their gifts; and, O too like   715
In sad event, when to the unwiser son
Of Japhet brought by Hermes, she ensnared
Mankind with her fair looks, to be avenged
On him who had stole Jove's authentic fire.

    Thus at their shady lodge arrived, both stood,   720
Both turned, and under open sky adored
The God that made both sky, air, earth and heaven,
Which they beheld, the moon's resplendent globe,
And starry pole: 'Thou also madest the night,
Maker omnipotent; and thou the day,   725
Which we in our appointed work employed,
Have finished, happy in our mutual help
And mutual love, the crown of all our bliss
Ordained by thee; and this delicious place,
For us too large, where thy abundance wants   730
Partakers, and uncropped falls to the ground.
But thou hast promised from us two a race
To fill the earth, who shall with us extol
Thy goodness infinite, both when we wake,
And when we seek, as now, thy gift of sleep.'   735
    This said unanimous, and other rites
Observing none, but adoration pure,
Which God likes best, into their inmost bower
Handed they went; and, eased the putting-off
These troublesome disguises which we wear,   740
Straight side by side were laid; nor turned, I ween,
Adam from his fair spouse, nor Eve the rites
Mysterious of connubial love refused:
Whatever hypocrites austerely talk
Of purity, and place, and innocence,   745
Defaming as impure what God declares
Pure, and commands to some, leaves free to all.
Our maker bids increase; who bids abstain
But our destroyer, foe to God and man?

714-19] Prometheus ('fore-thought') and Epimetheus ('after-thought') were
the two sons of the Titan Japhet. Prometheus 'stole Jove's authentic [i.e.
original] fire', and the gods took their revenge by having Hermes (see
Comus 637n.) present Pandora ('all . . . gifts') to Epimetheus ('the unwiser
son'), who opened Pandora's box of gifts and thus released all life's ills upon
the world.
724-5] Psalm lxxiv. 16. 'Pole' means 'sky'.
735 gift of sleep] Psalm cxxvii. 2; *Iliad* ix 712-13; *Aeneid* ii 268-9.
741 ween] surmise.
744-9] I Tim. iv. 1-3.

Hail, wedded love, mysterious law, true source   750
Of human offspring, sole propriety
In Paradise of all things common else.
By thee adulterous lust was driven from men
Among the bestial herds to range; by thee,
Founded in reason, loyal, just, and pure   755
Relations dear, and all the charities
Of father, son, and brother, first were known.
Far be it that I should write thee sin or blame,
Or think thee unbefitting holiest place,
Perpetual fountain of domestic sweets,   760
Whose bed is undefiled and chaste pronounced,
Present, or past, as saints and patriarchs used.
Here Love his golden shafts employs, here lights
His constant lamp, and waves his purple wings,
Reigns here and revels; not in the bought smile   765
Of harlots – loveless, joyless, unendeared,
Casual fruition; nor in court amours,
Mixed dance, or wanton mask, or midnight ball,
Or serenade, which the starved lover sings
To his proud fair, best quitted with disdain.   770
These, lulled by nightingales, embracing slept,
And on their naked limbs the flowery roof
Showered roses, which the morn repaired. Sleep on,
Blest pair; and O yet happiest if ye seek
No happier state, and know to know no more.   775
    Now had night measured with her shadowy cone
Half-way up-hill this vast sublunar vault,
And from their ivory port the cherubim
Forth issuing at the accustomed hour, stood armed
To their night-watches in warlike parade;   780

---

751 propriety] ownership, proprietorship.
756 charities] love, natural affections.
761] Heb. xiii. 4.
763 Cupid's sharp 'golden shafts' kindled love; his blunt leaden shafts put love
    to flight (*Metamorphoses* i 468–71).
769–70] Alludes to the ancient *paraklausithuron*, a serenade sung by a lover
    standing in the cold at his mistress' locked door. 'Starved' means both
    'benumbed with cold' and 'starved for love'.
773 repaired] replaced.
776–7] Because the earth is smaller than the sun, the earth's shadow is cone-
    shaped. When the axis of the cone is halfway between the horizon and the
    zenith ('Half-way up-hill'), the time in Paradise is nine o'clock.
778 ivory port] In classical literature false dreams pass through an ivory gate,
    so it is appropriate that cherubim about to interrupt a false dream do
    likewise (*Odyssey* xix 592 ff., *Aeneid* vi 893 f.).

When Gabriel to his next in power thus spake:
  'Uzziel, half these draw off, and coast the south
With strictest watch; these other wheel the north:
Our circuit meets full west.' As flame they part,
Half wheeling to the shield, half to the spear.   785
From these, two strong and subtle spirits he called
That near him stood, and gave them thus in charge:
  'Ithuriel and Zephon, with winged speed
Search through this garden; leave unsearched no nook;
But chiefly where those two fair creatures lodge,   790
Now laid perhaps asleep, secure of harm.
This evening from the sun's decline arrived
Who tells of some infernal spirit seen
Hitherward bent (who could have thought?) escaped
The bars of hell, on errand bad no doubt: 795
Such, where ye find, seize fast, and hither bring.'
  So saying, on he led his radiant files,
Dazzling the moon; these to the bower direct
In search of whom they sought; him there they found
Squat like a toad, close at the ear of Eve,   800
Assaying by his devilish art to reach
The organs of her fancy, and with them forge
Illusions as he list, phantasms and dreams;
Or if, inspiring venom, he might taint
The animal spirits, that from pure blood arise   805
Like gentle breaths from rivers pure, thence raise,
At least distempered, discontented thoughts,
Vain hopes, vain aims, inordinate desires,
Blown up with high conceits engendering pride.
Him thus intent Ithuriel with his spear   810
Touched lightly; for no falsehood can endure
Touch of celestial temper, but returns
Of force to its own likeness; up he starts,

---

782 Uzziel] means in Hebrew 'my strength is God'. The word is never used as an
    angel's name in the Bible, but according to a rabbinical tradition Uzziel
    was one of the seven angels in front of the throne of God.
785] 'shield' is left, 'spear' is right in classical military parlance.
788 Ithuriel] means in Hebrew 'discovery of God'. The name does not occur in
    the Bible.
    Zephon] means in Hebrew 'searcher'. The name is not used as an angel's
    name in the Bible.
793 Who] one who.
805] In Renaissance physiology 'spirits' were fluids permeating the blood and
    chief organs of the body; they were distinguished as animal, natural, and
    vital. Animal spirits (from *anima*, soul) were seated in the brain, and
    controlled sensation and voluntary motion.

Discovered and surprised. As when a spark
Lights on a heap of nitrous powder, laid   815
Fit for the tun, some magazine to store
Against a rumoured war, the smutty grain,
With sudden blaze diffused, inflames the air;
So started up, in his own shape, the fiend.
Back stepped those two fair angels, half amazed   820
So sudden to behold the grisly king;
Yet thus, unmoved with fear, accost him soon:
    'Which of those rebel spirits adjudged to hell
Com'st thou, escaped thy prison, and, transformed,
Why satt'st thou like an enemy in wait,   825
Here watching at the head of these that sleep?'
    'Know ye not, then,' said Satan, filled with scorn,
'Know ye not me? Ye knew me once no mate
For you, there sitting where ye durst not soar;
Not to know me argues yourselves unknown.   830
The lowest of your throng; or if ye know,
Why ask ye, and superfluous begin
Your message, like to end as much in vain?'
    To whom thus Zephon, answering scorn with scorn:
'Think not, revolted spirit, thy shape the same,   835
Or undiminished brightness, to be known
As when thou stood'st in heaven upright and pure;
That glory then, when thou no more wast good,
Departed from thee, and thou resemblest now
Thy sin and place of doom obscure and foul.   840
But come, for thou, be sure, shalt give account
To him who sent us, whose charge is to keep
This place inviolable, and these from harm.'
    So spake the cherub; and his grave rebuke,
Severe in youthful beauty, added grace   845
Invincible; abashed the devil stood,
And felt how awful goodness is, and saw
Virtue in her shape how lovely – saw, and pined
His loss; but chiefly to find here observed
His lustre visibly impaired; yet seemed   850
Undaunted. 'If I must contend,' said he,
'Best with the best – the sender, not the sent;
Or all at once: more glory will be won,
Or less be lost.' 'Thy fear,' said Zephon bold,
'Will save us trial what the least can do   855
Single against thee wicked, and thence weak.'

840 obscure] dark.
847 awful] awe-inspiring.

The fiend replied not, overcome with rage;
But, like a proud steed reined, went haughty on,
Champing his iron curb; to strive or fly
He held it vain; awe from above had quelled   860
His heart, not else dismayed. Now drew they nigh
The western point, where those half-rounding guards
Just met, and, closing, stood in squadron joined,
Awaiting next command. To whom their chief,
Gabriel, from the front thus called aloud: 865
    'O friends, I hear the tread of nimble feet
Hasting this way, and now by glimpse discern
Ithuriel and Zephon through the shade;
And with them comes a third, of regal port,
But faded splendour wan, who by his gait   870
And fierce demeanour seems the prince of hell –
Not likely to part hence without contest;
Stand firm, for in his look defiance lours.'
    He scarce had ended, when those two approached,
And brief related whom they brought, where found,   875
How busied, in what form and posture couched.
To whom, with stern regard, thus Gabriel spake:
    'Why hast thou, Satan, broke the bounds prescribed
To thy transgressions, and disturbed the charge
Of others, who approve not to transgress   880
By thy example, but have power and right
To question thy bold entrance on this place;
Employed, it seems, to violate sleep, and those
Whose dwelling God hath planted here in bliss?'
    To whom thus Satan, with contemptuous brow: 885
'Gabriel, thou hadst in heaven the esteem of wise,
And such I held thee; but this question asked
Puts me in doubt. Lives there who loves his pain?
Who would not, finding way, break loose from hell,
Though thither doomed? Thou wouldst thyself, no doubt,
And boldly venture to whatever place   891
Farthest from pain, where thou mightst hope to change
Torment with ease, and soonest recompense
Dole with delight, which in this place I sought;
To thee no reason, who know'st only good,   895
But evil hast not tried; and wilt object
His will who bound us? Let him surer bar

869 port] bearing.
879 transgressions] means both 'sins' and (etymologically) 'the action of
    passing over or beyond (a boundary)'.
896 object] adduce as an objection.

His iron gates, if he intends our stay
In that dark durance; thus much what was asked.
The rest is true, they found me where they say;   900
But that implies not violence or harm.'
  Thus he in scorn. The warlike angel moved,
Disdainfully half smiling, thus replied:
'O loss of one in heaven to judge of wise,
Since Satan fell, whom folly overthrew,   905
And now returns him from his prison scaped,
Gravely in doubt whether to hold them wise
Or not who ask what boldness brought him hither
Unlicensed from his bounds in hell prescribed;
So wise he judges it to fly from pain   910
However, and to scape his punishment.
So judge thou still, presumptuous, till the wrath,
Which thou incurr'st by flying, meet thy flight
Sevenfold, and scourge that wisdom back to hell,
Which taught thee yet no better that no pain   915
Can equal anger infinite provoked.
But wherefore thou alone? Wherefore with thee
Came not all hell broke loose? Is pain to them
Less pain, less to be fled, or thou than they
Less hardy to endure? Courageous chief,   920
The first in flight from pain, hadst thou alleged
To thy deserted host this cause of flight,
Thou surely hadst not come sole fugitive.'
  To which the fiend thus answered, frowning stern:
'Not that I less endure, or shrink from pain,   925
Insulting angel; well thou know'st I stood
Thy fiercest, when in battle to thy aid
The blasting volleyed thunder made all speed
And seconded thy else not dreaded spear.
But still thy words at random, as before,   930
Argue thy inexperience what behoves,
From hard assays and ill successes past,
A faithful leader – not to hazard all
Through ways of danger by himself untried;
I, therefore, I alone, first undertook   935
To wing the desolate abyss, and spy
This new-created world, whereof in hell
Fame is not silent, here in hope to find
Better abode, and my afflicted powers

899 durance] imprisonment, constraint.
911 However] howsoever.
926 stood] withstood.

To settle here on earth, or in mid air;   940
Though for possession put to try once more
What thou and thy gay legions dare against;
Whose easier business were to serve their Lord
High up in heaven, with songs to hymn his throne,
And practised distances to cringe, not fight.'   945
    To whom the warrior-angel soon replied:
'To say and straight unsay, pretending first
Wise to fly pain, professing next the spy,
Argues no leader, but a liar traced,
Satan; and couldst thou "faithful" add? O name;   950
O sacred name of faithfulness profaned!
Faithful to whom? To thy rebellious crew?
Army of fiends, fit body to fit head;
Was this your discipline and faith engaged,
Your military obedience, to dissolve   955
Allegiance to the acknowledged power supreme?
And thou, sly hypocrite, who now wouldst seem
Patron of liberty, who more than thou
Once fawned, and cringed, and servilely adored
Heaven's awful monarch? Wherefore, but in hope   960
To dispossess him, and thyself to reign?
But mark what I areed thee now – avaunt;
Fly thither whence thou fledd'st; if from this hour
Within these hallowed limits thou appear,
Back to the infernal pit I drag thee chained,   965
And seal thee so as henceforth not to scorn
The facile gates of hell too slightly barred.'
    So threatened he; but Satan to no threats
Gave heed, but waxing more in rage, replied:
    'Then, when I am thy captive, talk of chains,   970
Proud limitary cherub, but ere then
Far heavier load thyself expect to feel
From my prevailing arm, though heaven's king
Ride on thy wings, and thou with thy compeers,
Used to the yoke, draw'st his triumphant wheels   975
In progress through the road of heaven star-paved.'
    While thus he spake, the angelic squadron bright

940 mid air] See *Fair Infant* 16n.
942 gay] brilliantly good (here used ironically).
962 areed] advise.
965-7] Rev. xx. 1-3.
971] A 'limitary' is a guard at a boundary. On Gabriel's responsibility for the
    cherubim see 549n.
976 road of heaven] the Milky Way. Cf. VII 577-81.
977-1015] Cf. *Aeneid* xii 661-952.

Turned fiery red, sharpening in moonèd horns
Their phalanx, and began to hem him round
With ported spears, as thick as when a field   980
Of Ceres ripe for harvest waving bends
Her bearded grove of ears which way the wind
Sways them; the careful ploughman doubting stands
Lest on the threshing-floor his hopeful sheaves
Prove chaff. On the other side, Satan, alarmed,   985
Collecting all his might, dilated stood,
Like Tenerife or Atlas, unremoved:
His stature reached the sky, and on his crest
Sat Horror plumed; nor wanted in his grasp
What seemed both spear and shield; now dreadful deeds
Might have ensued, nor only Paradise,   991
In this commotion, but the starry cope
Of heaven perhaps, or all the elements
At least, had gone to wrack, disturbed and torn
With violence of this conflict, had not soon   995
The eternal, to prevent such horrid fray,
Hung forth in heaven his golden scales, yet seen
Betwixt Astrea and the Scorpion sign,
Wherein all things created first he weighed,
The pendulous round earth with balanced air   1000
In counterpoise, now ponders all events,
Battles and realms; in these he put two weights,
The sequel each of parting and of fight:
The latter quick up flew, and kicked the beam;
Which Gabriel spying thus bespake the fiend: 1005
    'Satan, I know thy strength, and thou know'st mine,
Neither our own, but given; what folly then
To boast what arms can do, since thine no more

---

987 moonèd horns] crescent formation.
980–5] *Iliad* ii 147–50; Virgil, *Georgics* i 226.
980 ported] held diagonally across and close to the body, so that the blade is
    opposite the middle of the left shoulder.
981 Ceres] corn (Ceres is the goddess of agriculture).
983 careful] anxious, full of care.
987 Tenerife] mountain on Canary Island of same name.
    Atlas] alludes to the Titan (see II 306n.) and to 'Mount Atlas' (see XI
    40sn.).
992 cope] vault.
997–8] The constellation Libra (the Scales) is between Scorpio and Virgo (here
    called Astrea because in the Golden Age she lived on earth; see *Nativity*
    141n.).
999–1001 a common Old Testament metaphor (e.g. Isa. xl. 12); 'ponders' means
    both 'weighs' and 'considers' (see I Sam. ii. 3).

Than heaven permits, nor mine, though doubled now
To trample thee as mire; for proof look up,   1010
And read thy lot in yon celestial sign,
Where thou art weighed, and shown how light, how weak
If thou resist.' The fiend looked up, and knew
His mounted scale aloft: nor more, but fled
Murmuring, and with him fled the shades of night.   1015

THE END OF THE FOURTH BOOK

1010] Isa. x. 6.
1012] Dan. v. 27.

BOOK V

THE ARGUMENT

Morning approached, Eve relates to Adam her troublesome dream; he likes it not, yet comforts her; they come forth to their day labours: their morning hymn at the door of their bower. God, to render man inexcusable, sends Raphael to admonish him of his obedience, of his free estate, of his enemy near at hand, who he is, and why his enemy, and whatever else may avail Adam to know. Raphael comes down to Paradise; his appearance described; his coming discerned by Adam afar off, sitting at the door of his bower; he goes out to meet him, brings him to his lodge, entertains him with the choicest fruits of Paradise, got together by Eve; their discourse at table. Raphael performs his message, minds Adam of his state and of his enemy; relates, at Adam's request, who that enemy is, and how he came to be so, beginning from his first revolt in heaven, and the occasion thereof; how he drew his legions after him to the parts of the north, and there incited them to rebel with him, persuading all but only Abdiel, a seraph, who in argument dissuades and opposes him, then forsakes him.

Now Morn, her rosy steps in the eastern clime
Advancing, sowed the earth with orient pearl,
When Adam waked, so customed; for his sleep
Was airy light, from pure digestion bred,
And temperate vapours bland, which the only sound   5
Of leaves and fuming rills, Aurora's fan,
Lightly dispersed, and the shrill matin song
Of birds on every bough; so much the more
His wonder was to find unwakened Eve,
With tresses discomposed, and glowing cheek,   10
As through unquiet rest; he on his side
Leaning half raised, with looks of cordial love
Hung over her enamoured, and beheld
Beauty which, whether waking or asleep,
Shot forth peculiar graces; then with voice   15
Mild as when Zephyrus on Flora breathes,
Her hand soft touching, whispered thus: 'Awake,

---

1 rosy steps] Imitates the description in Homer and Hesiod of the dawn (Eos, Aurora) as 'rosy-fingered' (ῥοδοδάκτυλος).

2] *Metamorphoses* xiii 621-2.

16] Zephyrus, the west wind, 'breathes the spring' (*L'Allegro* 18) and thus produces flowers, of which Flora was the goddess.

17-25] Cf. the aubade in Song of Solomon ii. 10-13. Satan's serenade (38-41) parodies the same passage.

My fairest, my espoused, my latest found,
Heaven's last, best gift, my ever-new delight;
Awake, the morning shines, and the fresh field   20
Calls us; we lose the prime to mark how spring
Our tended plants, how blows the citron grove,
What drops the myrrh, and what the balmy reed,
How nature paints her colours, how the bee
Sits on the bloom extracting liquid sweet.'   25
    Such whispering waked her, but with startled eye
On Adam; whom embracing, thus she spake:
    'O sole in whom my thoughts find all repose,
My glory, my perfection, glad I see
Thy face, and morn returned; for I this night –   30
Such night till this I never passed – have dreamed,
If dreamed, not as I oft am wont, of thee,
Works of day past, or morrow's next design,
But of offence and trouble, which my mind
Knew never till this irksome night; methought   35
Close at mine ear one called me forth to walk
With gentle voice; I thought it thine, it said,
"Why sleep'st thou, Eve? Now is the pleasant time,
The cool, the silent, save where silence yields
To the night-warbling bird, that now awake   40
Tunes sweetest his love-laboured song; now reigns
Full-orbed the moon, and with more pleasing light,
Shadowy sets off the face of things – in vain,
If none regard; heaven wakes with all his eyes,
Whom to behold but thee, nature's desire,   45
In whose sight all things joy, with ravishment
Attracted by thy beauty still to gaze?"
I rose as at thy call, but found thee not:
To find thee I directed then my walk;
And on, methought, alone I passed through ways   50
That brought me on a sudden to the tree
Of interdicted knowledge; fair it seemed,
Much fairer to my fancy than by day;
And as I wondering looked, beside it stood
One shaped and winged like one of those from heaven   55
By us oft seen: his dewy locks distilled
Ambrosia; on that tree he also gazed;
And, "O fair plant," said he, "with fruit surcharged,
Deigns none to ease thy load and taste thy sweet,
Nor God nor man? Is knowledge so despised?   60
Or envy, or what reserve forbids to taste?

56-7 dewy ... Ambrosia] *Aeneid* i 403-4.

Forbid who will, none shall from me withhold
Longer thy offered good, why else set here?"
This said, he paused not, but with venturous arm
He plucked, he tasted; me damp horror chilled   65
At such bold words vouched with a deed so bold;
But he thus, overjoyed: "O fruit divine,
Sweet of thyself, but much more sweet thus cropped,
Forbidden here, it seems, as only fit
For gods, yet able to make gods of men;   70
And why not gods of men, since good, the more
Communicated, more abundant grows,
The author not impaired, but honoured more?
Here, happy creature, fair angelic Eve,
Partake thou also: happy though thou art,   75
Happier thou may'st be, worthier canst not be;
Taste this, and be henceforth among the gods
Thyself a goddess, not to earth confined,
But sometimes in the air, as we; sometimes
Ascend to heaven, by merit thine, and see   80
What life the gods live there, and such live thou."
So saying, he drew nigh, and to me held,
Even to my mouth of that same fruit held part
Which he had plucked: the pleasant savoury smell
So quickened appetite that I, methought,   85
Could not but taste. Forthwith up to the clouds
With him I flew, and underneath beheld
The earth outstretched immense, a prospect wide
And various; wondering at my flight and change
To this high exaltation, suddenly   90
My guide was gone, and I, methought, sunk down,
And fell asleep; but O how glad I waked
To find this but a dream!' Thus Eve her night
Related, and thus Adam answered sad:
    'Best image of myself and dearer half,   95
The trouble of thy thoughts this night in sleep
Affects me equally; nor can I like
This uncouth dream – of evil sprung, I fear;
Yet evil whence? In thee can harbour none,
Created pure. But know that in the soul   100
Are many lesser faculties that serve
Reason as chief; among these Fancy next
Her office holds; of all external things,

---

84 savoury] means both 'gratifying to the sense of smell' and 'spiritually
    delightful or edifying'.
94 sad] gravely, seriously.

Which the five watchful senses represent,
She forms imaginations, airy shapes,   105
Which Reason, joining or disjoining, frames
All what we affirm or what deny, and call
Our knowledge or opinion; then retires
Into her private cell when nature rests.
Oft, in her absence, mimic Fancy wakes   110
To imitate her; but, misjoining shapes,
Wild work produces oft, and most in dreams,
Ill matching words and deeds long past or late.
Some such resemblances methinks I find
Of our last evening's talk in this thy dream,   115
But with addition strange; yet be not sad.
Evil into the mind of god or man
May come and go, so unapproved, and leave
No spot or blame behind; which gives me hope
That what in sleep thou did'st abhor to dream   120
Waking thou never wilt consent to do.
Be not disheartened then, nor cloud those looks,
That wont to be more cheerful and serene
Than when fair morning first smiles on the world;
And let us to our fresh employments rise   125
Among the groves, the fountains, and the flowers,
That open now their choicest bosomed smells,
Reserved from night, and kept for thee in store.'
    So cheered he his fair spouse; and she was cheered,
But silently a gentle tear let fall   130
From either eye, and wiped them with her hair:
Two other precious drops that ready stood,
Each in their crystal sluice, he, ere they fell,
Kissed as the gracious signs of sweet remorse
And pious awe, that feared to have offended.   135
    So all was cleared, and to the field they haste.
But first, from under shady arborous roof
Soon as they forth were come to open sight
Of day-spring, and the sun – who, scarce uprisen,
With wheels yet hovering o'er the ocean brim,   140
Shot parallel to the earth his dewy ray,
Discovering in wide landscape all the east
Of Paradise and Eden's happy plains –
Lowly they bowed, adoring, and began
Their orisons, each morning duly paid   145

117 God] means 'angel', but may also mean 'God'.
130–1] Luke vii. 38.
145 orisons] prayers.

In various style; for neither various style
Nor holy rapture wanted they to praise
Their maker, in fit strains pronounced, or sung
Unmeditated; such prompt eloquence
Flowed from their lips, in prose or numerous verse,   150
More tuneable than needed lute or harp
To add more sweetness; and they thus began:
  'These are thy glorious works, parent of good,
Almighty, thine this universal frame,
Thus wondrous fair: thyself how wondrous then!   155
Unspeakable, who sitt'st above these heavens
To us invisible, or dimly seen
In these thy lowest works; yet these declare
Thy goodness beyond thought, and power divine;
Speake ye who best can tell, ye sons of light,   160
Angels – for ye behold him, and with songs
And choral symphonies, day without night,
Circle his throne rejoicing – ye in heaven;
On earth join, all ye creatures, to extol
Him first, him last, him midst, and without end.   165
Fairest of stars, last in the train of night,
If better thou belong not to the dawn,
Sure pledge of day, that crown'st the smiling morn
With thy bright circlet, praise him in thy sphere
While day arises, that sweet hour of prime.   170
Thou sun, of this great world both eye and soul,
Acknowledge him thy greater; sound his praise
In thy eternal course, both when thou climb'st,
And when high noon hast gained, and when thou fall'st.
Moon, that now meet'st the orient sun, now fliest   175
With the fixed stars, fixed in their orb that flies;
And ye five other wandering fires that move

150 numerous] measured, rhythmic.
153-208] This hymn is based on Psalm cxlvii, and on The Song of the Three
    Holy Children (35-66), a LXX addition to the Book of Daniel. This
    apocryphal passage later became the Canticle *Benedicite*, which appears in
    the Book of Common Prayer.
165] Rev. xxii. 13.
166 Fairest of stars] Hesperus (IV 605) here re-appears as Phosphorous, or
    Lucifer.
177 five other wandering fires] Four of the planets are Mercury, Mars, Jupiter,
    and Saturn; the fifth may be Venus, or if 'other' excludes Venus (which
    appeared in l. 166), the earth may be intended (cf. VIII 128-9). 'Wandering
    fires' approximates the Greek phrase for planets, ἀστέρες πλανῆται (wander-
    ing stars).

In mystic dance, not without song, resound
His praise who out of darkness called up light.
Air, and ye elements, the eldest birth　　　　　　　180
Of nature's womb, that in quaternion run
Perpetual circle, multiform, and mix
And nourish all things, let your ceaseless change
Vary to our great maker still new praise.
Ye mists and exhalations, that now rise　　　　　　185
From hill or streaming lake, dusky or grey,
Till the sun paint your fleecy skirts with gold,
In honour to the world's great author rise;
Whether to deck with clouds the uncoloured sky,
Of wet the thirsty earth with falling showers,　　　190
Rising or falling, still advance his praise.
His praise, ye winds, that from four quarters blow,
Breathe soft or loud; and wave your tops, ye pines,
With every plant, in sign of worship wave.
Fountains, and ye that warble, as ye flow,　　　　　195
Melodious murmurs, warbling tune his praise.
Join voices, all ye living souls; ye birds,
That, singing, up to heaven-gate ascend,
Bear on your wings and in your notes his praise;
Ye that in waters glide, and ye that walk　　　　　200
The earth, and stately tread, or lowly creep,
Witness if I be silent, morn or even,
To hill or valley, fountain, or fresh shade,
Made vocal by my song, and taught his praise.
Hail universal Lord, be bounteous still　　　　　　205
To give us only good; and if the night
Have gathered aught of evil, or concealed,
Disperse it, as now light dispels the dark.'
　So prayed they innocent, and to their thoughts
Firm peace recovered soon, and wonted calm.　　　210
On to their morning's rural work they haste,
Among sweet dews and flowers, where any row
Of fruit-trees, over-woody, reached too far
Their pampered boughs, and needed hands to check
Fruitless embraces: or they led the vine　　　　　215
To wed her elm; she, spoused, about him twines
Her marriageable arms, and with her brings
Her dower, the adopted clusters, to adorn
His barren leaves. Them thus employed beheld

181-2] On the cycle of the group of four ('quaternion') elements see ll. 414-26.
215-19] A traditional idea, both in antiquity (e.g. Virgil, *Georgics* i 2, Horace,
　Odes II. xv. 4, IV. v. 30) and the Renaissance. Cf. *PL* IX 217.

With pity heaven's high king, and to him called   220
Raphael, the sociable spirit, that deigned
To travel with Tobias, and secured
His marriage with the seven-times-wedded maid.
    'Raphael,' said he, 'thou hear'st what stir on earth
Satan, from hell scaped through the darksome gulf,   225
Hath raised in Paradise, and how disturbed
This night the human pair; how he designs
In them at once to ruin all mankind.
Go, therefore; half this day, as friend with friend,
Converse with Adam, in what bower or shade   230
Thou find'st him from the heat of noon retired
To respite his day-labour with repast
Or with repose; and such discourse bring on
As may advise him of his happy state –
Happiness in his power left free to will,   235
Left to his own free will, his will though free
Yet mutable; whence warn him to beware
He swerve not, too secure: tell him withal
His danger, and from whom; what enemy,
Late fallen himself from heaven, is plotting now   240
The fall of others from like state of bliss;
By violence, no, for that shall be withstood;
But by deceit and lies; this let him know,
Lest wilfully transgressing he pretend
Surprisal, unadmonished, unforewarned.'   245
    So spake the eternal Father, and fulfilled
All justice. Nor delayed the wingèd saint
After his charge received; but from among
Thousand celestial ardours, where he stood
Veiled with his gorgeous wings, upspringing light,   250
Flew through the midst of heaven; the angelic choirs
On each hand parting, to his speed gave way
Through all the empyreal road, till, at the gate
Of heaven arrived, the gate self-opened wide,
On golden hinges turning, as by work   255
Divine the sovereign architect had framed.
From hence – no cloud or, to obstruct his sight,
Star interposed, however small – he sees,

224 Raphael] The name means 'God heals' in Hebrew; it does not occur in the
    canonical Scriptures, but the angel Raphael appears in both the apocryphal
    Book of Tobit and the pseudepigraphical Book of Enoch. On his functions
    see Tobit xii. 15; on the service rendered to Tobias (ll. 222–3) see IV
    166–71n.
249 ardours] flames; the word may indicate seraphim (cf. 'fiery seraphim', II
    512; the word 'seraph' derives from the Hebrew verbal root meaning 'to
    burn') or angels in general (Psalm civ. 4).

Not unconform to other shining globes,
Earth, and the garden of God with cedars crowned   260
Above all hills; as when by night the glass
Of Galileo, less assured, observes
Imagined lands and regions in the moon;
Or pilot from amidst the Cyclades
Delos or Samos first appearing kens   265
A cloudy spot. Down thither prone in flight
He speeds, and through the vast ethereal sky
Sails between worlds and worlds, with steady wing
Now on the polar winds; then with quick fan
Winnows the buxom air, till within soar   270
Of towering eagles, to all the fowls he seems
A phoenix, gazed by all, as that sole bird,
When, to enshrine his relics in the sun's
Bright temple, to Egyptian Thebes he flies.
At once on the eastern cliff of Paradise   275
He lights, and to his proper shape returns,
A seraph winged; six wings he wore, to shade
His lineaments divine. the pair that clad
Each shoulder broad came mantling o'er his breast
With regal ornament; the middle pair   280
Girt like a starry zone his waist, and round
Skirted his loins and thighs with downy gold
And colours dipped in heaven; the third his feet
Shadowed from either heel with feathered mail,
Sky-tinctured grain. Like Maia's son he stood,   285
And shook his plumes, that heavenly fragrance filled
The circuit wide. Straight knew him all the bands
Of angels under watch, and to his state
And to his message high in honour rise;
For on some message high they guessed him bound.   290
Their glittering tents he passed, and now is come

261-3] Cf. I 288-91n.

264-5] Delos is a tiny island regarded in antiquity as the centre of the Cyclades, the islands of the south Aegean. Samos is an island off the coast of western Asia Minor.

266-70] Cf. the descent of Mercury in *Aeneid* iv 238-58.

270 buxom] unresisting.

272-4] The phoenix is a mythical bird which every 500 years was consumed by fire in its own nest, whereupon a new phoenix would rise from the ashes and fly to Heliopolis, the city of the sun, to deposit 'his relics' in the temple. The names Thebes and Heliopolis were used interchangeably in the Renaissance. 'Egyptian' distinguishes this city from Boeotian Thebes. Cf. *SA* 1699-1707.

277-85] Isa. vi. 2.

285 Maia's son] Mercury. Cf. 266-70n.

Into the blissful field, through groves of myrrh,
And flowering odours, cassia, nard, and balm,
A wilderness of sweets; for nature here
Wantoned as in her prime, and played at will   295
Her virgin fancies, pouring forth more sweet,
Wild above rule or art; enormous bliss.
Him through the spicy forest onward come,
Adam discerned, as in the door he sat
Of his cool bower, while now the mounted sun   300
Shot down direct his fervid rays to warm
Earth's inmost womb, more warmth than Adam needs;
And Eve within, due at her hour, prepared
For dinner savoury fruits, of taste to please
True appetite, and not disrelish thirst   305
Of nectarous draughts between, from milky stream,
Berry or grape: to whom thus Adam called:
    'Haste hither, Eve, and, worth thy sight, behold
Eastward among those trees what glorious shape
Comes this way moving; seems another morn   310
Risen on mid-noon; some great behest from heaven
To us perhaps he brings, and will vouchsafe
This day to be our guest. But go with speed,
And what thy stores contain bring forth, and pour
Abundance fit to honour and receive   315
Our heavenly stranger; well we may afford
Our givers their own gifts, and large bestow
From large bestowed, where nature multiplies
Her fertile growth, and by disburdening grows
More fruitful; which instructs us not to spare.'   320
    To whom thus Eve: 'Adam, earth's hallowed mould,
Of God inspired, small store will serve where store,
All seasons, ripe for use hangs on the stalk;
Save what, by frugal storing, firmness gains
To nourish, and superfluous moist consumes;   325
But I will haste, and from each bough and brake,
Each plant and juiciest gourd, will pluck such choice
To entertain our angel guest, as he
Beholding shall confess that here on earth
God hath dispensed his bounties as in heaven.'   330

293 cassia, nard] Exod. xxx. 24; Mark xiv. 3. Cf. *Comus* 991.
297 enormous] deviating from ordinary rule, unusual.
299ff.] The scene in which Adam and Eve entertain Raphael is modelled on the
    scene in Gen. xviii in which Abraham and Sarah receive a theophanic
    visitation.
300-2] Cf. III 609n.

So saying, with dispatchful looks in haste
She turns, on hospitable thoughts intent
What choice to choose for delicacy best,
What order so contrived as not to mix
Tastes, not well joined, inelegant, but bring   335
Taste after taste upheld with kindliest change:
Bestirs her then, and from each tender stalk
Whatever Earth all-bearing mother yields
In India east or west, or middle shore
In Pontus or the Punic coast, or where   340
Alcinöus reigned, fruit of all kinds, in coat
Rough or smooth rined, or bearded husk, or shell,
She gathers, tribute large, and on the board
Heaps with unsparing hand; for drink the grape
She crushes, inoffensive must, and meaths   345
From many a berry, and from sweet kernels pressed
She tempers dulcet creams – nor these to hold
Wants her fit vessels pure; then strews the ground
With rose and odours from the shrub unfumed.

Meanwhile our primitive great sire, to meet   350
His godlike guest, walks forth, without more train
Accompanied than with his own complete
Perfections; in himself was all his state,
More solemn than the tedious pomp that waits
On princes, when their rich retinue long   355
Of horses led and grooms besmeared with gold
Dazzles the crowd and sets them all agape.
Nearer his presence, Adam, though not awed,
Yet with submiss approach and reverence meek,
As to a superior nature, bowing low,   360
Thus said: 'Native of heaven – for other place
None can than heaven such glorious shape contain –
Since by descending from the thrones above,
Those happy places thou hast deigned a while
To want, and honour these, vouchsafe with us,   365
Two only, who yet by sovereign gift possess

338 Earth all-bearing mother] translates the classical Greek title παμμήτωρ γῆ, the classical Latin *Magna Mater* (cf. VII 281n.) and the post-classical *Omniparens*.

339–41] 'middle shore' includes the Black Sea (indicated by Pontus, a district on the south coast) and the Mediterranean (indicated by the Punic, or Carthaginian coast). Alcinöus was the king of the Phaeacians on the mythical island of Scheria. On the Garden of Alcinöus cf. *PL* IX 441, and *Odyssey* vii 112–32.

345 must] unfermented wine.
   meaths] mead, here non-alcoholic.

349 unfumed] not burned for incense.

This spacious ground, in yonder shady bower
To rest, and what the garden choicest bears
To sit and taste, till this meridian heat
Be over, and the sun more cool decline.'   370
    Whom thus the angelic virtue answered mild:
'Adam, I therefore came; nor art thou such
Created, or such place hast here to dwell,
As may not oft invite, though spirits of heaven,
To visit thee; lead on then, where thy bower   375
O'ershades; for these mid-hours, till evening rise,
I have at will.' So to the sylvan lodge
They came, that like Pomona's arbour smiled,
With flowerets decked and fragrant smells; but Eve,
Undecked, save with herself, more lovely fair   380
Than wood-nymph, or the fairest goddess feigned
Of three that in Mount Ida naked strove,
Stood to entertain her guest from heaven; no veil
She needed, virtue-proof; no thought infirm
Altered her cheek. On whom the Angel 'Hail'   385
Bestowed – the holy salutation used
Long after to blest Mary, second Eve:
    'Hail mother of mankind, whose fruitful womb
Shall fill the world more numerous with thy sons
Than with these various fruits the trees of God   390
Have heaped this table.' Raised of grassy turf
Their table was, and mossy seats had round,
And on her ample square, from side to side,
All autumn piled, though spring and autumn here
Danced hand-in-hand. A while discourse they hold –   395
No fear lest dinner cool – when thus began
Our author: 'Heavenly stranger, please to taste
These bounties, which our nourisher, from whom
All perfect good, unmeasured-out, descends,
To us for food and for delight hath caused   400

371] Raphael is an archangel, not a virtue, so the phrase may imitate Homeric
    diction and mean 'the virtuous angel'. Cf. VI 355.
372 therefore] for that reason.
378 Pomona] Roman goddess of fruit trees, in Renaissance art often portrayed
    with a pruning-knife in her hand. Cf. IX 393.
381-2] Alludes to the judgement of Paris (on Mount Ida, now Kaz Dag, near
    Troy), who chose Venus over Juno and Minerva as the most beautiful
    goddess. On Eve as Venus see VIII 46-7n., 60-3n.
385-7] Luke i. 28. Cf. X 183n., XI 158-60, XII 379, PR II 67-8.
394-5] In a late tradition the Horae came to represent the four seasons, two of
    which are here represented as dancing hand-in-hand. On the simultaneity
    of spring and autumn in Paradise see IV 148.
397 author] ancestor.

The earth to yield: unsavoury food, perhaps,
To spiritual natures; only this I know,
That one celestial Father gives to all.'
    To whom the angel: 'Therefore, what he gives
(Whose praise be ever sung) to man, in part   405
Spiritual, may of purest spirits be found
No ingrateful food: and food alike those pure
Intelligential substances require
As doth your rational; and both contain
Within them every lower faculty   410
Of sense, whereby they hear, see, smell, touch, taste,
Tasting concoct, digest, assimilate,
And corporeal to incorporeal turn.
For know, whatever was created needs
To be sustained and fed; of elements   415
The grosser feeds the purer: earth the sea;
Earth and the sea feed air; the air those fires
Ethereal, and, as lowest, first the moon;
Whence in her visage round those spots, unpurged
Vapours not yet into her substance turned.   420
Nor doth the moon no nourishment exhale
From her moist continent to higher orbs.
The sun, that light imparts to all, receives
From all his alimental recompense
In humid exhalations, and at even   425
Sups with the ocean; though in heaven the trees
Of life ambrosial fruitage bear, and vines
Yield nectar – though from off the boughs each morn
We brush mellifluous dews and find the ground
Covered with pearly grain – yet God hath here   430
Varied his bounty so with new delights
As may compare with heaven; and to taste
Think not I shall be nice.' So down they sat,
And to their viands fell, nor seemingly

407-13] Milton's affirmation of the corporeity of angels is clarified by his
    description of 'first matter' in ll. 473-6. Broadly speaking, Milton's position
    aligns him with Platonic, Patristic, and Protestant views, and against the
    Aristotelian, Scholastic, and Counter-Reformation position.
433 nice] fastidious, difficult to please.
434-8] 'Seemingly' is almost a technical term, for it refers to the Docetist view
    (from δοκεῖν, to seem) that the earthly bodies of spiritual beings (especially
    Christ, but also the angels) were apparent rather than real. Milton's view
    that Raphael physically ate is resolutely Protestant, for in Tobit, which
    Catholics accepted as canonical and Protestants usually rejected from the
    canon, Raphael claims that his eating was illusory ('ye did see a vision'
    Tobit xii. 19). Milton's use of 'transubstantiate' as a digestive term is
    consonant with the anti-Catholic emphasis of the passage.

The angel, nor in mist – the common gloss   435
Of theologians – but with keen dispatch
Of real hunger, and concoctive heat
To transubstantiate: what redounds transpires
Through spirits with ease; nor wonder, if by fire
Of sooty coal the empiric alchemist   440
Can turn, or holds it possible to turn,
Metals of drossiest ore to perfect gold,
As from the mine. Meanwhile at table Eve
Ministered naked, and their flowing cups
With pleasant liquors crowned: O innocence   445
Deserving Paradise! If ever, then,
Then had the sons of God excuse to have been
Enamoured at that sight. But in those hearts
Love unlibidinous reigned, nor jealousy
Was understood, the injured lover's hell.   450
    Thus when with meats and drinks they had sufficed,
Not burdened nature, sudden mind arose
In Adam not to let the occasion pass,
Given him by this great conference, to know
Of things above his world, and of their being   455
Who dwell in heaven, whose excellence he saw
Transcend his own so far, whose radiant forms,
Divine effulgence, whose high power so far
Exceeded human; and his wary speech
Thus to the empyreal minister he framed: 460
    'Inhabitant with God, now know I well
Thy favour, in his honour done to man,
Under whose lowly roof thou hast vouchsafed
To enter, and these earthly fruits to taste,
Food not of angels, yet accepted so   465
As that more willingly thou could'st not seem
At heaven's high feasts to have fed: yet what compare?'
    To whom the wingèd hierarch replied:
'O Adam, one almighty is, from whom
All things proceed, and up to him return,   470
If not depraved from good, created all
Such to perfection; one first matter all,
Endued with various forms, various degrees
Of substance, and in things that live, of life;
But more refined, more spirituous and pure,   475
As nearer to him placed or nearer tending
Each in their several active spheres assigned,
Till body up to spirit work, in bounds
Proportioned to each kind. So from the root
Springs lighter the green stalk, from thence the leaves   480

More airy, last the bright consummate flower
Spirits odórous breathes; flowers and their fruit,
Man's nourishment, by gradual scale sublimed,
To vital spirits aspire, to animal,
To intellectual; give both life and sense,   485
Fancy and understanding; whence the soul
Reason receives, and reason is her being,
Discursive, or intuitive: discourse
Is oftest yours, the latter most is ours,
Differing but in degree, of kind the same.   490
Wonder not then, what God for you saw good
If I refuse not, but convert, as you,
To proper substance; time may come when men
With angels may participate, and find
No inconvenient diet, nor too light fare;   495
And from these corporal nutriments perhaps
Your bodies may at last turn all to spirit,
Improved by tract of time, and winged ascend
Ethereal, as we, or may at choice
Here or in heavenly paradises dwell,   500
If ye be found obedient, and retain
Unalterably firm his love entire
Whose progeny you are. Meanwhile enjoy
Your fill, what happiness this happy state
Can comprehend, incapable of more.'   505
     To whom the patriarch of mankind replied:
'O favourable spirit, propitious guest,
Well hast thou taught the way that might direct
Our knowledge, and the scale of nature set
From centre to circumference, whereon   510
In contemplation of created things,
By steps we may ascend to God. But say,
What meant that caution joined, "If ye be found
Obedient?" Can we want obedience, then,
To him, or possibly his love desert,   515
Who formed us from the dust, and placed us here
Full to the utmost measure of what bliss
Human desires can seek or apprehend?'
     To whom the angel: 'Son of heaven and earth,

484] On 'spirits' and 'animal' spirits see IV 805n. The 'vital spirits' were seated
     in the heart, and sustained life.
501] Isa. i. 19-20.
503 Whose progeny you are] Alludes to Paul's use of the phrase in Acts xvii. 28;
     Paul was quoting the phrase from Aratus' astronomical poem *Phaenomena*;
     cf. *Areopagitica* p. 586, note on 'sentences'.

Attend: that thou art happy, owe to God;   520
That thou continuest such, owe to thyself,
That is, to thy obedience; therein stand.
This was that caution given thee; be advised.
God made thee perfect, not immutable;
And good he made thee, but to persevere   525
He left it in thy power – ordained thy will
By nature free, not over-ruled by fate
Inextricable, or strict necessity;
Our voluntary service he requires,
Not our necessitated; such with him   530
Finds no acceptance, nor can find, for how
Can hearts not free be tried whether they serve
Willing or no, who will but what they must
By destiny, and can no other choose?
Myself, and all the angelic host, that stand   535
In sight of God enthroned, our happy state
Hold, as you yours, while our obedience holds;
On other surety none: freely we serve,
Because we freely love, as in our will
To love or not; in this we stand or fall;   540
And some are fallen, to disobedience fallen,
And so from heaven to deepest hell; O fall
From what high state of bliss into what woe!'
    To whom our great progenitor: 'Thy words
Attentive, and with more delighted ear,   545
Divine instructor, I have heard, than when
Cherubic songs by night from neighbouring hills
Aërial music send; nor knew I not
To be, both will and deed, created free;
Yet that we never shall forget to love   550
Our maker, and obey him whose command
Single is yet so just, my constant thoughts
Assured me, and still assure; though what thou tell'st
Hath passed in heaven some doubt within me move,
But more desire to hear, if thou consent,   555
The full relation, which must needs be strange,
Worthy of sacred silence to be heard;
And we have yet large day, for scarce the sun
Hath finished half his journey, and scarce begins
His other half in the great zone of heaven.'   560
    Thus Adam made request, and Raphael,
After short pause assenting, thus began:
    'High matter thou enjoin'st me, O prime of men –

557 Worthy of sacred silence] Horace, *Odes* II. xiii. 29.

Sad task and hard; for how shall I relate
To human sense the invisible exploits   565
Of warring spirits? How, without remorse,
The ruin of so many, glorious once
And perfect while they stood? How, last, unfold
The secrets of another world, perhaps
Not lawful to reveal? Yet for thy good   570
This is dispensed; and what surmounts the reach
Of human sense I shall delineate so,
By likening spiritual to corporal forms,
As may express them best – though what if earth
Be but the shadow of heaven, and things therein   575
Each to other like more than on earth is thought?
  'As yet this world was not, and Chaos wild
Reigned where these heavens now roll, where earth
       now rests
Upon her centre poised, when on a day
(For time, though in eternity, applied   580
To motion, measures all things durable
By present, past, and future), on such day
As heaven's great year brings forth, the empyreal host
Of angels, by imperial summons called,
Innumerable before the almighty's throne   585
Forthwith from all the ends of heaven appeared
Under their hierarchs in orders bright;
Ten thousand thousand ensigns high advanced,
Standards and gonfalons, 'twixt van and rear
Stream in the air, and for distinction serve   590
Of hierarchies, of orders, and degrees;
Or in their glittering tissues bear emblazed
Holy memorials, acts of zeal and love
Recorded eminent. Thus when in orbs
Of circuit inexpressible they stood,   595
Orb within orb, the Father infinite,
By whom in bliss embosomed sat the Son,
Amidst, as from a flaming mount, whose top

566 remorse] sorrow, pity, compassion.
571 dispensed] permitted.
580-2] Aristotle's description of time as the measure of motion (first used by
    Milton in *Hobson* II 7) is here used to discredit the Platonic and Aristotelian
    notion that time and motion cannot exist in eternity, i.e. without reference
    to the created world.
583] The 'great year' or Platonic year was the period (about 36,000 years,
    according to Plato) after which all the heavenly bodies were supposed to
    return to their original positions.
589] gonfalons] banners.

Brightness had made invisible, thus spake:
  '"Hear, all ye angels, progeny of light,   600
Thrones, dominations, princedoms, virtues, powers,
Hear my decree, which unrevoked shall stand.
This day I have begot whom I declare
My only Son, and on this holy hill
Him have anointed, whom ye now behold   605
At my right hand; your head I him appoint,
And by myself have sworn to him shall bow
All knees in heaven, and shall confess him Lord;
Under his great vicegerent reign abide,
United as one individual soul,   610
For ever happy; him who disobeys
Me disobeys, breaks union, and that day,
Cast out from God and blessed vision, falls
Into utter darkness, deep engulfed, his place
Ordained without redemption, without end."   615
  'So spake the Omnipotent, and with his words
All seemed well pleased; all seemed, but were not all.
That day, as other solemn days, they spent
In song and dance about the sacred hill –
Mystical dance, which yonder starry sphere   620
Of planets, and of fixed, in all her wheels
Resembles nearest; mazes intricate,
Eccentric, intervolved, yet regular
Then most when most irregular they seem;
And in their motions harmony divine   625
So smooths her charming tones that God's own ear
Listens delighted. Evening now approached
(For we have also our evening and our morn –
We ours for change delectable, not need),
Forthwith from dance to sweet repast they turn   630
Desirous: all in circles as they stood,
Tables are set, and on a sudden piled
With angels' food; and rubied nectar flows
In pearl, in diamond, and massy gold,
Fruit of delicious vines, the growth of heaven.   635
On flowes reposed, and with fresh flowerets crowned,
They eat, they drink, and in communion sweet

601] Col. i. 16.
603-6] See Heb. i.5, and Milton's translation of Psalm ii. 6-9 (ll. 11-21).
607-8] Isa. xlv. 23; Phil. ii. 9-11.
610 individual] cf. *Time* 12n.
613 blessed vision] cf. I 684n.
614 utter] outer.
618 solemn days] days marked by the celebration of special observances or
    rites.

Quaff immortality and joy, secure
Of surfeit where full measure only bounds
Excess, before the all-bounteous king, who showered   640
With copious hand, rejoicing in their joy.
Now when ambrosial night, with clouds exhaled
From that high mount of God, whence light and shade
Spring both, the face of brightest heaven had changed
To grateful twilight (for night comes not there   645
In darker veil), and roseate dews disposed
All but the unsleeping eyes of God to rest,
Wide over all the plain, and wider far
Than all this globous earth in plain outspread
(Such are the courts of God), the angelic throng,   650
Dispersed in bands and files, their camp extend
By living streams among the trees of life –
Pavilions numberless and sudden reared,
Celestial tabernacles, where they slept,   654
Fanned with cool winds; save those who, in their course,
Melodious hymns about the sovereign throne
Alternate all night long; but not so waked
Satan – so call him now; his former name
Is heard no more in heaven; he, of the first,
If not the first archangel, great in power,   660
In favour and pre-eminence, yet fraught
With envy against the Son of God, that day
Honoured by his great Father, and proclaimed
Messiah, king anointed, could not bear,   664
Through pride, that sight, and thought himself impaired.
Deep malice thence conceiving and disdain,
Soon as midnight brought on the dusky hour
Friendliest to sleep and silence, he resolved
With all his legions to dislodge, and leave
Unworshipped, unobeyed, the throne supreme,   670
Contemptuous, and, his next subordinate
Awakening, thus to him in secret spake:
   ' "Sleep'st thou, companion dear, what sleep can close
Thy eyelids? And rememberest what decree,
Of yesterday, so late hath passed the lips   675

645-6] Rev. xxi. 25.
647] Psalm cxxi. 4.
658 former name] According to a medieval tradition Satan's former name was
   Lucifer. Cf. VII 131-3.
664 Messiah, king anointed] Messiah means 'anointed' in Hebrew.
669 dislodge] a military term meaning 'to leave a place of encampment'.
671 subordinate] presumably Beëlzebub, who is not named in Book V.
673] Alludes to *Iliad* ii. 23; cf. *Aeneid* iv 267, 560.

Of heaven's almighty? Thou to me thy thoughts
Wast wont, I mine to thee was wont to impart;
Both waking we were one; how, then, can now
Thy sleep dissent? New laws thou seest imposed;
New laws from him who reigns new minds may raise   680
In us who serve – new counsels, to debate
What doubtful may ensue; more in this place
To utter is not safe. Assemble thou
Of all those myriads which we lead the chief;
Tell them that, by command, ere yet dim night   685
Her shadowy cloud withdraws, I am to haste,
And all who under me their banners wave,
Homeward with flying march where we possess
The quarters of the north, there to prepare
Fit entertainment to receive our king,   690
The great Messiah, and his new commands,
Who speedily through all the hierarchies
Intends to pass triumphant, and give laws."
  'So spake the false archangel, and infused
Bad influence into the unwary breast   695
Of his associate; he together calls,
Or several one by one, the regent powers,
Under him regent; tells, as he was taught,
That, the most high commanding, now ere night,
Now ere dim night had disencumbered heaven,   700
The great hierarchal standard was to move;
Tells the suggested cause, and casts between
Ambiguous words and jealousies, to sound
Or taint integrity; but all obeyed
The wonted signal, and superior voice   705
Of their great potentate; for great indeed
His name, and high was his degree in heaven:
His countenance, as the morning star that guides
The starry flock, allured them, and with lies
Drew after him the third part of heaven's host;   710
Meanwhile, the eternal eye, whose sight discerns
Abstrusest thoughts, from forth his holy mount,
And from within the golden lamps that burn
Nightly before him, saw without their light
Rebellion rising – saw in whom, how spread   715

---

689 north] the traditional home of Satan; cf. Isa. xiv. 13.
697 several] separately.
708-9] Satan imitates ('with lies') Christ as 'morning star'; both identifications
    are Biblical (Isa. xiv. 12; Rev. xxii. 16) Cf. *PR* I 294.
713] Rev. iv. 5.

Among the sons of morn, what multitudes
Were banded to oppose his high decree;
And, smiling, to his only Son thus said:
  ' "Son, thou in whom my glory I behold
In full resplendence, heir of all my might,   720
Nearly it now concerns us to be sure
Of our omnipotence, and with what arms
We mean to hold what anciently we claim
Of deity or empire: such a foe
Is rising, who intends to erect his throne   725
Equal to ours, throughout the spacious north;
Nor so content, hath in his thought to try
In battle what our power is or our right.
Let us advise, and to this hazard draw
With speed what force is left, and all employ   730
In our defence, lest unawares we lose
This our high place, our sanctuary, our hill."
  'To whom the Son, with calm aspéct and clear
Lightning divine, ineffable, serene
Made answer: "Mighty Father, thou thy foes   735
Justly hast in derision, and secure
Laugh'st at their vain designs and tumults vain –
Matter to me of glory, whom their hate
Illustrates, when they see all regal power
Given me to quell their pride, and in event   740
Know whether I be dextrous to subdue
Thy rebels, or be found the worst in heaven."
  'So spake the Son; but Satan with his powers
Far was advanced on winged speed, an host
Innumerable as the stars of night,   745
Or stars of morning, dew-drops which the sun
Impearls on every leaf and every flower.
Regions they passed, the mighty regencies
Of seraphim and potentates and thrones
In their triple degrees – regions to which   750
All thy dominion, Adam, is no more
Than what this garden is to all the earth
And all the sea, from one entire globose
Stretched into longitude; which having passed,

---

734 Lightning] Cf. Matt. xxvii. 3.
736 in derision] Cf. Milton's translation of Psalm ii. 4 (ll. 8–9).
739 Illustrates] renders illustrious.
750 triple degrees] In a tradition originating in the scheme of Dionysius the
    Pseudo-Areopagite, the nine orders of angels were divided into three
    groups of three.
754 into longitude] flat.

At length into the limits of the north   755
They came, and Satan to his royal seat
High on a hill, far blazing, as a mount
Raised on a mount, with pyramids and towers
From diamond quarries hewn and rocks of gold –
The palace of great Lucifer (so call   760
That structure, in the dialect of men
Interpreted) which not long after, he
Affecting all equality with God,
In imitation of that mount whereon
Messiah was declared in sight of heaven,   765
The Mountain of the Congregation called;
For thither he assembled all his train,
Pretending so commanded to consult
About the great reception of their king
Thither to come, and with calumnious art   770
Of counterfeited truth thus held their ears:
    ' "Thrones, dominations, princedoms, virtues, powers –
If these magnific titles yet remain
Not merely titular, since by decree
Another now hath to himself engrossed   775
All power, and us eclipsed under the name
Of king anointed; for whom all this haste
Of midnight march, and hurried meeting here,
This only to consult, how we may best,
With what may be devised of honours new,   780
Receive him coming to receive from us
Knee-tribute yet unpaid, prostration vile,
Too much to one, but double, how endured –
To one and to his image now proclaimed?
But what if better counsels might erect   785
Our minds, and teach us to cast off this yoke?
Will ye submit your necks, and choose to bend
The supple knee? Ye will not, if I trust
To know ye right, or if ye know yourselves
Natives and sons of heaven possessed before   790
By none, and, if not equal all, yet free,
Equally free; for orders and degrees
Jar not with liberty, but well consist.
Who can in reason, then, or right, assume
Monarchy over such as live by right   795
His equals – if in power and splendour less,
In freedom equal? Or can introduce
Law and edict on us, who without law
Err not, much less for this to be our lord,
And look for adoration, to the abuse   800

Of those imperial titles which assert
Our being ordained to govern, not to serve?"
   'Thus far his bold discourse without control
Had audience, when, among the seraphim,
Abdiel, than whom none with more zeal adored   805
The Deity, and divine commands obeyed,
Stood up, and in a flame of zeal severe
The current of his fury thus opposed:
   ' "O argument blasphémous, false, and proud –
Words which no ear ever to hear in heaven   810
Expected; least of all from thee, ingrate,
In place thyself so high above thy peers.
Canst thou with impious obloquy condemn
The just decree of God, pronounced and sworn,
That to his only Son, by right endued   815
With regal sceptre, every soul in heaven
Shall bend the knee, and in that honour due
Confess him rightful king? Unjust, thou say'st,
Flatly unjust, to bind with laws the free,
And equal over equals to let reign,   820
One over all with unsucceeded power.
Shalt thou give law to God, shalt thou dispute
With him the points of liberty, who made
Thee what thou art, and formed the powers of heaven
Such as he pleased, and circumscribed their being? 825
Yet, by experience taught, we know how good,
And of our good and of our dignity
How provident, he is – how far from thought
To make us less; bent rather to exalt
Our happy state, under one head more near   830
United. But – to grant it thee unjust
That equal over equals monarch reign –
Thyself, though great and glorious, dost thou count,
Or all angelic nature joined in one,
Equal to him, begotten Son, by whom   835
As by his word, the mighty Father made
All things, even thee, and all the spirits of heaven
By him created in their bright degrees,
Crowned them with glory, and to their glory named

---

805 Abdiel] The name means in Hebrew 'servant of God'; in the Bible it is used
    only as a human name.
821 unsucceeded] having no successor, everlasting.
822–5] See Rom. ix. 20 and A.V. marginal note, where 'disputest with God' is
    listed as an alternative reading.
835–40] Col. i. 16–17.

Thrones, dominations, princedoms, virtues, powers? –
Essential powers; nor by his reign obscured,   841
But more illustrious made, since he the head
One of our number thus reduced becomes,
His laws our laws, all honour to him done
Returns our own. Cease then this impious rage,   845
And tempt not these; but hasten to appease
The incensèd Father and the incensèd Son
While pardon may be found, in time besought."
  'So spake the fervent angel, but his zeal
None seconded, as out of season judged,   850
Or singular and rash; whereat rejoiced
The apostate, and, more haughty, thus replied:
  ' "That we were formed, then, say'st thou? And the
      work
Of secondary hands, by task transferred   855
From Father to his Son? Strange point and new!
Doctrine which we would know whence learned; who saw
When this creation was? Remember'st thou
Thy making, while the maker gave thee being?
We know no time when we were not as now;
Know none before us, self-begot, self-raised   860
By our own quickening power when fatal course
Had circled his full orb, the birth mature
Of this our native heaven, ethereal sons.
Our puissance is our own; our own right hand
Shall teach us highest deeds, by proof to try   865
Who is our equal; then thou shalt behold
Whether by supplication we intend
Address, and to begirt the almighty throne
Beseeching or besieging. This report,
These tidings, carry to the anointed king;   870
And fly, ere evil intercept thy flight."
  'He said, and, as the sound of waters deep,
Hoarse murmur echoed to his words applause
Through the infinite host; nor less for that
The flaming seraph, fearless, though alone,   875
Encompassed round with foes, thus answered bold:
  ' "O alienate from God, O spirit accursed,
Forsaken of all good; I see thy fall
Determined, and thy hapless crew involved
In this perfidious fraud, contagion spread
Both of thy crime and punishment; henceforth   880

864-5] Psalm xlv. 4.
872] Ezek. i. 24; Rev. xix. 6.

No more be troubled how to quit the yoke
Of God's Messiah; those indulgent laws
Will not be now vouchsafed; other decrees
Against thee are gone forth without recall;   885
That golden sceptre which thou didst reject
Is now an iron rod to bruise and break
Thy disobedience. Well thou didst advise;
Yet not for thy advice or threats I fly
These wicked tents devoted, lest the wrath   890
Impendent, raging into sudden flame,
Distinguish not: for soon expect to feel
His thunder on thy head, devouring fire.
Then who created thee lamenting learn,
When who can uncreate thee thou shalt know."   895
    'So spake the seraph Abdiel, faithful found;
Among the faithless faithful only he;
Among innumerable false unmoved,
Unshaken, unseduced, unterrified,
His loyalty he kept, his love, his zeal;   900
Nor number nor example with him wrought
To swerve from truth, or change his constant mind,
Though single. From amidst them forth he passed,
Long way through hostile scorn, which he sustained
Superior, nor of violence feared aught;   905
And with retorted scorn his back he turned
On those proud towers, to swift destruction doomed.'

THE END OF THE FIFTH BOOK

886–7] Cf. II 327–8 and 327n.
890 wicked tents] See Num. xvi. 26 and Milton's translation of Psalm lxxxiv. 10
    (ll. 37–40).
    devoted] consigned to destruction, doomed.
906 retorted] thrown back. In the phrase 'he turned' Milton recapitulates the
    root-meaning of retort, which is 'to turn or twist'.
907] II Pet. ii. 1.

BOOK VI

THE ARGUMENT

Raphael continues to relate how Michael and Gabriel were sent forth to battle against Satan and his angels. The first fight described: Satan and his powers retire under night; he calls a council; invents devilish engines, which, in the second day's fight, put Michael and his angels to some disorder; but they at length, pulling up mountains, overwhelmed both the force and machines of Satan. Yet, the tumult not so ending, God, on the third day, sends Messiah his Son, for whom he had reserved the glory of that victory; he, in the power of his Father, coming to the place, and causing all his legions to stand still on either side, with his chariot and thunder driving into the midst of his enemies pursued them, unable to resist, towards the wall of heaven; which opening, they leap down with horror and confusion into the place of punishment prepared for them in the deep. Messiah returns with triumph to his Father.

'All night the dreadless angel, unpursued,
Through heaven's wide champaign held his way, till Morn,
Waked by the circling Hours, with rosy hand
Unbarred the gates of light. There is a cave
Within the Mount of God, fast by his throne,   5
Where Light and Darkness in perpetual round
Lodge and dislodge by turns – which makes through
    heaven
Grateful vicissitude, like day and night;
Light issues forth, and at the other door
Obsequious Darkness enters, till her hour   10
To veil the heaven, though darkness there might well
Seem twilight here; and now went forth the Morn
Such as in highest heaven, arrayed in gold
Empyreal; from before her vanished night,
Shot through with orient beams; when all the plain   15
Covered with thick embattled squadrons bright,
Chariots, and flaming arms, and fiery steeds,
Reflecting blaze on blaze, first met his view;
War he perceived, war in procinct, and found
Already known what he for news had thought   20

---

1 angel] Abdiel.
2–4] *Metamorphoses* ii 112–14. On 'rosy hand' cf. V 1n.
4–7] Hesiod, *Theogony* 736–57.
19 in procinct] prepared, in readiness.

To have reported; gladly then he mixed
Among those friendly powers, who him received
With joy and acclamations loud, that one,
That of so many myriads fallen yet one,
Returned not lost; on to the sacred hill   25
They led him, high applauded, and present
Before the seat supreme; from whence a voice,
From midst a golden cloud, thus mild was heard:
  ' "Servant of God, well done; well hast thou fought
The better fight, who single hast maintained   30
Against revolted multitudes the cause
Of truth, in word mightier than they in arms,
And for the testimony of truth hast borne
Universal reproach, far worse to bear
Than violence; for this was all thy care –   35
To stand approved in sight of God, though worlds
Judged thee perverse; the easier conquest now
Remains thee – aided by this host of friends,
Back on thy foes more glorious to return
Than scorned thou didst depart, and to subdue   40
By force who reason for their law refuse –
Right reason for their law, and for their king
Messiah, who by right of merit reigns.
Go, Michael, of celestial armies prince,
And thou, in military prowess next,   45
Gabriel; lead forth to battle these my sons
Invincible; lead forth my armed saints,
By thousands and by millions ranged for fight,
Equal in number to that godless crew
Rebellious; them with fire and hostile arms   50
Fearless assault, and to the brow of heaven
Pursuing, drive them out from God and bliss
Into their place of punishment, the gulf
Of Tartarus, which ready opens wide
His fiery chaos to receive their fall."   55
  'So spake the sovereign voice, and clouds began

29-30] Matt. xxv. 21, II Tim. iv. 7. On 'Servant of God' cf. V 805n.
33-4] Psalm lxix. 7.
42 Right reason] a theological term, inherited from the Scholastic (and ultima-
    tely Stoic) idea of *recto ratio*, which describes the faculty implanted in man
    that manifests itself both as conscience and as an ability to distinguish
    truth from falsehood.
44 Michael] The archangel Michael (Hebrew 'who is like God?') was tradition-
    ally regarded as 'prince of angels (l.281), though Protestants often dis-
    sented from this tradition. On Michael's role in the war in heaven see Rev.
    xii. (cf. Dan. xii. 1).
56-60] Cf. *Nativity* 158-9n.

To darken all the hill, and smoke to roll
In dusky wreaths reluctant flames, the sign
Of wrath awaked; nor with less dread the loud
Ethereal trumpet from on high gan blow;   60
At which command the powers militant
That stood for heaven, in mighty quadrate joined
Of union irresistible, moved on
In silence their bright legions to the sound
Of instrumental harmony, that breathed   65
Heroic ardour to adventurous deeds
Under their godlike leaders, in the cause
Of God and his Messiah. On they move,
Indissolubly firm; nor obvious hill,
Nor straitening vale, nor wood, nor stream, divides   70
Their perfect ranks; for high above the ground
Their march was, and the passive air upbore
Their nimble tread; as when the total kind
Of birds, in orderly array on wing,
Came summoned over Eden to receive   75
Their names of thee; so over many a tract
Of heaven they marched, and many a province wide,
Tenfold the length of this terrene; at last,
Far in the horizon, to the north, appeared
From skirt to skirt a fiery region, stretched   80
In battailous aspect; and, nearer view,
Bristled with upright beams innumerable
Of rigid spears, and helmets thronged, and shields
Various, with boastful argument portrayed,
The banded powers of Satan hasting on   85
With furious expedition; for they weened
That self-same day, by fight or by surprise,
To win the Mount of God, and on his throne
To set the envier of his state, the proud
Aspirer; but their thoughts proved fond and vain   90
In the mid-way; though strange to us it seemed
At first that angel should with angel war,
And in fierce hosting meet, who wont to meet
So oft in festivals of joy and love

58 reluctant] means both 'struggling, writhing' (cf. X 515) and 'unwilling,
    averse'.
60 gan] began to.
62 quadrate] square or rectangle.
69 obvious] lying in the way.
73–6] Gen. ii. 20, *Iliad* ii 459–63, *Aeneid* vii 699–701.
78 terrene] earth.
93 hosting] hostile encounter.

Unanimous, as sons of one great sire,   95
Hymning the eternal Father; but the shout
Of battle now began, and rushing sound
Of onset ended soon each milder thought.
High in the midst, exalted as a god,
The apostate in his sun-bright chariot sat,   100
Idol of majesty divine, enclosed
With flaming cherubim and golden shields;
Then lighted from his gorgeous throne – for now
'Twixt host and host but narrow space was left,
A dreadful interval, and front to front   105
Presented stood, in terrible array
Of hideous length; before the cloudy van,
On the rough edge of battle ere it joined,
Satan with vast and haughty strides advanced,
Came towering, armed in adamant and gold;   110
Abdiel that sight endured not, where he stood
Among the mightiest, bent on highest deeds,
And thus his own undaunted heart explores:
    '"O heaven! That such resemblance of the highest
Should yet remain, where faith and realty   115
Remain not; wherefore should not strength and might
There fail where virtue fails, or weakest prove
Where boldest, though to sight unconquerable?
His puissance, trusting in the almighty's aid,
I mean to try, whose reason I have tried   120
Unsound and false; nor is it aught but just
That he who in debate of truth hath won
Should win in arms, in both disputes alike
Victor; though brutish that contést and foul,
When reason hath to deal with force, yet so   125
Most reason is that reason overcome."
    'So pondering, and from his armed peers
Forth stepping opposite, half-way he met
His daring foe, at this prevention more
Incensed, and thus securely him defied: 130
    '"Proud, art thou met? Thy hope was to have reached
The height of thy aspiring unopposed –
The throne of God unguarded, and his side
Abandoned at the terror of thy power
Or potent tongue; fool, not to think how vain   135

108 edge] cf. I 276n.
115 realty] sincerity, honesty.
120 tried] proved by trial.
129 prevention] stopping another person in the execution of his designs.

Against the omnipotent to rise in arms;
Who out of smallest things could without end
Have raised incessant armies to defeat
Thy folly; or with solitary hand,
Reaching beyond all limit, at one blow,   140
Unaided could have finished thee, and whelmed
Thy legions under darkness; but thou seest
All are not of thy train; there be who faith
Prefer, and piety to God, though then
To thee not visible when I alone   145
Seemed in thy world erroneous to dissent
From all: my sect thou seest; now learn too late
How few sometimes may know when thousands err."
   'Whom the grand foe, with scornful eye askance,
Thus answered: "Ill for thee, but in wished hour   150
Of my revenge, first sought for, thou return'st
From flight, seditious angel, to receive
Thy merited reward, the first assay
Of this right hand provoked, since first that tongue,
Inspired with contradiction, durst oppose   155
A third part of the gods, in synod met
Their deities to assert: who, while they feel
Vigour divine within them, can allow
Omnipotence to none. But well thou com'st
Before thy fellows, ambitious to win   160
From me some plume, that thy success may show
Destruction to the rest; this pause between
(Unanswered lest thou boast) to let thee know;
At first I thought that liberty and heaven
To heavenly souls had been all one; but now   165
I see that most through sloth had rather serve,
Ministering spirits, trained up in feast and song:
Such hast thou armed, the minstrelsy of heaven –
Servility with freedom to contend,
As both their deeds compared this day shall prove."   170
   'To whom in brief thus Abdiel stern replied:
"Apostate, still thou err'st, nor end wilt find
Of erring, from the path of truth remote;
Unjustly thou deprav'st it with the name
Of servitude, to serve whom God ordains,   175
Or nature: God and nature bid the same,

137-9] Matt. iii. 9.
148 my sect] the primary meaning is 'those of my party', but the phrase
   probably glances at the Royalists' derisive use of the word to describe
   various dissenting groups.

When he who rules is worthiest, and excels
Them whom he governs. This is servitude –
To serve the unwise, or him who hath rebelled
Against his worthier, as thine now serve thee,   180
Thyself not free, but to thyself enthralled;
Yet lewdly dar'st our ministering upbraid.
Reign thou in hell, thy kingdom; let me serve
In heaven God ever blest, and his divine
Behests obey, worthiest to be obeyed.   185
Yet chains in hell, not realms, expect: meanwhile,
From me returned, as erst thou saidst, from flight,
This greeting on thy impious crest receive.''
    'So saying, a noble stroke he lifted high,
Which hung not, but so swift with tempest fell   190
On the proud crest of Satan that no sight,
Nor motion of swift thought, less could his shield,
Such ruin intercept; ten paces huge
He back recoiled; the tenth on bended knee
His massy spear upstayed: as if on earth   195
Winds under ground, or waters forcing way
Sidelong had pushed a mountain from his seat,
Half-sunk with all his pines. Amazement seized
The rebel thrones, but greater rage, to see
Thus foiled their mightiest; ours joy filled, and shout,   200
Presage of victory, and fierce desire
Of battle: whereat Michaël bid sound
The archangel trumpet; through the vast of heaven
It sounded, and the faithful armies rung
Hosanna to the highest; nor stood at gaze   205
The adverse legions, nor less hideous joined
The horrid shock; now storming fury rose,
And clamour such as heard in heaven till now
Was never; arms on armour clashing brayed
Horrible discord, and the madding wheels   210
Of brazen chariots raged; dire was the noise
Of conflict; overhead the dismal hiss
Of fiery darts in flaming volleys flew,
And, flying, vaulted either host with fire.
So under fiery cope together rushed   215
Both battles main with ruinous assault

182 lewdly] means both 'foolishly' and 'wickedly'.
209 brayed] made the harsh jarring sound of thunder (not of an animal).
210 madding] frenzied.
216 battles main] the main bodies of the armies, as distinct from the van (l. 107)
    or the wings.

And inextinguishable rage; all heaven
Resounded; and had earth been then, all earth
Had to her centre shook. What wonder, when
Millions of fierce encountering angels fought   220
On either side, the least of whom could wield
These elements, and arm him with the force
Of all their regions? How much more of power
Army against army numberless to raise
Dreadful combustion warring, and disturb,   225
Though not destroy, their happy native seat;
Had not the eternal king omnipotent
From his strong hold of heaven high overruled
And limited their might, though numbered such
As each divided legion might have seemed   230
A numerous host, in strength each armed hand
A legion; led in fight, yet leader seemed
Each warrior single as in chief; expert
When to advance, or stand, or turn the sway
Of battle, open when, and when to close   235
The ridges of grim war; no thought of flight,
None of retreat, no unbecoming deed
That argued fear; each on himself relied
As only in his arm the moment lay
Of victory; deeds of eternal fame   240
Were done, but infinite; for wide was spread
That war, and various: sometimes on firm ground
A standing fight; then, soaring on main wing,
Tormented all the air; all air seemed then
Conflicting fire; long time in even scale   245
The battle hung; till Satan, who that day
Prodigious power had shown, and met in arms
No equal, ranging through the dire attack
Of fighting seraphim confused, at length
Saw where the sword of Michael smote, and felled   250
Squadrons at once: with huge two-handed sway
Brandished aloft, the horrid edge came down
Wide-wasting; such destruction to withstand
He hasted, and opposed the rocky orb
Of tenfold adamant, his ample shield   255
A vast cirumference; at his approach

225 combustion] commotion, tumult.
229 numbered such] so numerous.
236 ridges of ... war] probably imitates an Homeric phrase (πολέμοιο γέφυραι),
   the precise meaning of which is uncertain: it refers either to the ground that
   divides two lines of battle or to the passage that links them.

The great archangel from his warlike toil
Surceased, and glad as hoping here to end
Intestine war in heaven, the arch-foe subdued,
Or captive dragged in chains, with hostile frown   260
And visage all inflamed, first thus began:
'"Author of evil, unknown till thy revolt,
Unnamed in heaven, now plenteous as thou seest
These acts of hateful strife – hateful to all,
Though heaviest, by just measure, on thyself   265
And thy adherents – how hast thou disturbed
Heaven's blessed peace, and into nature brought
Misery, uncreated till the crime
Of thy rebellion! How hast thou instilled
Thy malice into thousands, once upright   270
And faithful, now proved false. But think not here
To trouble holy rest; heaven casts thee out
From all her confines. Heaven, the seat of bliss,
Brooks not the works of violence and war.
Hence then, and evil go with thee along,   275
Thy offspring, to the place of evil, hell –
Thou and thy wicked crew; there mingle broils,
Ere this avenging sword begin thy doom,
Or some more sudden vengeance, winged from God,
Precipitate thee with augmented pain."   280
'So spake the prince of angels; to whom thus
The adversary: "Nor think thou with wind
Of airy threats to awe whom yet with deeds
Thou canst not. Hast thou turned the least of these
To flight – or if to fall, but that they rise   285
Unvanquished – easier to transact with me
That thou shouldst hope, imperious, and with threats
To chase me hence? Err not that so shall end
The strife which thou call'st evil, but we style
The strife of glory; which we mean to win,   290
Or turn this heaven itself into the hell
Thou fablest; here, however, to dwell free,
If not to reign; meanwhile, thy utmost force –
And join him named Almighty to thy aid –
I fly not, but have sought thee far and nigh."   295
'They ended parle, and both addressed for fight
Unspeakable; for who, though with the tongue
Of angels, can relate, or to what things;

259] Intestine war] civil war.
282 adversary] See I 82n.
296 parle] discussion between enemies under a truce.

Liken on earth conspicuous, that may lift
Human imagination to such height   300
Of godlike power? For likest gods they seemed,
Stood they or moved, in stature, motion, arms,
Fit to decide the empire of great heaven.
Now waved their fiery swords, and in the air
Made horrid circles; two broad suns their shields   305
Blazed opposite, while Expectation stood
In horror; from each hand with speed retired,
Where erst was thickest fight, the angelic throng,
And left large field, unsafe within the wind
Of such commotion: such as – to set forth   310
Great things by small – if, nature's concord broke,
Among the constellations war were sprung,
Two planets, rushing from aspéct malign
Of fiercest opposition, in mid sky
Should combat, and their jarring spheres confound   315
Together both, with next to almighty arm
Uplifted imminent, one stroke they aimed
That might determine, and not need repeat
As not of power, at once; nor odds appeared
In might or swift prevention; but the sword   320
Of Michael from the armoury of God
Was given him tempered so, that neither keen
Nor solid might resist that edge: it met
The sword of Satan with steep force to smite
Descending, and in half cut sheer; nor stayed,   325
But, with swift wheel reverse, deep entering, shared
All his right side; then Satan first knew pain,
And writhed him to and fro convolved; so sore
The griding sword with discontinuous wound
Passed through him; but the ethereal substance closed,
Not long divisible, and from the gash   331
A stream of nectarous humour issuing flowed
Sanguine, such as celestial spirits may bleed,

313 aspéct] the relative positions of the heavenly bodies. Renaissance astro-
    logers distinguished five positions, two of which (including 'opposition',
    l. 314) were deemed 'malign'. Cf. X 658-9.
320 prevention] anticipation.
321] Jer. i. 25.
326 shared] cut into parts.
329 griding] piercing, wounding.
    discontinuous] producing a separation of the tissues of the body; gaping.
332-3] 'Sanguine' means 'blood-red', but also modifies 'humour', and thus
    refers (in the physiological theory of the 'cardinal humours') to Satan's loss
    of confidence of success. Sanguine humour is 'nectarous' because it is
    produced by the digestion of food and drink, and the angelic drink is nectar
    (V 633).

And all his armour stained, erewhile so bright.
Forthwith, on all sides, to his aid was run   335
By angels many and strong, who interposed
Defence, while others bore him on their shields
Back to his chariot where it stood retired
From off the files of war: there they him laid
Gnashing for anguish, and despite, and shame   340
To find himself not matchless, and his pride
Humbled by such rebuke, so far beneath
His confidence to equal God in power.
Yet soon he healed; for spirits, that live throughout
Vital in every part – not, as frail man,   345
In entrails, heart or head, liver or reins –
Cannot but by annihilating die;
Nor in their liquid texture mortal wound
Receive, no more than can the fluid air:
All heart they live, all head, all eye, all ear,   350
All intellect, all sense; and as they please
They limb themselves, and colour, shape, or size
Assume, as likes them best, condense or rare.
    'Meanwhile, in other parts, like deeds deserved
Memorial, where the might of Gabriel fought,   355
And with fierce ensigns pierced the deep array
Of Moloch, furious king, who him defied,
And at his chariot wheels to drag him bound
Threatened, nor from the holy one of heaven
Refrained his tongue blasphémous, but anon,   360
Down cloven to the waist, with shattered arms
And uncouth pain fled bellowing. On each wing
Uriel and Raphaël his vaunting foe,
Though huge and in a rock of diamond armed,
Vanquished – Adramelech and Asmadai,   365
Two potent thrones, that to be less than gods
Disdained, but meaner thoughts learned in their flight,
Mangled with ghastly wounds through plate and mail;
Nor stood unmindful Abdiel to annoy
The atheist crew, but with redoubled blow   370

346 reins] kidneys.
355 might of] imitates Homeric diction, and means 'mighty'.
357 king] See I 392n.
359–60] II Kings xix. 22.
363 vaunting] means both 'vain-glorious' and 'in the van (i.e. front) of the
    army'.
365 Vanquished] The grammatical object of 'vanquished' is 'foe'. Uriel's foe is
    Adramelech, a god of Assyrian origin brought to Samaria from Sepharvaim
    (II Kings xvii. 31); Raphael's foe is Asmadai (see IV 166–71n.).
370 atheist] impious.

Ariel, and Arioch, and the violence
Of Ramiel, scorched and blasted, overthrew.
I might relate of thousands, and their names
Eternize here on earth; but those elect
Angels, contented with their fame in heaven,   375
Seek not the praise of men: the other sort,
In might though wondrous and in acts of war,
Nor of renown less eager, yet by doom
Cancelled from heaven and sacred memory,
Nameless in dark oblivion let them dwell   380
For strength from truth divided, and from just,
Illaudable, naught merits but dispraise
And ignominy, yet to glory aspires,
Vain-glorious, and through infamy seeks fame:
Therefore eternal silence be their doom.   385
  'And now, their mightiest quelled, the battle swerved,
With many an inroad gored; deformèd rout
Entered, and foul disorder; all the ground
With shivered armour strown, and on a heap
Chariot and charioteer lay overturned,   390
And fiery foaming steeds; what stood recoiled,
O'er-wearied, through the faint Satanic host,
Defensive scarce, or with pale fear surprised –
Then first with fear surprised and sense of pain –
Fled ignominious, to such evil brought   395
By sin of disobedience, till that hour
Not liable to fear, or flight, or pain.
Far otherwise the inviolable saints
In cubic phalanx firm advanced entire,
Invulnerable, impenetrably armed;   400
Such high advantages their innocence
Gave them above their foes – not to have sinned,
Not to have disobeyed; in fight they stood
Unwearied, unobnoxious to be pained   404
By wound, though from their place by violence moved.
  'Now night her course began, and over heaven
Inducing darkness, grateful truce imposed,
And silence on the odious din of war;

371] Ariel means 'lion of God' in Hebrew, and in the O.T. is used as a human
     name and a name for Jerusalem; in a later tradition he was thought to be an
     angel or an evil demon. Arioch means 'like a Lion' and in the O.T. is used of
     various kings; in a later tradition he was identified with the spirit of
     revenge.
372] Ramiel means 'thunder of God' in Hebrew, and in the Book of Enoch
     refers to a fallen angel.
393 Defensive scarce] scarcely capable of defence.
404 unobnoxious] not liable.

Under her cloudy covert both retired,
Victor and vanquished; on the foughten field   410
Michaël and his angels, prevalent
Encamping, placed in guard their watches round,
Cherubic waving fires: on the other part,
Satan with his rebellious disappeared,
Far in the dark dislodged, and void of rest,   415
His potentates to council called by night,
And in the midst thus undismayed began:
     '"O now in danger tried, now known in arms
Not to be overpowered, companions dear,
Found worthy not of liberty alone –   420
Too mean pretence – but, what we more affect,
Honour, dominion, glory, and renown;
Who have sustained one day in doubtful fight
(And, if one day, why not eternal days?)
What heaven's lord had powerfullest to send   425
Against us from about his throne, and judged
Sufficient to subdue us to his will,
But proves not so: then fallible, it seems,
Of future we may deem him, though till now
Omniscient thought. True is, less firmly armed,   430
Some disadvantage we endured, and pain –
Till now not known, but, known, as soon contemned;
Since now we find this our empyreal form
Incapable of mortal injury,
Imperishable, and though pierced with wound,   435
Soon closing, and by native vigour healed.
Of evil, then, so small, as easy think
The remedy: perhaps more valid arms,
Weapons more violent, when next we meet
May serve to better us and worse our foes,   440
Or equal what between us made the odds,
In nature none; if other hidden cause
Left them superior, while we can preserve
Unhurt our minds, and understanding sound,
Due search and consultation will disclose."   445
     'He sat; and in the assembly next upstood
Nisroch, of principalities the prime.
As one he stood escaped from cruel fight
Sore toiled, his riven arms to havoc hewn,

---

410 foughten field] battlefield.
411 prevalent] prevailing, victorious.
429 Of] in.
447 Nisroch] The Hebrew name for an Assyrian god (II Kings xix. 37).

And, cloudy in aspéct, thus answering spake: 450
   '"Deliverer from new lords, leader to free
Enjoyment of our rights as gods; yet hard
For gods, and too unequal work, we find
Against unequal arms to fight in pain,
Against unpained, impassive; from which evil   455
Ruin must needs ensue; for what avails
Valour or strength, though matchless, quelled with pain,
Which all subdues, and makes remiss the hands
Of mightiest? Sense of pleasure we may well
Spare out of life perhaps, and not repine,   460
But live content – which is the calmest life;
But pain is perfect misery, the worst
Of evils, and, excessive, overturns
All patience. He who therefore can invent
With what more forcible we may offend   465
Our yet unwounded enemies, or arm
Ourselves with like defence, to me deserves
No less than for deliverance what we owe."
   'Whereto with look composed Satan replied:
"Not uninvented that, which thou aright   470
Believ'st so main to our success, I bring;
Which of us who beholds the bright surfáce
Of this ethereous mould whereon we stand –
This continent of spacious heaven, adorned
With plant, fruit, flower ambrosial, gems and gold   475
Whose eye so superficially surveys
These things as not to mind from whence they grow
Deep under ground: materials dark and crude,
Of spiritous and fiery spume, till touched
With heaven's ray, and tempered, they shoot forth   480
So beauteous, opening to the ambient light?
These in their dark nativity the deep
Shall yield us, pregnant with infernal flame;
Which, into hollow engines long and round
Thick-rammed, at the other bore with touch of fire   485
Dilated and infuriate, shall send forth
From far, with thundering noise, among our foes
Such implements of mischief as shall dash
To pieces and o'erwhelm whatever stands
Adverse, that they shall fear we have disarmed   490
The thunderer of his only dreaded bolt.
Nor long shall be our labour; yet ere dawn

471 main] highly important.
485 other bore] the touch-hole.

Effect shall end our wish. Meanwhile revive;
Abandon fear; to strength and counsel joined
Think nothing hard, much less to be despaired."   495
  'He ended, and his words their drooping cheer
Enlightened, and their languished hope revived.
The invention all admired, and each how he
To be the inventor missed; so easy it seemed
Once found, which yet unfound most would have thought
Impossible; yet haply of thy race,   501
In future days, if malice should abound,
Some one, intent on mischief, or inspired
With devilish machination, might devise
Like instrument to plague the sons of men   505
For sin, on war and mutual slaughter bent.
Forthwith from council to the work they flew;
None arguing stood; innumerable hands
Were ready; in a moment up they turned
Wide the celestial soil, and saw beneath   510
The originals of nature in their crude
Conception; sulphurous and nitrous foam
They found, they mingled, and with subtle art
Concocted and adusted, they reduced
To blackest grain, and into store conveyed;   515
Part hidden veins digged up (nor hath this earth
Entrails unlike) of mineral and stone,
Whereof to found their engines and their balls
Of missive ruin; part incentive reed
Provide, pernicious with one touch to fire.   520
So all ere day-spring, under conscious night,
Secret they finished, and in order set,
With silent circumspection, unespied.
  'Now, when fair morn orient in heaven appeared,
Up rose the victor angels, and to arms   525
The matin trumpet sung; in arms they stood
Of golden panoply, refulgent host,
Soon banded; others from the dawning hills
Looked round, and scouts each coast light-armèd scour,
Each quarter, to descry the distant foe,   530
Where lodged, or whither fled, or if for fight,

---

514 Concocted] maturated (i.e. purified) by heating (an alchemical term).
   adjusted] dried up with heat (cf. XII 635).
518 found] cast, mould.
519 incentive] kindling.
520 pernicious] means both 'rapid' (from *pernix*) and 'destructive' (from
   perniciosus).
521 conscious] possessing a guilty knowledge.

In motion or in halt; him soon they met
Under spread ensigns moving nigh, in slow
But firm battalion: back with speediest sail
Zophiel, of cherubim the swiftest wing,   535
Came flying, and in mid air aloud thus cried:
  ' "Arm, warriors, arm for fight – the foe at hand,
Whom fled we thought, will save us long pursuit
This day; fear not his flight; so thick a cloud
He comes, and settled in his face I see   540
Sad resolution and secure; let each
His adamantine coat gird well, and each
Fit well his helm, gripe fast his orbed shield,
Borne even or high; for this day will pour down,
If I conjecture aught, no drizzling shower,   545
But rattling storm of arrows barbed with fire."
  'So warned he them, aware themselves, and soon
In order, quit of all impediment;
Instant without disturb they took alarm,
And onward move embattled: when behold   550
Not distant far, with heavy pace the foe
Approaching gross and huge, in hollow cube
Training his devilish enginery, impaled
On every side with shadowing squadrons deep,
To hide the fraud. At interview both stood   555
A while, but suddenly at head appeared
Satan, and thus was heard commanding loud:
  ' "Vanguard, to right and left the front unfold,
That all may see who hate us how we seek
Peace and composure, and with open breast   560
Stand ready to receive them, if they like
Our overture, and turn not back perverse:
But that I doubt; however, witness heaven;
Heaven, witness thou anon, while we discharge

535 Zophiel] The name means 'spy of God'; it does not occur in the Bible.
541 Sad] grave, serious.
549 took alarm] took up arms.
553 Training] hauling.
555 At interview] within mutual view.
560 composure] settlement.
560-7] As Raphael observes (l. 568), the lines contain 'ambiguous words':
    'breast' means 'heart' (as the seat of affections) and, as a military term, 'the
    broad even front of a moving company'; 'overture' means 'opening of
    negotiations with a view to a settlement', and 'orifice', i.e. the mouths of
    the cannons (l. 577); 'touch' plays on the technical meaning of 'touch-
    powder', i.e. the priming powder for the cannons (the same pun occurs in ll.
    479, 485, 520, 584); the puns on 'discharge' and 'loud' are obvious.

Freely our part; ye who appointed stand   565
Do as you have in charge, and briefly touch
What we propound, and loud that all may hear."
    'So scoffing in ambiguous words, he scarce
Had ended, when to right and left the front
Divided, and to either flank retired;   570
Which to our eyes discovered, new and strange,
A triple mounted row of pillars laid
On wheels (for like to pillars most they seemed,
Or hollowed bodies made of oak or fir,
With branches lopped, in wood or mountain felled),   575
Brass, iron, stony mould, had not their mouths
With hideous orifice gaped on us wide,
Portending hollow truce; at each, behind,
A seraph stood, and in his hand a reed
Stood waving tipped with fire; while we, suspense,   580
Collected stood within our thoughts amused,
Not long, for sudden all at once their reeds
Put forth, and to a narrow vent applied
With nicest touch. Immediate in a flame,
But soon obscured with smoke, all heaven appeared,   585
From those deep-throated engines belched, whose roar
Embowelled with outrageous noise the air,
And all her entrails tore, disgorging foul
Their devilish glut, chained thunderbolts and hail
Of iron globes; which on the victor host   590
Levelled, with such impetuous fury smote,
That whom they hit none on their feet might stand
Though standing else as rocks, but down they fell
By thousands, angel on archangel rolled,
The sooner for their arms; unarmed, they might   595
Have easily, as spirits, evaded swift
By quick contraction or remove; but now
Foul dissipation followed, and forced rout;
Nor served it to relax their serried files.
What should they do? If on they rushed, repulse   600
Repeated, and indecent overthrow
Doubled, would render them yet more despised,
And to their foes a laughter – for in view
Stood ranked of seraphim another row,
In posture to displode their second tire   605

581 amused] put in a muse, absorbed.
587 Embowelled] 'disembowelled', or possibly 'filled the bowels of'.
598 dissipation] scattering, dispersal.
605] means 'in position to fire their second volley'.

Of thunder; back defeated to return
They worse abhorred. Satan beheld their plight,
And to his mates thus in derision called:
   ' "O friends, why come not on these victors proud?
Erewhile they fierce were coming, and when we,   610
To entertain them fair with open front
And breast (what could we more?) propounded terms
Of composition, straight they changed their minds,
Flew off, and into strange vagaries fell,
As they would dance, yet for a dance they seemed   615
Somewhat extravagant and wild, perhaps
For joy of offered peace; but I suppose,
If our proposals once again were heard,
We should compel them to a quick result."
   'To whom thus Belial, in like gamesome mood;   620
"Leader, the terms we sent were terms of weight,
Of hard contents, and full of force urged home,
Such as we might perceive amused them all,
And stumbled many; who receives them right
Had need from head to foot well understand;   625
Not understood, this gift they have besides –
They show us when our foes walk not upright."
   'So they among themselves in pleasant vein
Stood scoffing, heightened in their thoughts beyond
All doubt of victory; eternal might   630
To match with their inventions they presumed
So easy, and of his thunder made a scorn,
And all his host derided, while they stood
A while in trouble; but they stood not long;
Rage prompted them at length, and found them arms 635
Against such hellish mischief fit to oppose.
Forthwith (behold the excellence, the power,
Which God hath in his mighty angels placed)
Their arms away they threw, and to the hills
(For earth hath his variety from heaven   640
Of pleasure situate in hill and dale)
Light as the lightning-glimpse they ran, they flew;
From their foundations, loosening to and fro,
They plucked the seated hills with all their load,

611-12] 'Breast' repeats the pun of l. 560, and 'front' introduces a parallel play
    on the meanings 'the face as expressive of emotion' (here candour) and 'the
    foremost line of an army'.
613 composition] truce.
625 understand] means both 'comprehend' and 'be supported'.
635] *Aeneid* i 150.

Rocks, waters, woods, and, by the shaggy tops　　　645
Uplifting, bore them in their hands; amaze,
Be sure, and terror, seized the rebel host,
When coming towards them so dread they saw
The bottom of the mountains upward turned,
Till on those cursed engines' triple row　　　650
They saw them whelmed, and all their confidence
Under the weight of mountains buried deep;
Themselves invaded next, and on their heads
Main promontories flung, which in the air
Came shadowing, and oppressed whole legions armed;　655
Their armour helped their harm, crushed in and bruised,
Into their substance pent – which wrought them pain
Implacable, and many a dolorous groan,
Long struggling underneath, ere they could wind
Out of such prison, though spirits of purest light,　　　660
Purest at first, now gross by sinning grown.
The rest, in imitation, to like arms
Betook them, and the neighbouring hills uptore;
So hills amid the air encountered hills,
Hurled to and fro with jaculation dire,　　　665
That underground they fought in dismal shade:
Infernal noise; war seemed a civil game
To this uproar; horrid confusion heaped
Upon confusion rose; and now all heaven
Had gone to wrack, with ruin overspread,　　　670
Had not the almighty Father, where he sits
Shrined in his sanctuary of heaven secure,
Consulting on the sum of things, foreseen
This tumult, and permitted all, advised,
That his great purpose he might so fulfil,　　　675
To honour his anointed Son, avenged
Upon his enemies, and to declare
All power on him transferred; whence to his Son,
The assessor of his throne, he thus began:
　'"Effulgence of my glory, Son beloved,　　　680
Son in whose face invisible is beheld
Visibly, what by deity I am,
And in whose hand what by decree I do,

646 amaze] panic.
654 Main] entire, solid.
665 jaculation] hurling.
674 advised] advisedly.
679 assessor] 'one who sits beside', hence sharing his rank and dignity.
681–2] Col. i. 15.

Second omnipotence; two days are passed,
Two days, as we compute the days of heaven, 685
Since Michael and his powers went forth to tame
These disobedient; sore hath been their fight,
As likeliest was when two such foes met armed:
For to themselves I left them; and thou know'st
Equal in their creation they were formed, 690
Save what sin hath impaired – which yet hath wrought
Insensibly, for I suspend their doom:
Whence in perpetual fight they needs must last
Endless, and no solution will be found:
War wearied hath performed what war can do, 695
And to disordered rage let loose the reins,
With mountains, as with weapons, armed, which
    makes
Wild work in heaven, and dangerous to the main.
Two days are therefore passed; the third is thine:
For thee I have ordained it, and thus far 700
Have suffered, that the glory may be thine
Of ending this great war, since none but thou
Can end it. Into thee such virtue and grace
Immense I have transfused, that all may know
In heaven and hell thy power above compare, 705
And this perverse commotion governed thus,
To manifest thee worthiest to be heir
Of all things – to be heir, and to be king
By sacred unction, thy deserved right.
Go then, thou mightiest, in thy Father's might; 710
Ascend my chariot; guide the rapid wheels
That shake heaven's basis; bring forth all my war;
My bow and thunder, my almighty arms,
Gird on, and sword upon thy puissant thigh;
Pursue these sons of darkness, drive them out 715
From all heaven's bounds into the utter deep;
There let them learn, as likes them, to despise
God, and Messiah his anointed king."
    'He said, and on his Son with rays direct
Shone full; he all his Father full expressed 720
Ineffably into his face received;
And thus the filial Godhead answering spake:
    ' "O Father, O supreme of heavenly thrones,

---

692 Insensibly] imperceptibly.
698 main] entirety, i.e. the universe.
701 suffered] allowed.
709 unction] anointing (cf. III 317, V 605).

First, highest, holiest, best, thou always seek'st
To glorify thy Son; I always thee,　　　　　　　　725
As is most just; this I my glory account,
My exaltation, and my whole delight,
That thou in me, well pleased, declar'st thy will
Fulfilled, which to fulfil is all my bliss.
Sceptre and power, thy giving, I assume,　　　　730
And gladlier shall resign when in the end
Thou shalt be all in all, and I in thee
For ever, and in me all whom thou lov'st;
But whom thou hat'st I hate, and can put on
Thy terrors, as I put thy mildness on,　　　　735
Image of thee in all things: and shall soon,
Armed with thy might, rid heaven of these rebelled,
To their prepared ill mansion driven down,
To chains of darkness and the undying worm,
That from thy just obedience could revolt,　　　740
Whom to obey, is happiness entire.
Then shall thy saints, ummixed, and from the impure
Far separate, circling thy holy mount,
Unfeignèd halleluiahs to thee sing,
Hymns of high praise, and I among them chief."　745
　'So said, he, o'er his sceptre bowing, rose
From the right hand of glory where he sat;
And the third sacred morn began to shine,
Dawning through heaven; forth rushed with whirlwind
　　　sound
The chariot of paternal deity,　　　　　　　　750
Flashing thick flames, wheel within wheel; undrawn,
Itself instinct with spirit, but convoyed
By four cherubic shapes; four faces each
Had wondrous; as with stars, their bodies all
And wings were set with eyes; with eyes the wheels　755
Of beryl, and careering fires between;
Over their heads a crystal firmament,
Whereon a sapphire throne, inlaid with pure
Amber and colours of the showery arch.
He, in celestial panoply all armed　　　　　　760
Of radiant Urim, work divinely wrought,
Ascended; at his right hand Victory

734] Psalm cxxxix. 21.
749-59] The imagery is based on Ezek. i. and x. Cf *Penseroso* 53 and *Passion*
　36-40n.
752 instinct] impelled, moved.
761 Urim] Exod. xxviii. 30. See *PR* III 13-15n.

Sat eagle-winged; beside him hung his bow,
And quiver, with three-bolted thunder stored;
And from about him fierce effusion rolled   765
Of smoke and bickering flame and sparkles dire;
Attended with ten thousand thousand saints,
He onward came; far off his coming shone;
And twenty thousand (I their number heard)
Chariots of God, half on each hand, were seen;   770
He on the wings of cherub rode sublime
On the crystalline sky, in sapphire throned –
Illustrious far and wide, but by his own
First seen; them unexpected joy surprised
When the great ensign of Messiah blazed   775
Aloft, by angels borne, his sign in heaven;
Under whose conduct Michael soon reduced
His army, circumfused on either wing,
Under their head embodied all in one.
Before him power divine his way prepared;   780
At his command the uprooted hills retired
Each to his place; they heard his voice, and went
Obsequious; heaven his wonted face renewed,
And with fresh flowerets hill and valley smiled.

'This saw his hapless foes, but stood obdured,   785
And to rebellious fight rallied their powers,
Insensate, hope conceiving from despair.
In heavenly spirits could such perverseness dwell?
But to convince the proud what signs avail,
Or wonders move the obdurate to relent?   790
They, hardened more by what might most reclaim,
Grieving to see his glory, at the sight
Took envy, and, aspiring to his height,
Stood re-embattled fierce, by force or fraud
Weening to prosper, and at length prevail   795
Against God and Messiah, or to fall

763-4] The eagle is the imperial bird of Jove, and the thunderbolt his weapon
    and the weapon of God in the O.T.
766 bickering] flashing, gleaming.
767] Rev. v. 11.
769-70] Psalm lxviii. 17.
771] Psalm xviii. 10; II Sam. xxii. 11.
773 Ilustrious] lustrous, shining.
776] Matt. xxiv. 30.
777 reduced] led back.
785 obdured] hardened in wickedness.
788] imitates *Aeneid* i 11.
789-91, 801] Exod. xiv. 4, 8, 13.

In universal ruin last; and now
To final battle drew, disdaining flight,
Or faint retreat: when the great Son of God
To all his host on either hand thus spake: 800
    '"Stand still in bright array, ye saints; here stand,
Ye angels armed; this day from battle rest;
Faithful hath been your warfare, and of God
Accepted, fearless in his righteous cause;
And as ye have received, so have ye done,   805
Invincibly; but of this cursed crew
The punishment to other hand belongs;
Vengeance is his, or whose he sole appoints;
Number to this day's work is not ordained,
Nor multitude; stand only and behold   810
God's indignation on these godless poured
By me; not you, but me, they have despised,
Yet envied; against me is all their rage,
Because the Father, to whom in heaven supreme
Kingdom and power and glory appertains,   815
Hath honoured me according to his will.
Therefore to me their doom he hath assigned,
That they may have their wish, to try with me
In battle which the stronger proves – they all,
Or I alone against them; since by strength   820
They measure all, of other excellence
Not emulous, nor care who them excels;
Nor other strife with them do I vouchsafe."
    'So spake the Son, and into terror changed
His countenance, too severe to be beheld,   825
And full of wrath bent on his enemies.
At once the four spread out their starry wings
With dreadful shade contiguous, and the orbs
Of his fierce chariot rolled, as with the sound
Of torrent floods, or of a numerous host.   830
He on his impious foes right onward drove,
Gloomy as night; under his burning wheels
The steadfast empyrean shook throughout,
All but the throne itself of God. Full soon
Among them he arrived, in his right hand   835

808] a Biblical commonplace (e.g. Deut. xxxii. 35).
815] the concluding doxology of the Lord's Prayer (Matt. vi. 13), which was not
    part of the English liturgy until it was incorporated in the 1662 Book of
    Common Prayer.
827–32] See 749–59n.
833] II Sam. xxii. 8.

Grasping ten thousand thunders, which he sent
Before him, such as in their souls infixed
Plagues. They, astonished, all resistance lost,
All courage; down their idle weapons dropped;
O'er shields, and helms, and helmed heads he rode   840
Of thrones and mighty seraphim prostráte,
That wished the mountains now might be again
Thrown on them, as a shelter from his ire.
Nor less on either side tempestuous fell
His arrows, from the fourfold-visaged four,   845
Distinct with eyes, and from the living wheels,
Distinct alike with multitude of eyes;
One spirit in them ruled, and every eye
Glared lightning, and shot forth pernicious fire
Among the accursed, that withered all their strength,   850
And of their wonted vigour left them drained,
Exhausted, spiritless, afflicted, fallen.
Yet half his strength he put not forth, but checked
His thunder in mid-volley; for he meant
Not to destroy, but root them out of heaven;   855
The overthrown he raised, and as a herd
Of goats or timorous flock together thronged,
Drove them before him thunderstruck, pursued
With terrors and with furies to the bounds
And crystal wall of heaven, which, opening wide,   860
Rolled inward, and a spacious gap disclosed
Into the wasteful deep; the monstrous sight
Strook them with horror backward; but far worse
Urged them behind: headlong themselves they threw
Down from the verge of heaven: eternal wrath   865
Burnt after them to the bottomless pit.
   'Hell heard the unsufferable noise; hell saw
Heaven ruining from heaven, and would have fled
Affrighted; but strict fate had cast too deep
Her dark foundations, and too fast had bound.   870
Nine days they fell; confounded Chaos roared,
And felt tenfold confusion in their fall
Through his wild anarchy; so huge a rout
Encumbered him with ruin; hell at last,
Yawning, received them whole, and on them closed –   875
Hell, their fit habitation, fraught with fire

838 Plagues] used in the Greek and Latin sense of 'blows, strokes, wounds'.
845-6] Ezek. x. 9-14. 'Distinct' means 'adorned'.
868 ruining] falling headlong.
874-5] Isa. v. 14.

Unquenchable, the house of woe and pain.
Disburdened heaven rejoiced, and soon repaired
Her mural breach, returning whence it rolled.
Sole victor, from the expulsion of his foes   880
Messiah his triumphal chariot turned;
To meet him all his saints, who silent stood
Eye-witnesses of his almighty acts,
With jubilee advanced; and as they went,
Shaded with branching palm, each order bright   885
Sung triumph, and him sung victorious king,
Son, heir, and Lord, to him dominion given,
Worthiest to reign; he celebrated rode,
Triumphant through mid heaven, into the courts
And temple of his mighty Father throned   890
On high; who into glory him received,
Where now he sits at the right hand of bliss.
    'Thus, measuring things in heaven by things on earth,
At thy request, and that thou may'st beware
By what is past, to thee I have revealed   895
What might have else to human race been hid –
The discord which befell, and war in heaven
Among the angelic powers, and the deep fall
Of those too high aspiring who rebelled
With Satan: he who envies now thy state,   900
Who now is plotting how he may seduce
Thee also from obedience, that with him
Bereaved of happiness, thou may'st partake
His punishment, eternal misery;
Which would be all his solace and revenge,   905
As a despite done against the most high,
Thee once to gain companion of his woe.
But listen not to his temptations; warn
Thy weaker; let it profit thee to have heard,
By terrible example, the reward   910
Of disobedience; firm they might have stood,
Yet fell; remember, and fear to transgress.'

THE END OF THE SIXTH BOOK

---

909 weaker] i.e. weaker vessel (I Pet. iii. 7).

BOOK VII

THE ARGUMENT

Raphael, at the request of Adam, relates how and wherefore this
world was first created: that God, after the expelling of Satan and
his angels out of heaven, declared his pleasure to create another
world, and other creatures to dwell therein; sends his Son with
glory, and attendance of angels, to perform the work of creation in
six days: the angels celebrate with hymns the performance thereof,
and his reascension into heaven.

Descend from heaven, Urania, by that name
If rightly thou art called, whose voice divine
Following, above the Olympian hill I soar,
Above the flight of Pegasean wing.
The meaning, not the name, I call; for thou   5
Nor of the Muses nine, nor on the top
Of old Olympus dwell'st; but, heavenly-born,
Before the hills appeared or fountain flowed,
Thou with eternal wisdom didst converse,
Wisdom thy sister, and with her didst play   10
In presence of the almighty Father, pleased
With thy celestial song. Up led by thee,
Into the heaven of heavens I have presumed,
An earthly guest, and drawn empyreal air,
Thy tempering; with like safety guided down,   15
Return me to my native element;
Lest, from this flying steed unreined (as once
Bellerophon, though from a lower clime)

---

1 Urania] In early antiquity Urania ('heavenly one') was the name of one of the
nine muses, and in late Roman times she was identified specifically as the
muse of astronomy. In the Renaissance she was transformed by Pontanus
and Du Bartas into the muse of Christian poetry.

3 Olympian hill] Mount Olympus, the home of the gods on the border of
Macedonia and Thessaly.

4] Pegasus, the winged horse, created with his hoof Hippocrene (literally 'horse-
spring'), the Muses' spring on Mount Helicon.

8-12] See Prov. viii. 22-31. Milton's 'play' reflects the Vulgate (*ludens*) rather
than the A.V. ('rejoicing') or the LXX (εὐφραινόμην, rejoicing). Cf. the
apocryphal Wisdom of Solomon vii-viii.

17-20] Bellerophon tried to ride Pegasus to heaven, and was toppled from his
mount by Jove, whereupon he fell on to the 'Aleian field', Homer's 'plain of
wandering'. 'Clime' means both 'region' and 'climb'; 'erroneous' refers to
both physical and moral wandering.

Dismounted, on the Aleian field I fall,
Erroneous there to wander and forlorn.   20
Half yet remains unsung, but narrower bound
Within the visible diurnal sphere;
Standing on earth, not rapt above the pole,
More safe I sing with mortal voice, unchanged
To hoarse or mute, though fallen on evil days,   25
On evil days though fallen, and evil tongues,
In darkness, and with dangers compassed round,
And solitude; yet not alone, while thou
Visit'st my slumbers nightly, or when morn
Purples the east; still govern thou my song,   30
Urania, and fit audience find, though few.
But drive far off the barbarous dissonance
Of Bacchus and his revellers, the race
Of that wild rout that tore the Thracian bard
In Rhodope, where woods and rocks had ears   35
To rapture, till the savage clamour drowned
Both harp and voice; nor could the Muse defend
Her son. So fail not thou who thee implores;
For thou art heavenly, she an empty dream.

    Say, Goddess, what ensued when Raphael,   40
The affable archangel, had forewarned
Adam by dire example to beware
Apostasy, by what befell in heaven
To those apostates, lest the like befall
In Paradise to Adam or his race,   45
Charged not to touch the interdicted tree,
If they transgress, and slight that sole command,
So easily obeyed amid the choice
Of all tastes else to please their appetite,
Though wandering. He with his consorted Eve   50
The story heard attentive, and was filled
With admiration and deep muse, to hear
Of things so high and strange – things to their thought
So unimaginable as hate in heaven,
And war so near the peace of God in bliss,   55

22 diurnal sphere] the firmament, which appears to revolve daily around the
    earth.
23 rapt above the pole] carried away in spirit above the celestial pole.
24–8] The lines refer to the 'dangers' of Milton's situation after the Restoration,
    when those who had served in Cromwell's government became liable to
    persecution.
32–8] Cf. *Lycidas* 58–63n. Rhodope is a mountain range on the border of Thrace
    and Macedonia.
52 admiration] wonder, astonishment.

With such confusion; but the evil, soon
Driven back, redounded as a flood on those
From whom it sprung, impossible to mix
With blessedness. Whence Adam soon repealed
The doubts that in his heart arose; and now   60
Led on, yet sinless, with desire to know
What nearer might concern him – how this world
Of heaven and earth conspicuous first began;
When, and whereof, created; for what cause;
What within Eden, or without, was done   65
Before his memory – as one whose drouth,
Yet scarce allayed, still eyes the current stream,
Whose liquid murmur heard new thirst excites,
Proceeded thus to ask his heavenly guest:
    'Great things, and full of wonder in our ears,   70
Far differing from this world, thou hast revealed,
Divine interpreter, by favour sent
Down from the empyrean to forewarn
Us timely of what might else have been our loss,
Unknown, which human knowledge could not reach;   75
For which to the infinitely good we owe
Immortal thanks, and his admonishment
Receive with solemn purpose to observe
Immutably his sovereign will, the end
Of what we are. But, since thou hast vouchsafed   80
Gently, for our instruction, to impart
Things above earthly thought, which yet concerned
Our knowing, as to highest wisdom seemed,
Deign to descend now lower, and relate
What may no less perhaps avail us known –   85
How first began this heaven which we behold
Distant so high, with moving fires adorned
Innumerable; and this which yields or fills
All space, the ambient air, wide interfused,
Embracing round this florid earth; what cause   90
Moved the creator, in his holy rest
Through all eternity, so late to build
In chaos; and the work begun, how soon
Absolved: if unforbid thou may'st unfold

59 repealed] abandoned.
63 conspicuous] visible.
67 current] flowing.
72 Divine interpreter] a comparison of Raphael to Mercury, messenger of the
    gods ('*interpres divum*', *Aeneid* iv 378).
83 seemed] seemed fitting, appropriate.
94 Absolved] completed.

What we not to explore the secrets ask   95
Of his eternal empire, but the more
To magnify his works the more we know.
And the great light of day yet wants to run
Much of his race, though steep; suspense in heaven
Held by thy voice, thy potent voice he hears,   100
And longer will delay, to hear thee tell
His generation, and the rising birth
Of nature from the unapparent deep:
Of if the star of evening and the moon
Haste to thy audience, night with her will bring   105
Silence, and sleep listening to thee will watch;
Or we can bid his absence till thy song
End, and dismiss thee ere the morning shine.'
  Thus Adam his illustrious guest besought;
And thus the godlike angel answered mild: 110
  'This also thy request, with caution asked,
Obtain; though to recount almighty works
What words or tongue of seraph can suffice,
Or heart of man suffice to comprehend?
Yet what thou canst attain, which best may serve   115
To glorify the maker, and infer
Thee also happier, shall not be withheld
Thy hearing; such commission from above
I have received, to answer thy desire
Of knowledge within bounds; beyond abstain   120
To ask, nor let thine own inventions hope
Things not revealed, which the invisible king,
Only omniscient, hath suppressed in night,
To none communicable in earth or heaven;
Enough is left beside to search and know;   125
But knowledge is as food, and needs no less
Her temperance over appetitie, to know
In measure what the mind may well contain;
Oppresses else with surfeit, and soon turns
Wisdom to folly, as nourishment to wind.   130
  'Know then that, after Lucifer from heaven
(So call him, brighter once amidst the host
Of angels than that star the stars among)
Fell with his flaming legions through the deep

95] Job xxxvi. 24.
103 unapparent deep] invisible chaos.
106 watch] stay awake (cf. I 332).
116 infer] cause to be, render.
131 Lucifer] See V 658n.

Into his place, and the great Son returned   135
Victorious with his saints, the omnipotent
Eternal Father from his throne beheld
Their multitude, and to his Son thus spake:
  ' "At least our envious foe hath failed, who thought
All like himself rebellious; by whose aid   140
This inaccessible high strength, the seat
Of deity supreme, us dispossessed,
He trusted to have seized, and into fraud
Drew many whom their place knows here no more;
Yet far the greater part have kept, I see,   145
Their station; heaven, yet populous, retains
Number sufficient to possess her realms,
Though wide, and this high temple to frequent
With ministeries due and solemn rites;
But, lest his heart exalt him in the harm   150
Already done, to have dispeopled heaven –
My damage fondly deemed – I can repair
That detriment, if such it be to lose
Self-lost, and in a moment will create
Another world; out of one man a race   155
Of men innumerable, there to dwell,
Not here, till by degrees of merit raised,
They open to themselves at length the way
Up hither, under long obedience tried,
And earth be changed to heaven, and heaven to earth,
One kingdom, joy and union without end.   161
Meanwhile inhabit lax, ye powers of heaven;
And thou, my Word, begotten Son, by thee
This I perform; speak thou, and be it done;
My overshadowing spirit and might with thee   165
I send along; ride forth, and bid the deep
Within appointed bounds be heaven and earth;
Boundless the deep, because I am who fill
Infinitude; nor vacuous the space,
Though I, uncircumscribed, myself retire,   170
And put not forth my goodness, which is free
To act or not; necessity and chance
Approach not me, and what I will is fate."

---

143 fraud] Milton's occasional use of the word in a passive sense (meaning 'in
  the state of being defrauded or deceived') may imitate the Latin *fraus*; the
  usage is unique to Milton. Cf. *PL* IX 643, *PR* I 372.
144] Job vii. 10.
162 inhabit lax] 'Lax' means 'so as to have ample room'. The phrase is a
  Latinism, and imitates *Habitare laxe et magnifice voluit* (Cicero, *De domo sua*
  xliv. 115).

'So spake the almighty, and to what he spake
His Word, the filial Godhead, gave effect.   175
Immediate are the acts of God, more swift
Than time or motion, but to human ears
Cannot without process of speech be told,
So told as earthly notion can receive.
Great triumph and rejoicing was in heaven   180
When such was heard declared the almighty's will;
Glory they sung to the most high, good-will
To future men, and in their dwellings peace –
Glory to him whose just avenging ire
Had driven out the ungodly from his sight   185
And the habitations of the just; to him
Glory and praise whose wisdom had ordained
Good out of evil to create – instead
Of spirits malign, a better race to bring
Into their vacant room, and thence diffuse   190
His good to worlds and ages infinite.
'So sang the hierarchies; meanwhile the Son
On his great expedition now appeared,
Girt with omnipotence, with radiance crowned
Of majesty divine, sapience and love   195
Immense; and all his Father in him shone.
About his chariot numberless were poured
Cherub and seraph, potentates and thrones,
And virtues, winged spirits, and chariots winged
From the armoury of God, where stand of old   200
Myriads, between two brazen mountains lodged
Against a solemn day, harnessed at hand,
Celestial equipage; and now came forth
Spontaneous, for within them spirit lived,
Attendant on their Lord: heaven opened wide   205
Her ever-during gates, harmonious sound
On golden hinges moving, to let forth
The king of glory, in his powerful Word
And Spirit coming to create new worlds.
On heavenly ground they stood, and from the shore   210
They viewed the vast immeasurable abyss,
Outrageous as a sea, dark, wasteful, wild,
Up from the bottom turned by furious winds
And surging waves, as mountains to assault

182-3 Luke ii. 14.
201] Zech. vi. 1.
204] Ezek. i. 20.
205-9] Psalm xxiv. 7.

Heaven's height, and with the centre mix the pole.   215
  ' "Silence, ye troubled waves, and thou deep, peace,"
Said then the omnific Word: "Your discord end;"
Nor stayed, but, on the wings of cherubim
Uplifted, in paternal glory rode
Far into chaos and the world unborn;   220
For chaos heard his voice; him all his train
Followed in bright procession to behold
Creation and the wonders of his might.
Then stayed the fervid wheels, and in his hand
He took the golden compasses, prepared   225
In God's eternal store, to circumscribe
This universe, and all created things;
One foot he centred, and the other turned
Round through the vast profundity obscure,
And said, "Thus far extend, thus far thy bounds;   230
This be thy just circumference, O world."
Thus God the heaven created, thus the earth,
Matter unformed and void; darkness profound
Covered the abyss; but on the watery calm
His brooding wings the spirit of God outspread,   235
And vital virtue infused, and vital warmth,
Throughout the fluid mass, but downward purged
The black tartareous cold infernal dregs,
Adverse to life; then founded, then conglobed,
Like things to like, the rest to several place   240
Disparted, and between spun out the air,
And earth, self-balanced, on her centre hung.
  ' "Let there be light," said God, and forthwith light
Ethereal, first of things, quintessence pure,
Sprung from the deep, and from her native east   245
To journey through the airy gloom began,
Sphered in a radiant cloud – for yet the sun
Was not; she in a cloudy tabernacle
Sojourned the while. God saw the light was good;
And light from darkness by the hemisphere   250

217 omnific] all-creating.
224 fervid] burning. Cf. VI 832.
225] Prov. viii. 27; Dante, *Paradiso* xix. 40–2.
236] 'Virtue' is divine power and influence; 'Vital warmth' alludes to the
    primus calor which figures in Renaissance Neoplatonist accounts of the
    creation.
239] 'Founded' means 'moulded, cast'; 'conglobed' means 'formed into a ball'.
243–4] See III 716n.
247–9] Milton recapitulates the traditional solution to the problem that light
    was created on the first day, but the sun, moon and stars on the fourth. On
    the 'tabernacle' see Psalm xix. 4.

Divided: light the day, and darkness night,
He named. Thus was the first day even and morn;
Nor passed uncelebrated, nor unsung
By the celestial choirs, when orient light
Exhaling first from darkness they beheld,   255
Birth-day of heaven and earth; with joy and shout
The hollow universal orb they filled,
And touched their golden harps, and hymning praised
God and his works; creator him they sung,
Both when first evening was, and when first morn.   260
    'Again God said, "Let there be firmament
Amid the waters, and let it divide
The waters from the waters"; and God made
The firmament, expanse of liquid, pure,
Transparent, elemental air diffused   265
In circuit to the uttermost convex
Of this great round – partition firm and sure,
The waters underneath from those above
Dividing; for as earth, so he the world
Built on circumfluous waters calm, in wide   270
Crystalline ocean, and the loud misrule
Of chaos far removed, lest fierce extremes
Contiguous might distemper the whole frame:
And heaven he named the firmament; so even
And morning chorus sung the second day.   275
    'The earth was formed, but in the womb as yet
Of waters, embryon immature, involved,
Appeared not; over all the face of earth
Main ocean flowed, not idle, but with warm
Prolific humous softening all her globe,   280
Fermented the great mother to conceive,
Satiate with genial moisture; when God said,
"Be gathered now, ye waters under heaven,
Into one place, and let dry land appear."
Immediately the mountains huge appear   285
Emergent, and their broad bare backs upheave
Into the clouds; their tops ascend the sky;
So high as heaved the tumid hills, so low

---

264 expanse] Cf. A.V. and R.V. marginal notes to Gen. i. 6, and *PL* VII 340.
267, 269 round, world] the universe.
277 involved] enveloped.
279-82] Renaissance Neoplatonists assumed the existence of a *primus humor*
      (cf. 236n.), which was a generative ('genial') moisture.
281 great mother] in antiquity Cybele was honoured as Magna Mater. Cf. V
      338n. and *Arcades* 21n.
283-306] Psalm civ. 6-10.

Down sunk a hollow bottom broad and deep,
Capacious bed of waters; thither they   290
Hasted with glad precipitance, uprolled
As drops on dust conglobing from the dry:
Part rise in crystal wall, or ridge direct,
For haste; such flight the great command impressed
On the swift floods; as armies at the call   295
Of trumpet (for of armies thou hast heard)
Troop to their standard, so the watery throng,
Wave rolling after wave, where way they found –
If steep, with torrent rapture, if through plain,
Soft-ebbing; nor withstood them rock or hill;   300
But they, or underground, or circuit wide
With serpent error wandering, found their way,
And on the washy ooze deep channels wore:
Easy, ere God had bid the ground be dry,
All but within those banks where rivers now   305
Stream, and perpetual draw their humid train.
The dry land earth, and the great receptacle
Of congregated waters he called seas;
And saw that it was good, and said, "Let the earth
Put forth the verdant grass, herb yielding seed,   310
And fruit-tree yielding fruit after her kind,
Whose seed is in herself upon the earth."
He scarce had said when the bare earth, till then
Desert and bare, unsightly, unadorned,
Brought forth the tender grass, whose verdure clad   315
Her universal face with pleasant green;
Then herbs of every leaf, that sudden flowered,
Opening their various colours, and made gay
Her bosom, smelling sweet; and these scarce blown,
Forth flourished thick the clustering vine, forth crept   320
The swelling gourd, up stood the corny reed
Embattled in her field: and the humble shrub,
And bush with frizzled hair implicit: last
Rose, as in dance, the stately trees, and spread
Their branches hung with copious fruit, or gemmed   325

---

302 error] the primary (Latinate) sense is 'winding course', but the juxtaposi-
     tion of the word with 'serpent' brings out the secondary sense, and thus
     connects the phrase with the fall.
308 congregated waters] cf. *congregationesque aquarum*, the Vulgate rendering
     of Gen. i. 10.
317–19] Cf. the apocryphal II Esdras vi. 44.
322 humble] low-growing.
323 implicit] entangled.
325 gemmed] budded (a Latinism).

Their blossoms; with high woods the hills were crowned,
With tufts the valleys and each fountain-side,
With borders long the rivers, that earth now
Seemed like to heaven, a seat where gods might dwell,
Or wander with delight, and love to haunt   330
Her sacred shades; though God had yet not rained
Upon the earth, and man to till the ground
None was, but from the earth a dewy mist
Went up and watered all the ground, and each
Plant of the field, which ere it was in the earth   335
God made, and every herb before it grew
On the green stem; God saw that it was good;
So even and morn recorded the third day.
   'Again the almighty spake, "Let there be lights
High in the expanse of heaven, to divide   340
The day from night; and let them be for signs,
For seasons, and for days, and circling years;
And let them be for lights, as I ordain
Their office in the firmament of heaven,
To give light on the earth;" and it was so.   345
And God made two great lights, great for their use
To man, the greater to have rule by day,
The less by night, altern; and made the stars,
And set them in the firmament of heaven
To illuminate the earth, and rule the day   350
In their vicissitude, and rule the night,
And light from darkness to divide. God saw,
Surveying his great work, that it was good:
For, of celestial bodies, first the sun
A mighty sphere he framed, unlightsome first,   355
Though of ethereal mould; then formed the moon
Globose, and every magnitude of stars,
And sowed with stars the heaven thick as a field;
Of light by far the greater part he took,
Transplanted from her cloudy shrine, and placed   360
In the sun's orb, made porous to receive
And drink the liquid light, firm to retain
Her gathered beams, great palace now of light.
Hither, as to their fountain, other stars
Repairing in their golden urns draw light.   365
And hence the morning planet gilds her horns;
By tincture or reflection they augment

366] Venus has 'horns' when near to the conjunction, like the moon (cf. Milton's
     translation of Psalm cxxxvi. 9, l. 34).
367 tincture] an infusion of a quality.

Their small peculiar, though, from human sight
So far remote, with diminution seen.
First in his east the glorious lamp was seen,   370
Regent of day, and all the horizon round
Invested with bright rays, jocund to run
His longitude through heaven's high road; the grey
Dawn, and the Pleiades before him danced,
Shedding sweet influence; less bright the moon,   375
But opposite in levelled west, was set,
His mirror, with full face borrowing her light
From him, for other light she needed none
In that aspect, and still that distance keeps
Till night; then in the east her turn she shines,   380
Revolved on heaven's great axle, and her reign
With thousand lesser lights dividual holds,
With thousand thousand stars, that then appeared
Spangling the hemisphere; then first adorned
With their bright luminaries, that set and rose,   385
Glad evening and glad morn crowned the fourth day.

   'And God said, "Let the waters generate
Reptile with spawn abundant, living soul;
And let fowl fly above the earth, with wings
Displayed on the open firmament of heaven."   390
And God created the great whales, and each
Soul living, each that crept, which plenteously
The waters generated by their kinds,
And every bird of wing after his kind,
And saw that it was good, and blessed them, saying,   395
"Be fruitful, multiply, and in the seas,
And lakes and running streams the waters fill;
And let the fowl be multiplied on the earth."
Forthwith the sounds and seas, each creek and bay,
With fry innumerable swarm, and shoals   400
Of fish that with their fins and shining scales
Glide under the green wave in sculls that oft
Bank the mid-sea; part, single or with mate,
Graze the sea-weed, their pasture, and through groves
Of coral stray, or sporting with quick glance   405
Show to the sun their waved coats dropped with gold,

368 Their small peculiar] i.e. the small amount of light inherent in them.
373 longitude] course.
376] Job xxxviii. 31.
382 dividual] divided.
402 sculls] schools.
406 dropped] speckled.

Or in their pearly shells at ease, attend
Moist nutriment, or under rocks their food
In jointèd armour watch; on smooth the seal
And bended dolphins play: part, huge of bulk,   410
Wallowing unwieldy, enormous in their gait,
Tempest the ocean; there leviathan,
Hugest of living creatures, on the deep
Stretched like a promontory, sleeps or swims,
And seems a moving land, and at his gills   415
Draws in, and at his trunk spouts out, a sea.
Meanwhile the tepid caves, and fens, and shores,
Their brood as numerous hatch from the egg, that soon,
Bursting with kindly rupture, forth disclosed
Their callow young; but feathered soon and fledge   420
They summed their pens, and soaring the air sublime,
With clang despised the ground, under a cloud
In prospect; there the eagle and the stork
On cliffs and cedar-tops their eyries build;
Part loosely wing the region; part, more wise,   425
In common, ranged in figure, wedge their way,
Intelligent of seasons, and set forth
Their airy caravan, high over seas
Flying, and over lands, with mutual wing
Easing their flight: so steers the prudent crane   430
Her annual voyage, borne on winds: the air
Floats as they pass, fanned with unnumbered plumes;
From branch to branch the smaller birds with song
Solaced the woods, and spread their painted wings,
Till even; nor then the solemn nightingale   435
Ceased warbling, but all night tuned her soft lays;
Others, on silver lakes and rivers, bathed
Their downy breast; the swan, with archèd neck
Between her white wings mantling proudly, rows
Her state with oary feet; yet oft they quit   440
The dank, and, rising on stiff pennons, tower
The mid aerial sky; others on ground
Walked firm – the crested cock, whose clarion sounds

409 smooth] smooth sea.
412-15] Cf. I 200-8n.
419 kindly] pertaining to nature or birth.
421 summed their pens] brought their feathers to full growth. Cf. *PR* I 14.
422 despised] looked down upon.
429-30 mutual ... flight] Birds flying in a 'wedge' were thought to rest their
    beaks on those in front.
432 floats] undulates.
439 mantling] forming a mantle.

The silent hours, and the other, whose gay train
Adorns him, coloured with the florid hue   445
Of rainbows and starry eyes. The waters thus
With fish replenished, and the air with fowl,
Evening and morn solemnised the fifth day.
    'The sixth, and of creation last, arose
With evening harps and matin; when God said,   450
"Let the earth bring forth soul living in her kind,
Cattle, and creeping things, and beast of the earth,
Each in their kind." The earth obeyed, and, straight
Opening her fertile womb, teemed at a birth
Innumerous living creatures, perfect forms,   455
Limbed and full-grown; out of the ground up rose,
As from his lair, the wild beast, where he wons
In forest wild, in thicket, brake, or den –
Among the trees in pairs they rose, they walked;
The cattle in the fields and meadows green: 460
Those rare and solitary, these in flocks
Pasturing at once and in broad herds, upsprung.
The grassy clods now calved; now half appeared
The tawny lion pawing to get free
His hinder parts – then springs, as broke from bonds, 465
And rampant shakes his brinded mane; the ounce,
The libbard, and the tiger, as the mole
Rising, the crumbled earth above them threw
In hillocks; the swift stag from underground
Bore up his branching head; scarce from his mould   470
Behemoth, biggest born of earth, upheaved
His vastness; fleeced the flocks and bleating rose,
As plants; ambiguous between sea and land,
The river-horse and scaly crocodile.
At once came forth whatever creeps the ground,   475
Insect or worm; those waved their limber fans
For wings, and smallest lineaments exact
In all the liveries decked of summer's pride,
With spots of gold and purple, azure and green;
These as a line their long dimension drew,   480
Streaking the ground with sinuous trace; not all
Minims of nature; some of serpent kind,

444 other] the peacock.
457 wons] lives.
466 ounce] See *Comus* 71n.
467 libbard] leopard.
471 Behemoth] tentatively identified as the elephant in the A.V. marginal note
    to Job xl. 15.
474 river-horse] translates the Greek 'hippopotamus'.
482 Minims of nature] the smallest forms of animal life.

Wondrous in length and corpulence, involved
Their snaky folds, and added wings. First crept
The parsimonious emmet, provident   485
Of future, in small room large heart enclosed –
Pattern of just equality perhaps
Hereafter – joined in her popular tribes
Of commonalty; swarming next appeared
The female bee, that feeds her husband drone   490
Deliciously, and builds her waxen cells
With honey stored; the rest are numberless,
And thou their natures know'st, and gav'st them names,
Needless to thee repeated; nor unknown
The serpent, subtlest beast of all the field,   495
Of huge extent sometimes, with brazen eyes,
And hairy mane terrific, though to thee
Not noxious, but obedient at thy call.
     'Now heaven in all her glory shone, and rolled
Her motions, as the great first mover's hand   500
First wheeled their course; earth, in her rich attire
Consummate, lovely smiled; air, water, earth,
By fowl, fish, beast, was flown, was swum, was walked,
Frequent; and of the sixth day yet remained;
There wanted yet the master-work, the end   505
Of all yet done – a creature who not prone
And brute as other creatures, but endued
With sanctity of reason, might erect
His stature, and upright with front serene
Govern the rest, self-knowing, and from thence   510
Magnanimous to correspond with heaven,
But grateful to acknowledge whence his good
Descends; thither with heart and voice and eyes
Directed in devotion, to adore
And worship God supreme, who made him chief   515
Of all his works; therefore the omnipotent
Eternal Father (for where is not he

483 corpulence] bulk.
    involved] coiled.
484] Isa. xxx. 6.
485 emmet] ant.
490] Worker bees were thought to be female, and drones male.
497 terrific] terrifying.
504 Frequent] abundantly.
509 front] face.
511 Magnanimous] An Aristotelian term meaning 'greatsouledness' or 'high-
    mindedness'; when blended with Christian ideas by scholastic philosophers
    it came to mean 'fortitude' or 'lofty courage'.

Present?) thus to his Son audibly spake:
"Let us make now man in our image, man
In our similitude, and let them rule   520
Over the fish and fowl of sea and air,
Beast of the field, and over all the earth,
And every creeping thing that creeps the ground."
This said, he formed thee, Adam, thee O man,
Dust of the ground, and in thy nostrils breathed   525
The breath of life; in his own image he
Created thee, in the image of God
Express, and thou becam'st a living soul.
Male he created thee, but thy consort
Female, for race; then blessed mankind, and said,   530
"Be fruitful, multiply, and fill the earth;
Subdue it, and throughout dominion hold
Over fish of the sea, and fowl of the air,
And every living thing that moves on the earth."
Wherever thus created – for no place   535
Is yet distinct by name – thence, as thou know'st,
He brought thee into this delicious grove,
This garden, planted with the trees of God,
Delectable both to behold and taste,
And freely all their pleasant fruit for food   540
Gave thee: all sorts are here that all the earth yields,
Variety without end; but of the tree
Which tasted works knowledge of good and evil
Thou may'st not; in the day thou eat'st, thou diest.
Death is the penalty imposed; beware,   545
And govern well thy appetite, lest Sin
Surprise thee, and her black attendant Death.
   'Here finished he, and all that he had made
Viewed, and behold all was entirely good;
So even and morn accomplished the sixth day;   550
Yet not till the creator from his work
Desisting, though unwearied, up returned,
Up to the heaven of heavens, his high abode,
Thence to behold this new-created world,
The addition of his empire, how it showed   555
In prospect from his throne, how good, how fair,
Answering his great idea. Up he rode,

519-20] See the Vulgate rendering of Gen. i. 26. Expositors of this verse usually
   distinguished between the *Imago Dei*, which was obscured but not lost at
   the fall, and the *Similitudo Dei*, which was destroyed by original sin but
   could be restored by God (traditionally through baptism). For Milton's
   view, see XI 511-25.
557 idea] The term is used in the Platonic sense of 'ideal form'.

Followed with acclamation, and the sound
Symphonious of ten thousand harps, that tuned
Angelic harmonies; the earth, the air   560
Resounded (thou remember'st, for thou heard'st),
The heavens and all the constellations rung,
The planets in their stations listening stood,
While the bright pomp ascended jubilant.
"Open, ye everlasting gates," they sung;   565
"Open, ye heavens, your living doors; let in
The great creator, from his work returned
Magnificent, his six days' work, a world;
Open, and henceforth oft; for God will deign
To visit oft the dwellings of just men   570
Delighted, and with frequent intercourse
Thither will send his winged messengers
On errands of supernal grace." So sung
The glorious train ascending; he through heaven,
That opened wide her blazing portals, led   575
To God's eternal house direct the way –
A broad and ample road, whose dust is gold,
And pavement stars, as stars to thee appear
Seen in the galaxy, that milky way
Which nightly as a circling zone thou seest   580
Powdered with stars. And now on earth the seventh
Evening arose in Eden – for the sun
Was set, and twilight from the east came on,
Forerunning night, when at the holy mount
Of heaven's high-seated top, the imperial throne   585
Of Godhead, fixed for ever firm and sure,
The filial power arrived, and sat him down
With his great Father (for he also went
Invisible, yet stayed: such privilege
Hath omnipresence) and the work ordained,   590
Author and end of all things, and, from work
Now resting, blessed and hallowed the seventh day,
As resting on that day from all his work,
But not in silence holy kept: the harp
Had work, and rested not; the solemn pipe   595

563 station] an astronomical term which refers to the apparent standing still of
    a planet at its apogee and perigee, here applied to the position of the
    planets at creation.
564 pomp] triumphal procession.
565-7] Psalm xxiv. 7-9.
577-9] On the Milky Way as a road to the house of Jove see *Metamorphoses* i
    168-71.

And dulcimer, all organs of sweet stop,
All sounds on fret by string or golden wire,
Tempered soft tunings, intermixed with voice
Choral or unison; of incense clouds,
Fuming from golden censers, hid the mount.   600
Creation and the six days' acts they sung:
"Great are thy works, Jehovah, infinite
Thy power; what thought can measure thee, or tongue
Relate thee – greater now in thy return
Than from the giant angels; thee that day   605
Thy thunders magnified; but to create
Is greater than created to destroy.
Who can impair thee, mighty king, or bound
Thy empire? Easily the proud attempt
Of spirits apostate, and their counsels vain,   610
Thou hast repelled, while impiously they thought
Thee to diminish, and from thee withdraw
The number of thy worshippers. Who seeks
To lessen thee, against his purpose serves
To manifest the more thy might; his evil   615
Thou usest, and from thence creat'st more good.
Witness this new-made world, another heaven
From heaven-gate not far, founded in view
On the clear hyaline, the glassy sea;
Of amplitude almost immense, with stars   620
Numerous, and every star perhaps a world
Of destined habitation – but thou know'st
Their seasons; among these the seat of men,
Earth, with her nether ocean circumfused,
Their pleasant dwelling-place. Thrice happy men,   625
And sons of men, whom God hath thus advanced,
Created in his image, there to dwell
And worship him, and in reward to rule
Over his works, on earth, in sea, or air,
And multiply a race of worshippers   630

596 dulcimer] not the stringed instrument, but the bagpipe of Dan. iii. 5, 15,
    translated in the A.V. as 'dulcimer'.
599-600] Rev. viii. 3-5.
605 giant angels] a comparison of Satan and his followers to the giants who in
    . classical mythology rebelled against Jove.
619 hyaline] the 'sea of glass like unto crystal' (θάλασσα ὑαλίνη) of Rev. iv. 6, xv.
    2, and the waters above the firmament of *PL* III 518-19, VII 268-71.
620 immense] immeasurable.
624 nether ocean] i.e. the ocean of the earth, as opposed to the waters above the
    firmament.

Holy and just; thrice happy, if they know
Their happiness, and persevere upright."
    'So sung they, and the empyrean rung
With halleluiahs; thus was Sabbath kept.
And thy request think now fulfilled, that asked   635
How first this world and face of things began,
And what before thy memory was done
From the beginning, that posterity,
Informed by thee, might know; if else thou seek'st
Aught, not surpassing human measure, say.'   640

THE END OF THE SEVENTH BOOK

631-2] Virgil, *Georgics* ii 458-60.
632 persevere] a technical theological term referring to steady continuance in
    the faith and life proper to the attainment of eternal life.
634 halleluiahs] See II 243n.

BOOK VIII

THE ARGUMENT

Adam enquires concerning celestial motions; is doubtfully ans-
wered, and exhorted to search rather things more worthy of
knowledge; Adam assents, and still desirous to detain Raphael,
relates to him what he remembered since his own creation – his
placing in Paradise; his talk with God concerning solitude and fit
society; his first meeting and nuptials with Eve; his discourse with
the angel thereupon; who, after admonitions repeated, departs.

The angel ended, and in Adam's ear
So charming left his voice that he a while
Thought him still speaking, still stood fixed to hear;
Then, as new-waked, thus gratefully replied:
   'What thanks sufficient, or what recompense   5
Equal, have I to render thee, divine
Historian, who thus largely hast allayed
The thirst I had of knowledge, and vouchsafed
This friendly condescension, to relate
Things else by me unsearchable – now heard   10
With wonder, but delight, and, as is due,
With glory áttributed to the high
Creator? Something yet of doubt remains,
Which only thy solution can resolve.
When I behold this goodly frame, this world   15
Of heaven and earth consisting, and compute
Their magnitudes – this earth a spot, a grain,
An atom, with the firmament compared
And all her numbered stars, that seem to roll
Spaces incomprehensible (for such   20
Their distance argues, and their swift return
Diurnal) merely to officiate light
Round this opacous earth, this punctual spot,
One day and night, in all their vast survey
Useless besides – reasoning, I oft admire   25
How nature, wise and frugal, could commit

---

2 charming] In Milton's time the word was still strongly felt as a metaphor, and
    meant 'acting upon as with a charm'.
14 solution] explanation, answer.
19 numbered] numerous.
22 officiate] supply.
23 punctual] like a point, minute.

Such disproportions, with superfluous hand
So many nobler bodies to create,
Greater so manifold, to this one use,
For aught appears, and on their orbs impose   30
Such restless revolution day by day
Repeated, while the sedentary earth,
That better might with far less compass move,
Served by more noble than herself, attains
Her end without least motion, and receives,   35
As tribute, such a sumless journey brought
Of incorporeal speed, her warmth and light:
Speed, to describe whose swiftness number fails.'
    So spake our sire, and by his countenance seemed
Entering on studious thoughts abstruse; which Eve   40
Perceiving, where she sat retired in sight,
With lowliness majestic from her seat,
And grace that won who saw to wish her stay,
Rose, and went forth among her fruits and flowers,
To visit how they prospered, bud and bloom,   45
Her nursery; they at her coming sprung,
And, touched by her fair tendance, gladlier grew.
Yet went she not as not with such discourse
Delighted, or not capable her ear
Of what was high; such pleasure she reserved,   50
Adam relating, she sole auditress;
Her husband the relater she preferred
Before the angel, and of him to ask
Chose rather; he, she knew, would intermix
Grateful digressions, and solve high dispute   55
With conjugal caresses: from his lip
Not words alone pleased her. O when meet now
Such pairs, in love and mutual honour joined?
With goddess-like demeanour forth she went,
Not unattended; for on her as queen   60
A pomp of winning Graces waited still,
And from about her shot darts of desire
Into all eyes, to wish her still in sight.
And Raphael now to Adam's doubt proposed

36 sumless] incalculable.
45 visit] examine.
46-7] The response of the fruit and flowers constitutes a comparison of Eve to
    Venus, who was in early antiquity an Italic goddess of vegetation, the
    guardian of gardens.
60-3] Another comparison of Eve to Venus, here as the goddess of love on
    whom the Graces (see *L'Allegro* 12-16n.) attended. Cf. V 381-2. 'Pomp'
    means 'train'.

Benevolent and facile thus replied: 65
   'To ask or search I blame thee not, for heaven
Is as the book of God before thee set,
Wherein to read his wondrous works, and learn
His seasons, hours, or days, or months, or years;
This to attain, whether heaven move or earth   70
Imports not, if thou reckon right: the rest
From man or angel the great architect
Did wisely to conceal, and not divulge
His secrets, to be scanned by them who ought
Rather admire; or if they list to try   75
Conjecture, he his fabric of the heavens
Hath left to their disputes – perhaps to move
His laughter at their quaint opinions wide
Hereafter, when they come to model heaven,
And calculate the stars; how they will wield   80
The mighty frame; how build, unbuild, contrive
To save appearances; how gird the sphere
With centric and eccentric scribbled o'er,
Cycle and epicycle, orb in orb;
Already by thy reasoning this I guess,   85
Who art to lead thy offspring, and supposest
That bodies bright and greater should not serve
The less not bright, nor heaven such journeys run,
Earth sitting still, when she alone receives
The benefit; consider, first, that great   90
Or bright infers not excellence; the earth,
Though, in comparison of heaven, so small,
Nor glistering, may of solid good contain
More plenty than the sun that barren shines,
Whose virtue on itself works no effect,   95
But in the fruitful earth; there first received,
His beams, unactive else, their vigour find.
Yet not to earth are those bright luminaries
Officious, but to thee, earth's habitant.
And, for the heaven's wide circuit, let it speak   100
The maker's high magnificence, who built
So spacious, and his line stretched out so far,
That man may know he dwells not in his own –

65   facile] mild, courteous, fluent.
78   wide] wide of the mark, mistaken.
82   To save appearances] a scholastic term (originally Greek) referring to the
     construction of hypotheses which satisfactorily explain the observed facts.
83–4] See III 575n.
99   Officious] attentive.
102] Job xxxviii. 5.

An edifice too large for him to fill,
Lodged in a small partition, and the rest   105
Ordained for uses to his Lord best known.
The swiftness of those circles attribute,
Though numberless, to his omnipotence,
That to corporeal substances could add
Speed almost spiritual; me thou think'st not slow,   110
Who since the morning-hour set out from heaven
Where God resides, and ere mid-day arrived
In Eden – distance inexpressible
By numbers that have name. But this I urge,
Admitting motion in the heavens, to show   115
Invalid that which thee to doubt it moved;
Not that I so affirm, though so it seem
To thee who hast thy dwelling here on earth.
God, to remove his ways from human sense,
Placed heaven from earth so far, that earthly sight,   120
If it presume, might err in things too high,
And no advantage gain. What if the sun
Be centre to the world, and other stars,
By his attractive virtue and their own
Incited, dance about him various rounds?   125
Their wandering course now high, now low, then hid,
Progressive, retrograde, or standing still,
In six thou seest; and what if, seventh to these,
The planet earth, so steadfast though she seem,
Insensibly three different motions move?   130
Which else to several spheres thou must ascribe,
Moved contrary with thwart obliquities,
Or save the sun his labour, and that swift

126 wandering] See V 177n.
127] Kepler showed that the stations (see VII 563n.) and retrogressions
    (apparent movements from east to west) of the planets were necessary
    consequences of the revolution of the planets (including the earth) around
    the sun in elliptical orbits.
128-9] The six planets are the moon, Mercury, Venus, Mars, Jupiter, and
    Saturn. In Ptolemaic astronomy the seventh planet is the sun; in Coperni-
    can astronomy, the earth.
130] Two of the motions are the daily rotation of the earth, and its annual
    revolution around the sun. If Raphael is speaking proleptically of the
    postlapsarian universe, the third motion would be the alteration in the
    plane of the earth's equator which causes its axis to describe a cone in
    space, a phenomenon to which Copernicus attributed the precession of the
    seasons (cf. III 481-3n.). If, as seems more likely, he is speaking of the
    prelapsarian universe, then the third motion would probably be Coperni-
    cus' notion of the progressive (but fluctuating) motion of the earth's
    apse-line.
132] i.e. moving in contrary directions on inclined ecliptic planes.

Nocturnal and diurnal rhomb supposed,
Invisible else above all stars, the wheel   135
Of day and night; which needs not thy belief,
If earth, industrious of herself, fetch day,
Travelling east, and with her part averse
From the sun's beam meet night, her other part
Still luminous by his ray. What if that light,   140
Sent from her through the wide transpicuous air,
To the terrestrial moon be as a star,
Enlightening her by day, as she by night
This earth – reciprocal, if land be there,
Fields and inhabitants? Her spots thou seest   145
As clouds, and clouds may rain, and rain produce
Fruits in her softened soil, for some to eat
Allotted there; and other suns perhaps
With their attendant moons, thou wilt descry,
Communicating male and female light –   150
Which two great sexes animate the world,
Stored in each orb perhaps with some that live.
For such vast room in nature unpossessed
By living soul, desert and desolate,
Only to shine, yet scarce to contribute   155
Each orb a glimpse of light, conveyed so far
Down to this habitable, which returns
Light back to them, is obvious to dispute.
But whether thus these things, or whether not –
Whether the sun, predominant in heaven,   160
Rise on the earth, or earth rise on the sun;
He from the east his flaming road begin,
Or she from west her silent course advance
With inoffensive pace that spinning sleeps
On her soft axle, while she paces even,   165
And bears thee soft with the smooth air along –
Solicit not thy thoughts with matters hid;

---

134 rhomb] the *primum mobile* (see *Fair Infant* 39n.).
141 transpicuous] pervious to vision.
150 male and female] original and reflected.
157 this habitable] imitates ἡ οἰκουμένη (sc. γῆ), the inhabited (world), a term
   used by the Greeks to designate the Greek world, as opposed to barbarian
   lands.
164 inoffensive] means both 'unoffending' and (etymologically) 'free from
   hindrance'.
166] Copernican cosmology assumed an atmosphere which moved with the
   earth to account for the absence of high winds caused by the rotation of the
   earth.
167 Solicit] disturb, disquiet.

Leave them to God above; him serve and fear;
Of other creatures as him pleases best,
Wherever placed, let him dispose; joy thou   170
In what he gives to thee, this Paradise
And thy fair Eve; heaven is for thee too high
To know what passes there; be lowly wise;
Think only what concerns thee and thy being;
Dream not of other worlds, what creatures there   175
Live, in what state, condition, or degree –
Contented that thus far hath been revealed
Not of earth only, but of highest heaven.'
     To whom thus Adam, cleared of doubt, replied:
'How fully hast thou satisfied me, pure   180
Intelligence of heaven, angel serene,
And, freed from intricacies, taught to live
The easiest way, nor with perplexing thoughts
To interrupt the sweet of life, from which
God hath bid dwell far off all anxious cares,   185
And not molest us, unless we ourselves
Seek them with wandering thoughts, and notions vain.
But apt the mind or fancy is to rove
Unchecked, and of her roving is no end,
Till warned, or by experience taught, she learn   190
That not to know at large of things remote
From use, obscure and subtle, but to know
That which before us lies in daily life,
Is the prime wisdom: what is more is fume,
Or emptiness, or fond impertinence,   195
And renders us in things that most concern
Unpractised, unprepared, and still to seek.
Therefore from this high pitch let us descend
A lower flight, and speak of things at hand
Useful; whence, haply, mention may arise   200
Of something not unseasonable to ask,
By sufferance, and thy wonted favour, deigned.
Thee I have heard relating what was done
Ere my remembrance; now hear me relate
My story, which perhaps thou hast not heard;   205
And day is yet not spent; till then thou seest
How subtly to detain thee I devise,
Inviting thee to hear while I relate –
Fond, were it not in hope of thy reply;
For while I sit with thee, I seem in heaven,   210

168] Eccles. xii. 13.
195 fond impertinence] foolish irrelevance.
197 to seek] deficient.

And sweeter thy discourse is to my ear
Than fruits of palm-tree, pleasantest to thirst
And hunger both, from labour, at the hour
Of sweet repast; they satiate, and soon fill,
Though pleasant; but thy words, with grace divine   215
Imbued, bring to their sweetness no satiety.'
    To whom thus Raphael answered, heavenly meek:
'Nor are thy lips ungraceful, sire of men,
Nor tongue ineloquent; for God on thee
Abundantly his gifts hath also poured,   220
Inward and outward both, his image fair:
Speaking or mute, all comeliness and grace
Attends thee, and each word, each motion, forms.
Nor less think we in heaven of thee on earth
Than of our fellow-servant, and enquire   225
Gladly into the ways of God with man;
For God, we see, hath honoured thee, and set
On man his equal love; say therefore on;
For I that day was absent, as befell,
Bound on a voyage uncouth and obscure,   230
Far on excursion toward the gates of hell,
Squared in full legion (such command we had)
To see that none thence issued forth a spy
Or enemy, while God was in his work,
Lest he incensed at such eruption bold,   235
Destruction with creation might have mixed.
Not that they durst without his leave attempt;
But us he sends upon his high behests
For state, as sovereign king, and to inure
Our prompt obedience. Fast we found, fast shut,   240
The dismal gates, and barricadoed strong,
But, long ere our approaching, heard within
Noise, other than the sound of dance or song –
Torment, and loud lament, and furious rage.
Glad we returned up to the coasts of light   245
Ere Sabbath-evening; so we had in charge.
But thy relation now; for I attend,
Pleased with thy words no less than thou with mine.'
    So spake the godlike power, and thus our sire:
'For man to tell how human life began   250
Is hard; for who himself beginning knew?
Desire with thee still longer to converse

225] Rev. xxii. 8-9.
230 uncouth] strange, unfamiliar.
239 state] dignified observance of ceremony.
242-4] *Aeneid* vi 557-9.

Induced me. As new-waked from soundest sleep,
Soft on the flowery herb I found me laid,
In balmy sweat, which with his beams the sun   255
Soon dried, and on the reeking moisture fed.
Straight toward heaven my wondering eyes I turned,
And gazed a while the ample sky, till, raised
By quick instinctive motion, up I sprung,
As thitherward endeavouring, and upright   260
Stood on my feet; about me round I saw
Hill, dale, and shady woods, and sunny plains,
And liquid lapse of murmuring streams; by these,
Creatures that lived and moved, and walked or flew,
Birds on the branches warbling; all things smiled;   265
With fragrance and with joy my heart o'erflowed.
Myself I then perused, and limb by limb
Surveyed, and sometimes went, and sometimes ran
With supple joints, as lively vigour led;
But who I was, or where, or from what cause,   270
Knew not; to speak I tried, and forthwith spake;
My tongue obeyed, and readily could name
What'er I saw. "Thou sun," said I, "fair light,
And thou enlightened earth, so fresh and gay,
Ye hills and dales, ye rivers, woods, and plains,   275
And ye that live and move, fair creatures, tell,
Tell, if ye saw, how came I thus, how here.
Not of myself; by some great maker then,
In goodness and in power pre-eminent;
Tell me, how may I know him, how adore,   280
From whom I have that thus I move and live,
And feel that I am happier than I know."
While thus I called, and strayed I knew not whither,
From where I first drew air, and first beheld
This happy light, when answer none returned,   285
On a green shady bank, profuse of flowers,
Pensive I sat me down; there gentle sleep
First found me, and with soft oppression seized
My drowsed sense, untroubled, though I thought
I then was passing to my former state   290
Insensible, and forthwith to dissolve:
When suddenly stood at my head a dream,

256 reeking] steaming.
263 lapse] flow.
268 went] walked.
281] Acts xvii. 28.
292] Imitates *Iliad* 20, where Oneiros, god of dreams, stands at the bedside of
    Agamemnon.

Whose inward apparition gently moved
My fancy to believe I yet had being,
And lived; one came, methought, of shape divine,   295
And said, "Thy mansion wants thee, Adam; rise,
First man, of men innumerable ordained
First father; called by thee, I come thy guide
To the garden of bliss, thy seat prepared."
So saying, by the hand he took me, raised,   300
And over fields and waters, as in air
Smooth sliding without step, last led me up
A woody mountain, whose high top was plain,
A circuit wide, enclosed, with goodliest trees
Planted, with walks and bowers, that what I saw   305
Of earth before scarce pleasant seemed. Each tree
Loaden with fairest fruit, that hung to the eye
Tempting, stirred in me sudden appetite
To pluck and eat; whereat I waked, and found
Before mine eyes all real, as the dream   310
Had lively shadowed; here had new begun
My wandering, had not he who was my guide
Up hither from among the trees appeared,
Presence divine. Rejoicing, but with awe,
In adoration at his feet I fell   315
Submiss; he reared me, and, "Whom thou sought'st I am,"
Said mildly, "author of all this thou seest
Above, or round about thee, or beneath.
This Paradise I give thee; count it thine
To till and keep, and of the fruit to eat;   320
Of every tree that in the garden grows
Eat freely with glad heart; fear here no dearth;
But of the tree whose operation brings
Knowledge of good and ill, which I have set
The pledge of thy obedience and thy faith,   325
Amid the garden by the tree of life –
Remember what I warn thee – shun to taste,
And shun the bitter consequence: for know,
The day thou eat'st thereof, my sole command
Transgressed, inevitably thou shalt die,   330

---

320 till and keep] The A.V. makes 'dressing' the garden a prelapsarian
    obligation (Gen. ii. 15) and 'tilling' a postlapsarian obligation (Gen. iii. 23).
    In the Hebrew, Greek (LXX) and Latin (Vulgate) versions, however, the
    same word is used in both verses.
330-1 inevitably . . . mortal] a traditional interpretation of Gen. ii. 17, overcom-
    ing the difficulty that Adam did not die on the day that he ate the fruit by
    interpreting death as inevitable mortality. Cf. X 49-52, 210-11.

From that day mortal, and this happy state
Shalt loose, expelled from hence into a world
Of woe and sorrow." Sternly he pronounced
The rigid interdiction, which resounds
Yet dreadful in mine ear, though in my choice   335
Not to incur; but soon his clear aspéct
Returned, and gracious purpose thus renewed:
"Not only these fair bounds, but all the earth
To thee and to thy race I give; as lords
Possess it, and all things that therein live,   340
Or live in sea or air, beast, fish, and fowl.
In sign whereof, each bird and beast behold
After their kinds; I bring them to receive
From thee their names, and pay thee fealty
With low subjection; understand the same   345
Of fish within their watery residence,
Not hither summoned, since they cannot change
Their element to draw the thinner air."
As thus he spake, each bird and beast behold
Approaching two and two – these cowering low   350
With blandishment; each bird stooped on his wing.
I named them as they passed, and understood
Their nature; with such knowledge God endued
My sudden apprehension; but in these
I found not what methought I wanted still,   355
And to the heavenly vision thus presumed:
    ' "O by what name – for thou above all these,
Above mankind, or aught than mankind higher,
Surpassest far my naming – how may I
Adore thee, author of this universe,   360
And all this good to man, for whose well-being
So amply, and with hands so liberal,
Thou hast provided all things? but with me
I see not who partakes. In solitude
What happiness, who can enjoy alone,   365
Or, all enjoying, what contentment find?"
Thus I, presumptuous; and the vision bright,
As with a smile more brightened, thus replied:
    ' "What call'st thou solitude? Is not the earth
With various living creatures, and the air,   370
Replenished, and all these at thy command

332 loose] means both 'dissolve, violate' and 'lose'.
337 purpose] discourse.
371 Replenished] fully and abundantly stocked.

To come and play before thee? Know'st thou not
Their language and their ways? They also know,
And reason not contemptibly; with these
Find pastime, and bear rule; thy realm is large."   375
So spake the universal Lord, and seemed
So ordering. I with leave of speech implored,
And humble deprecation, thus replied:
    '"Let not my words offend thee, heavenly power;
My maker, be propitious while I speak.   380
Hast thou not made me here thy substitute,
And these inferior far beneath me set?
Among unequals what society
Can sort, what harmony or true delight?
Which must be mutual, in proportion due   385
Given and received; but, in disparity,
The one intense, the other still remiss,
Cannot well suit with either, but soon prove
Tedious alike; of fellowship I speak
Such as I seek, fit to participate   390
All rational delight, wherein the brute
Cannot be human consort; they rejoice
Each with their kind, lion with lioness;
So fitly them in pairs thou hast combined:
Much less can bird with beast, or fish with fowl,   395
So well converse, nor with the ox the ape;
Worse, then, can man with beast, and least of all."
    'Whereto the almighty answered, not displeased:
"A nice and subtle happiness, I see,
Thou to thyself proposest, in the choice   400
Of thy associates, Adam, and wilt taste
No pleasure, though in pleasure, solitary.
What think'st thou, then, of me, and this my state?
Seem I to thee sufficiently possessed
Of happiness, or not, who am alone   405
From all eternity? For none I know
Second to me or like, equal much less.
How have I, then, with whom to hold converse,
Save with the creatures which I made, and those
To me inferior infinite descents   410

379-80] Gen. xviii. 30.
384-9] an extended musical metaphor. 'Intense' means 'taut' (etymologically),
    and 'remiss' means 'diminished in tension'; the human string is thus higher
    in pitch than the animal string.
396 converse] associate familiarly, consort.
402 in pleasure] plays on 'pleasure' as the literal meaning of 'Eden' in Hebrew.
406-7] Cf. Horace, *Odes* I. xii. 17-18.

Beneath what other creatures are to thee?"
  'He ceased, I lowly answered: "To attain
The height and depth of thy eternal ways
All human thoughts come short, supreme of things;
Thou in thyself art perfect, and in thee   415
Is no deficience found; not so is man,
But in degree – the cause of his desire
By conversation with his like to help
Or solace his defects. No need that thou
Should'st propagate, already infinite,   420
And through all numbers absolute, though one;
But man by number is to manifest
His single imperfection, and beget
Like of his like, his image multiplied,
In unity defective, which requires   425
Collateral love and dearest amity.
Thou in thy secrecy although alone,
Best with thyself accompanied, seek'st not
Social communication – yet, so pleased,
Canst raise thy creature to what height thou wilt   430
Of union or communion, deified;
I by conversing cannot these erect
From prone, nor in their ways complacence find."
Thus I emboldened spake, and freedom used
Permissive, and acceptance found; which gained   435
This answer from the gracious voice divine:
  '"Thus far to try thee, Adam, I was pleased,
And find thee knowing not of beasts alone,
Which thou hast rightly named, but of thyself –
Expressing well the spirit within thee free,   440
My image, not imparted to the brute,
Whose fellowship, therefore, unmeet for thee,
Good reason was thou freely shouldst dislike;
And be so minded still; I, ere thou spak'st,
Knew it not good for man to be alone,   445
And no such company as then thou saw'st
Intended thee – for trial only brought,
To see how thou could'st judge of fit and meet;

415–20] Aristotle, *Eudemian Ethics* 1244b, 1245b.
421] 'Numbers' carries the Latin sense of 'parts' as well as its modern sense; 'absolute' means 'complete, perfect'.
427–8 Imitates Cicero's famous phrase, *Numquam minus solum, quam cum solus* ('never less alone than when alone'). *De Officiis* III. i. 1. Cf. *PL* IX 249, *PR* I 301–2.
433 complacence] See III 276n.
435 permissive] acting under permission.

What next I bring shall please thee, be assured,
Thy likeness, thy fit help, thy other self,   450
Thy wish exactly to thy heart's desire.''
    'He ended, or I heard no more; for now
My earthly, by his heavenly overpowered,
Which it had long stood under, strained to the height
In that celestial colloquy sublime,   455
As with an object that excels the sense,
Dazzled and spent, sunk down, and sought repair
Of sleep, which instantly fell on me, called
By nature as in aid, and closed mine eyes.
Mine eyes he closed, but open left the cell   460
Of fancy, my internal sight, by which,
Abstract as in a trance, methought I saw,
Though sleeping, where I lay, and saw the shape
Still glorious before whom awake I stood;
Who, stooping, opened my left side, and took   465
From thence a rib, with cordial spirits warm,
And life-blood streaming fresh; wide was the wound,
But suddenly with flesh filled up and healed;
The rib he formed and fashioned with his hands;
Under his forming hands a creature grew,   470
Man-like, but different sex, so lovely fair
That what seemed fair in all the world seemed now
Mean, or in her summed up, in her contained
And in her looks, which from that time infused
Sweetness into my heart unfelt before   475
And into all things from her air inspired
The spirit of love and amorous delight.
She disappeared, and left me dark; I waked
To find her, or for ever to deplore
Her loss, and other pleasures all abjure: 480
When, out of hope, behold her not far off,
Such as I saw her in my dream, adorned
With what all earth and heaven could bestow
To make her amiable; on she came,

450 other self] translates the Greek ἕτερος αὑτός and the Latin *alter ego*, both of
    which are used of very intimate friends. Cf. l. 495, and X 128.
453 earthly, heavenly] i.e. nature.
462 Abstract] withdrawn.
    as in a trance] Milton follows the LXX version of Gen. ii. 21 (ἔκστασιν, the
    word translated in Acts x. 10, xxii. 17 as 'trance'); in the A.V. and Vulgate
    Adam falls into a 'deep sleep'.
466 cordial spirits] the 'vital spirits' of V 484; 'cordial' means 'of the heart'.
476 her air inspired] means both 'her manner and appearance inspired' and 'her
    breath breathed'.

Led by her heavenly maker, though unseen   485
And guided by his voice, nor uninformed
Of nuptial sanctity and marriage rites;
Grace was in all her steps, heaven in her eye,
In every gesture dignity and love.
I, overjoyed, could not forbear aloud: 490
  ' "This turn hath made amends; thou hast fulfilled
Thy words, creator bounteous and benign,
Giver of all things fair – but fairest this
Of all thy gifts – nor enviest. I now see
Bone of my bone, flesh of my flesh, my self   495
Before me; woman is her name, of man
Extracted; for this cause he shall forgo
Father and mother, and to his wife adhere,
And they shall be one flesh, one heart, one soul."
  'She heard me thus, and, though divinely brought,
Yet innocence and virgin modesty,   501
Her virtue and the conscience of her worth,
That would be wooed, and not unsought be won,
Not obvious, not obtrusive, but retired,
The more desirable – or, to say all,   505
Nature herself, though pure of sinful thought –
Wrought in her so, that seeing me, she turned;
I followed her; she what was honour knew,
And with obsequious majesty approved
My pleaded reason. To the nuptial bower   510
I led her blushing like the morn; all heaven,
And happy constellations, on that hour
Shed their selectest influence; the earth
Gave sign of gratulation, and each hill;
Joyous the birds; fresh gales and gentle airs   515
Whispered it to the woods, and from their wings
Flung rose, flung odours from the spicy shrub,
Disporting, till the amorous bird of night
Sung spousal, and bid haste the evening star
On his hill-top to light the bridal lamp.   520
  'Thus have I told thee all my state, and brought
My story to the sum of earthly bliss
Which I enjoy, and must confess to find

490 aloud] i.e. saying aloud.
502 conscience] inward knowledge, consciousness.
504 obvious] open to influence.
508 honour] Heb. xiii. 4.
509 obsequious] obedient, dutiful, prompt to serve.
518 bird] the nightingale.
519 evening star] Hesperus. Cf. XI 588-9.

In all things else delight indeed, but such
As, used or not, works in the mind no change,   525
Nor vehement desire – these delicacies
I mean of taste, sight, smell, herbs, fruits, and flowers,
Walks, and the melody of birds: but here,
Far otherwise, transported I behold,
Transported touch: here passion first I felt,   530
Commotion strange, in all enjoyments else
Superior and unmoved, here only weak
Against the charm of beauty's powerful glance.
Or nature failed in me, and left some part
Not proof enough such object to sustain,   535
Or, from my side subducting, took perhaps
More than enough – at least on her bestowed
Too much of ornament, in outward show
Elaborate, of inward less exact.
For well I understand in the prime end   540
Of nature her inferior, in the mind
And inward faculties, which most excel;
In outward also her resembling less
His image who made both, and less expressing
The character of that dominion given   545
O'er other creatures; yet when I approach
Her loveliness, so absolute she seems
And in herself complete, so well to know
Her own, that what she wills to do or say
Seems wisest, virtuousest, discreetest, best;   550
All higher knowledge in her presence falls
Degraded; wisdom in discourse with her
Looses, discountenanced, and like folly shows;
Authority and reason on her wait,
As one intended first, not after made   555
Occasionally; and to consummate all,
Greatness of mind and nobleness their seat
Build in her loveliest, and create an awe
About her, as a guard angelic placed.'
    To whom the angel, with contracted brow: 560
'Accuse not nature, she hath done her part;
Do thou but thine, and be not diffident

536 subducting] taking away.
547 absolute] See l. 421n.
553 Looses] means both 'dissolves' and 'loses'; cf. l. 332.
556 Occasionally] incidentally, i.e. on the occasion of Adam's request for a
    companion.
557 Greatness of mind] magnanimity. See VII 511n.

Of wisdom; she deserts thee not, if thou
Dismiss not her, when most thou need'st her nigh,
By attributing overmuch to things   565
Less excellent, as thou thyself perceiv'st.
For, what admir'st thou, what transports thee so,
An outside? Fair, no doubt, and worthy well
Thy cherishing, thy honouring, and thy love,
Not thy subjection; weigh with her thyself;   570
Then value; oft-times nothing profits more
Than self-esteem, grounded on just and right
Well managed; of that skill the more thou know'st,
The more she will acknowledge thee her head,
And to realities yield all her shows –   575
Made so adorn for thy delight the more,
So awful, that with honour thou may'st love
Thy mate, who sees when thou art seen least wise.
But if the sense of touch whereby mankind
Is propagated seem such dear delight   580
Beyond all other, think the same vouchsafed
To cattle and each beast; which would not be
To them made common and divulged, if aught
Therein enjoyed were worthy to subdue
The soul of man, or passion in him move.   585
What higher in her society thou find'st
Attractive, human, rational, love still:
In loving thou dost well; in passion not,
Wherein true love consists not; love refines
The thoughts, and heart enlarges – hath his seat   590
In reason, and is judicious, is the scale
By which to heavenly love thou may'st ascend,
Not sunk in carnal pleasure; for which cause
Among the beasts no mate for thee was found.'
    To whom thus, half-abashed, Adam replied: 595
'Neither her outside formed so fair, nor aught
In procreation, common to all kinds
(Though higher of the genial bed by far,
And with mysterious reverence, I deem),
So much delights me as those graceful acts,   600
Those thousand decencies, that daily flow
From all her words and actions, mixed with love
And sweet compliance, which declare unfeigned
Union of mind, or in us both one soul –

574 head] I Cor. xi. 3.
577 awful] awe-inspiring.
598 genial] see IV 712n.

Harmony to behold in wedded pair   605
More grateful than harmonious sound to the ear.
Yet these subject not; I to thee disclose
What inward thence I feel, not therefore foiled,
Who meet with various subjects, from the sense
Variously representing, yet, still free,   610
Approve the best, and follow what I approve.
To love thou blam'st me not – for love, thou say'st,
Leads up to heaven, is both the way and guide;
Bear with me, then, if lawful what I ask:
Love not the heavenly spirits, and how their love   615
Express they – by looks only, or do they mix
Irradiance, virtual or immediate touch?'
    To whom the angel, with a smile that glowed
Celestial rosy-red, love's proper hue,
Answered: 'Let it suffice thee that thou know'st   620
Us happy, and without love no happiness.
Whatever pure thou in the body enjoy'st
(And pure thou wert created) we enjoy
In eminence, and obstacle find none
Of membrane, joint, or limb, exclusive bars;   625
Easier than air with air, if spirits embrace,
Total they mix, union of pure with pure
Desiring, nor restrained conveyance need
As flesh to mix with flesh, or soul with soul.
But I can now no more: the parting sun   630
Beyond the earth's green cape and verdant isles
Hesperean sets, my signal to depart.
Be strong, live happy, and love, but first of all
Him whom to love is to obey, and keep
His great command; take heed lest passion sway   635
Thy judgement to do aught which else free will
Would not admit; thine and of all thy sons
The weal or woe in thee is placed; beware.
I in thy persevering shall rejoice,
And all the blest; stand fast; to stand or fall   640
Free in thine own arbitrament it lies.
Perfect within, no outward aid require;
And all temptation to transgress repel.'

608 foiled] overcome.
510-11] *Metamorphoses* vii 20-1.
631 green cape] Cape Verde.
      verdant isles] the Cape Verde Islands.
632 Hesperean sets] i.e. sets in the west.
634-5] I John v. 3.
639 persevering] See VII 632n.

So saying, he arose; whom Adam thus
Followed with benediction: 'Since to part,   645
Go, heavenly guest, ethereal messenger,
Sent from whose sovereign goodness I adore.
Gentle to me and affable hath been
Thy condescension, and shall be honoured ever
With graceful memory; thou to mankind   650
Be good and friendly still, and oft return.'
So parted they, the angel up to heaven
From the thick shade, and Adam to his bower.

THE END OF THE EIGHTH BOOK

647 whose] him whose.

BOOK IX

THE ARGUMENT

Satan, having compassed the earth, with meditated guile returns
as a mist by night into Paradise; enters into the serpent sleeping.
Adam and Eve in the morning go forth to their labours, which Eve
proposes to divide in several places, each labouring apart: Adam
consents not, alleging the danger lest that enemy of whom they
were forewarned should attempt her found alone; Eve, loath to be
thought not circumspect or firm enough, urges her going apart, the
rather desirous to make trial of her strength; Adam at last yields;
the serpent finds her alone: his subtle approach, first gazing, then
speaking, with much flattery extolling Eve above all other
creatures. Eve, wondering to hear the serpent speak, asks how he
attained to human speech and such understanding not till now; the
serpent answers that by tasting of a certain tree in the garden he
attained both to speech and reason, till then void of both; Eve
requires him to bring her to that tree, and finds it to be the tree of
knowledge forbidden: the serpent, now grown bolder, with many
wiles and arguments induces her at length to eat; she, pleased with
the taste, deliberates a while whether to impart thereof to Adam or
not; at last brings him of the fruit; relates what persuaded her to
eat thereof; Adam, at first amazed, but perceiving her lost,
resolves, through vehemence of love, to perish with her, and
extenuating the trespass, eats also of the fruit; the effects thereof
in them both; they seek to cover their nakedness; then fall to
variance and accusation of one another.

No more of talk where God or angel guest
With man, as with his friend, familiar used
To sit indulgent, and with him partake
Rural repast, permitting him the while
Venial discourse unblamed; I now must change   5
Those notes to tragic – foul distrust, and breach
Disloyal, on the part of man, revolt
And disobedience; on the part of heaven,
Now alienated, distance and distaste,
Anger and just rebuke, and judgement given,   10
That brought into this world a world of woe,
Sin and her shadow Death, and Misery,
Death's harbinger; sad task, yet argument
Not less but more heroic than the wrath

2 familiar] The primary meaning is 'as in a family', but the word also evokes the
    phrase 'familiar (i.e. guardian) angel'.
5 Venial] permissible, blameless.
14–16] 'The wrath/Of stern Achilles' is the subject announced at the beginning
    of the *Iliad*; 'his foe' is Hector.

Of stern Achilles on his foe pursued   15
Thrice fugitive about Troy wall; or rage
Of Turnus for Lavinia disespoused;
Or Neptune's ire, or Juno's, that so long
Perplexed the Greek, and Cytherea's son:
In answerable style I can obtain   20
Of my celestial patroness, who deigns
Her nightly visitation unimplored,
And dictates to me slumbering, or inspires
Easy my unpremeditated verse,
Since first this subject for heroic song   25
Pleased me, long choosing and beginning late,
Not sedulous by nature to indite
Wars, hitherto the only argument
Heroic deemed, chief mastery to dissect
With long and tedious havoc fabled knights   30
In battles feigned – the better fortitude
Of patience and heroic martyrdom
Unsung – or to describe races and games,
Or tilting furniture, emblazoned shields,
Impreses quaint, caparisons and steeds,   35
Bases and tinsel trappings, gorgeous knights
At joust and tournament; then marshalled feast
Served up in hall with sewers and seneschals:
The skill of artifice or office mean,
Not that which justly gives heroic name   40
To person or to poem. Me, of these
Nor skilled nor studious, higher argument
Remains, sufficient of itself to raise
That name, unless an age too late, or cold
Climate, or years, damp my intended wing   45
Depressed; and much they may if all be mine,
Not hers who brings it nightly to my ear.
      The sun was sunk, and after him the star

17] In the *Aeneid* Turnus is the suitor of Lavinia; he is killed by Aeneas, who
      marries Lavinia himself.
18-19] In the *Odyssey* 'Neptune's ire' is directed against Odysseus ('the Greek')
      who had blinded Neptune's son, the Cyclops Polyphemus; in the *Aeneid*
      Juno's ire is directed against Aeneas, 'Cytherea's (i.e. Venus') son', who is so
      described because Juno's ire was prompted by Paris' judgement in favour
      of Venus (See V 381-2n.). 'Perplexed' means 'tormented'.
21 celestial patroness] Urania. See VII 1n.
34-8] Alludes to the characteristic preoccupations of romance epic. 'Tilting
      furniture' is armour; 'impreses' are emblems or devices, usually with a
      motto; 'caparisons' are the armour of horses; 'bases' are the cloth housings
      of horses; 'sewers' are waiters, and 'senseschals' are stewards.

Of Hesperus, whose office is to bring
Twilight upon the earth, short arbiter   50
'Twixt day and night, and now from end to end
Night's hemisphere had veiled the horizon round,
When Satan, who late fled before the threats
Of Gabriel out of Eden, now improved
In meditated fraud and malice, bent   55
On man's destruction, maugre what might hap
Of heavier on himself, fearless returned.
By night he fled, and at midnight returned
From compassing the earth – cautious of day
Since Uriel, regent of the sun, descried   60
His entrance, and forewarned the cherubim
That kept their watch; thence, full of anguish, driven,
The space of seven continued nights he rode
With darkness – thrice the equinoctial line
He circled, four times crossed the car of Night   65
From pole to pole, traversing each colure –
On the eighth returned, and on the coast averse
From entrance or cherubic watch by stealth
Found unsuspected way. There was a place –
Now not, though Sin, not Time, first wrought the change –
Where Tigris, at the foot of Paradise,   71
Into a gulf shot under ground, till part
Rose up a fountain by the tree of life;
In with the river sunk, and with it rose
Satan, involved in rising mist, then sought   75
Where to lie hid; sea he had searched and land
From Eden over Pontus, and the Pool
Maeotis, up beyond the river Ob;
Downward as far antarctic; and in length

54 improved] increased or augmented (in evil).
56 maugre] in spite of.
63–6] For the first three nights Satan circles the earth at the equator, which
    before the fall was on the same plane as the ecliptic. For the next four
    nights he follows the lines of the colures, i.e. the two great circles
    intersecting rectangularly at the poles, one passing through the equinoctial
    points of the ecliptic, and the other the solstitial points. It is difficult to
    understand how Satan could have stayed in continual darkness, for before
    the fall both poles were in perpetual light (cf. X, 680–7), and even after the
    fall one is always light.
73 fountain] See IV 229n.
75 involved] enveloped.
76–8] Satan travels northwards past Pontus (Pontus Euxinus, the Black Sea),
    'the Pool/Maeotis' (Palus Maeotis, the Sea of Asov), and 'the river Ob',
    which flows into Obskaya Guba and thence into the Arctic Ocean.

West from Orontes to the ocean barred   80
At Darien, thence to the land where flows
Ganges and Indus; thus the orb he roamed
With narrow search, and with inspection deep
Considered every creature, which of all
Most opportune might serve his wiles, and found   85
The serpent subtlest beast of all the field.
Him, after long debate, irresolute
Of thoughts revolved, his final sentence chose
Fit vessel, fittest imp of fraud, in whom
To enter, and his dark suggestions hide   90
From sharpest sight; for in the wily snake
Whatever sleights none would suspicious mark,
As from his wit and native subtlety
Proceeding, which, in other beasts observed,
Doubt might beget of diabolic power   95
Active within beyond the sense of brute.
Thus he resolved, but first from inward grief
His bursting passion into plaints thus poured:
    'O earth, how like to heaven, if not preferred
More justly, seat worthier of gods, as built   100
With second thought, reforming what was old!
For what god, after better, worse would build?
Terrestrial heaven, danced round by other heavens,
That shine, yet bear their bright officious lamps,
Light above light, for thee alone, as seems,   105
In thee concentring all their precious beams
Of sacred influence; as God in heaven
Is centre, yet extends to all, so thou
Centring receiv'st from all those orbs; in thee,
Not in themselves, all their known virtue appears,   110
Productive in herb, plant, and nobler birth
Of creatures animate with gradual life
Of growth, sense, reason, all summed up in man.
With what delight could I have walked thee round,
If I could joy in aught – sweet interchange   115
Of hill and valley, rivers, woods, and plains,
Now land, now sea, and shores with forest crowned,
Rocks, dens, and caves; but I in none of these

80-2] Satan travels westwards past the Orontes River, in Turkey and Syria (see
    IV 272-4n.) to the Pacific Ocean, which is 'barred' (see Job xxxviii. 8-11)
    by Darien (a district in Panama), and thence to India.
89 imp] child.
95 Doubt] suspicion.
112 gradual] arranged in grades (cf. V 483).

Find place or refuge; and the more I see
Pleasures about me, so much more I feel   120
Torment within me, as from the hateful siege
Of contraries; all good to me becomes
Bane, and in heaven much worse would be my state.
But neither here seek I, no, nor in heaven,
To dwell, unless by mastering heaven's supreme;   125
Nor hope to be myself less miserable
By what I seek, but others to make such
As I, though thereby worse to me redound;
For only in destroying I find ease
To my relentless thoughts; and him destroyed,   130
Or won to what may work his utter loss,
For whom all this was made, all this will soon
Follow, as to him linked in weal or woe:
In woe then, that destruction wide may range;
To me shall be the glory sole among   135
The infernal powers, in one day to have marred
What he, almighty styled, six nights and days
Continued making, and who knows how long
Before had been contriving, though perhaps
Not longer than since I in one night freed   140
From servitude inglorious well-nigh half
The angelic name, and thinner left the throng
Of his adorers; he, to be avenged,
And to repair his numbers thus impaired –
Whether such virtue, spent of old, now failed   145
More angels to create – if they at least
Are his created – or to spite us more,
Determined to advance into our room
A creature formed of earth, and him endow,
Exalted from so base original,   150
With heavenly spoils, our spoils; what he decreed
He effected; man he made, and for him built
Magnificent this world, and earth his seat,
Him lord pronounced, and, O indignity!
Subjected to his service angel wings   155
And flaming ministers, to watch and tend
Their earthy charge; of these the vigilance
I dread, and to elude, thus wrapped in mist
Of midnight vapour, glide obscure, and pry
In every bush and brake, where hap may find   160
The serpent sleeping, in whose mazy folds
To hide me, and the dark intent I bring.

155-7] Psalms civ. 4, xci. 11, Heb. i. 14.

O foul descent! That I, who erst contended
With gods to sit the highest, am now constrained
Into a beast, and mixed with bestial slime,   165
This essence to incarnate and imbrute,
That to the height of deity aspired;
But what will not ambition and revenge
Descend to? Who aspires must down as low
As high he soared, obnoxious, first or last,   170
To basest things. Revenge, at first though sweet,
Bitter ere long back on itself recoils;
Let it; I reck not, so it light well aimed,
Since higher I fall short, on him who next
Provokes my envy, this new favourite   175
Of heaven, this man of clay, son of despite,
Whom, us the more to spite, his maker raised
From dust: spite then with spite is best repaid.'
    So saying, through each thicket, dank or dry,
Like a black mist low creeping, he held on   180
His midnight search, where soonest he might find
The serpent; him fast sleeping soon he found
In labyrinth of many a sound self-rolled,
His head the midst, well stored with subtle wiles:
Not yet in horrid shade or dismal den,   185
Nor nocent yet, but on the grassy herb,
Fearless, unfeared, he slept; in at his mouth
The devil entered, and his brutal sense,
In heart or head, possessing soon inspired
With act intelligential; but his sleep   190
Disturbed not, waiting close the approach of morn.
    Now, whenas sacred light began to dawn
In Eden on the humid flowers, that breathed
Their morning incense, when all things that breathe
From the earth's great altar send up silent praise   195
To the creator, and his nostrils fill
With grateful smell, forth came the human pair,
And joined their vocal worship to the choir
Of creatures wanting voice; that done, partake
The season, prime for sweetest scents and airs;   200
Then commune how that day they best may ply

170 obnoxious] exposed, liable (to an influence).
185 horrid] means both 'shaggy, rough' and 'causing horror'.
186 nocent] means both 'guilty' and 'harmful'.
188 brutal] pertaining to animals.
195-7] Gen. viii. 21.
200 season] i.e. early morning.

Their growing work – for much their work outgrew
The hands' dispatch of two, gardening so wide.
And Eve first to her husband thus began:
   'Adam, well may we labour still to dress   205
This garden, still to tend plant, herb, and flower,
Our pleasant task enjoined; but, till more hands
Aid us, the work under our labour grows,
Luxurious by restraint: what we by day
Lop overgrown, or prune, or prop, or bind,   210
One night or two with wanton growth derides,
Tending to wild. Thou, therefore, now advise,
Or hear what to my mind first thoughts present;
Let us divide our labours – thou where choice
Leads thee, or where most needs, whether to wind   215
The woodbine round this arbour, or direct
The clasping ivy where to climb, while I
In yonder spring of roses intermixed
With myrtle find what to redress till noon;
For, while so near each other thus all day   220
Our task we choose, what wonder if so near
Looks intervene and smiles, or objects new
Casual discourse draw on, which intermits
Our day's work, brought to little, though begun
Early, and the hour of supper comes unearned.'   225
   To whom mild answer Adam thus returned:
'Sole Eve, associate sole, to me beyond
Compare above all living creatures dear,
Well hast thou motioned, well thy thoughts employed
How we might best fulfil the work which here   230
God hath assigned us, nor of me shalt pass
Unpraised; for nothing lovelier can be found
In woman than to study household good,
And good works in her husband to promote.
Yet not so strictly hath our Lord imposed   235
Labour as to debar us when we need
Refreshment, whether food or talk between,
Food of the mind, or this sweet intercourse
Of looks and smiles; for smiles from reason flow
To brute denied, and are of love the food –   240
Love, not the lowest end of human life.

217 where to climb] i.e. on the elm. See V 215-19n.
218 spring] a plantation of young trees.
219 redress] set upright again, direct to the right course.
229 motioned] offered a plan.
233] Prov. xxxi. 27.

For not to irksome toil, but to delight,
He made us, and delight to reason joined.
These paths and bowers doubt not but our joint hands
Will keep from wilderness with ease, as wide   245
As we need walk, till younger hands ere long
Assist us; but, if much converse perhaps
Thee satiate, to short absence I could yield;
For solitude sometimes is best society,
And short retirement urges sweet return.   250
But other doubt possesses me, lest harm
Befall thee, severed from me; for thou know'st
What hath been warned us – what malicious foe,
Envying our happiness, and of his own
Despairing, seeks to work us woe and shame   255
By sly assault, and somewhere nigh at hand
Watches, no doubt, with greedy hope to find
His wish and best advantage, us asunder,
Hopeless to circumvent us joined, where each
To other speedy aid might lend at need;   260
Whether his first design be to withdraw
Our fealty from God, or to disturb
Conjugal love – than which perhaps no bliss
Enjoyed by us excites his envy more –
Or this, or worse, leave not the faithful side   265
That gave thee being, still shades thee and protects.
The wife, where danger or dishonour lurks,
Safest and seemliest by her husband stays,
Who guards her, or with her the worst endures.'
        To whom the virgin majesty of Eve,   270
As one who loves, and some unkindness meets,
With sweet austere composure thus replied:
        'Offspring of heaven and earth, and all earth's lord,
That such an enemy we have, who seeks
Our ruin, both by thee informed I learn,   275
And from the parting angel overheard,
As in a shady nook I stood behind,
Just then returned at shut of evening flowers.
But that thou shouldst my firmness therefore doubt
To God or thee, because we have a foe   280
May tempt it, I expected not to hear.
His violence thou fear'st not, being such
As we, not capable of death or pain,

249] Cf. VIII 427-8n.
265 Or] whether.
270 virgin] innocent, chaste.

Can either not receive, or can repel.
His fraud is, then, thy fear; which plain infers   285
Thy equal fear that my firm faith and love
Can by his fraud be shaken or seduced:
Thoughts, which how found they harbour in thy breast,
Adam, misthought of her to thee so dear?'
  To whom, with healing words, Adam replied: 290
'Daughter of God and man, immortal Eve –
For such thou art, from sin and blame entire –
Not diffident of thee do I dissuade
Thy absence from my sight, but to avoid
The attempt itself, intended by our foe.   295
For he who tempts, though in vain, at least asperses
The tempted with dishonour foul, supposed
Not incorruptible of faith, not proof
Against temptation; thou thyself with scorn
And anger wouldst resent the offered wrong,   300
Though ineffectual found; misdeem not then,
If such affront I labour to avert
From thee alone, which on us both at once
The enemy, though bold, will hardly dare;
Or daring, first on me the assault shall light.   305
Nor thou his malice and false guile contemn –
Subtle he needs must be who could seduce
Angels – nor think superfluous others' aid.
I from the influence of thy looks receive
Access in every virtue – in thy sight   310
More wise, more watchful, stronger, if need were
Of outward strength; while shame, thou looking on,
Shame to be overcome or overreached,
Would utmost vigour raise, and raised unite.
Why shouldst not thou like sense within thee feel   315
When I am present, and thy trial choose
With me, best witness of thy virtue tried?'
  So spake domestic Adam in his care
And matrimonial love; but Eve, who thought
Less áttributed to her faith sincere,   320
Thus her reply with accent sweet renewed –
  'If this be our condition, thus to dwell

292 entire] free from reproach, blameless.
293 diffident] distrustful (cf. VIII 562).
296 asperses] injuriously and falsely bespatters.
310 Access] increase.
320 Less] too little (by analogy to the Latin comparative *minor*).
    sincere] pure. The Protestant catch-phrase *fides sincera* derives from the
    use of the word in I Pet. ii. 2.

In narrow circuit straitened by a foe,
Subtle or violent, we not endued
Single with like defence wherever met,   325
How are we happy, still in fear of harm?
But harm precedes not sin: only our foe
Tempting affronts us with his foul esteem
Of our integrity: his foul esteem
Sticks no dishonour on our front, but turns   330
Foul on himself; when wherefore shunned or feared
By us, who rather double honour gain
From his surmise proved false, find peace within,
Favour from heaven, our witness, from the event?
And what is faith, love, virtue, unassayed   335
Alone, without exterior help sustained?
Let us not then suspect our happy state
Left so imperfect by the maker wise
As not secure to single or combined;
Frail is our happiness, if this be so,   340
And Eden were no Eden, thus exposed.'
     To whom thus Adam fervently replied:
'O woman, best are all things as the will
Of God ordained them; his creating hand
Nothing imperfect or deficient left   345
Of all that he created – much less man,
Or aught that might his happy state secure,
Secure from outward force; within himself
The danger lies, yet lies within his power;
Against his will he can receive no harm.   350
But God left free the will, for what obeys
Reason is free; and reason he made right,
But bid her well beware, and still erect,
Lest by some fair appearing good surprised,
She dictate false, and misinform the will   355
To do what God expressly hath forbid.
Not then mistrust, but tender love enjoins
That I should mind thee oft; and mind thou me.
Firm we subsist, yet possible to swerve,
Since reason not impossibly may meet   360
Some specious object by the foe suborned,
And fall into deception unaware,

328 affronts] means both 'insults' and, as Eve's use of 'front' in l. 330 indicates,
    'sets face to face'.
341 no Eden] i.e. no pleasure. See IV 27-8n.
352 reason ... right] See VI 42n.
353 still erect] unceasingly alert (with a suggestion of 'directed upwards').

Not keeping strictest watch, as she was warned.
Seek not temptation, then, which to avoid
Were better, and most likely if from me   365
Thou sever not: trial will come unsought.
Wouldst thou approve thy constancy, approve
First thy obedience; the other who can know,
Not seeing thee attempted, who attest?
But if thou think trial unsought may find   370
Us both securer than thus warned thou seem'st,
Go; for thy stay, not free, absents thee more;
Go in thy native innocence; rely
On what thou hast of virtue; summon all;
For God towards thee hath done his part: do thine.'   375
    So spake the patriarch of mankind; but Eve
Persisted; yet submiss, though last, replied:
    'With thy permission, then, and thus forewarned,
Chiefly by what thy own last reasoning words
Touched only, that our trial, when least sought,   380
May find us both perhaps far less prepared,
The willinger I go, nor much expect
A foe so proud will first the weaker seek;
So bent, the more shall shame him his repulse.'
    Thus saying, from her husband's hand her hand   385
Soft she withdrew, and like a wood-nymph light,
Oread or dryad, or of Delia's train,
Betook her to the groves, but Delia's self
In gait surpassed and goddess-like deport,
Though not as she with bow and quiver armed,   390
But with such gardening tools as art, yet rude,
Guiltless of fire had formed, or angels brought.
To Pales, or Pomona, thus adorned,
Likest she seemed – Pomana when she fled
Vertumnus – or to Ceres in her prime,   395

---

367 approve] prove.
371 securer] more overconfident.
385–6] Cf. IV 321n.; 'light' means both 'swift, agile' and 'unsteady, susceptible
    to slight pressure'.
387] Oreads are mountain nymphs, the favourite companions of Diana (*Aeneid* i
    500), and dryads are nymphs of forests and groves; both are mortal
    (*Metamorphoses* viii 771). Delia is Diana, who is so called after her
    birthplace, Delos.
393] Pales was the Roman goddess of flocks and shepherds; on Pomona see V
    378n.
395 Vertumnus] a Roman deity associated with the changing seasons and the
    effect of the seasons on vegetation; he assumed a series of disguises, and was
    thus able to seduce Pomona (*Metamorphoses* xiv 623–771).

Yet virgin of Proserpina from Jove.
Her long with ardent look his eye pursued
Delighted, but desiring more her stay.
Oft he to her his charge of quick return
Repeated; she to him as oft engaged   400
To be returned by noon amid the bower,
And all things in best order to invite
Noontide repast, or afternoon's repose.
O much deceived, much failing, hapless Eve,
Of thy presumed return! Event perverse!   405
Thou never from that hour in Paradise
Found'st either sweet repast or sound repose;
Such ambush, hid among sweet flowers and shades,
Waited, with hellish rancour imminent,
To intercept thy way, or send thee back   410
Despoiled of innocence, of faith, of bliss.
For now, and since first break of dawn, the fiend,
Mere serpent in appearance, forth was come,
And on his quest where likeliest he might find
The only two of mankind, but in them   415
The whole included race, his purposed prey.
In bower and field he sought, where any tuft
Of grove or garden-plot more pleasant lay,
Their tendance or plantation for delight;
By fountain or by shady rivulet   420
He sought them both, but wished his hap might find
Eve separate; he wished, but not with hope
Of what so seldom chanced, when to his wish,
Beyond his hope, Eve separate he spies,
Veiled in a cloud of fragrance, where she stood,   425
Half-spied, so thick the roses bushing round
About her glowed, oft stooping to support
Each flower of tender stalk, whose head, though gay
Carnation, purple, azure, or specked with gold,
Hung drooping unsustained; them she upstays   430
Gently with myrtle band, mindless the while
Herself, though fairest unsupported flower,
From her best prop so far, and storm so nigh.
Nearer he drew, and many a walk traversed
Of stateliest covert, cedar, pine, or palm;   435
Then voluble and bold, now hid, now seen
Among thick-woven arborets, and flowers

395-6] See IV 268-72n.
421 hap] fortune, chance.
436 voluble] moving rapidly with an undulating movement.
437 arborets] little trees, shrubs.

Embordered on each bank, the hand of Eve:
Spot more delicious than those gardens feigned
Or of revived Adonis, or renowned   440
Alcinous, host of old Laertes' son,
Or that, not mystic, where the sapient king
Held dalliance with his fair Egyptian spouse.
Much he the place admired, the person more.
As one who long in populous city pent,   445
Where houses thick and sewers annoy the air,
Forth issuing on a summer's morn, to breathe
Among the pleasant villages and farms
Adjoined, from each thing met conceives delight –
The smell of grain, or tedded grass, or kine,   450
Or dairy, each rural sight, each rural sound –
If chance with nymph-like step fair virgin pass,
What pleasing seemed, for her now pleases more,
She most, and in her look sums all delight:
Such pleasure took the serpent to behold   455
This flowery plat, the sweet recess of Eve
Thus early, thus alone; her heavenly form
Angelic, but more soft and feminine,
Her graceful innocence, her every air
Of gesture or least action, overawed   460
His malice, and with rapine sweet bereaved
His fierceness of the fierce intent it brought.
That space the evil one abstracted stood
From his own evil, and for the time remained
Stupidly good, of enmity disarmed,   465
Of guile, of hate, of envy, of revenge;
But the hot hell that always in him burns,
Though in mid heaven, soon ended his delight
And tortures him now more, the more he sees
Of pleasure not for him ordained; then soon   470
Fierce hate he recollects, and all his thoughts

---

438 hand] handiwork.
440] See *Comus* 996-1011n.
441] See V 339-41n. Laertes' son is Odysseus.
442-3] Solomon married a daughter of the Pharaoh (I Kings iii. 1); on the
    garden see Song of Solomon, passim. Solomon is 'sapient' in Kings and
    Chronicles, but Milton also exploits the Latin sense of wisdom (*sapientia*) as
    a kind of taste. (cf. ll. 1017-20).
46 annoy] affect injuriously.
450 tedded] spread out for drying.
    kine] cows.
453 for] because of.
456 plat] patch of ground.

Of mischief, gratulating, thus excites:
　'Thoughts, whither have ye led me? With what sweet
Compulsion thus transported to forget
What hither brought us? Hate, not love, nor hope　　　475
Of Paradise for hell, hope here to taste
Of pleasure, but all pleasure to destroy,
Save what is in destroying; other joy
To me is lost. Then let me not let pass
Occasion which now smiles; behold alone　　　　　　480
The woman, opportune to all attempts –
Her husband, for I view far round, not nigh,
Whose higher intellectual more I shun,
And strength, of courage haughty, and of limb
Heroic built, though of terrestrial mould;　　　　485
Foe not informidable, exempt from wound –
I not; so much hath hell debased, and pain
Enfeebled me, to what I was in heaven.
She fair, divinely fair, fit love for gods,
Not terrible, though terror be in love,　　　　　490
And beauty, not approached by stronger hate,
Hate stronger under show of love well feigned –
The way which to her ruin now I tend.'
　So spake the enemy of mankind, enclosed
In serpent, inmate bad, and toward Eve　　　　　495
Addressed his way – not with indented wave,
Prone on the ground, as since, but on his rear,
Circular base of rising folds, that towered
Fold above fold, a surging maze; his head
Crested aloft, and carbuncle his eyes;　　　　　500
With burnished neck of verdant gold, erect
Amidst his circling spires, that on the grass
Floated redundant; pleasing was his shape
And lovely; never since of serpent kind
Lovelier – not those that in Illyria changed　　　505
Hermione and Cadmus, or the god

---

472 gratulating] manifesting joy (in meeting Eve).
481 opportune] conveniently exposed.
491 not] if not.
496 indented] having a zigzag course.
503 redundant] in swelling waves.
505-6] Cadmus, son of the King of Tyre, went in his old age to Illyria (an
　　ancient kingdom which corresponds to modern Albania), where he and his
　　wife Harmonia (Hermione) were turned into serpents (*Metamorphoses* iv
　　563-603).
506-7] Epidaurus was the sanctuary of Aesculapius (the god of healing), who
　　turned himself into a serpent to travel to Rome to deal with a plague
　　(*Metamorphoses* xv 622-744).

In Epidaurus; nor to which transformed
Ammonian Jove, or Capitoline, was seen,
He with Olympias, this with her who bore
Scipio, the height of Rome. With tract oblique　　　510
At first, as one who sought access but feared
To interrupt, sidelong he works his way.
As when a ship, by skilful steersman wrought
Nigh river's mouth, or foreland, where the wind
Veers oft, as oft so steers, and shifts her sail,　　　515
So varied he, and of his tortuous train
Curled many a wanton wreath in sight of Eve,
To lure her eye; she, busied, heard the sound
Of rustling leaves, but minded not, as used
To such disport before her through the field　　　520
From every beast, more duteous at her call
Than at Circean call the herd disguised.
He bolder now, uncalled before her stood,
But as in gaze admiring; oft he bowed
His turret crest and sleek enamelled neck,　　　525
Fawning, and licked the ground whereon she trod.
His gentle dumb expression turned at length
The eye of Eve to mark his play; he, glad
Of her attention gained, with serpent tongue
Organic, or impulse of vocal air,　　　530
His fraudulent temptation thus began:
　'Wonder not, sovereign mistress – if perhaps
Thou canst who are sole wonder – much less arm
Thy looks, the heaven of mildness, with disdain,
Displeased that I approach thee thus, and gaze　　　535
Insatiate, I thus single, nor have feared

507–9] Ammonian Jove (see IV 275–9n.) assumed the form of a serpent and
became the father of Alexander the Great, whose mother was Olympias.
Cf. *PR* III 84.

508–10] The Capitol is the hill in Rome on which stood the Temple of Jupiter
(hence Capitoline). In antiquity many parallels were drawn between the
lives of Scipio Africanus and Alexander, and Scipio was accordingly said to
have been the son of Jupiter Capitolinus, who took the form of a serpent.

510 tract] track, course.

510–14] The initial letters of these lines may be a deliberate acrostic:
S-A-T-A-N.

522] The 'herd disguised' are those who had been turned into wolves and lions
by Circe. Homer compares them to dogs fawning on their master (*Odyssey* x
212–19).

525 enamelled] Cf. IV 149n.

530 Organic] like an organ or instrument.
impulse] the primary meaning is 'application of sudden force', but the word
also carries the secondary meaning of 'a suggestion coming from an evil
spirit'.

Thy awful brow, more awful thus retired.
Fairest resemblance of thy maker fair,
Thee all things living gaze on, all things thine
By gift, and thy celestial beauty adore,   540
With ravishment beheld – there best beheld
Where universally admired; but here
In this enclosure wild, these beasts among,
Beholders rude, and shallow to discern
Half what in thee is fair, one man except,   545
Who sees thee (and what is one?) who shouldst be seen
A goddess among gods, adored and served
By angels numberless, thy daily train?'
So glozed the tempter, and his proem tuned.
Into the heart of Eve his words made way,   550
Though at the voice much marvelling; at length,
Not unamazed, she thus in answer spake:
    'What may this mean? Language of man pronounced
By tongue of brute, and human sense expressed?
The first at least of these I thought denied   555
To beasts, whom God on their creation-day
Created mute to all articulate sound;
The latter I demur, for in their looks
Much reason, and in their actions, oft appears.
Thee, serpent, subtlest beast of all the field   560
I knew, but not with human voice endued;
Redouble then this miracle, and say,
How cam'st thou speakable of mute, and how
To me so friendly grown above the rest
Of brutal kind that daily are in sight: 565
Say, for such wonder claims attention due.'
    To whom the guileful tempter thus replied:
'Empress of this fair world, resplendent Eve,
Easy to me it is to tell thee all
What thou command'st, and right thou shouldst be
        obeyed;
I was at first as other beasts that graze   571
The trodden herb, of abject thoughts and low,
As was my food, nor aught but food discerned
Or sex, and apprehended nothing high:
Till on a day, roving the field, I chanced   575
A goodly tree far distant to behold,
Loaden with fruit of fairest colours mixed,
Ruddy and gold; I nearer drew to gaze,
When from the boughs a savoury odour blown,

549 proem] prelude.
558 demur] to hesitate about.
579 savoury] Cf. V 84n.

Grateful to appetite, more pleased my sense   580
Than smell of sweetest fennel, or the teats
Of ewe or goat dropping with milk at even,
Unsucked of lamb or kid, that tend their play.
To satisfy the sharp desire I had
Of tasting those fair apples, I resolved   585
Not to defer; hunger and thirst at once,
Powerful persuaders, quickened at the scent
Of that alluring fruit, urged me so keen.
About the mossy trunk I wound me soon,
For, high from ground, the branches would require   590
Thy utmost reach, or Adam's: round the tree
All other beasts that saw, with like desire
Longing and envying stood, but could not reach.
Amid the tree now got, where plenty hung
Tempting so nigh, to pluck and eat my fill   595
I spared not, for such pleasure till that hour
At feed or fountain never had I found.
Sated at length, ere long I might perceive
Strange alteration in me, to degree
Of reason in my inward powers, and speech   600
Wanted not long, though to this shape retained.
Thenceforth to speculations high or deep
I turned my thoughts, and with capacious mind
Considered all things visible in heaven,
Or earth, or middle, all things fair and good;   605
But all that fair and good in thy divine
Semblance and in thy beauty's heavenly ray,
United I beheld – no fair to thine
Equivalent or second; which compelled
Me thus, though importune perhaps, to come   610
And gaze, and worship thee of right declared
Sovereign of creatures, universal dame.'
      So talked the spirited sly snake; and Eve,
Yet more amazed, unwary thus replied:
      'Serpent, thy overpraising leaves in doubt   615
The virtue of that fruit, in thee first proved;
But say, where grows the tree? From hence how far?

581-3] Serpents were believed to sharpen their sight with fennel, and to suck
    milk from animals. Fennel was also a common emblem of pride.
605 middle] i.e. between heaven and earth.
609] Horace. *Odes* I. xii. 18.
612 universal dame] mistress of the universe.
613 spirited] means both 'lively' and 'possessed by a spirit'.
614 amazed] means 'bewildered', but also refers to the agent of bewilderment,
    the serpent's 'maze' (l. 499).

For many are the trees of God that grow
In Paradise, and various, yet unknown
To us; in such abundance lies our choice   620
As leaves a greater store of fruit untouched,
Still hanging incorruptible, till men
Grow up to their provision, and more hands
Help to disburden nature of her birth.'
    To whom the wily adder, blithe and glad: 625
'Empress, the way is ready, and not long –
Beyond a row of myrtles, on a flat,
Fast by a fountain, one small thicket past
Of blowing myrrh and balm; if thou accept
My conduct, I can bring thee thither soon.'   630
    'Lead, then,' said Eve. He leading swiftly rolled
In tangles, and made intricate seem straight,
To mischief swift. Hope elevates, and joy
Brightens his crest; as when a wandering fire,
Compact of unctuous vapour, which the night   635
Condenses, and the cold environs round,
Kindled through agitation to a flame –
Which oft, they say, some evil spirit attends –
Hovering and blazing with delusive light,
Misleads the amazed night-wanderer from his way   640
To bogs and mires, and oft through pond or pool,
There swallowed up and lost, from succour far;
So glistered the dire snake, and into fraud
Led Eve, our credulous mother, to the tree
Of prohibition, root of all our woe;   645
Which when she saw, thus to her guide she spake:
    'Serpent, we might have spared our coming hither,
Fruitless to me, though fruit be here to excess,
The credit of whose virtue rest with thee –
Wondrous indeed, if cause of such effects.   650
But of this tree we may not taste nor touch;
God so commanded, and left that command
Sole daughter of his voice: the rest, we live
Law to ourselves; our reason is our law.'
    To whom the tempter guilefully replied: 655
'Indeed? Hath God then said that of the fruit
Of all these garden-trees ye shall not eat,
Yet lords declared of all in earth or air?'

629 blowing] blooming.
635 Compact] composed.
643 fraud] Cf. VII 143n.
654 Rom. ii. 14.

To whom thus Eve, yet sinless: 'Of the fruit
Of each tree in the garden we may eat;   660
But of the fruit of this fair free, amidst
The garden, God hath said, "Ye shall not eat
Thereof, nor shall ye touch it, lest ye die." '
She scarce had said, though brief, when now more bold
The tempter, but with show of zeal and love   665
To man, and indignation at his wrong,
New part puts on, and as to passion moved,
Fluctuates disturbed, yet comely, and in act
Raised, as of some great matter to begin.
As when of old some orator renowned   670
In Athens or free Rome, where eloquence
Flourished, since mute, to some great cause addressed,
Stood in himself collected, while each part,
Motion, each act, won audience ere the tongue
Sometimes in height began, as no delay   675
Of preface brooking through his zeal of right:
So standing, moving, or to height upgrown,
The tempter, all impassioned, thus began:
     'O sacred, wise, and wisdom-giving plant,
Mother of science, now I feel thy power   680
Within me clear, not only to discern
Things in their causes, but to trace the ways
Of highest agents, deemed however wise.
Queen of this universe, do not believe
Those rigid threats of death; ye shall not die;   685
How should ye? By the fruit? It gives you life
To knowledge. By the threatener? Look on me,
Me who have touched and tasted, yet both live,
And life more perfect have attained than fate
Meant me, by venturing higher than my lot.   690
Shall that be shut to man which to the beast
Is open? Or will God incense his ire
For such a petty trespass, and not praise
Rather your dauntless virtue, whom the pain
Of death denounced, whatever thing death be,   695
Deterred not from achieving what might lead
To happier life, knowledge of good and evil?
Of good, how just! Of evil – if what is evil
Be real, why not known, since easier shunned?
God therefore cannot hurt ye, and be just;   700
Not just, not God; not feared then, nor obeyed;

680 science] knowledge.
687 To] as well as.

Your fear itself of death removes the fear.
Why then was this forbid? Why but to awe,
Why but to keep ye low and ignorant,
His worshippers? He knows that in the day   705
Ye eat thereof your eyes that seem so clear,
Yet are but dim, shall perfectly be then
Opened and cleared, and ye shall be as gods,
Knowing both good and evil, as they know.
That ye should be as gods, since I as man,   710
Internal man, is but proportion meet –
I, of brute, human; ye, of human, gods.
So ye shall die perhaps, by putting off
Human, to put on gods – death to be wished,
Though threatened, which no worse than this can bring.
And what are gods, that man may not become   716
As they, participating godlike food?
The gods are first, and that advantage use
On our belief, that all from them proceeds;
I question it, for this fair earth I see,   720
Warmed by the sun, producing every kind,
Them nothing; if they all things, who enclosed
Knowledge of good and evil in this tree,
That whoso eats thereof forthwith attains
Wisdom without their leave? And wherein lies   725
The offence, that man should thus attain to know?
What can your knowledge hurt him, or this tree
Impart against his will, if all be his?
Or is it envy? And can envy dwell
In heavenly breasts? These, these and many more   730
Causes import your need of this fair fruit.
Goddess humane, reach then, and freely taste.'

He ended, and his words, replete with guile,
Into her heart too easy entrance won;
Fixed on the fruit she gazed, which to behold   735
Might tempt alone; and in her ears the sound
Yet rung of his persuasive words, impregned
With reason, to her seeming, and with truth;
Meanwhile the hour of noon drew on, and waked
An eager appetite, raised by the smell   740
So savoury of that fruit, which with desire,

713-14] parodies a common N.T. metaphor (e.g. Eph. iv. 22-4, Col. iii. 1-10).
717 participating] partaking of.
722 they all] i.e. they produce all.
731 import] involve as a consequence.
732 humane] means both 'human' and 'gracious'.

Inclinable now grown to touch or taste,
Solicited her longing eye; yet first,
Pausing a while, thus to herself she mused:
   'Great are thy virtues, doubtless, best of fruits   745
Though kept from man, and worthy to be admired,
Whose taste, too long forborne, at first assay
Gave elocution to the mute, and taught
The tongue not made for speech to speak thy praise;
Thy praise he also who forbids thy use   750
Conceals not from us, naming thee the tree
Of knowledge, knowledge both of good and evil;
Forbids us then to taste; but his forbidding
Commends thee more, while it infers the good
By thee communicated, and our want;   755
For good unknown sure is not had, or had
And yet unknown, is as not had at all.
In plain, then, what forbids he but to know?
Forbids us good, forbids us to be wise!
Such prohibitions bind not. But, if death   760
Bind us with after-bands, what profits then
Our inward freedom? In the day we eat
Of this fair fruit, our doom is we shall die.
How dies the serpent? He hath eaten, and lives,
And knows, and speaks, and reasons, and discerns,   765
Irrational till then. For us alone
Was death invented? Or to us denied
This intellectual food, for beasts reserved?
For beasts it seems; yet that one beast which first
Hath tasted envies not, but brings with joy   770
The good befallen him, author unsuspect,
Friendly to man, far from deceit or guile.
What fear I, then? Rather, what know to fear
Under this ignorance of good and evil,
Of God or death, of law or penalty?   775
Here grows the cure of all, this fruit divine,
Fair to the eye, inviting to the taste,
Of virtue to make wise; what hinders, then,
To reach, and feed at once both body and mind?'
   So saying, her rash hand in evil hour   780
Forth reaching to the fruit, she plucked, she ate;
Earth felt the wound, and nature from her seat,
Sighing through all her works, gave signs of woe
That all was lost. Back to the thicket slunk

758 In plain] plainly.
7712 author unsuspect] authority not subject to suspicion.

The guilty serpent, and well might, for Eve,   785
Intent now only on her taste, naught else
Regarded; such delight till then, as seemed,
In fruit she never tasted, whether true,
Or fancied so through expectation high
Of knowledge; nor was godhead from her thought.   790
Greedily she engorged without restraint,
And knew not eating death; satiate at length,
And heightened as with wine, jocund and boon,
Thus to herself she pleasingly began:
    'O sovereign, virtuous, precious of all trees   795
In Paradise, of operation blest
To sapience, hitherto obscured, infamed,
And thy fair fruit let hang, as to no end
Created; but henceforth my early care,
Not without song, each morning, and due praise,   800
Shall tend thee, and the fertile burden ease
Of thy full branches, offered free to all;
Till dieted by thee I grow mature
In knowledge, as the gods who all things know;
Though others envy what they cannot give –   805
For had the gift been theirs, it had not here
Thus grown. Experience, next to thee I owe,
Best guide: not following thee, I had remained
In ignorance; thou open'st wisdom's way,
And giv'st access, though secret she retire.   810
And I perhaps am secret: heaven is high –
High, and remote to see from thence distinct
Each thing on earth; and other care perhaps
May have diverted from continual watch
Our great forbidder, safe with all his spies   815
About him. But to Adam in what sort
Shall I appear? Shall I to him make known
As yet my change, and give him to partake
Full happiness with me, or rather not,
But keep the odds of knowledge in my power   820
Without copartner? So to add what wants
In female sex, the more to draw his love,
And render me more equal, and perhaps –

---

792 eating] i.e. that she was eating. The phrase imitates a Greek construction in
     which the verb 'to know' is followed by a participle (in the nominative)
     without repetition of subject.
795 virtuous, precious] most virtuous, most precious; in Greek and Latin the
     positive can stand for the superlative.
811–13] Job xxii. 13–14, Psalms x. 11, xciv. 7.
815 safe] unlikely to intervene, not at present dangerous.

A thing not undesirable – sometime
Superior; for, inferior, who is free?   825
This may be well; but what if God have seen,
And death ensue? Then I shall be no more;
And Adam, wedded to another Eve,
Shall live with her enjoying, I extinct;
A death to think. Confirmed, then, I resolve   830
Adam shall share with me in bliss or woe;
So dear I love him that with him all deaths
I could endure, without him live no life.'
   So saying, from the tree her step she turned,
But first low reverence done, as to the power   835
That dwelt within, whose presence had infused
Into the plant sciential sap, derived
From nectar, drink of gods. Adam the while,
Waiting desirous her return, had wove
Of choicest flowers a garland to adorn   840
Her tresses, and her rural labours crown,
As reapers oft are wont their harvest queen.
Great joy he promised to his thoughts, and new
Solace in her return, so long delayed;
Yet oft his heart, divine of something ill,   845
Misgave him; he the faltering measure felt,
And forth to meet her went, the way she took
That morn when first they parted; by the tree
Of knowledge he must pass; there he her met,
Scarce from the tree returning; in her hand   850
A bough of fairest fruit, that downy smiled,
New gathered, and ambrosial smell diffused.
To him she hasted; in her face excuse
Came prologue, and apology to prompt,
Which with bland words at will, she thus addressed: 855
   'Hast thou not wondered, Adam, at my stay?
Thee I have missed, and thought it long, deprived
Thy presence – agony of love till now
Not felt, nor shall be twice; for never more
Mean I to try, what rash untried I sought,   860
The pain of absence from thy sight. But strange
Hath been the cause, and wonderful to hear;

832-3] Horace, *Odes* III. ix. 24.
837 sciential] infused with knowledge.
838-41] Cf. *Iliad* xxii 437 ff.
845 divine] diviner.
846 measure] i.e. his heartbeat.
854 apology] defence (not an expression of regret).

This tree is not, as we are told, a tree
Of danger tasted, nor to evil unknown
Opening the way, but of divine effect   865
To open eyes, and make them gods who taste;
And hath been tasted such; the serpent wise,
Or not restrained as we, or not obeying,
Hath eaten of the fruit, and is become
Not dead, as we are threatened, but thenceforth   870
Endued with human voice and human sense,
Reasoning to admiration, and with me
Persuasively hath so prevailed that I
Have also tasted, and have also found
The effects to correspond – opener mine eyes,   875
Dim erst, dilated spirits, ampler heart,
And growing up to godhead; which for thee
Chiefly I sought, without thee can despise.
For bliss, as thou hast part, to me is bliss;
Tedious, unshared with thee, and odious soon.   880
Thou therefore also taste, that equal lot
May join us, equal joy, as equal love;
Lest thou not tasting, different degree
Disjoin us, and I then too late renounce
Deity for thee, when fate will not permit.'   885
    Thus Eve with countenance blithe her story
        told;
But in her cheek distemper flushing glowed.
On the other side, Adam, soon as he heard
The fatal trespass done by Eve, amazed,
Astonied stood and blank, while horror chill   890
Ran through his veins, and all his joints relaxed.
From his slack hand the garland wreathed for Eve
Down dropped, and all the faded roses shed;
Speechless he stood and pale, till thus at length
First to himself he inward silence broke: 895
    'O fairest of creation, last and best
Of all God's works, creature in whom excelled
Whatever can to sight or thought be formed,
Holy, divine, good, amiable, or sweet!
How art thou lost, how on a sudden lost,   900

---

864 tasted] if tasted.
887 distemper] an imbalance of the humours, or (possiby) intoxication
    (cf. l. 793).
890 Astonied] dazed, dismayed.
    blank] means both 'speechless' and 'pale' (cf. l. 894).
892-3] Cf. Statius, *Thebaid* vii. 148-50.

Defaced, deflowered, and now to death devote?
Rather, how hast thou yielded to transgress
The strict forbiddance, how to violate
The sacred fruit forbidden? Some cursed fraud
Of enemy hath beguiled thee, yet unknown,   905
And me with thee hath ruined; for with thee
Certain my resolution is to die;
How can I live without thee, how forgo
Thy sweet converse, and love so dearly joined,
To live again in these wild woods forlorn?   910
Should God create another Eve, and I
Another rib afford, yet loss of thee
Would never from my heart; no, no, I feel
The link of nature draw me: flesh of flesh,
Bone of my bone thou art, and from thy state   915
Mine never shall be parted, bliss or woe.'
      So having said, as one from sad dismay
Recomforted, and after thoughts disturbed
Submitting to what seemed remediless,
Thus in calm mood his words to Eve he turned: 920
      'Bold deed thou hast presumed, adventurous Eve,
And peril great provoked, who thus hast dared
Had it been only coveting to eye
That sacred food, sacred to abstinence;
Much more to taste it, under ban to touch.   925
But past who can recall, or done undo?
Not God omnipotent, nor fate; yet so
Perhaps thou shalt not die; perhaps the fact
Is not so heinous now – foretasted fruit,
Profaned first by the serpent, by him first   930
Made common and unhallowed ere our taste,
Nor yet on him found deadly; he yet lives –
Lives, as thou saidst, and gains to live, as man,
Higher degree of life: inducement strong
To us, as likely tasting to attain   935
Proportional ascent, which cannot be
But to be gods, or angels, demi-gods.
Nor can I think that God, creator wise,
Though threatening, will in earnest so destroy
Us, his prime creatures, dignified so high,   940
Set over all his works; which in our fall,
For us created, needs with us must fail,
Dependent made; so God shall uncreate,

901 devote] doomed.
928 fact] evil deed.

Be frustrate, do, undo, and labour loose –
Not well conceived of God, who though his power   945
Creation could repeat, yet would be loath
Us to abolish, lest the adversary
Triumph and say: "Fickle their state whom God
Most favours; who can please him long? Me first
He ruined, now mankind; whom will he next?" –   950
Matter of scorn not to be given the foe;
However, I with thee have fixed my lot,
Certain to undergo like doom; if death
Consort with thee, death is to me as life;
So forcible within my heart I feel   955
The bond of nature draw me to my own –
My own in thee, for what thou art is mine;
Our state cannot be severed; we are one,
One flesh; to lose thee were to lose myself.'
    So Adam; and thus Eve to him replied: 960
'O glorious trial of exceeding love,
Illustrious evidence, example high!
Engaging me to emulate; but, short
Of thy perfection, how shall I attain,
Adam, from whose dear side I boast me sprung,   965
And gladly of our union hear thee speak,
One heart, one soul in both? Whereof good proof
This day affords, declaring thee resolved,
Rather than death, or aught than death more dread,
Shall separate us, linked in love so dear,   970
To undergo with me one guilt, one crime,
If any be, of tasting this fair fruit;
Whose virtue – for of good still good proceeds,
Direct, or by occasion – hath presented
This happy trial of thy love, which else   975
So eminently never had been known.
Were it I thought death menaced would ensue
This my attempt, I would sustain alone
The worst, and not persuade thee – rather die
Deserted than oblige thee with a fact   980
Pernicious to thy peace, chiefly assured

---

944 labour loose] means either 'undo labour already performed' or 'lose labour'.
947–8] Deut. xxxii. 27; on 'adversary' see I 82n.
953 Certain] resolved.
976 eminently] According to a scholastic tradition which survived in Reforma-
    tion theology God was said to possess the excellencies of human character –
    in this case love – not 'formally', as animals possess them, but 'eminently',
    i.e. in a higher sense. Eve's use of the word is thus blasphemous.
980 oblige] make subject to a penalty.

Remarkably so late of thy so true,
So faithful, love unequalled; but I feel
Far otherwise the event – not death, but life
Augmented, opened eyes, new hopes, new joys,   985
Taste so divine that what of sweet before
Hath touched my sense flat seems to this and
    harsh.
On my experience, Adam, freely taste,
And fear of death deliver to the winds.'
    So saying, she embraced him, and for joy   990
Tenderly wept, much won that he his love
Had so ennobled, as of choice to incur
Divine displeasure for her sake, or death.
In recompense (for such compliance bad
Such recompense best merits), from the bough   995
She gave him of that fair enticing fruit
With liberal hand; he scrupled not to eat,
Against his better knowledge, not deceived,
But fondly overcome with female charm.
Earth trembled from her entrails, as again   1000
In pangs, and nature gave a second groan;
Sky loured, and muttering thunder, some sad drops
Wept at completing of the mortal sin
Original; while Adam took no thought,
Eating his fill, nor Eve to iterate   1005
Her former trespass feared, the more to soothe
Him with her loved society; that now,
As with new wine intoxicated both,
They swim in mirth, and fancy that they feel
Divinity within them breeding wings   1010
Wherewith to scorn the earth; but that false fruit
Far other operation first displayed,
Carnal desire inflaming; he on Eve
Began to cast lascivious eyes, she him
As wantonly repaid; in lust they burn,   1015
Till Adam thus 'gan Eve to dalliance move:
    'Eve, now I see thou art exact of taste
And elegant – of sapience no small part;
Since to each meaning savour we apply,

984 event] outcome, consequence.
998-9] I Tim. ii. 14.
1003-4] Original sin is the theological doctrine according to which the sin of
    Adam was transmitted to all his descendants.
1017-20] Cf. 442-3n. for the play on 'sapience'. 'Savour' refers to both taste
    and perception (cf. V 84n.).

And palate call judicious; I the praise   1020
Yield thee, so well this day thou hast purveyed.
Much pleasure we have lost, while we abstained
From this delightful fruit, nor known till now
True relish, tasting; if such pleasure be
In things to us forbidden, it might be wished   1025
For this one tree had been forbidden ten.
But come; so well refreshed, now let us play,
As meet is, after such delicious fare;
For never did thy beauty since the day
I saw thee first and wedded thee, adorned   1030
With all perfections, so inflame my sense
With ardour to enjoy thee, fairer now
Than ever – bounty of this virtuous tree.'
     So said he, and forbore not glance or toy
Of amorous intent, well understood   1035
Of Eve, whose eye darted contagious fire.
Her hand he seized, and to a shady bank
Thick overhead with verdant roof embowered
He led her, nothing loath; flowers were the couch,
Pansies, and violets, and asphodel,   1040
And hyacinth – earth's freshest, softest lap.
There they their fill of love and love's disport
Took largely, of their mutual guilt the seal,
The solace of their sin, till dewy sleep
Oppressed them, wearied with their amorous play.   1045
     Soon as the force of that fallacious fruit,
That with exhilarating vapour bland
About their spirits had played, and inmost powers
Made err, was now exhaled, and grosser sleep,
Bred of unkindly fumes, with conscious dreams   1050
Encumbered, now had left them, up they rose
As from unrest, and each the other viewing,
Soon found their eyes how opened, and their minds
How darkened; innocence, that as a veil
Had shadowed them from knowing ill, was gone;   1055
Just confidence, and native righteousness
And honour, from about them, naked left
To guilty shame: he covered, but his robe

1029–33] Cf. *Iliad* iii 442 ff., xiv 292 ff.
1034 toy] caressing.
1037] Cf. IV 321n.
1042–4] Prov. vii., esp. v. 18.
1050 unkindly fumes] unnatural vapours. Cf. V 5.
       conscious] Cf. VI 521n.

Uncovered more; so rose the Danite strong,
Herculean Samson, from the harlot-lap   1060
Of Philistean Dalila, and waked
Shorn of his strength; they destitute and bare
Of all their virtue; silent, and in face
Confounded, long they sat, as stricken mute,
Till Adam, though not less than Eve abashed,   1065
At length gave utterance to these words constrained:
  'O Eve, in evil hour thou didst give ear
To that false worm, of whomsoever taught
To counterfeit man's voice – true in our fall,
False in our promised rising; since our eyes   1070
Opened we find indeed, and find we know
Both good and evil, good lost and evil got:
Bad fruit of knowledge, if this be to know,
Which leaves us naked thus, of honour void,
Of innocence, of faith, of purity,   1075
Our wonted ornaments now soiled and stained,
And in our faces evident the signs
Of foul concupiscence; whence evil store,
Even shame, the last of evils; of the first
Be sure then. How shall I behold the face   1080
Henceforth of God or angel, erst with joy
And rapture so oft beheld? Those heavenly shapes
Will dazzle now this earthly with their blaze
Insufferably bright. O might I here
In solitude live savage, in some glade   1085
Obscured, where highest woods, impenetrable
To star or sunlight, spread their umbrage broad,
And brown as evening; cover me, ye pines;
Ye cedars, with innumerable boughs
Hide me, where I may never see them more.   1090
But let us now, as in bad plight, devise
What best may, for the present, serve to hide
The parts of each from other that seem most
To shame obnoxious, and unseemliest seen –   1094
Some tree, whose broad smooth leaves together sewed,
And girded on our loins, may cover round
Those middle parts, that this new comer, shame,
There sit not, and reproach us as unclean.'
  So counselled he, and both together went

1059–62] Judges xvi. Samson is a Danite because his father Manoah was 'of the
    family of the Danites' (Judges xiii. 2); on Dalila as Philistine see *SA* 216n.
1090 them] the 'shapes' of l. 1082.
1094 obnoxious] liable (Cf. *SA* 106).

Into the thickest wood; there soon they choose   1100
The fig-tree – not that kind for fruit renowned,
But such as at this day to Indians known,
In Malabar or Decan spreads her arms
Branching so broad and long that in the ground
The bended twigs take root, and daughters grow   1105
About the mother tree, a pillared shade
High overarched, and echoing walks between:
There oft the Indian herdsman, shunning heat,
Shelters in cool, and tends his pasturing herds
At loop-holes cut through thickest shade; those leaves
They gathered, broad as Amazonian targe,   1111
And with what skill they had together sewed,
To gird their waist – vain covering, if to hide
Their guilt and dreaded shame; O how unlike
To that first naked glory! Such of late   1115
Columbus found the American, so girt
With feathered cincture, naked else and wild,
Among the trees on isles and woody shores.
Thus fenced, and as they thought, their shame in part
Covered, but not at rest or ease of mind,   1120
They sat them down to weep; nor only tears
Rained at their eyes, but high winds worse within
Began to rise, high passions – anger, hate,
Mistrust, suspicion, discord – and shook sore
Their inward state of mind, calm region once   1125
And full of peace, now tossed and turbulent:
For understanding ruled not, and the will
Heard not her lore, both in subjection now
To sensual appetite, who from beneath
Usurping over sovereign reason, claimed   1130
Superior sway; from thus distempered breast
Adam, estranged in look and altered style,
Speech intermitted thus to Eve renewed:
    'Would thou hadst hearkened to my words, and stayed
With me, as I besought thee, when that strange   1135
Desire of wandering, this unhappy morn,
I know not whence possessed thee; we had then
Remained still happy – not, as now, despoiled

1102] refers to the banyan, or Indian fig tree (*ficus religiosa*).
1103 Malabar] (modern Kerala) is on the south-west coast of India; Decan is the
    Indian peninsula.
1111 Amazonian targe] the crescent-shaped shield of the Amazons, a mythical
    race of warrior women.
1121] Psalm cxxxvii. 1.

Of all our good, shamed, naked, miserable.
Let none henceforth seek needless cause to approve   1140
The faith they owe; when earnestly they seek
Such proof, conclude they then begin to fail.'
   To whom, soon moved with touch of blame, thus Eve:
'What words have passed thy lips, Adam severe?
Imput'st thou that to my default, or will   1145
Of wandering, as thou call'st it, which who knows
But might as ill have happened thou being by,
Or to thyself perhaps? Hadst thou been there,
Or here the attempt, thou couldst not have discerned
Fraud in the serpent, speaking as he spake;   1150
No ground of enmity between us known,
Why he should mean me ill or seek to harm;
Was I to have never parted from thy side?
As good have grown there still a lifeless rib.
Being as I am, why didst not thou the head   1155
Command me absolutely not to go,
Going into such danger, as thou saidst?
Too facile then, thou didst not much gainsay,
Nay didst permit, approve, and fair dismiss.
Hadst thou been firm and fixed in thy dissent,   1160
Neither had I transgressed, nor thou with me.'
   To whom, then first incensed, Adam replied:
'Is this the love, is this the recompense
Of mine to thee, ingrateful Eve, expressed
Immutable when thou wert lost, not I –   1165
Who might have lived, and joyed immortal bliss,
Yet willingly chose rather death with thee?
And am I now upbraided as the cause
Of thy transgressing? Not enough severe,
It seems, in thy restraint; what could I more?   1170
I warned thee, I admonished thee, foretold
The danger, and the lurking enemy
That lay in wait; beyond this had been force,
And force upon free will hath here no place.
But confidence then bore thee on, secure   1175
Either to meet no danger, or to find
Matter of glorious trial; and perhaps

1140 approve] prove.
1141 owe] means both 'owe' and 'own'.
1144] *Iliad* xiv 83.
1155 head] I Cor. xi. 3.
1175 confidence, secure] both words mean 'overconfident'.
1177 Matter] pretext, occasion.

I also erred in overmuch admiring
What seemed in thee so perfect that I thought
No evil durst attempt thee; but I rue   1180
That error now, which is become my crime,
And thou the accuser. Thus it shall befall
Him who to worth in women overtrusting,
Lets her will rule: restraint she will not brook,
And left to herself, if evil thence ensue,   1185
She first his weak indulgence will accuse.'
   Thus they in mutual accusation spent
The fruitless hours, but neither self-condemning;
And of their vain contest appeared no end.

THE END OF THE NINTH BOOK

BOOK X

THE ARGUMENT

Man's transgression known, the guardian angels forsake Paradise, and return up to heaven to approve their vigilance, and are approved; God declaring that the entrance of Satan could not be by them prevented. He sends his Son to judge the transgressors; who descends, and gives sentence accordingly; then, in pity, clothes them both, and reascends. Sin and Death sitting till then at the gates of hell, by wondrous sympathy feeling the success of Satan in this new world, and the sin by man there committed, resolve to sit no longer confined in hell, but to follow Satan, their sire, up to the place of man: to make the way easier from hell to this world to and fro, they pave a broad highway or bridge over chaos, according to the track that Satan first made; then, preparing for earth, they meet him, proud of his success, returning to hell; their mutual gratulation. Satan arrives at Pandemonium; in full assembly relates, with boasting, his success against man; instead of applause is entertained with a general hiss by all his audience, transformed, with himself also, suddenly into serpents, according to his doom given in Paradise; then, deluded with a show of the forbidden tree springing up before them, they, greedily reaching to take of the fruit, chew dust and bitter ashes. The proceedings of Sin and Death: God foretells the final victory of his Son over them, and the renewing of all things; but, for the present, commands his angels to make several alterations in the heavens and elements. Adam, more and more perceiving his fallen condition, heavily bewails, rejects the condolement of Eve; she persists, and at length appeases him: then, to evade the curse likely to fall on their offspring, proposes to Adam violent ways which he approves not, but, conceiving better hope, puts her in mind of the late promise made them, that her seed should be revenged on the serpent, and exhorts her, with him, to seek peace of the offended Deity by repentance and supplication.

Meanwhile the heinous and despiteful act
Of Satan done in Paradise, and how
He in the serpent, had perverted Eve,
Her husband she, to taste the fatal fruit,
Was known in heaven; for what can scape the eye   5
Of God all-seeing, or deceive his heart
Omniscient, who, in all things wise and just,
Hindered not Satan to attempt the mind
Of man, with strength entire and free will armed,
Complete to have discovered and repulsed   10
Whatever wiles of foe or seeming friend.

10 Complete] fully equipped or endowed (modifies 'mind').

For still they knew, and ought to have still remembered,
The high injunction not to taste that fruit,
Whoever tempted; which they not obeying
Incurred – what could they less? – the penalty, 15
And, manifold in sin, deserve to fall.
Up into heaven from Paradise in haste
The angelic guards ascended, mute and sad
For man, for of his state by this they knew,
Much wondering how the subtle fiend had stolen 20
Entrance unseen. Soon as the unwelcome news
From earth arrived at heaven-gate, displeased
All were who heard; dim sadness did not spare
That time celestial visages, yet mixed
With pity, violated not their bliss. 25
About the new-arrived, in multitudes,
The ethereal people ran, to hear and know
How all befell; they towards the throne supreme,
Accountable made haste to make appear
With righteous plea, their utmost vigilance, 30
And easily approved; when the most high,
Eternal Father, from his secret cloud
Amidst, in thunder uttered thus his voice:
　'Assembled angels, and ye powers returned
From unsuccessful charge, be not dismayed 35
Nor troubled at these tidings from the earth,
Which your sincerest care could not prevent,
Foretold so lately what would come to pass,
When first this tempter crossed the gulf from hell.
I told ye then he should prevail, and speed 40
On his bad errand – man should be seduced,
And flattered out of all, believing lies
Against his maker; no decree of mine,
Concurring to necessitate his fall,
Or touch with lightest moment of impulse 45
His free will, to her own inclining left
In even scale. But fallen he is; and now
What rests, but that the mortal sentence pass
On his transgression, death denounced that day,
Which he presumes already vain and void, 50

12 still] invariably, always.
19 this] this time.
31 approved] confirmed. Cf. Argument, 'approve their vigilance'.
33] Rev. iv. 5.
40 speed] attain his purpose.
48 rests] remains.
49-52] See VIII 330-1n.

Because not yet inflicted, as he feared,
By some immediate stroke, but soon shall find
Forbearance no acquittance ere day end.
Justice shall not return, as bounty, scorned.
But whom send I to judge them? Whom but thee,   55
Vicegerent Son? To thee I have transferred
All judgement, whether in heaven, or earth, or hell.
Easy it may be seen that I intend
Mercy colleague with justice, sending thee,
Man's friend, his mediator, his designed   60
Both ransom and redeemer voluntary,
And destined man himself to judge man fallen.'
   So spake the Father, and unfolding bright
Toward the right hand his glory, on the Son
Blazed forth unclouded deity; he full   65
Resplendent all his Father manifest
Expressed, and thus divinely answered mild:
   'Father Eternal, thine is to decree;
Mine both in heaven and earth to do thy will
Supreme, that thou in me, thy Son beloved,   70
May'st ever rest well pleased. I go to judge
On earth these thy transgressors; but thou know'st,
Whoever judged, the worst on me must light,
When time shall be; for so I undertook
Before thee, and, not repenting, this obtain   75
Of right, that I may mitigate their doom
On me derived; yet I shall temper so
Justice with mercy as may illustrate most
Them fully satisfied, and thee appease.
Attendance none shall need, nor train, where none   80
Are to behold the judgement but the judged,
Those two; the third best absent is condemned,
Convict by flight, and rebel to all law;
Conviction to the serpent none belongs.'
   Thus saying, from his radiant seat he rose   85
Of high collateral glory; him thrones and powers,
Princedoms, and dominations ministrant,
Accompanied to heaven-gate, from whence
Eden and all the coast in prospect lay.
Down he descended straight; the speed of gods   90
Time counts not, though with swiftest minutes winged.

56–7] John v. 22.
70–1] Matt. iii. 17, xii. 18.
77 derived] diverted.
79 Them] justice and mercy.

Now was the sun in western cadence low
From noon, and gentle airs due at their hour
To fan the earth now waked, and usher in
The evening cool, when he, from wrath more cool,   95
Came, the mild judge and intercessor both,
To sentence man; the voice of God they heard
Now walking in the garden, by soft winds
Brought to their ears, while day declined; they heard,
And from his presence hid themselves among   100
The thickest trees, both man and wife, till God,
Approaching, thus to Adam called aloud:
    'Where art thou, Adam, wont with joy to meet
My coming, seen far off? I miss thee here,
Not pleased, thus entertained with solitude,   105
Where obvious duty erewhile apeared unsought;
Or come I less conspicuous, or what change
Absents thee, or what chance detains? Come forth.'
    He came, and with him Eve, more loath, though first
To offend, discountenanced both, and discomposed;   110
Love was not in their looks, either to God
Or to each other, but apparent guilt,
And shame, and perturbation, and despair,
Anger, and obstinacy, and hate, and guile.
Whence Adam, faltering long, thus answered brief: 115
    'I heard thee in the garden, and of thy voice
Afraid, being naked, hid myself.' To whom
The gracious judge, without revile, replied:
    'My voice thou oft hast heard, and hast not feared,
But still rejoiced; how is it now become   120
So dreadful to thee? That thou art naked, who
Hath told thee? Hast thou eaten of the tree
Whereof I gave thee charge thou shouldst not eat?'
To whom thus Adam, sore beset, replied:
    'O heaven! In evil strait this day I stand   125
Before my judge – either to undergo
Myself the total crime, or to accuse
My other self, the partner of my life,
Whose failing, while her faith to me remains,
I should conceal, and not expose to blame   130

92 cadence] used in the Latin sense of 'falling, sinking down'.
98 soft winds] The A.V. marginal note to Gen. iii. 8 proposes 'wind' instead of
      'cool' and the Vulgate has *aura* (gentle breeze).
106 obvious] coming in the way (i.e. to meet).
112 apparent] evident.
128 other self] see VIII 450n.

By my complaint; but strict necessity
Subdues me, and calamitous constraint,
Lest on my head both sin and punishment,
However insupportable, be all
Devolved; though should I hold my peace, yet thou   135
Wouldst easily detect what I conceal.
This woman, whom thou mad'st to be my help,
And gav'st me as thy perfect gift, so good,
So fit, so acceptable, so divine,
That from her hand I could suspect no ill,   140
And what she did, whatever in itself,
Her doing seemed to justify the deed –
She gave me of the tree, and I did eat.'
To whom the sovereign presence thus replied:
    'Was she thy God, that her thou didst obey   145
Before his voice, or was she made thy guide,
Superior, or but equal, that to her
Thou didst resign thy manhood, and the place
Wherein God set thee above her, made of thee
And for thee, whose perfection far excelled   150
Hers in all real dignity? Adorned
She was indeed, and lovely, to attract
Thy love, not thy subjection; and her gifts
Were such as under government well seemed –
Unseemly to bear rule, which was thy part   155
And person, hadst thou known thyself aright.'
    So having said, he thus to Eve in few:
'Say, woman, what is this which thou hast done?'
    To whom sad Eve, with shame nigh overwhelmed,
Confessing soon, yet not before her judge   160
Bold or loquacious, thus abashed replied:
'The serpent me beguiled, and I did eat.'
    Which when the Lord God heard, without delay
To judgement he proceeded on the accused
Serpent, though brute, unable, to transfer   165
The guilt on him who made him instrument
Of mischief, and polluted from the end
Of his creation – justly then accursed,
As vitiated in nature; more to know
Concerned not man (since he no further knew),   170
Nor altered his offence; yet God at last

149–50] I Cor. xi. 8–9.
151 real] royal.
156 person] rôle.
157 few] few words.

To Satan, first in sin, his doom applied,
Though in mysterious terms, judged as then best;
And on the serpent thus his curse let fall:
   'Because thou hast done this, thou art accursed   175
Above all cattle, each beast of the field;
Upon thy belly grovelling thou shalt go,
And dust shalt eat all the days of thy life.
Between thee and the woman I will put
Enmity, and between thine and her seed;   180
Her seed shall bruise thy head, thou bruise his heel.'
   So spake this oracle – then verified
When Jesus, son of Mary, second Eve,
Saw Satan fall like lightning down from heaven,
Prince of the air; then rising from his grave,   185
Spoiled principalities and powers, triumphed
In open show, and with ascension bright,
Captivity led captive through the air,
The realm itself of Satan, long usurped,
Whom he shall tread at last under our feet,   190
Even he who now foretold his fatal bruise,
And to the woman thus his sentence turned:
   'Thy sorrow I will greatly multiply
By thy conception; children thou shalt bring
In sorrow forth, and to thy husband's will   195
Thine shall submit; he over thee shall rule.'
   On Adam last thus judgement he pronounced:
'Because thou hast hearkened to the voice of thy wife,
And eaten of the tree concerning which
I charged thee, saying "Thou shalt not eat thereof",   200
Cursed is the ground for thy sake; thou in sorrow
Shalt eat thereof all the days of thy life;
Thorns also and thistles it shall bring thee forth
Unbid, and thou shalt eat the herb of the field;
In the sweat of thy face thou shalt eat bread,   205
Till thou return unto the ground; for thou

---

183 Mary, second Eve] a common Patristic idea, often illustrated in the middle
    ages by the conceit that the Latin form of her name (*Eva*) spelt backwards
    was the first word (*Ave*) of the angel's address to Mary.
184] Luke x. 18.
185] Eph. ii. 2.
186–7] Col. ii. 14–15.
188] Psalm lxviii. 18, Eph. iv. 8.
189–90] Rom. xvi. 20. See the A.V. marginal note, which proposes 'tread'
    instead of 'bruise', presumably reflecting an uneasiness which Milton may
    have shared about the precise meaning of the word translated as 'bruise' in
    Gen. iii. 15.

Out of the ground wast taken: know thy birth,
For dust thou art, and shalt to dust return.'
  So judged he man, both judge and saviour sent,
And the instant stroke of death, denounced that day,   210
Removed far off; then pitying how they stood
Before him naked to the air, that now
Must suffer change, disdained not to begin
Thenceforth the form of servant to assume;
As when he washed his servants' feet, so now,   215
As father of his family, he clad
Their nakedness with skins of beasts, or slain,
Or as the snake, with youthful coat repaid;
And thought not much to clothe his enemies;
Nor he their outward only with the skins   220
Of beasts, but inward nakedness, much more
Opprobrious, with his robe of righteousness
Arraying, covered from his Father's sight.
To him with swift ascent he up returned,
Into his blissful bosom reassumed   225
In glory as of old; to him, appeased,
All, though all-knowing, what had passed with man
Recounted, mixing intercession sweet.
  Meanwhile, ere thus was sinned and judged on earth,
Within the gates of hell sat Sin and Death,   230
In counterview within the gates, that now
Stood open wide, belching outrageous flame
Far into chaos, since the fiend passed through,
Sin opening; who thus now to Death began:
  'O son, why sit we here, each other viewing   235
Idly, while Satan our great author thrives
In other worlds, and happier seat provides
For us, his offspring dear? It cannot be
But that success attends him; if mishap,
Ere this he had returned, with fury driven   240
By his avengers, since no place like this
Can fit his punishment, or their revenge.

210-11] See VIII 330-1n.; 'denounced' means 'proclaimed in the manner of a
    warning'.
214] Phil. ii. 7.
215] John xiii. 5.
216] Heb. ii. 13.
217-18 or ... or] either ... or.
222] Isa. lxi. 10.
232 outrageous] enormous, raging.
235] II Kings vii. 3.
236 author] begetter.

Methinks I feel new strength within me rise,
Wings growing, and dominion given me large
Beyond this deep – whatever draws me on,   245
Or sympathy, or some connatural force,
Powerful at greatest distance to unite
With secret amity things of like kind
By secretest conveyance. Thou, my shade
Inseparable, must with me along;   250
For Death from Sin no power can separate.
But, lest the difficulty of passing back
Stay his return perhaps over this gulf
Impassable, impervious, let us try
Adventurous work – yet to thy power and mine   255
Not unagreeable – to found a path
Over this main from hell to that new world
Where Satan now prevails: a monument
Of merit high to all the infernal host,
Easing their passage hence, for intercourse   260
Or transmigration, as their lot shall lead.
Nor can I miss the way, so strongly drawn
By this new-felt attraction and instinct.'
    Whom thus the meagre shadow answered soon:
'Go whither fate and inclination strong   265
Leads thee; I shall not lag behind, nor err
The way, thou leading: such a scent I draw
Of carnage, prey innumerable, and taste
The savour of death from all things there that live;
Nor shall I to the work thou enterprisest   270
Be wanting, but afford thee equal aid.'
    So saying, with delight he snuffed the smell
Of mortal change on earth. As when a flock
Of ravenous fowl, though many a league remote,
Against the day of battle, to a field   275
Where armies lie encamped come flying, lured
With scent of living carcasses designed
For death the following day in bloody fight;
So scented the grim feature, and upturned
His nostril wide into the murky air,   280
Sagacious of his quarry from so far.
Then both from out hell gates into the waste

---

257 main] sea (i.e. chaos).
260-1 intercourse/Or transmigration] travel between two places, either both
    ways ('intercourse') or one way ('transmigration').
266 err] mistake.
281 Sagacious] acute in olfactory perception.

Wide anarchy of chaos, damp and dark,
Flew diverse, and with power (their power was great)
Hovering upon the waters, what they met   285
Solid or slimy, as in raging sea
Tossed up and down, together crowded drove,
From each side shoaling, towards the mouth of hell;
As when two polar winds, blowing adverse
Upon the Cronian sea, together drive   290
Mountains of ice, that stop the imagined way
Beyond Petsora eastward to the rich
Cathaian coast. The aggregated soil
Death with his mace petrific, cold and dry,
As with a trident smote, and fixed as firm   295
As Delos, floating once; the rest his look
Bound with Gorgonian rigour not to move,
And with asphaltic slime; broad as the gate,
Deep to the roots of hell the gathered beach
They fastened, and the mole immense wrought on   300
Over the foaming deep high-arched, a bridge
Of length prodigious, joining to the wall
Immovable of this now fenceless world,
Forfeit to Death – from hence a passage broad,
Smooth, easy, inoffensive, down to hell.   305
So, if great things to small may be compared,

288 shoaling] assembling in shoals.
290 Cronian sea] The Arctic Ocean.
291 the imagined way] the north-east passage.
292 Petsora] Pechora, a river in northern Russia.
294 petrific] having the power to petrify.
296 Delos] See V 264-5n. Delos was created as a floating island by Neptune, and later anchored by Jove to provide a place for Latona to give birth to her twins (see *Sonnet* XII 5-7n.).
297] On Gorgonian see *Comus* 447-52n.; 'rigour' means 'stiffness, hardness'.
298 asphaltic slime] 'Asphaltic' renders the LXX of Gen. xi. 3 (ἀσφαλτος); 'slime' is the A.V. reading. The Vulgate says *bitumen*, which Milton uses in XII 41.
299 gathered beach] assembled ridge of stone.
300 mole] a stone causeway.
302 wall] the 'orb' of II 1029, and the 'firm ... globe' of III 418.
303 fenceless] defenceless.
305 inoffensive] used in the Latin sense of 'free from hindrance, uninterrupted'.
306-11] Xerxes, King of Persia, was the son of Darius, who had built his palace in Susa (now Shush, in Iran), a city associated by Aeschylus and Herodotus with Memnon (on whom see *Penseroso* 18n.). In 480 BC Xerxes began his preparations for a punitive invasion of Greece by building a bridge across the Hellespont (the modern Dardanelles); when this bridge was swept away by a storm, Xerxes ordered the sea to be scourged.

Xerxes, the liberty of Greece to yoke,
From Susa, his Memnonian palace high,
Came to the sea, and over Hellespont
Bridging his way, Europe with Asia joined,   310
And scourged with many a stroke the indignant waves.
Now had they brought the work by wondrous art
Pontifical – a ridge of pendant rock
Over the vexed abyss, following the track
Of Satan, to the self-same place where he   315
First lighted from his wing and landed safe
From out of chaos – to the outside bare
Of this round world; with pins of adamant
And chains they made all fast, too fast they made
And durable; and now in little space   320
The confines met of empyrean heaven
And of this world, and on the left hand hell,
With long reach interposed; three several ways
In sight to each of these three places led.
And now their way to earth they had descried,   325
To Paradise first tending, when, behold
Satan, in likeness of an angel bright,
Betwixt the Centaur and the Scorpion steering
His zenith, while the sun in Aries rose;
Disguised he came, but those his children dear   330
Their parent soon discerned, though in disguise.
He after Eve seduced, unminded slunk
Into the wood fast by, and changing shape
To observe the sequel, saw his guileful act
By Eve, though all unweeting, seconded   335
Upon her husband – saw their shame that sought
Vain covertures; but, when he saw descend
The Son of God to judge them, terrified
He fled, not hoping to escape, but shun
The present – fearing, guilty, what his wrath   340
Might suddenly inflict; that past, returned
By night, and, listening where the hapless pair
Sat in their sad discourse and various plaint,
Thence gathered his own doom, which understood
Not instant, but of future time, with joy   345
And tidings fraught, to hell he now returned,

---

313 Pontifical] Milton plays on the apparent etymology of the word – *pontem*
    (from *pons*, bridge), -*ficus* (making, from *facere*) – and also utilizes the
    ordinary meaning of 'episcopal' or 'popish'.
328–9] The Centaur (Sagittarius), Scorpion, and Aries (the Ram) are respect-
    ively the ninth, eighth, and first signs of the zodiac.

And at the brink of chaos, near the foot
Of this new wondrous pontifice, unhoped
Met who to meet him came, his offspring dear.
Great joy was at their meeting, and at sight   350
Of that stupendous bridge his joy increased.
Long he admiring stood, till Sin, his fair
Enchanting daughter, thus the silence broke:
      'O parent, these are thy magnific deeds,
Thy trophies, which thou view'st as not thine own;   355
Thou art their author and prime architect;
For I no sooner in my heart divined –
My heart, which by a secret harmony
Still moves with thine, joined in connection sweet –
That thou on earth hadst prospered, which thy looks   360
Now also evidence, but straight I felt –
Though distant from thee worlds between, yet felt –
That I must after thee with this thy son;
Such fatal consequence unites us three;
Hell could no longer hold us in her bounds,   365
Nor this unvoyageable gulf obscure
Detain from following thy illustrious track.
Thou hast achieved our liberty, confined
Within hell gates till now; thou us empowered
To fortify thus far, and overlay   370
With this portentous bridge the dark abyss.
Thine now is all this world; thy virtue hath won
What thy hands builded not; thy wisdom gained,
With odds, what war hath lost, and fully avenged
Our foil in heaven; here thou shalt monarch reign,   375
There didst not; there let him still victor sway,
As battle hath adjudged, from this new world
Retiring, by his own doom alienated,
And henceforth monarchy with thee divide
Of all things, parted by the empyreal bounds,   380
His quadrature, from thy orbicular world,
Or try thee now more dangerous to his throne.'
      Whom thus the prince of darkness answered glad:

347 foot] the end of the slope of the bridge.
348 pontifice] means both 'bridge' and 'priest, bishop, pope'.
364 consequence] the relation of a result to its cause.
375 foil] defeat, disgrace. The etymological sense of 'that which is trampled
    under foot' may be relevant in view of Milton's repeated allusions to Gen.
    iii. 15.
378 doom] judgement, condemnation.
381 quadrature] square. See II 1048-50n.
382 try] demonstrate.

'Fair daughter, and thou son and grandchild both,
High proof ye now have given to be the race 385
Of Satan (for I glory in the name,
Antagonist of heaven's almighty king),
Amply have merited of me, of all
The infernal empire, that so near heaven's door
Triumphal with triumphal act have met, 390
Mine with this glorious work, and made one realm
Hell and this world – one realm, one continent
Of easy thoroughfare. Therefore while I
Descend through darkness, on your road with ease,
To my associate powers, them to acquaint 395
With these successes, and with them rejoice,
You two this way, among these numerous orbs,
All yours, right down to Paradise descend;
There dwell and reign in bliss; thence on the earth
Dominion exercise and in the air, 400
Chiefly on man, sole lord of all declared;
Him first make sure your thrall, and lastly kill.
My substitutes I send ye, and create
Plenipotent on earth, of matchless might
Issuing from me; on your joint vigour now 405
My hold of this new kingdom all depends,
Through Sin to Death exposed by my exploit.
If your joint power prevail, the affairs of hell
No detriment need fear; go, and be strong.'
　　So saying, he dismissed them; they with speed 410
Their course through thickest constellations held,
Spreading their bane; the blasted stars looked wan,
And planets, planet-strook, real eclipse
Then suffered. The other way Satan went down
The causey to hell gate; on either side 415
Disparted Chaos overbuilt exclaimed,

386-7] See I 82n.
399-402] Rom. v. 12-21.
409 No detriment] alludes to the charge given when the *decretum ultimum* was
　　passed by the Roman Senate in times of national crisis giving the two
　　consuls dictatorial power: *ne quid respublica detrimenti capiat* ('that the
　　state suffer no harm'); cf. *Areopagitica* p. 597.
　　be strong] Deut. xxxi. 7.
412-13] 'Blasted' means 'perniciously breathed upon'; malign planets normally
　　'blasted', and were not themselves the objects of a blast. Similarly, planets
　　'struck' ('strook'), and were not themselves stricken by malign influence,
　　and eclipses were normally apparent rather than real.
415 causey] causeway.

And with rebounding surge the bars assailed,
That scorned his indignation; through the gate,
Wide open and unguarded, Satan passed,
And all about found desolate; for those   420
Appointed to sit there had left their charge,
Flown to the upper world; the rest were all
Far to the inland retired, about the walls
Of Pandemonium, city and proud seat
Of Lucifer, so by allusion called   425
Of that bright star to Satan paragoned.
There kept their watch the legions, while the grand
In council sat, solicitous what chance
Might intercept their emperor sent; so he
Departing gave command, and they observed.   430
As when the Tartar from his Russian foe,
By Astracan, over the snowy plains,
Retires, or Bactrian sophy, from the horns
Of Turkish crescent, leaves all waste beyond
The realm of Aladule, in his retreat   435
To Tauris or Casbeen; so these, the late
Heaven-banished host, left desert utmost hell
Many a dark league, reduced in careful watch
Round their metropolis, and now expecting
Each hour their great adventurer from the search   440
Of foreign worlds; he through the midst unmarked,
In show plebeian angel militant
Of lowest order, passed, and from the door
Of that Plutonian hall, invisible
Ascended his high throne, which under state   445
Of richest texture spread, at the upper end
Was placed in regal lustre. Down a while
He sat, and round about him saw, unseen;
At last, as from a cloud, his fulgent head
And shape star-bright appeared, or brighter, clad   450
With what permissive glory since his fall

425–6] Cf. V 658n.
432 Astracan] Astrakhan, a Tartan khanate on the lower Volga.
433 Bactrian sophy] Bactria (modern Afghanistan) was subject to Persia, and
   the Bactrian sophy was the Shah of Persia.
434 crescent] the emblem of the Turkish sultans.
435 realm of Aladule] Armenia, of which Aladule was the last king before the
   Turkish conquest.
436 Tauris, Casbeen] now Tabriz and Kasvin, in Iran; both are former Persian
   capitals.
444 Plutonian] refers to Pluto, god of the underworld.
445 state] canopy.

Was left him, or false glitter; all amazed
At that so sudden blaze, the Stygian throng
Bent their aspéct, and whom they wished beheld,
Their mighty chief returned: loud was the acclaim;   455
Forth rushed in haste the great consulting peers,
Raised from their dark divan, and with like joy
Congratulant approached him, who with hand
Silence, and with these words attention, won:
    'Thrones, dominations, princedoms, virtues, powers,
For in possession such, not only of right,   461
I call ye, and declare ye now, returned
Successful beyond hope, to lead ye forth
Triumphant out of this infernal pit
Abominable, accursed, the house of woe,   465
And dungeon of our tyrant; now possess,
As lords, a spacious world, to our native heaven
Little inferior, by my adventure hard
With peril great achieved. Long were to tell
What I have done, what suffered, with what pain   470
Voyaged the unreal, vast, unbounded deep
Of horrible confusion – over which
By Sin and Death a broad way now is paved,
To expedite your glorious march; but I
Toiled out my uncouth passage, forced to ride   475
The untractable abyss, plunged in the womb
Of unoriginal Night and Chaos wild,
That, jealous of their secrets, fiercely opposed
My journey strange, with clamorous uproar
Protesting fate supreme; thence how I found   480
The new-created world, which fame in heaven
Long had foretold, a fabric wonderful,
Of absolute perfection; therein man
Placed in a paradise, by our exile
Made happy; him by fraud I have seduced   485
From his creator, and the more to increase
Your wonder, with an apple; he, thereat
Offended – worth your laughter – hath given up
Both his beloved man and all his world
To Sin and Death a prey, and so to us,   490
Without our hazard, labour, or alarm,

457 divan] an oriental council of state, especially the Turkish council.
471 unreal] unformed.
475 uncouth] strange, unfamiliar.
477 unoriginal] uncreated.
480 Protesting] appealing to.

To range in, and to dwell, and over man
To rule, as over all he should have ruled.
True is, me also he hath judged; or rather
Me not, but the brute serpent in whose shape   495
Man I deceived; that which to me belongs
Is enmity, which he will put between
Me and mankind: I am to bruise his heel;
His seed – when, is not set – shall bruise my head;
A world who would not purchase with a bruise,   500
Or much more grievous pain? Ye have the account
Of my performance; what remains, ye gods,
But up and enter now into full bliss?'
    So having said, a while he stood, expecting
Their universal shout and high applause   505
To fill his ear; when, contrary, he hears,
On all sides, from innumerable tongues
A dismal universal hiss, the sound
Of public scorn; he wondered, but not long
Had leisure, wondering at himself now more;   510
His visage drawn he felt to sharp and spare,
His arms clung to his ribs, his legs entwining
Each other, till supplanted down he fell,
A monstrous serpent on his belly prone,
Reluctant, but in vain; a greater power   515
Now ruled him, punished in the shape he sinned,
According to his doom; he would have spoke,
But hiss for hiss returned with forked tongue
To forked tongue; for now were all transformed
Alike, to serpents all, as accessories   520
To his bold riot; dreadful was the din
Of hissing through the hall, thick-swarming now
With complicated monsters, head and tail –
Scorpion, and asp, and amphisbaena dire,
Cerastes horned, hydrus, and ellops drear,   525
And dipsas (not so thick swarmed once the soil

506-14] Cf. the transformation of Cadmus (IX 505-6n.), and similar transfor-
    mations described in Lucan, *Pharsalia* ix. 700-33, Dante, *Inferno* xxiv,
    xxv. 'Supplanted' means 'tripped up'.
515 Reluctant] struggling, writhing.
523 complicated] means both 'complex' and 'turned together'.
524 amphisbaena] The name means 'going both ways' in Greek, and refers to a
    serpent with a head at each end.
525 Cerastes] a horned serpent.
    hydrus] a water-snake (not the Hydras of *Comus* 605, nor the Hydras of *PL*
    II 628 and *Sonnet* XV. 7).
    ellops] here refers to a kind of serpent.
526 dipsas] a serpent whose bite caused raging thirst.

Bedropped with blood of Gorgon, or the isle
Ophiusa); but still greatest he the midst,
Now dragon grown, larger than whom the sun
Engendered in the Pythian vale on slime,   530
Huge python; and his power no less he seemed
Above the rest still to retain; they all
Him followed, issuing forth to the open field,
Where all yet left of that revolted rout,
Heaven-fallen, in station stood or just array,   535
Sublime with expectation when to see
In triumph issuing forth their glorious chief;
They saw, but other sight instead – a crowd
Of ugly serpents; horror on them fell,
And horrid sympathy; for what they saw   540
They felt themselves now changing; down their arms,
Down fell both spear and shield; down they as fast,
And the dire hiss renewed, and the dire form
Catched by contagion, like in punishment
As in their crime. Thus was the applause they meant   545
Turned to exploding hiss, triumph to shame
Cast on themselves from their own mouths. There stood
A grove hard by, sprung up with this their change,
His will who reigns above, to aggravate
Their penance, laden with fair fruit, like that   550
Which grew in Paradise, the bait of Eve
Used by the tempter; on that prospect strange
Their earnest eyes they fixed, imagining
For one forbidden tree a multitude
Now risen, to work them further woe or shame;   555
Yet parched with scalding thirst and hunger fierce,
Though to delude them sent, could not abstain,
But on they rolled in heaps, and up the trees
Climbing, sat thicker than the snaky locks
That curled Megaera; greedily they plucked   560
The fruitage fair to sight, like that which grew

526-7] When Perseus was crossing Libya, drops of blood from the head of the
   Gorgon (Medusa) fell on the soil and were changed into snakes, which is
   why Libya is full of deadly serpents (*Metamorphoses* iv 617-20).
528 Ophiusa] in Greek means 'full of serpents'. In antiquity the name was
   applied to at least three different islands.
529-31] The Pythian vale is Delphi, where the serpent that Apollo slew had
   lived. In the Greek of the LXX and the N.T. a python is a possessing spirit
   (e.g. Acts xvi. 16).
536 Sublime] exalted in feeling, elated.
546 exploding] used in the Latin sense of 'hissing (an actor) off the stage'.
560 Megaera] a Fury; see II 596n.

Near that bituminous lake where Sodom flamed;
This, more delusive, not the touch, but taste
Deceived; they, fondly thinking to allay
Their appetite with gust, instead of fruit   565
Chewed bitter ashes, which the offended taste
With spattering noise rejected; oft they assayed,
Hunger and thirst constraining; drugged as oft,
With hatefulest disrelish writhed their jaws
With soot and cinders filled; so oft they fell   570
Into the same illusion, not as man
Whom they triumphed once lapsed. Thus were they
        plagued,
And worn with famine long, and ceaseless hiss,
Till their lost shape, permitted, they resumed –
Yearly enjoined, some say, to undergo   575
This annual humbling certain numbered days,
To dash their pride, and joy for man seduced.
However, some tradition they dispersed
Among the heathen of their purchase got,
And fabled how the serpent, whom they called   580
Ophion, with Eurynome – the wide-
Encroaching Eve perhaps – had first the rule
Of high Olympus, thence by Saturn driven
And Ops, ere yet Dictaean Jove was born.
        Meanwhile in Paradise the hellish pair   585
Too soon arrived – Sin, there in power before
Once actual, now in body, and to dwell
Habitual habitant; behind her Death,
Close following pace for pace, not mounted yet
On his pale horse; to whom Sin thus began: 590

562] The Dead Sea ('bituminous lake') is associated with Sodom in the
    apocryphal II Esdras v. 7. In a popular tradition originating in Josephus
    (*Bellum Judaicum* IV viii. 4) the fruit growing on the site of Sodom was said
    to contain ashes from the fire which destroyed the city. (Gen. xix. 24, Deut.
    xxxii. 32).
565 gust] gusto.
568 drugged] nauseated.
579 purchase] booty.
581] The name Ophion derives from the Greek word 'serpent', and refers to a
    Titan, the husband of Eurynome (which means 'wide-ruling' in Greek);
    they ruled Olympus (see VII 3n.) until they were overthrown by Saturn
    and Rhea (Ops), whose son Jove was associated with Mount Dicte, in Crete.
    Dictaean was one of Jove's epithets. Cf. I 509-21n. Ophion was tradition-
    ally associated with Satan.
587 actual] Actual sin is a technical theological term for a sin which is the
    outcome of a free personal act of the individual will, and is therefore to be
    contrasted with original sin (see IX 1003-4n.). On sin 'in body' see 816n.
590 pale horse] Rev. vi. 8.

'Second of Satan sprung, all-conquering Death,
What think'st thou of our empire now? Though earned
With travail difficult, not better far
Than still at hell's dark threshold to have sat watch,
Unnamed, undreaded, and thyself half-starved?'   595
    Whom thus the Sin-born monster answered soon:
'To me, who with eternal famine pine,
Alike is hell, or Paradise, or heaven –
There best where most with ravin I may meet:
Which here, though plenteous, all too little seems   600
To stuff this maw, this vast unhidebound corpse.'
    To whom the incestuous mother thus replied:
'Thou therefore on these herbs, and fruits, and flowers,
Feed first, on each beast next, and fish, and fowl –
No homely morsels; and whatever thing   605
The scythe of time mows down, devour unspared,
Till I, in man residing through the race,
His thoughts, his looks, words, actions, all infect,
And season him thy last and sweetest prey.'
    This said, they both betook them several ways,   610
Both to destroy, or unimmortal make
All kinds, and for destruction to mature
Sooner or later; which the almighty seeing,
From his transcendent seat the saints among,
To those bright orders uttered thus his voice: 615
    'See with what heat these dogs of hell advance
To waste and havoc yonder world, which I
So fair and good created, and had still
Kept in that state, had not the folly of man
Let in these wasteful furies, who impute   620
Folly to me – so doth the prince of hell
And his adherents – that with so much ease
I suffer them to enter and possess
A place so heavenly, and conniving seem
To gratify my scornful enemies,   625
That laugh, as if, transported with some fit
Of passion, I to them had quitted all,
At random yielded up to their misrule;
And know not that I called and drew them thither,
My hell-hounds, to lick up the draff and filth   630
Which man's polluting sin with taint hath shed
On what was pure; till crammed and gorged, nigh burst

599 ravin] prey
601 unhidebound] having loose skin.
624 conniving] remaining inactive.

With sucked and glutted offal, at one sling
Of thy victorious arm, well-pleasing Son,
Both Sin and Death, and yawning grave, at last   635
Through chaos hurled, obstruct the mouth of hell
For ever, and seal up his ravenous jaws.
Then heaven and earth, renewed, shall be made pure
To sanctity that shall receive no stain:
Till then the curse pronounced on both precedes.'   640
    He ended, and the heavenly audience loud
Sung Halleluiah, as the sound of seas,
Through multitude that sung: 'Just are thy ways,
Righteous are thy decrees on all thy works;
Who can extenuate thee? Next, to the Son,   645
Destined restorer of mankind, by whom
New heaven and earth shall to the ages rise,
Or down from heaven descend.' Such was their song,
While the creator, calling forth by name
His mighty angels, gave them several charge,   650
As sorted best with present things. The sun
Had first his precept so to move, so shine,
As might affect the earth with cold and heat
Scarce tolerable, and from the north to call
Decrepit winter, from the south to bring   655
Solstitial summer's heat. To the blank moon
Her office they prescribed; to the other five
Their planetary motions and aspécts,
In sextile, square, and trine, and opposite,
Of noxious efficacy, and when to join   660
In synod unbenign; and taught the fixed
Their influence malignant when to shower –
Which of them, rising with the sun or falling,
Should prove tempestuous; to the winds they set
Their corners, when with bluster to confound   665
Sea, air, and shore; the thunder when to roll

633] I Sam. xxv. 29.
638-9] II Pet. iii. 7-13.
641-3] Rev. xix. 6.
643-4] Rev. xv. 3, xvi. 7.
645 extenuate] disparage.
648] Rev. xxi. 2.
656 blank] white, pale.
657] See V 177n.
659 Sextile, square, trine, and opposite are 'aspects' (see VI 313n.) of 60, 90,
    120, and 180 degrees respectively.
661 synod] conjunction, the fifth 'position' (often not called an aspect) of the
    heavenly bodies. Cf. PR IV 385n.

With terror through the dark aerial hall.
Some say he bid his angels turn askance
The poles of earth twice ten degrees and more
From the sun's axle; they with labour pushed   670
Oblique the centric globe: some say the sun
Was bid turn reins from the equinoctial road
Like distant breadth – to Taurus with the seven
Atlantic Sisters, and the Spartan Twins,
Up to the Tropic Crab; thence down amain   675
By Leo and the Virgin and the Scales,
As deep as Capricorn, to bring in change
Of seasons to each clime; else had the spring
Perpetual smiled on earth with verdant flowers,
Equal in days and nights, except to those   680
Beyond the polar circles; to them day
Had unbenighted shone, while the low sun,
To recompense his distance, in their sight
Had rounded still the horizon, and not known
Or east or west – which had forbid the snow   685
From cold Estotiland, and south as far
Beneath Magellan. At that tasted fruit,
The sun, as from Thyestean banquet, turned
His course intended; else how had the world
Inhabited, though sinless, more than now   690
Avoided pinching cold and scorching heat?

668 Some] Those who advocate the Copernican model, according to which the
    axis of the earth ('centric globe') is tilted.
671 some] Those who advocate the Ptolemaic model, according to which the
    plane of the sun's orbit is tilted.
673–8] The sun travels through the signs of the zodiac. Before the fall it is in
    Aries, the first sign (l. 329); it now travels to the second sign, Taurus (in
    which are the Pleiades, 'the seven Atlantic Sisters'), the third sign, Gemini
    ('the Spartan Twins'), and the fourth sign, Cancer ('the Tropic Crab').
    Cancer represents the furthest retreat of the sun (i.e. the summer solstice),
    after which the sun descends quickly ('thence down amain') to the fifth
    sign, Leo (the Lion), the sixth, Virgo ('the Virgin'), the seventh, Libra ('the
    Scales'), and continues on this route through Scorpio and Sagittarius 'as
    deep as Capricorn' (the Goat), the tenth sign (i.e. the winter solstice). This
    journey brings the seasons to each region ('clime').
686 Estotiland] the name referred vaguely to the coast of modern Labrador, or
    to an island off its coast.
687 Magellan] either Argentina or the Straits of Magellan.
688 Thyestean banquet] Thyestes, the son of Pelops, suffered from the curse
    that weighed on 'Pelops' line' (see *Penseroso* 99n.). His brother Atreus
    (whose wife Thyestes had seduced) killed one of Thyestes' sons and served
    him to Thyestes as food. According to Seneca, the sun changed course to
    avoid seeing the banquet (*Thyestes* 776–8).

These change in the heavens, though slow, produced
Like change on sea and land – sideral blast,
Vapour, and mist, and exhalation hot,
Corrupt and pestilent; now from the north   695
Of Norumbega, and the Samoed shore,
Bursting their brazen dungeon, armed with ice,
And snow, and hail, and stormy gust and flaw,
Boreas and Caecius and Argeste loud
And Thrascias rend the woods, and seas upturn;   700
With adverse blast upturns them from the south
Notus and Afer, black with thunderous clouds
From Serraliona; thwart of these, as fierce
Forth rush the Levant and the ponent winds,
Eurus and Zephir, with their lateral noise,   705
Sirocco and Libeccio; thus began
Outrage from lifeless things; but Discord first,
Daughter of Sin, among the irrational
Death introduced through fierce antipathy;
Beast now with beast 'gan war, and fowl with fowl,   710
And fish with fish; to graze the herb all leaving
Devoured each other; nor stood much in awe
Of man, but fled him, or with countenance grim
Glared on him passing; these were from without
The growing miseries, which Adam saw   715
Already in part, though hid in gloomiest shade,
To sorrow abandoned, but worse felt within,
And in a troubled sea of passion tossed,
Thus to disburden sought with sad complaint:
    'O miserable of happy! Is this the end   720
Of this new glorious world, and me so late
The glory of that glory? who now, become
Accursed of blessed, hide me from the face

693 sideral] from the stars.
696 Norumbega] New England and the maritime provinces of Canada.
    Samoed] north-eastern Siberia.
697 dungeon] Aeolus imprisoned the winds in a cave on Aeolia, a floating island
    near Sicily.
699–706] Milton is naming the winds in a plan based on the anemology of
    antiquity (Aristotle, *Meteorologica* ii 4–6, *Problemata* xxvi, and Theophras-
    tus, *De Ventis*), in which the horizon is divided into twelve sections of 30
    degrees each and winds blow in opposition to each other. Boreas, the north
    wind, opposes Afer (from Sierra Leone, then a Portuguese possession on the
    west coast of Africa) and Notus, the south wind; Thrascias (NW by 30°)
    opposes Sirocco (SE by 30°); Argestes (NW by 60°) opposes Eurus (SE by
    60°); Zephir (a 'ponent', i.e. western wind) opposes Levant (E); Libeccio
    (SW by 60°) opposes Caecius (NE by 60°).
718] Isa. lvii. 20 may be the ultimate source of this commonplace.

Of God, whom to behold was then my height
Of happiness; yet well, if here would end   725
The misery; I deserved it, and would bear
My own deservings; but this will not serve:
All that I eat or drink, or shall beget,
Is propagated curse. O voice, once heard
Delightfully, "Increase and multiply;"   730
Now death to hear! For what can I increase
Or multiply, but curses on my head?
Who of all ages to succeed, but feeling
The evil on him brought by me, will curse
My head? "Ill fare our ancestor impure;   735
For this we may thank Adam;" but his thanks
Shall be the execration; so besides
Mine own that bide upon me, all from me
Shall with a fierce reflux on me redound –
On me, as on their natural centre, light;   740
Heavy, though in their place. O fleeting joys
Of Paradise, dear bought with lasting woes!
Did I request thee, maker, from my clay
To mould me man? Did I solicit thee
From darkness to promote me, or here place   745
In this delicious garden? As my will
Concurred not to my being, it were but right
And equal to reduce me to my dust,
Desirous to resign and render back
All I received, unable to perform   750
Thy terms too hard, by which I was to hold
The good I sought not. To the loss of that,
Sufficient penalty, why hast thou added
The sense of endless woes? Inexplicable
Thy justice seems; yet, to say truth, too late   755
I thus contest; then should have been refused
Those terms, whatever, when they were proposed;
Thou didst accept them: wilt thou enjoy the good,
Then cavil the conditions? And though God
Made thee without thy leave, what if thy son   760
Prove disobedient, and reproved, retort,
"Wherefore didst thou beget me? I sought it not;"
Wouldst thou admit for his contempt of thee
That proud excuse? Yet him not thy election,

738 own] own curses.
740 light] plays on the meanings 'alight' and 'not heavy'.
743-4] Isa. xiv. 9.
748 equal] used in the Latin sense of 'fair, equitable, just'.
762] Isa. xiv. 10.

But natural necessity, begot.   765
God made thee of choice his own, and of his own
To serve him; thy reward was of his grace;
Thy punishment, then, justly is at his will.
Be it so, for I submit; his doom is fair,
That dust I am, and shall to dust return;   770
O welcome hour, whenever! Why delays
His hand to execute what his decree
Fixed on this day? Why do I overlive,
Why am I mocked with death, and lengthened out
To deathless pain? How gladly would I meet   775
Mortality, my sentence, and be earth
Insensible; how glad would lay me down
As in my mother's lap! There I should rest,
And sleep secure; his dreadful voice no more
Would thunder in my ears; no fear of worse   780
To me and to my offspring would torment me
With cruel expectation. Yet one doubt
Pursues me still – lest all I cannot die;
Lest that pure breath of life, the spirit of man
Which God inspired, cannot together perish   785
With this corporeal clod; then in the grave,
Or in some other dismal place, who knows
But I shall die a living death? O thought
Horrid, if true! Yet why? It was but breath
Of life that sinned: what dies but what had life   790
And sin? The body properly hath neither.
All of me, then, shall die: let this appease
The doubt, since human reach no further knows.
For though the Lord of all be infinite,
Is his wrath also? Be it, man is not so,   795
But mortal doomed. How can he exercise
Wrath without end on man, whom death must end?
Can he make deathless death? That were to make
Strange contradiction, which to God himself
Impossible is held, as argument   800
Of weakness, not of power. Will he draw out,
For anger's sake, finite to infinite
In punished man, to satisfy his rigour

792] Adam temporarily advocates the mortalist heresy, according to which
     both the spiritual and corporeal elements in man die at the same time (and
     are later resurrected together).
803-4] Satisfaction is a technical theological term for the payment of a penalty
     due to God on account of sin. Protestant theologians inherited Anselm's
     doctrine that Christ's death was a sufficient vicarious satisfaction for the
     sins of the world (cf. XII 419).

Satisfied never? That were to extend
His sentence beyond dust and nature's law;   805
By which all causes else according still
To the reception of their matter act,
Not to the extent of their own sphere. But say
That death be not one stroke, as I supposed,
Bereaving sense, but endless misery   810
From this day onward, which I feel begun
Both in me and without me, and so last
To perpetuity – ay me, that fear
Comes thundering back with dreadful revolution
On my defenceless head; both death and I   815
Am found eternal, and incorporate both:
Nor I on my part single; in me all
Posterity stands cursed; fair patrimony
That I must leave ye, sons; O were I able
To waste it all myself, and leave ye none!   820
So disinherited, how would ye bless
Me, now your curse! Ah, why should all mankind,
For one man's fault, thus guiltless be condemned,
If guiltless? But from me what can proceed
But all corrupt – both mind and will depraved   825
Not to do only, but to will the same
With me? How can they, then, acquitted stand
In sight of God? Him after all disputes,
Forced I absolve; all my evasions vain
And reasonings, though through mazes, lead me still   830
But to my own conviction: first and last
On me, me only, as the source and spring
Of all corruption, all the blame lights due;
So might the wrath. Fond wish! Couldst thou support
That burden, heavier than the earth to bear –   835
Than all the world much heavier, though divided
With that bad woman? Thus, what thou desir'st,
And what thou fear'st, alike destroys all hope
Of refuge, and concludes thee miserable
Beyond all past example and futúre –   840
To Satan only like, both crime and doom.
O Conscience! Into what abyss of fears
And horrors hast thou driven me; out of which

804-8] Adam appeals to a scholastic axiom, according to which *omne efficiens agit secundum vires recipientis, non suas* (every cause acts according to the powers of its recipient, not its own powers).
816] incorporate] refers to Paul's doctrine of the 'body of sin' (*corpus peccati*; Rom. vi. 6).

I find no way, from deep to deeper plunged!'
   Thus Adam to himself lamented loud   845
Through the still night – not now, as ere man fell,
Wholesome and cool and mild, but with black air
Accompanied, with damps and dreadful gloom;
Which to his evil conscience represented
All things with double terror; on the ground   850
Outstretched he lay, on the cold ground, and oft
Cursed his creation; death as oft accused
Of tardy execution, since denounced
The day of his offence. 'Why comes not death,'
Said he, 'with one thrice-acceptable stroke   855
To end me? Shall truth fail to keep her word,
Justice divine not hasten to be just?
But death comes not at call, justice divine
Mends not her slowest pace for prayers or cries.
O woods, O fountains, hillocks, dales, and bowers,   860
With other echo late I taught your shades
To answer, and resound far other song.'
Whom thus afflicted when sad Eve beheld,
Desolate where she sat, approaching nigh,
Soft words to his fierce passion she assayed;   865
But her, with stern regard, he thus repelled:
   'Out of my sight, thou serpent! That name best
Befits thee, with him leagued, thyself as false
And hateful: nothing wants, but that thy shape
Like his, and colour serpentine, may show   870
Thy inward fraud, to warn all creatures from thee
Henceforth, lest that too heavenly form, pretended
To hellish falsehood, snare them. But for thee
I had persisted happy, had not thy pride
And wandering vanity, when least was safe,   875
Rejected my forewarning, and disdained
Not to be trusted – longing to be seen,
Though by the devil himself; him overweening
To overreach; but with the serpent meeting,
Fooled and beguiled; by him thou, I by thee,   880
To trust thee from my side, imagined wise,
Constant, mature, proof against all assaults,
And understood not all was but a show,
Rather than solid virtue, all but a rib

867] According to a patristic tradition which drew on Philo, the Hebrew word
   for Eve means 'serpent'.
872 pretended] held in front as a covering.
884–8] Eve was traditionally thought to have been formed from a bent (hence
   morally defective) supernumerary rib. Sinister means 'left' (the original
   Latin sense) as well as 'corrupt, evil'.

Crooked by nature – bent, as now appears,   885
More to the part sinister – from me drawn;
Well if thrown out, as supernumerary
To my just number found. O why did God,
Creator wise, that peopled highest heaven
With spirits masculine, create at last   890
This novelty on earth, this fair defect
Of nature, and not fill the world at once
With men as angels, without feminine;
Or find some other way to generate
Mankind? This mischief had not then befallen,   895
And more that shall befall – innumerable
Disturbances on earth through female snares,
And strait conjunction with this sex; for either
He never shall find out fit mate, but such
As some misfortune brings him, or mistake;   900
Or whom he wishes most shall seldom gain,
Through her perverseness, but shall see her gained
By a far worse, or if she love, withheld
By parents; or his happiest choice too late
Shall meet, already linked and wedlock-bound   905
To a fell adversary, his hate or shame:
Which infinite calamity shall cause
To human life, and household peace confound.'
     He added not, and from her turned; but Eve,
Not so repulsed, with tears that ceased not flowing,   910
And tresses all disordered, at his feet
Fell humble, and embracing them, besought
His peace, and thus proceeded in her plaint:
     'Forsake me not thus, Adam, witness heaven
What love sincere and reverence in my heart   915
I bear thee, and unweeting have offended,
Unhappily deceived; thy suppliant
I beg, and clasp thy knees; bereave me not
Whereon I live, thy gentle looks, thy aid,
Thy counsel in this uttermost distress,   920
My only strength and stay; forlorn of thee,
Whither shall I betake me, where subsist?
While yet we live, scarce one short hour perhaps,
Between us two let there be peace, both joining,
As joined in injuries, one enmity   925
Against a foe by doom express assigned us,
That cruel serpent; on me exercise not
Thy hatred for this misery befallen –

888–95] Cf. Euripides, *Hippolytus* 616–19.

On me already lost, me than thyself
More miserable; both have sinned, but thou   930
Against God only, I against God and thee,
And to the place of judgement will return,
There with my cries importune heaven, that all
The sentence, from thy head removed, may light
On me, sole cause to thee of all this woe,   935
Me, me only, just object of his ire.'
　　She ended, weeping; and her lowly plight,
Immovable till peace obtained from fault
Acknowledged and deplored, in Adam wrought
Commiseration; soon his heart relented   940
Towards her, his life so late, and sole delight,
Now at his feet submissive in distress –
Creature so fair his reconcilement seeking,
His counsel whom she had displeased, his aid;
As one disarmed, his anger all he lost,   945
And thus with peaceful words upraised her soon:
　　'Unwary, and too desirous, as before
So now, of what thou know'st not, who desir'st
The punishment all on thyself; alas,
Bear thine own first, ill able to sustain   950
His full wrath whose thou feel'st as yet least part,
And my displeasure bear'st so ill. If prayers
Could alter high decrees, I to that place
Would speed before thee, and be louder heard,
That on my head all might be visited,   955
Thy frailty and infirmer sex forgiven,
To me committed, and by me exposed.
But rise; let us no more contend, nor blame
Each other, blamed enough elsewhere, but strive
In offices of love how we may lighten   960
Each other's burden in our share of woe;
Since this day's death denounced, if aught I see,
Will prove no sudden, but a slow-paced evil,
A long day's dying, to augment our pain,
And to our seed (O hapless seed!) derived.'   965
　　To whom thus Eve, recovering heart, replied:
'Adam, by sad experiment I know
How little weight my words with thee can find,
Found so erroneous, thence by just event
Found so unfortunate; nevertheless,   970

930–1] Psalm li. 4.
959 elsewhere] probably heaven, but possibly 'the place of judgement' (l. 932).
969 event] outcome, consequence.

Restored by thee, vile as I am, to place
Of new acceptance, hopeful to regain
Thy love, the sole contentment of my heart,
Living or dying from thee I will not hide
What thoughts in my unquiet breast are risen,   975
Tending to some relief of our extremes,
Or end, though sharp and sad, yet tolerable,
As in our evils, and of easier choice.
If care of our descent perplex us most
Which must be born to certain woe, devoured   980
By death at last – and miserable it is
To be to others cause of misery,
Our own begotten, and of our loins to bring
Into this cursed world a woeful race,
That after wretched life must be at last   985
Food for so foul a monster – in thy power
It lies, yet ere conception, to prevent
The race unblest, to being yet unbegot.
Childless thou art; childless remain; so death
Shall be deceived his glut, and with us two   990
Be forced to satisfy his ravenous maw.
But if thou judge it hard and difficult,
Conversing, looking, loving, to abstain
From love's due rites, nuptial embraces sweet,
And with desire to languish without hope   995
Before the present object languishing
With like desire – which would be misery
And torment less than none of what we dread –
Then both ourselves and seed at once to free
From what we fear for both, let us make short;   1000
Let us seek death, or, he not found, supply
With our own hands his office on ourselves;
Why stand we longer shivering under fears
That show no end but death, and have the power,
Of many ways to die the shortest choosing,   1005
Destruction with destruction to destroy?'
    She ended here, or vehement despair
Broke off the rest; so much of death her thoughts
Had entertained as dyed her cheeks with pale.
But Adam, with such counsel nothing swayed,   1010
To better hopes his more attentive mind

979 our descent perplex] our descendants torment.
989 so death] in early editions, printed at beginning of next line.
995] Cf. Dante, *Inferno* iv. 42.
996 object] Eve.

Labouring had raised, and thus to Eve replied:
    'Eve, thy contempt of life and pleasure seems
To argue in thee something more sublime
And excellent than what thy mind contemns: 1015
But self-destruction therefore sought refutes
That excellence thought in thee, and implies
Not thy contempt, but anguish and regret
For loss of life and pleasure overloved.
Or if thou covet death, as utmost end   1020
Of misery, so thinking to evade
The penalty pronounced, doubt not but God
Hath wiselier armed his vengeful ire than so
To be forestalled; much more I fear lest death
So snatched will not exempt us from the pain   1025
We are by doom to pay; rather such acts
Of contumacy will provoke the highest
To make death in us live; then let us seek
Some safer resolution – which methinks
I have in view, calling to mind with heed   1030
Part of our sentence, that thy seed shall bruise
The serpent's head; piteous amends, unless
Be meant whom I conjecture, our grand foe,
Satan, who in the serpent hath contrived
Against us this deceit; to crush his head   1035
Would be revenge indeed – which will be lost
By death brought on ourselves, or childless days
Resolved as thou proposest; so our foe
Shall scape his punishment ordained, and we
Instead shall double ours upon our heads.   1040
No more be mentioned, then, of violence
Against ourselves, and wilful barrenness
That cuts us off from hope, and savours only
Rancour and pride, impatience and despite,
Reluctance against God and his just yoke   1045
Laid on our necks. Remember with what mild
And gracious temper he both heard and judged,
Without wrath or reviling; we expected
Immediate dissolution, which we thought
Was meant by death that day, when lo, to thee   1050
Pains only in child-bearing were foretold,
And bringing forth, soon recompensed with joy,
Fruit of thy womb; on me the curse aslope

1045 Reluctance] resistance, opposition.
1052] John xvi. 21.
1053] Luke i. 42.

Glanced on the ground: with labour I must earn
My bread; what harm? Idleness had been worse;   1055
My labour will sustain me; and lest cold
Or heat should injure us, his timely care
Hath, unbesought, provided, and his hands
Clothed us unworthy, pitying while he judged;
How much more, if we pray him, will his ear   1060
Be open, and his heart to pity incline,
And teach us further by what means to shun
The inclement seasons, rain, ice, hail, and snow,
Which now the sky with various face begins
To show us in this mountain, while the winds   1065
Blow moist and keen, shattering the graceful locks
Of these fair spreading trees; which bids us seek
Some better shroud, some better warmth to cherish
Our limbs benumbed – ere this diurnal star
Leave cold the night, how we his gathered beams   1070
Reflected may with matter sere foment,
Or by collision of two bodies grind
The air attrite to fire; as late the clouds
Justling, or pushed with winds, rude in their shock,
Tine the slant lightning, whose thwart flame, driven down,
Kindles the gummy bark of fir or pine,   1076
And sends a comfortable heat from far,
Which might supply the sun; such fire to use,
And what may else be remedy or cure
To evils which our own misdeeds have wrought,   1080
He will instruct us praying, and of grace
Beseeching him; so as we need not fear
To pass commodiously this life, sustained
By him with many comforts, till we end
In dust, our final rest and native home.   1085
What better can we do than to the place
Repairing where he judged us, prostrate fall
Before him reverent, and there confess

1068 shroud] shelter. Cf. *Comus* 147.
1069 diurnal star] the sun.
1071 foment] means 'cherish with heat, warm' (cf. IV 669) and also draws on
    the Latin *fomentum*, which could mean 'kindling-wood'; 'sere' means 'dry'.
1073 attrite] means 'worn or ground down by friction', but inasmuch as the
    word may be thought to reflect Adam's state of mind, it may carry some of
    its usual theological sense (originally Scholastic, and later Protestant) of
    'having a sorrow for sin which proceeds from a sense of fear rather than (as
    does contrition, l. 1103) from the love of God'.
1075 Tine] kindle.
1078 supply] serve as a substitute for.

Humbly our faults, and pardon beg, with tears
Watering the ground, and with our sighs the air   1090
Frequenting, sent from hearts contrite, in sign
Of sorrow unfeigned and humiliation meek?
Undoubtedly he will relent, and turn
From his displeasure, in whose look serene,
When angry most he seemed and most severe,   1095
What else but favour, grace, and mercy shone?'
   So spake our father penitent, nor Eve
Felt less remorse; they forthwith to the place
Repairing where he judged them, prostrate fell
Before him reverent, and both confessed   1100
Humbly their faults, and pardon begged, with tears
Watering the ground, and with their sighs the air
Frequenting, sent from hearts contrite, in sign
Of sorrow unfeigned and humiliation meek.

THE END OF THE TENTH BOOK

1090-1] Dante, *Inferno* iv. 25-7 (cf. l. 995n.). 'Frequenting' means 'filling'.

BOOK XI

THE ARGUMENT

The Son of God presents to his Father the prayers of our first
parents now repenting, and intercedes for them; God accepts
them, but declares that they must no longer abide in Paradise;
sends Michael with a band of cherubim to dispossess them but first
to reveal to Adam future things: Michael's coming down. Adam
shows to Eve certain ominous signs: he discerns Michael's
approach; goes out to meet him: the angel denounces their
departure. Eve's lamentation. Adam pleads, but submits; the
angel leads him up to a high hill; sets before him in vision what
shall happen till the flood.

Thus they in lowliest plight repentant stood
Praying; for from the mercy-seat above
Prevenient grace descending had removed
The stony from their hearts, and made new flesh
Regenerate grow instead, that sighs now breathed   5
Unutterable, which the spirit of prayer
Inspired, and winged for heaven with speedier flight
Than loudest oratory; ye their port
Not of mean suitors; nor important less
Seemed their petition, than when the ancient pair   10
In fables old, less ancient yet than these,
Deucalion and chaste Pyrrha to restore
The race of mankind drowned, before the shrine
Of Themis stood devout. To heaven their prayers
Flew up, nor missed the way, by envious winds   15
Blown vagabond or frustrate: in they passed

2 mercy-seat] Exod. xxv. 17–22.
3 Prevenient grace] An ancient technical theological term (*gratia praeveniens*)
    for the kind of grace that precedes the free determination of the will. Cf. III
    231n.
3–5] Ezek. xi. 19.
5–7] Rom. viii. 26.
8 port] bearing (cf. IV 869).
10–14] Deucalion (the son of Prometheus) and Pyrrha built a small boat and so
    became the sole survivers when Zeus destroyed mankind with a universal
    flood. When the waters receded the ship landed on Mount Parnassus, and
    Deucalion and Pyrrha consulted the Delphic oracle (which was dedicated
    to Themis, i.e. Justitia, before it became Apollo's) about repopulating the
    earth (*Metamorphoses* i. 313–437).
15–16 nor ... frustrate] Alludes to Milton's 'Paradise of Fools' (III 444–97, esp.
    487–9).

Dimensionless through heavenly doors; then clad
With incense, where the golden altar fumed,
By their great intercessor, came in sight
Before the Father's throne; them the glad Son   20
Presenting thus to intercede began:
　'See, Father, what first-fruits on earth are sprung
From thy implanted grace in man – these sighs
And prayers, which in this golden censer, mixed
With incense, I thy priest before thee bring;   25
Fruits of more pleasing savour, from thy seed
Sown with contrition in his heart, than those
Which, his own hand manuring, all the trees
Of Paradise could have produced, ere fallen
From innocence. Now therefore bend thine ear   30
To supplication; hear his sighs, though mute;
Unskilful with what words to pray, let me
Interpret for him, me his advocate
And propitiation; all his words on me,
Good or not good, engraft; my merit those   35
Shall perfect, and for these my death shall pay.
Accept me, and in me from these receive
The smell of peace toward mankind; let him live,
Before thee reconciled, at least his days
Numbered, though sad, till death, his doom (which I   40
To mitigate thus plead, not to reverse),
To better life shall yield him, where with me
All my redeemed may dwell in joy and bliss,
Made one with me, as I with thee am one.'
　To whom the Father, without cloud, serene: 45
'All thy request for man, accepted Son,
Obtain; all thy request was my decree;
But longer in that Paradise to dwell
The law I gave to nature him forbids;
Those pure immortal elements, that know   50
No gross, no unharmonious mixture foul,
Eject him, tainted now, and purge him off
As a distemper, gross, to air as gross,
And mortal food, as may dispose him best
For dissolution wrought by sin, that first   55
Distempered all things, and of incorrupt
Corrupted. I at first with two fair gifts

18, 24] Rev. viii. 3.
33-4] I John ii. 1-2.
35 engraft] Rom. xi. 16-24. See III 293n.
44] John xvii. 11, 21-3.

Created him endowed – with happiness
And immortality; that fondly lost,
This other served but to eternize woe,   60
Till I provided death; so death becomes
His final remedy, and after life
Tried in sharp tribulation, and refined
By faith and faithful works, to second life,
Waked in the renovation of the just,   65
Resigns him up with heaven and earth renewed.
But let us call to synod all the blest
Through heaven's wide bounds; from them I will not hide
My judgements – how with mankind I proceed,
As how with peccant angels late they saw,   70
And in their state, though firm, stood more confirmed.'
  He ended, and the Son gave signal high
To the bright minister that watched; he blew
His trumpet, heard in Oreb since perhaps
When God descended, and perhaps once more   75
To sound at general doom. The angelic blast
Filled all the regions: from their blissful bowers
Of amarantine shade, fountain or spring,
By the waters of life, where'er they sat
In fellowships of joy, the sons of light   80
Hasted, resorting to the summons high,
And took their seats, till from his throne supreme
The almighty thus pronounced his sovereign will:
  'O sons, like one of us man is become
To know both good and evil, since his taste   85
Of that defended fruit; but let him boast
His knowledge of good lost and evil got,
Happier had it sufficed him to have known
Good by itself and evil not at all.
He sorrows now, repents, and prays contrite –   90
My motions in him; longer than they move,
His heart I know how variable and vain,
Self-left. Lest therefore his now bolder hand

59 fondly] foolishly.
65 renovation] renewal of the body at the resurrection.
66] II Pet. iii. 13.
70 peccant] sinning.
74 Oreb] See I 7–8n.
78 amarantine] See III 352–61n.
86 defended] forbidden.
91 motions] stirring of the soul, inward promptings. Cf. *PR* I 290, *SA* 1382.
93 Self-left] left to itself.

Reach also of the tree of life, and eat,
And live for ever, dream at least to live   95
For ever, to remove him I decree,
And send him from the garden forth, to till
The ground whence he was taken, fitter soil.
Michael, this my behest have thou in charge:
Take to thee from among the cherubim   100
Thy choice of flaming warriors, lest the fiend,
Or in behalf of man, or to invade
Vacant possession, some new trouble raise;
Haste thee, and from the Paradise of God
Without remorse drive out the sinful pair,   105
From hallowed ground the unholy, and denounce
To them and to their progeny, from thence
Perpetual banishment. Yet lest they faint
At the sad sentence rigorously urged –
For I behold them softened, and with tears   110
Bewailing their excess – all terror hide.
If patiently thy bidding they obey,
Dismiss them not disconsolate; reveal
To Adam what shall come in future days,
As I shall thee enlighten; intermix   115
My covenant in the woman's seed renewed;
So send them forth, though sorrowing, yet in peace;
And on the east side of the garden place,
Where entrance up from Eden easiest climbs,
Cherubic watch, and of a sword the flame   120
Wide-waving, all approach far off to fright,
And guard all passage to the tree of life;
Lest Paradise a receptacle prove
To spirits foul, and all my trees their prey,
With whose stolen fruit man once more to delude.'   125
   He ceased, and the archangelic power prepared
For swift descent; with him the cohort bright
Of watchful cherubim; four faces each
Had, like a double Janus; all their shape
Spangled with eyes more numerous than those   130

99 Michael] See VI 44n.
102 in behalf of] with regard to.
106 denounce] See X 210-11n.
111 excess] Cf. *Circumcision* 24n.
128] See VI 753 ('four faces each') and VI 749-59n.
129 double Janus] Janus, the god of gates and of the course of the year, was
    described and depicted in late antiquity as *quadrifrons* (four-faced).

Of Argus, and more wakeful than to drowse,
Charmed with Arcadian pipe, the pastoral reed
Of Hermes, or his opiate rod. Meanwhile,
To resalute the world with sacred light,
Leucothea waked, and with fresh dews embalmed   135
The earth, when Adam and first matron Eve
Had ended now their orisons, and found
Strength added from above, new hope to spring
Out of despair, joy, but with fear yet linked;
Which thus to Eve his welcome words renewed: 140
    'Eve, easily may faith admit that all
The good which we enjoy from heaven descends;
But that from us aught should ascend to heaven
So prevalent as to concern the mind
Of God high-blest, or to incline his will,   145
Hard to belief may seem; yet this will prayer,
Or one short sigh of human breath, upborne
Even to the seat of God. For since I sought
By prayer the offended Deity to appease,
Kneeled and before him humbled all my heart,   150
Methought I saw him placable and mild,
Bending his ear; persuasion in me grew
That I was heard with favour; peace returned
Home to my breast, and to my memory
His promise that thy seed shall bruise our foe;   155
Which, then not minded in dismay, yet now
Assures me that the bitterness of death
Is past, and we shall live. Whence hail to thee,
Eve rightly called, mother of all mankind,
Mother of all things living, since by thee   160
Man is to live, and all things live for man.'
    To whom thus Eve with sad demeanour meek:
'Ill-worthy I such title should belong
To me transgressor, who for thee ordained

131-3] Argus, the son of Arestor, was a giant with one hundred eyes, of which
    only one pair slept at a time. Juno ordered him to guard Io, whom Jove had
    turned into a heifer. Hermes (Mercury) charmed Argus to sleep with his
    pipe of reeds ('pastoral reed') and his sleep-producing wand ('opiate rod'),
    and then slew him (*Metamorphoses* i 568-779).
135] Leucothea (see *Comus* 875n.) was identified by the Romans with Mater
    Matuta, a goddess of dawn.
142] James i. 17.
144 prevalent] powerful.
157-8] I Sam. xv. 32.
158] Cf. V. 385-7n.

A help, became thy snare; to me reproach   165
Rather belongs, distrust and all dispraise;
But infinite in pardon was my judge,
That I, who first brought death on all, am graced
The source of life; next favourable thou,
Who highly thus to entitle me vouchsaf'st,   170
Far other name deserving. But the field
To labour calls us now with sweat imposed,
Though after sleepless night; for see the morn,
All unconcerned with our unrest, begins
Her rosy progress smiling; let us forth,   175
I never from thy side henceforth to stray,
Where'er our day's work lies, though now enjoined
Laborious, till day droop; while here we dwell,
What can be toilsome in these pleasant walks?
Here let us live, though in fallen state, content.'   180
     So spake, so wished, much-humbled Eve, but fate
Subscribed not; nature first gave signs, impressed
On bird, beast, air – air suddenly eclipsed,
After short blush of morn; nigh in her sight
The bird of Jove, stooped from his airy tower,   185
Two birds of gayest plume before him drove;
Down from a hill the beast that reigns in woods,
First hunter then, pursued a gentle brace,
Goodliest of all the forest, hart and hind;
Direct to the eastern gate was bent their flight.   190
Adam observed, and with his eye the chase
Pursuing, not unmoved to Eve thus spake:
     'O Eve, some further change awaits us nigh,
Which heaven by these mute signs in nature shows,
Forerunners of his purpose, or to warn   195
Us, haply too secure of our discharge
From penalty because from death released
Some days: how long, and what till then our life,
Who knows, or more than this, that we are dust,
And thither must return, and be no more?   200
Why else this double object in our sight,
Of flight pursued in the air and o'er the ground
One way the self-same hour? Why in the east
Darkness ere day's mid-course, and morning light
More orient in yon western cloud, that draws   205

180] Phil. iv. 11.
185 bird of Jove, stooped] the eagle, having swooped.
187 beast] lion.
204 Isa. xvi. 3.

O'er the blue firmament a radiant white,
And slow descends, with something heavenly fraught?'
    He erred not, for by this the heavenly bands
Down from a sky of jasper lighted now
In Paradise, and on a hill made halt –   210
A glorious apparition, had not doubt
And carnal fear that day dimmed Adam's eye.
Not that more glorious, when the angels met
Jacob in Mahanaim, where he saw
The field pavilioned with his guardians bright;   215
Nor that which on the flaming mount appeared
In Dothan, covered with a camp of fire,
Against the Syrian king, who to surprise
One man, assassin-like, had levied war,
War unproclaimed. The princely hierarch   220
In their bright stand there left his powers to seize
Possession of the garden; he alone,
To find where Adam sheltered, took his way,
Not unperceived of Adam, who to Eve,
While the great visitant approached, thus spake: 225
    'Eve, now expect great tidings, which perhaps
Of us will soon determine, or impose
New laws to be observed; for I descry
From yonder blazing cloud that veils the hill,
One of the heavenly host, and by his gait,   230
None of the meanest – some great potentate
Or of the thrones above, such majesty
Invests him coming; yet not terrible,
That I should fear, nor sociably mild,
As Raphael, that I should much confide,   235
But solemn and sublime; whom, not to offend,
With reverence I must meet, and thou retire.'
    He ended; and the archangel soon drew nigh,
Not in his shape celestial, but as man
Clad to meet man; over his lucid arms   240
A military vest of purple flowed,

209] Rev. xxi. 11.
213-15] Gen. xxxii. 1-2 *Mahanaim* means 'two camps' in Hebrew (cf. LXX,
    παρεμβολαί, and Vulgate, *id est, Castra*), Milton's 'field pavilioned'.
216-20] II Kings vi. 13-18. 'One man' is Elisha, for the capture of whom 'the
    Syrian king' besieged Dothan.
    assassin] then felt as a metaphor, with reference to the Assassins (literally
    'hashish-eaters'), a Shi'te sect feared for its practice of murdering enemies
    by stealth.
227 determine] cause to end.

Livelier than Meliboean, or the grain
Of Sarra, worn by kings and heroes old
In time of truce; Iris had dipped the woof;
His starry helm unbuckled showed him prime   245
In manhood where youth ended; by his side,
As in glistering zodiac, hung the sword,
Satan's dire dread, and in his hand the spear.
Adam bowed low; he, kingly, from his state
Inclined not, but his coming thus declared: 250
  'Adam, heaven's high behest no preface needs;
Sufficient that thy prayers are heard, and Death,
Then due by sentence when thou didst transgress,
Defeated of his seizure many days,
Given thee of grace, wherein thou may'st repent,   255
And one bad act with many deeds well done
May'st cover; well may then thy Lord, appeased,
Redeem thee quite from Death's rapacious claim;
But longer in this Paradise to dwell
Permits not; to remove thee I am come,   260
And send thee from the garden forth to till
The ground whence thou wast taken, fitter soil.'
He added not, for Adam, at the news
Heart-strook, with chilling gripe of sorrow stood,
That all his senses bound; Eve, who unseen   265
Yet all had heard, with audible lament
Discovered soon the place of her retire:
  'O unexpected stroke, worse than of Death!
Must I leave thee, Paradise? Thus leave
Thee, native soil, these happy walks and shades,   270
Fit haunt of gods, where I had hope to spend,
Quiet, though sad, the respite of that day
That must be mortal to us both? O flowers,
That never will in other climate grow,
My early visitation, and my last   275
At even, which I bred up with tender hand
From the first opening bud, and gave ye names,
Who now shall rear ye to the sun, or rank

242 Meliboean] Meliboea, in Thessaly, was famous in antiquity for its purple
    dye.
243 Sarra] Tyre, which was also famous for its dye.
244] See *Comus* 83n.
247] Cf. VI 250, 320-23.
249 state] stateliness of bearing.
264 gripe] spasm.
267 discovered] revealed.

Your tribes, and water from the ambrosial fount?
Thee lastly nuptial bower, by me adorned　　　　280
With what to sight or smell was sweet, from thee
How shall I part, and whither wander down
Into a lower world, to this obscure
And wild? How shall we breathe in other air
Less pure, accustomed to immortal fruits?'　　　　285
　　Whom thus the angel interrupted mild:
'Lament not, Eve, but patiently resign
What justly thou hast lost; nor set thy heart,
Thus over-fond, on that which is not thine;
Thy going is not lonely; with thee goes　　　　290
Thy husband; him to follow thou art bound;
Where he abides, think there thy native soil.'
　　Adam, by this from the cold sudden damp
Recovering, and his scattered spirits returned,
To Michael thus his humble words addressed:　　　　295
　　'Celestial, whether among the thrones, or named
Of them the highest – for such of shape may seem
Prince above princes – gently hast thou told
Thy message, which might else in telling wound,
And in performing end us; what besides　　　　300
Of sorrow and dejection and despair,
Our frailty can sustain, thy tidings bring –
Departure from this happy place, our sweet
Recess, and only consolation left
Familiar to our eyes; all places else　　　　305
Inhospitable appear, and desolate,
Nor knowing us, nor known; and if by prayer
Incessant I could hope to change the will
Of him who all things can, I would not cease
To weary him with my assiduous cries;　　　　310
But prayer against his absolute decree
No more avails than breath against the wind,
Blown stifling back on him that breathes it forth:
Therefore to his great bidding I submit.
This most afflicts me – that, departing hence,　　　　315
As from his face I shall be hid, deprived
His blessed countenance; here I could frequent,
With worship, place by place where he vouchsafed

283 to] compared with.
293 damp] dazed or stupefied condition (i.e. the bound senses of l. 265).
298] Dan. x. 13, and A.V. marginal note.
309 can] knows.
316] Gen. iv. 14.

Presence divine, and to my sons relate,
"On this mount he appeared; under this tree   320
Stood visible; among these pines his voice
I heard; here with him at this fountain talked;"
So many grateful altars I would rear
Of grassy turf, and pile up every stone
Of lustre from the brook, in memory   325
Or monument to ages, and thereon
Offer sweet-smelling gums, and fruits, and flowers;
In yonder nether world where shall I seek
His bright appearances, or footstep trace?
For though I fled him angry, yet recalled   330
To life prolonged and promised race, I now
Gladly behold though but his utmost skirts
Of glory, and far off his steps adore.'
    To whom thus Michael, with regard benign:
'Adam, thou know'st heaven his, and all the earth,   335
Not this rock only; his omnipresence fills
Land, sea, and air, and every kind that lives,
Fomented by his virtual power and warmed;
All the earth he gave thee to possess and rule,
No despicable gift; surmise not then   340
His presence to these narrow bounds confined
Of Paradise or Eden; this had been
Perhaps thy capital seat, from whence had spread
All generations, and had hither come,
From all the ends of the earth, to celebrate   345
And reverence thee their great progenitor.
But this pre-eminence thou hast lost, brought down
To dwell on even ground now with thy sons:
Yet doubt not but in valley and in plain
God is as here, and will be found alike   350
Present, and of his presence many a sign
Still following thee, still compassing thee round
With goodness and paternal love, his face
Express, and of his steps the track divine.
Which that thou may'st believe, and be confirmed   355
Ere thou from hence depart, know I am sent
To show thee what shall come in future days
To thee and to thy offspring; good with bad
Expect to hear, supernal grace contending
With sinfulness of men – thereby to learn   360
True patience, and to temper joy with fear
And pious sorrow, equally inured

338 virtual] effective, potent, powerful.

By moderation either state to bear,
Prosperous or adverse: so shalt thou lead
Safest thy life, and best prepared endure   365
Thy mortal passage when it comes. Ascend
This hill; let Eve (for I have drenched her eyes)
Here sleep below while thou to foresight wak'st,
As once thou slept'st while she to life was formed.'
To whom thus Adam gratefully replied: 370
'Ascend; I follow thee, safe guide, the path
Thou lead'st me, and to the hand of heaven submit,
However chastening – to the evil turn
My obvious breast, arming to overcome
By suffering, and earn rest from labour won,   375
If so I may attain.' So both ascend
In the visions of God; it was a hill,
Of Paradise the highest, from whose top
The hemisphere of earth in clearest ken
Stretched out to the amplest reach of prospect lay.   380
Not higher that hill, nor wider looking round,
Whereon for different cause the tempter set
Our second Adam in the wilderness,
To show him all earth's kingdoms and their glory.
His eye might there command wherever stood   385
City of old or modern fame, the seat
Of mightiest empire, from the destined walls
Of Cambalu, seat of Cathaian khan,
And Samarkand by Oxus, Temir's throne,
To Paquin, of Sinaean kings, and thence   390
To Agra and Lahore of Great Mogul,
Down to the golden Chersonese, or where

---

374 obvious] exposed.

377] Ezek. xl. 2.

381-4] Cf. *PR* III 251 ff.

388 Cambalu] capital of Cathay, and seat of the khan.

389 Samarkand] Samarkand, in modern Uzbekistan, about 150 miles from the Oxus River (now Amu-Darya), was the seat of Temir Lang, Marlowe's Tamburlaine.

390] Peking (Paquin) was the seat of the Chinese (Sinaean) kings; here China is clearly distinguished from Cathay (l. 388). Contrast III 438n.

391] Agra, in Uttar Pradesh (northern India), and Lahore, in the Punjab (Pakistan), are both former Mogul capitals. 'Great Mogul' was the usual European designation for the emperor of Delhi, which after 1526 was the capital of a huge Mogul empire.

392 colden Chersonese] *Aurea Chersonesus*, so called because of its fabled wealth, was rather vaguely identified with the area east of India, possibly the Malay Peninsula. Cf. *PR* IV 74.

The Persian in Ecbatan sat, or since
In Hispahan, or where the Russian czar
In Moscow, or the Sultan in Bizance,   395
Turkestan-born; nor could his eye not ken
The empire of Negus to his utmost port
Ercoco, and the less maritime kings,
Mombaza, and Quiloa, and Melind,
And Sofala – thought Ophir – to the realm   400
Of Congo, and Angola farthest south,
Or thence from Niger flood to Atlas mount,
The kingdoms of Almansor, Fez and Sus,
Marocco, and Algiers, and Tremisen;
On Europe thence, and where Rome was to sway   405
The world: in spirit perhaps he also saw
Rich Mexico, the seat of Montezume,
And Cuzco in Peru, the richer seat
Of Atabalipa, and yet unspoiled

393] Ecbatan, now Hamadan, a Median city which was the summer capital of
    Persian kings.
394] Hispahan, now Isfahan, replaced Kasvin (X 436n.) as the Persian capital
    in the sixteenth century.
395-6] Bizance (Byzantium, later Constantinople and now Istanbul) was after
    1453 the seat of the Turkish Sultans, who belonged to a tribe that had
    originally come from Turkestan, in central Asia. The form 'Bizance' derives
    from the English bezant, a coin first struck in Byzantium.
397 Negus] the Amharic term for the title of the supreme ruler of Abyssinia
    (now Ethiopia).
398] Ercoco (modern Arkiks) is a port on the Red Sea near Massawa.
399] Mombaza (Mombasa, in Kenya), Quiloa (Kilwa Kisiwani, in Tanzania),
    and Melind (Malindi, in Kenya) were all Muslim colonies on the coast of
    East Africa.
400] Sofala, a port south of the Zambezi (in modern Mozambique), was
    sometimes identified with Ophir, which is mentioned many times in the
    O.T. as the source of Solomon's gold.
402] The Niger River in modern Guinea and Mali, and the Atlas mountains in
    Morocco.
403 Almansor] The Arabic regnal title 'al-Mansur' ('the Victorious') was
    applied to many rulers, in this case to the twelfth-century Almohad emir
    Abu-Yusuf Ya'qub al-Mansur, the only 'al-Mansur' described in the
    accounts of North Africa (all based on Leo Africanus) available to Milton.
    Fez] part of the sultanate of Fez and Morocco.
    Sus] a province of southern Morocco, once an independent kingdom.
404] On Marocco, see I 583-4n. Tremisen, now Tlemcen, in Algeria, was once an
    independent sultanate.
407 Montezume] Montezuma II, last ruler of the Aztec empire, in Mexico, was
    defeated by Cortés.
408-9] Cuzco, the Inca capital (in modern Peru), was the seat of Atahuallpa
    ('Atabalipa'), who was defeated by Pizarro.

Guiana, whose great city Geryon's sons   410
Call El Dorado; but to nobler sights
Michael from Adam's eyes the film removed,
Which that false fruit that promised clearer sight
Had bred; then purged with euphrasy and rue
The visual nerve, for he had much to see,   415
And from the well of life three drops instilled.
So deep the power of these ingredients pierced,
Even to the inmost seat of mental sight,
That Adam, now enforced to close his eyes,
Sunk down, and all his spirits became entranced;   420
But him the gentle angel by the hand
Soon raised, and his attention thus recalled:
  'Adam, now ope thine eyes, and first behold
The effects which thy original crime hath wrought
In some to spring from thee, who never touched   425
The excepted tree, nor with the snake conspired,
Nor sinned thy sin, yet from that sin derive
Corruption to bring forth more violent deeds.'
  His eyes he opened, and beheld a field,
Part arable and tilth, whereon were sheaves   430
New-reaped, the other part sheep-walks and folds;
I' the midst an altar as the landmark stood,
Rustic, of grassy sward; thither anon
A sweaty reaper from his tillage brought
First-fruits, the green ear and the yellow sheaf,   435
Unculled, as came to hand; a shepherd next,
More meek, came with the firstlings of his flock,
Choicest and best; then sacrificing, laid
The inwards and their fat, with incense strewed,

410-11] Manoa, the mythical golden city of Guiana, was called El Dorado by
    the Spanish, who are here (following Spenser, *Faerie Queene* V. x. 8-10)
    called Geryon's sons. Geryon was a three-headed monster who ruled
    Erythea, a mythical island vaguely situated to the west of Europe. On 21
    July 1667, about a month before *PL* was published, Guiana was ceded (in
    the Peace of Breda) by the English to the Dutch (in exchange for New
    York), so 'yet unspoiled' would have been seen as (and conceivably could
    have been) a topical reference.
412] Cf. *Iliad* v 127, *Aeneid* ii 604-5.
414 euphrasy] a medicinal plant (eyebright) and (etymologically, from
    εὐφρασία) 'good cheer'.
    rue] a medicinal plant, and (in a common play on the word) 'pity,
    compassion'; Shakespeare twice calls it 'herb of grace'.
416] Psalm xxxvi. 9.
427-60] For the story of Cain and Abel see Gen. iv.
436 Unculled] not selected.

On the cleft wood, and all due rites performed.   440
His offering soon propitious fire from heaven
Consumed, with nimble glance and grateful steam;
The other's not, for his was not sincere:
Whereat he inly raged, and as they talked,
Smote him into the midriff with a stone   445
That beat out life; he fell, and deadly pale,
Groaned out his soul, with gushing blood effused.
Much at that sight was Adam in his heart
Dismayed, and thus in haste to the angel cried:
    'O teacher, some great mischief hath befallen   450
To that meek man, who well had sacrificed;
Is piety thus and pure devotion paid?'
    To whom Michael thus, he also moved, replied:
'These two are brethren, Adam, and to come
Out of thy loins; the unjust the just hath slain,   455
For envy that his brother's offering found
From heaven acceptance; but the bloody fact
Will be avenged, and the other's faith approved
Lose no reward, though here thou see him die,
Rolling in dust and gore.' To which our sire: 460
    'Alas, both for the deed and for the cause!
But have I now seen death? Is this the way
I must return to native dust? O sight
Of terror, foul and ugly to behold;
Horrid to think, how horrible to feel!'   465
    To whom thus Michael: 'Death thou hast seen
In his first shape on man; but many shapes
Of Death, and many are the ways that lead
To his grim cave – all dismal, yet to sense
More terrible at the entrance than within.   470
Some, as thou saw'st, by violent stroke shall die,
By fire, flood, famine; by intemperance more
In meats and drinks, which on the earth shall bring
Diseases dire, of which a monstrous crew
Before thee shall appear, that thou may'st know   475
What misery the inabstinence of Eve
Shall bring on men.' Immediately a place
Before his eyes appeared, sad, noisome, dark;
A lazar-house it seemed, wherein were laid
Numbers of all diseased – all maladies   480

457 fact] evil deed.
458–60] Heb. xi. 4.
468–70] The details are those of the classical underworld (see *Metamorphoses* iv
    432–45, and the famous description in *Aeneid* vi).

Of ghastly spasm, or racking torture, qualms
Of heart-sick agony, all feverous kinds,
Convulsions, epilepsies, fierce catarrhs,
Intestine stone and ulcer, colic pangs,
Demoniac frenzy, moping melancholy,   485
And moon-struck madness, pining atrophy,
Marasmus, and wide-wasting pestilence,
Dropsies and asthmas, and joint-racking rheums.
Dire was the tossing, deep the groans; Despair
Tended the sick, busiest from couch to couch;   490
And over them triumphant Death his dart
Shook, but delayed to strike, though oft invoked
With vows, as their chief good and final hope.
Sight so deform what heart of rock could long
Dry-eyed behold? Adam could not, but wept,   495
Though not of woman born: compassion quelled
His best of man, and gave him up to tears
A space, till firmer thoughts restrained excess,
And, scarce recovering words, his plaint renewed:
    'O miserable mankind, to what fall   500
Degraded, to what wretched state reserved!
Better end here unborn. Why is life given
To be thus wrested from us? Rather why
Obtruded on us thus? Who, if we knew
What we receive, would either not accept   505
Life offered, or soon beg to lay it down,
Glad to be so dismissed in peace. Can thus
The image of God in man, created once
So goodly and erect, though faulty since,
To such unsightly sufferings be debased   510
Under inhuman pains? Why should not man,
Retaining still divine similitude
In part, from such deformities be free,
And for his maker's image sake exempt?'
    'Their maker's image,' answered Michael, 'then   515
Forsook them, when themselves they vilified
To serve ungoverned appetite, and took
His image whom they served – a brutish vice,
Inductive mainly to the sin of Eve.

---

486 moon-struck madness] lunacy, i.e. intermittent insanity caused by the
     changes of the moon (*luna*).
487 Marasmus] wasting away of the body.
504-6] Adam's response is Stoical (cf. Seneca, *Ad Marciam: De Consolatione*
     xxii. 3).
511-25] See VII 519-20n.
519 Inductive] inducing, leading on.

Therefore so abject is their punishment,   520
Disfiguring not God's likeness, but their own;
Or if his likeness, by themselves defaced
While they pervert pure nature's healthful rules
To loathsome sickness – worthily, since they
God's image did not reverence in themselves.'   525
    'I yield it just,' said Adam, 'and submit.
But is there yet no other way, besides
These painful passages, how we may come
To death, and mix with our connatural dust?'
    'There is,' said Michael, 'if thou well observe   530
The rule of "not too much", by temperance taught
In what thou eat'st and drink'st, seeking from thence
Due nourishment, not gluttonous delight,
Till many years over thy head return;
So may'st thou live, till like ripe fruit thou drop   535
Into thy mother's lap, or be with ease
Gathered, not harshly plucked, for death mature:
This is old age; but then thou must outlive
Thy youth, thy strength, thy beauty, which will change
To withered, weak, and grey; thy senses then,   540
Obtuse, all taste of pleasure must forgo
To what thou hast; and for the air of youth,
Hopeful and cheerful, in thy blood will reign
A melancholy damp of cold and dry,
To weigh thy spirits down, and last consume   545
The balm of life.' To whom our ancestor:
    'Henceforth I fly not death, nor would prolong
Life much – bent rather how I may be quit,
Fairest and easiest, of this cumbrous charge,
Which I must keep till my appointed day   550
Of rendering up, and patiently attend
My dissolution.' Michael replied:
    'Nor love thy life, nor hate; but what thou liv'st
Live well; how long or short permit to heaven;
And now prepare thee for another sight.'   555
    He looked, and saw a spacious plain, whereon
Were tents of various hue: by some were herds
Of cattle grazing: others whence the sound
Of instruments that made melodious chime

---

531 not too much] Alludes to the ancient aphorism μηδὲν ἄγαν (or *ne quid nimis*), nothing in excess.
535-7] The ultimate source of the comparison is Cicero's essay *De Senectute* 19.
553-4] A classical commonplace (e.g. Horace, *Odes*, I. ix. 9, Martial, *Epigrams* X. xlvii. 13, Seneca, *Epistles* lxv. 18).

Was heard, of harp and organ, and who moved   560
Their stops and chords was seen: his volant touch
Instinct through all proportions low and high
Fled and pursued transverse the resonant fugue.
In other part stood one who, at the forge
Labouring, two massy clods of iron and brass   565
Had melted (whether found where casual fire
Had wasted woods, on mountain or in vale,
Down to the veins of earth, thence gliding hot
To some cave's mouth, or whether washed by stream
From underground); the liquid ore he drained   570
Into fit moulds prepared; from which he formed
First his own tools, then what might else be wrought
Fusile or graven in metal. After these,
But on the hither side, a different sort   574
From the high neighbouring hills, which was their seat,
Down to the plain descended: by their guise
Just men they seemed, and all their study bent
To worship God aright, and know his works
Not hid, nor those things last which might preserve
Freedom and peace to men; they on the plain   580
Long had not walked when from the tents behold
A bevy of fair women, richly gay
In gems and wanton dress; to the harp they sung
Soft amorous ditties, and in dance came on;
The men, though grave, eyed them, and let their eyes   585
Rove without rein, till, in the amorous net
Fast caught, they liked, and each his liking chose;
And now of love they treat, till the evening star,
Love's harbinger, appeared; then all in heat,
They light the nuptial torch, and bid invoke   590
Hymen, then first to marriage rites invoked:

560 who] Jubal, 'the father of all such as handle the harp and organ', Gen. iv.
     21.
561 volant] moving rapidly and lightly.
562 Instinct] impelled, animated.
     proportions] melodies, harmony.
564 one] Tubal-cain, 'an instructor of every artificer in brass and iron', Gen. iv.
     22.
566 casual] accidental (used of unfortunate events).
573 Fusile] formed by melting or casting.
574-627] Gen. vi. 2-4, the substance of which is recapitulated in ll. 621-2; cf.
     III 463-5, V 447-8.
578-9] According to an ancient tradition (e.g. Josephus, *Antiquities* I. ii. 3) the
     descendants of Seth discovered astronomy, the study of God's 'works/Not
     hid'.
588 evening star] Hesperus, which is also 'love's harbinger' in VIII 519-20.
590-1 invoke/Hymen] See IV 711n.

With feast and music all the tents resound.
Such happy interview, and fair event
Of love and youth not lost, songs, garlands, flowers,
And charming symphonies, attached the heart   595
Of Adam, soon inclined to admit delight,
The bent of nature; which he thus expressed:
    'True opener of mine eyes, prime angel blest,
Much better seems this vision, and more hope
Of peaceful days portends, than those two past: 600
Those were of hate and death, or pain much worse;
Here nature seems fulfilled in all her ends.'
    To whom thus Michael: 'Judge not what is best
By pleasure, though to nature seeming meet,
Created, as thou art, to nobler end,   605
Holy and pure, conformity divine.
Those tents thou saw'st so pleasant were the tents
Of wickedness, wherein shall dwell his race
Who slew his brother: studious they appear
Of arts that polish life; inventors rare;   610
Unmindful of their maker, though his spirit
Taught them; but they his gifts acknowledge none.
Yet they a beauteous offspring shall beget;
For that fair female troop thou saw'st, that seemed
Of goddesses, so blithe, so smooth, so gay,   615
Yet empty of all good wherein consists
Woman's domestic honour and chief praise;
Bred only and completed to the taste
Of lustful appetence, to sing, to dance,
To dress, and troll the tongue, and roll the eye;   620
To these that sober race of men, whose lives
Religious titled them the sons of God,
Shall yield up all their virtue, all their fame,
Ignobly, to the trains and to the smiles
Of these fair atheists, and now swim in joy   625
(Erelong to swim at large) and laugh; for which
The world erelong a world of tears must weep.'

607–8] Psalm lxxxiv. 10. Cain's descendant Jabal 'was the father of such as
    dwell in tents' (Gen. iv. 20).
609–12] The children of Cain were believed to have invented the arts (Gen. iv.
    16–22).
619 appetence] desire, appetite.
620 troll] wag.
621–2] See 574–627n. Milton dissents from the common patristic idea that the
    'sons of God' were fallen angels, and aligns himself with those (such as
    Augustine) who identified them with the descendants of Seth.
624 trains] deceits, snares.

   To whom thus Adam, of short joy bereft:
'O pity and shame, that they who to live well
Entered so fair, should turn aside to tread   630
Paths indirect, or in the midway faint!
But still I see the tenor of man's woe
Holds on the same, from woman to begin.'
   'From man's effeminate slackness it begins,'
Said the angel, 'who should better hold his place   635
By wisdom, and superior gifts received.
But now prepare thee for another scene.'
   He looked, and saw wide territory spread
Before him – towns, and rural works between,
Cities of men with lofty gates and towers,   640
Concourse in arms, fierce faces threatening war,
Giants of mighty bone and bold emprise;
Part wield their arms, part curb the foaming steed,
Single or in array of battle ranged
Both horse and foot, nor idly mustering stood;   645
One way a band select from forage drives
A herd of beeves, fair oxen and fair kine,
From a fat meadow-ground, or fleecy flock,
Ewes and their bleating lambs, over the plain,
Their booty; scarce with life the shepherds fly,   650
But call in aid, which makes a bloody fray:
With cruel tournament the squadrons join;
Where cattle pastured late, now scattered lies
With carcasses and arms the ensanguined field
Deserted; others to a city strong   655
Lay siege, encamped, by battery, scale, and mine,
Assaulting; others from the wall defend
With dart and javelin, stones and sulphurous fire;
On each hand slaughter and gigantic deeds.
In other part the sceptred heralds call   660
To council in the city-gates: anon
Grey-headed men and grave, with warriors mixed,
Assemble, and harangues are heard; but soon
In factious opposition, till at last
Of middle age one rising, eminent   665

632-3] In sixteenth- and seventeenth-century etymology 'woman' was said to
    mean 'woe of man'.
638-73] Imitates the scenes depicted on the shields of Achilles (*Iliad* xviii
    478-540) and Aeneas (*Aeneid* viii 626-728).
641 Concourse] hostile encounter.
642 emprise] chivalric prowess.
656 scale] ladder.
665 one] Enoch (Gen. v. 21-4, Heb. xi. 5, Jude 14-15).

In wise deport, spake much of right and wrong,
Of justice, of religion, truth, and peace,
And judgement from above: him old and young
Exploded, and had seized with violent hands,
Had not a cloud descending snatched him thence,   670
Unseen amid the throng; so violence
Proceeded, and oppression, and sword-law,
Through all the plain, and refuge none was found.
Adam was all in tears, and to his guide
Lamenting turned full sad: 'O what are these,   675
Death's ministers, not men, who thus deal death
Inhumanly to men, and multiply
Ten thousandfold the sin of him who slew
His brother; for of whom such massacre
Make they but of their brethren, men of men?   680
But who was that just man, whom had not heaven
Rescued, had in his righteousness been lost?'
    To whom thus Michael: 'These are the product
Of those ill-mated marriages thou saw'st   684
Where good with bad were matched; who of themselves
Abhor to join, and by imprudence mixed,
Produce prodigious births of body or mind.
Such were these giants, men of high renown;
For in those days might only shall be admired,
And valour and heroic virtue called;   690
To overcome in battle, and subdue
Nations, and bring home spoils with infinite
Manslaughter, shall be held the highest pitch
Of human glory, and for glory done,
Of triumph, to be styled great conquerors,   695
Patrons of mankind, gods, and sons of gods –
Destroyers rightlier called, and plagues of men.
Thus fame shall be achieved, renown on earth,
And what most merits fame in silence hid.
But he, the seventh from thee, whom thou beheld'st   700
The only righteous in a world perverse,
And therefore hated, therefore so beset
With foes, for daring single to be just,
And utter odious truth, that God would come

669 Exploded] See X 546n.
670-1] Milton probably had access to the tradition embodied in the pseudepi-
    graphical Ethiopic Book of Enoch (xiv. 8-9) that the translation of Enoch
    (see III 461n.) was initiated by an invitation extended by the clouds.
688-9] Gen. vi. 4.
700 seventh from thee] Jude 14; Gen. v. 3-18.

To judge them with his saints – him the most high,　　705
Rapt in a balmy cloud, with winged steeds,
Did, as thou saw'st, receive, to walk with God
High in salvation and the climes of bliss,
Exempt from death, to show thee what reward
Awaits the good, the rest what punishment;　　　　710
Which now direct thine eyes and soon behold.'
　　He looked, and saw the face of things quite changed;
The brazen throat of war had ceased to roar;
All now was turned to jollity and game,
To luxury and riot, feast and dance,　　　　　　715
Marrying or prostituting, as befell,
Rape or adultery, where passing fair
Allured them; thence from cups to civil broils.
At length a reverend sire among them came,
And of their doings great dislike declared,　　　720
And testified against their ways; he oft
Frequented their assemblies, whereso met,
Triumphs or festivals, and to them preached
Conversion and repentance, as to souls
In a prison, under judgements imminent;　　　　725
But all in vain; which when he saw, he ceased
Contending, and removed his tents far off;
Then from the mountain hewing timber tall,
Began to build a vessel of huge bulk,
Measured by cubit, length, and breadth, and height,　730
Smeared round with pitch, and in the side a door
Contrived, and of provisions laid in large
For man and beast: when lo a wonder strange!
Of every beast, and bird, and insect small,
Came sevens and pairs, and entered in, as taught　735
Their order; last the sire and his three sons,

706] A conflation of the tradition described in 670–1n. with the description of
　　the translation of Elijah (II Kings ii. 11).
707 walk with God] Gen. v. 24.
714–18] Luke xvii. 26–7; 'luxury' means 'lust'.
717 passing fair] 'Fair' means 'beautiful woman', and 'passing' plays on the
　　senses 'passing by' and 'exceedingly'.
719–53] Gen. vi. 5–vii. 24; Heb. xi. 7.
719 reverend sire] Noah.
723–5] I Pet. iii. 18–21.
734] Insects were added to the Biblical passenger-list by those Renaissance
　　commentators on Genesis who had rejected the traditional belief that
　　insects arose spontaneously from putrefaction and instead believed with
　　Milton that insects were generated in the same way as other animals (cf. IV
　　704, VII 476).

With their four wives; and God made fast the door.
Meanwhile the south-wind rose, and with black wings
Wide-hovering, all the clouds together drove
From under heaven; the hills to their supply   740
Vapour, and exhalation dusk and moist,
Sent up amain; and now the thickened sky
Like a dark ceiling stood: down rushed the rain
Impetuous, and continued till the earth
No more was seen; the floating vessel swum   745
Uplifted, and secure with beaked prow
Rode tilting o'er the waves; all dwellings else
Flood overwhelmed, and them with all their pomp
Deep under water rolled; sea covered sea,
Sea without shore: and in their palaces,   750
Where luxury late reigned, sea-monsters whelped
And stabled: of mankind, so numerous late,
All left in one small bottom swum embarked.
How didst thou grieve then, Adam, to behold
The end of all thy offspring, end so sad,   755
Depopulation; thee another flood,
Of tears and sorrow a flood thee also drowned,
And sunk thee as thy sons; till gently reared
By the angel, on thy feet thou stood'st at last,
Though comfortless, as when a father mourns   760
His children, all in view destroyed at once,
And scarce to the angel utter'dst thus thy plaint:
     'O visions ill foreseen! Better had I
Lived ignorant of future – so had borne
My part of evil only, each day's lot   765
Enough to bear; those now that were dispensed
The burden of many ages on me light
At once, by my foreknowledge gaining birth
Abortive, to torment me, ere their being,
With thought that they must be. Let no man seek   770
Henceforth to be foretold what shall befall
Him or his children – evil, he may be sure,
Which neither his foreknowing can prevent,
And he the future evil shall no less
In apprehension than in substance feel   775
Grievous to bear; but that care now is past;

738–53] Many of the details are drawn from Ovid's account of the universal
     flood in *Metamorphoses* i 253–347. Cf. ll. 10–14n.
753 bottom] boat.
765–6] Matt. vi. 34.
773–4 neither ... And] Imitates the Latin construction '*neque ... et*'.

Man is not whom to warn; those few escaped,
Famine and anguish will at last consume,
Wandering that watery desert; I had hope,
When violence was ceased and war on earth,   780
All would have then gone well, peace would have crowned
With length of happy days, the race of man;
But I was far deceived, for now I see
Peace to corrupt no less than war to waste.
How comes it thus? Unfold, celestial guide,   785
And whether here the race of man will end.'
        To whom thus Michael: 'Those whom last thou saw'st
In triumph and luxurious wealth, are they
First seen in acts of prowess eminent
And great exploits, but of true virtue void;   790
Who having spilt much blood, and done much waste,
Subduing nations, and achieved thereby
Fame in the world, high titles, and rich prey,
Shall change their course to pleasure, ease, and sloth,
Surfeit, and lust, till wantonness and pride   795
Raise out of friendship hostile deeds in peace.
The conquered also, and enslaved by war,
Shall, with their freedom lost, all virtue lose,
And fear of God – from whom their piety feigned
In sharp contest of battle found no aid   800
Against invaders; therefore, cooled in zeal,
Thenceforth shall practise how to live secure,
Worldly or dissolute, on what their lords
Shall leave them to enjoy; for the earth shall bear
More than enough, that temperance may be tried;   805
So all shall turn degenerate, all depraved,
Justice and temperance, truth and faith, forgot;
One man except, the only son of light
In a dark age, against example good,
Against allurement, custom, and a world   810
Offended; fearless of reproach and scorn,
Or violence, he of their wicked ways
Shall them admonish, and before them set
The paths of righteousness, how much more safe
And full of peace, denouncing wrath to come   815
On their impenitence, and shall return
Of them derided, but of God observed
The one just man alive: by his command
Shall build a wondrous ark, as thou beheld'st,

787–807] Milton's description is designed to embrace the seventeenth century
        as well as the time of the flood.

To save himself and household from amidst   820
A world devote to universal rack.
No sooner he, with them of man and beast
Select for life, shall in the ark be lodged
And sheltered round, but all the cataracts
Of heaven set open on the earth shall pour   825
Rain day and night; all fountains of the deep,
Broke up, shall heave the ocean to usurp
Beyond all bounds, till inundation rise
Above the highest hills; then shall this mount
Of Paradise by might of waves be moved   830
Out of his place, pushed by the horned flood,
With all his verdure spoiled, and trees adrift,
Down the great river to the opening gulf,
And there take root, an island salt and bare,
The haunt of seals, and orcs, and sea-mews' clang –   835
To teach thee that God attributes to place
No sanctity, if none be thither brought
By men who there frequent or therein dwell.
And now what further shall ensue behold.'

    He looked, and saw the ark hull on the flood,   840
Which now abated; for the clouds were fled,
Driven by a keen north-wind, that blowing dry,
Wrinkled the face of deluge, as decayed;
And the clear sun on his wide watery glass
Gazed hot, and of the fresh wave largely drew,   845
As after thirst; which made their flowing shrink
From standing lake to tripping ebb, that stole
With soft foot towards the deep, who now had stopped
His sluices, as the heaven his windows shut.
The ark no more now floats, but seems on ground,   850

---

821 devote] doomed.
824-7] Gen. vii. 11. 'Cataracts' transliterates the LXX (καταρράκται) or the
    Vulgate *cataractae*); the Greek term probably and the Latin term certainly
    mean 'flood-gates', which is the A.V. marginal reading. The A.V. 'windows'
    translates the Hebrew word for 'lattices, windows' (cf. Isa. lx. 8, where the
    same Hebrew word is used).
833] The 'great river' is probably the Euphrates (Gen. xv. 18), and the 'gulf' the
    Persian Gulf.
834 salt] i.e. barren (a common O.T. usage).
835 orcs] whales, ferocious sea-monsters.
    sea-mews] gulls.
840 hull] drift.
842 north-wind] Gen. viii. 1; *Metamorphoses* i 328.
848-9] Gen. viii. 2.
850-4] Gen. viii. 4-5; *Metamorphoses* i. 343-5.

Fast on the top of some high mountain fixed.
And now the tops of hills as rocks appear;
With clamour thence the rapid currents drive
Towards the retreating sea their furious tide.
Forthwith from out the ark a raven flies,　　　855
And after him, the surer messenger,
A dove sent forth once and again to spy
Green tree or ground whereon his foot may light;
The second time returning, in his bill
An olive-leaf he brings, pacific sign;　　　860
Anon dry ground appears, and from his ark
The ancient sire descends, with all his train;
Then with uplifted hands, and eyes devout,
Grateful to heaven, over his head beholds
A dewy cloud, and in the cloud a bow　　　865
Conspicuous with three listed colours gay,
Betokening peace from God, and covenant new.
Whereat the heart of Adam, erst so sad,
Greatly rejoiced, and thus his joy broke forth:
　'O thou, who future things canst represent　　　870
As present, heavenly instructor, I revive
At this last sight, assured that man shall live,
With all the creatures, and their seed preserve.
Far less I now lament for one whole world
Of wicked sons destroyed, than I rejoice　　　875
For one man found so perfect, and so just,
That God vouchsafes to raise another world
From him, and all his anger to forget.
But say, what mean those coloured streaks in heaven,
Distended as the brow of God appeased?　　　880
Or serve they as a flowery verge to bind
The fluid skirts of that same watery cloud,
Lest it again dissolve and shower the earth?'
　To whom the archangel: 'Dextrously thou aim'st;
So willingly doth God remit his ire:　　　885
Though late repenting him of man depraved,
Grieved at his heart, when looking down he saw
The whole earth filled with violence, and all flesh
Corrupting each their way; yet those removed,
Such grace shall one just man find in his sight　　　890
That he relents, not to blot out mankind,

865-701] Gen. ix. 8-17.
866] The three colours (red, yellow, blue) are arranged in bands ('listed').
886-90] Gen. vi. 6-12.

And makes a covenant never to destroy
The earth again by flood, nor let the sea
Surpass his bounds, nor rain to drown the world
With man therein or beast; but when he brings   895
Over the earth a cloud, will therein set
His triple-coloured bow, whereon to look
And call to mind his covenant; day and night,
Seed-time and harvest, heat and hoary frost,
Shall hold their course, till fire purge all things new,   900
Both heaven and earth, wherein the just shall dwell.'

THE END OF THE ELEVENTH BOOK

898–901] Gen. viii. 22; II Pet. iii. 6–13.

BOOK XII

THE ARGUMENT

The angel Michael continues, from the flood, to relate what shall
succeed; then, in the mention of Abraham, comes by degrees to explain
who that seed of the woman shall be which was promised
Adam and Eve in the fall: his incarnation, death, resurrection, and
ascension; the state of the Church till his second coming. Adam,
greatly satisfied and recomforted by these relations and promises,
descends the hill with Michael; wakens Eve, who all this while had
slept, but with gentle dreams composed to quietness of mind and
submission. Michael in either hand leads them out of Paradise, the
fiery sword waving behind them, and the cherubim taking their
stations to guard the place.

As one who in his journey baits at noon,
Though bent on speed, so here the archangel paused
Betwixt the world destroyed and world restored,
If Adam aught perhaps might interpose;
Then, with transition sweet, new speech resumes: 5
    'Thus thou hast seen one world begin and end,
And man as from a second stock proceed.
Much thou hast yet to see, but I perceive
Thy mortal sight to fail; objects divine
Must needs impair and weary human sense;   10
Henceforth what is to come I will relate;
Thou therefore give due audience, and attend.
    'This second source of men, while yet but few,
And while the dread of judgement past remains
Fresh in their minds, fearing the Deity,   15
With some regard to what is just and right
Shall lead their lives, and multiply apace,
Labouring the soil, and reaping plenteous crop,
Corn, wine, and oil; and from the herd or flock
Oft sacrificing bullock, lamb, or kid,   20
With large wine offerings poured, and sacred feast,
Shall spend their days in joy unblamed, and dwell
Long time in peace, by families and tribes,
Under paternal rule: till one shall rise,

---

1 baits] used of travellers who stop at an inn.
7 second stock] literally Noah, and typologically Christ, in whom believers were
    said to be 'engrafted'. Cf. III 293n.
18-21] Deut. xiv. 23-6.
24-37] On Nimrod see Gen. x. 8-10.

Of proud, ambitious heart, who not content   25
With fair equality, fraternal state,
Will arrogate dominion undeserved
Over his brethren, and quite dispossess
Concord and law of nature from the earth –
Hunting (and men, not beasts, shall be his game)   30
With war and hostile snare such as refuse
Subjection to his empire tyrannous;
A mighty hunter thence he shall be styled
Before the Lord, as in despite of heaven,
Or from heaven claiming second sovereignty,   35
And from rebellion shall derive his name,
Though of rebellion others he accuse.
He with a crew, whom like ambition joins
With him or under him to tyrannize,
Marching from Eden towards the west, shall find   40
The plain, wherein a black bituminous gurge
Boils out from under ground, the mouth of hell;
Of brick, and of that stuff, they cast to build
A city and tower, whose top may reach to heaven;
And get themselves a name, lest far dispersed   45
In foreign lands, their memory be lost –
Regardless whether good or evil fame.
But God, who oft descends to visit men
Unseen, and through their habitations walks,
To mark their doings, them beholding soon,   50
Comes down to see their city, ere the tower
Obstruct heaven-towers, and in derision sets
Upon their tongues a various spirit, to raze
Quite out their native language, and instead
To sow a jangling noise of words unknown;   55
Forthwith a hideous gabble rises loud
Among the builders; each to other calls,
Not understood – till, hoarse and all in rage,
As mocked they storm; great laughter was in heaven,
And looking down to see the hubbub strange   60
And hear the din; thus was the building left

36] The popular derivation of Nimrod from *marad*, to rebel, rests on a false
    etymology.
38–62] On the Tower of Babel see Gen. xi. 1–9 and cf. *PL* III 466–8. Although
    Nimrod is associated with Babel in Gen. x. 10, the tradition that he built
    the tower seems to have been initiated by Josephus (*Antiquities* I iv. 2,
    vi. 2).
41 bituminous] see X 298n.
   gurge] whirlpool.
43 cast] resolve.
53 various] causing difference or dissimilarity.

Ridiculous, and the work Confusion named.'
   Whereto thus Adam, fatherly displeased:
'O execrable son, so to aspire
Above his brethren, to himself assuming   65
Authority usurped, from God not given;
He gave us only over beast, fish, fowl,
Dominion absolute; that right we hold
By his donation: but man over men
He made not lord – such title to himself   70
Reserving, human left from human free.
But this usurper his encroachment proud
Stays not on man; to God his tower intends
Siege and defiance. Wretched man! What food
Will he convey up thither, to sustain   75
Himself and his rash army, where thin air
Above the clouds will pine his entrails gross,
And famish him of breath, if not of bread?'
   To whom thus Michael: 'Justly thou abhorr'st
That son, who on the quiet state of men   80
Such trouble brought, affecting to subdue
Rational liberty; yet know withal,
Since thy original lapse; true liberty
Is lost, which always with right reason dwells
Twinned, and from her hath no dividual being;   85
Reason in man obscured, or not obeyed,
Immediately inordinate desires
And upstart passions catch the government
From reason, and to servitude reduce
Man, till then free. Therefore, since he permits   90
Within himself unworthy powers to reign
Over free reason, God in judgement just,
Subjects him from without to violent lords,
Who oft as undeservedly enthral
His outward freedom; tyranny must be,   95
Though to the tyrant thereby no excuse.
Yet sometimes nations will decline so low
From virtue, which is reason, that no wrong,
But justice and some fatal curse annexed,
Deprives them of their outward liberty,   100
Their inward lost: witness the irreverent son

---

62 Confusion] See Gen. xi. 9, A.V. marginal note. The Hebrew text contains a
    play on the words 'confound' (*balal*) and *Babel* (Babylon). Cf. l. 343.
84 right reason] see VI 42n.
85 dividual] separate, distinct, particular.
101–4] On Ham and Canaan see Gen. ix. 22–7.

Of him who built the ark, who for the shame
Done to his father, heard this heavy curse,
"Servant of servants", on his vicious race.
Thus will this latter, as the former world,   105
Still tend from bad to worse, till God at last,
Wearied with their iniquities, withdraw
His presence from among them, and avert
His holy eyes, resolving from thenceforth
To leave them to their own polluted ways,   110
And one peculiar nation to select
From all the rest, of whom to be invoked –
A nation from one faithful man to spring;
Him on this side Euphrates yet residing,
Bred up in idol-worship – O that men   115
(Canst thou believe?) should be so stupid grown,
While yet the patriarch lived who scaped the flood,
As to forsake the living God, and fall
To worship their own work in wood and stone
For gods! Yet him God the most high vouchsafes   120
To call by wisdom from his father's house,
His kindred, and false gods, into a land
Which he will show him, and from him will raise
A mighty nation, and upon him shower
His benediction so that in his seed   125
All nations shall be blest; he straight obeys,
Not knowing to what land, yet firm believes;
I see him, but thou canst not, with what faith
He leaves his gods, his friends, and native soil,
Ur of Chaldaea, passing now the ford   130
To Haran – after him a cumbrous train
Of herds and flocks, and numerous servitude –

111-13] Among the several kinds of election distinguished by Protestant
    theologians were the general, or national election of the Jews (who are thus
    called 'peculiar', i.e. specially chosen) and the election of an individual
    (such as Abraham, or the apostles) to a particular office. Neither of these
    should be confused with the individual election to salvation (a doctrine
    related to predestination). Cf. 'race elect', l. 214.
113-64] On Abraham see Gen. xi. 27-xxv. 10.
114-15] Joshua xxiv. 2.
117] Gen. ix. 28.
120-30] Gen. xii. 1-3, Gal. iii. 6-18, Acts vii. 2-7, Heb. xi. 8.
130-1] Haran is a city of north-western Mesopotamia (now Turkey). Line 114
    suggests that Milton thought Ur was east of the Euphrates (cf. Acts vii. 2),
    so the 'ford/To Haran' cannot be across the Euphrates, but must rather be
    across one of the tributaries coming from the north-east (cf. PR III 257).
132 servitude] slaves and servants.

Not wandering poor, but trusting all his wealth
With God, who called him, in a land unknown.
Canaan he now attains; I see his tents   135
Pitched about Sechem, and the neighbouring plain
Of Moreh; there by promise he receives
Gift to his progeny of all that land,
From Hamath northward to the desert south
(Things by their names I call, though yet unnamed),   140
From Hermon east to the great western sea;
Mount Hermon, yonder sea, each place behold
In prospect, as I point them: on the shore,
Mount Carmel; here, the double-founted stream,
Jordan, true limit eastward; but his sons   145
Shall dwell to Senir, that long ridge of hills.
This ponder, that all nations of the earth
Shall in his seed be blessed; by that seed
Is meant thy great deliverer, who shall bruise
The serpent's head; whereof to thee anon   150
Plainlier shall be revealed. This patriarch blest,
Whom "faithful Abraham" due time shall call,
A son, and of his son a grandchild leaves,
Like him in faith, in wisdom, and renown;
The grandchild, with twelve sons increased, departs   155
From Canaan to a land hereafter called
Egypt, divided by the river Nile;
See where it flows, disgorging at seven mouths
Into the sea; to sojourn in that land
He comes, invited by a younger son   160

135-7] Gen. xii. 5-6.
139 Hamath] a city and ancient kingdom on the Orontes (now Hama, in Syria).
141] Mount Hermon, on the border of Lebanon and Syria, was the highest
    mountain of Palestine. In the Hebrew of the O.T. the Mediterranean is
    variously called the 'Hinder (i.e. western) Sea' (e.g. Zech. xiv. 8), the 'Great
    Sea' (e.g. Num. xxxiv. 6), or simply 'The Sea' (e.g. Num. xxxiv. 5).
144-5] Mount Carmel is a promontory near Haifa. The belief that the Jordan is
    'double-founted' is at least as old as Jerome, who argued that the springs
    'Jor' and 'Dan' ran together into a river appropriately called 'Jordan'. In
    fact the Hebrew word for Jordan is not related to 'Dan'.
146] Senir was the Amorite name for Mount Hermon (Deut. iii. 9), which was
    commonly represented on seventeenth-century maps as a range of hills.
147-8] Gen. xxii. 18.
152] In Gen. xvii. 5 Abram's name is changed to Abraham, and the termination
    -raham is connected with the Hebrew word for multitude to make the name
    mean 'father of a multitude' (see A.V. marginal note).
153] The son is Isaac, the grandchild Jacob.
155-64] Gen. xxxix-1. The 'younger son' is Joseph.

In time of dearth – a son whose worthy deeds
Raise him to be the second in that realm
Of Pharaoh; there he dies, and leaves his race
Growing into a nation, and now grown
Suspected to a sequent king, who seeks   165
To stop their overgrowth, as inmate guests
Too numerous; whence of guests he makes them slaves
Inhospitably, and kills their infant males:
Till by two brethren (those two brethren call
Moses and Aaron) sent from God to claim   170
His people from enthralment, they return
With glory and spoil, back to their Promised Land.
But first the lawless tyrant, who denies
To know their God, or message to regard,
Must be compelled by signs and judgements dire: 175
To blood unshed the rivers must be turned;
Frogs, lice, and flies must all his palace fill
With loathed intrusion, and fill all the land;
His cattle must of rot and murrain die;
Botches and blains must all his flesh emboss,   180
And all his people; thunder mixed with hail,
Hail mixed with fire, must rend the Egyptian sky,
And wheel on the earth, devouring where it rolls;
What it devours not, herb, or fruit, or grain,
A darksome cloud of locusts swarming down   185
Must eat, and on the ground leave nothing green;
Darkness must overshadow all his bounds,
Palpable darkness, and blot out three days;
Last, with one midnight-stroke, all the first-born
Of Egypt must lie dead. Thus with ten wounds   190
The river-dragon tamed at length submits
To let his sojourners depart, and oft
Humbles his stubborn heart, but still as ice
More hardened after thaw; till in his rage,
Pursuing whom he late dismissed, the sea   195
Swallows him with his host, but them lets pass,

164-8] Exod. i. The king is named as Busiris in I 307 (see I 306-11n.).
169-90] Exod. iii-xii.
173 denies] refuses.
179 murrain] cattle plague.
180 Botches, blains] boils, blisters.
184-8] Cf. I 338-43. The darkness is palpable in Eox. x. 21, where the Vulgate
      reading is *palpari queant*.
191] Pharaoh is identified with the crocodile ('river-dragon') in Ezek. xxix. 3.
194-214] Exod. xiv. 5-31.

As on dry land, between two crystal walls,
Awed by the rod of Moses so to stand
Divided till his rescued gain their shore:
Such wondrous power God to his saint will lend,   200
Though present in his angel, who shall go
Before them in a cloud, and pillar of fire –
By day a cloud, by night a pillar of fire –
To guide them in their journey, and remove
Behind them, while the obdurate king pursues;   205
All night he will pursue, but his approach
Darkness defends between till morning-watch;
Then through the fiery pillar and the cloud
God looking forth will trouble all his host,
And craze their chariot-wheels: when, by command,   210
Moses once more his potent rod extends
Over the sea; the sea his rod obeys;
On their embattled ranks the waves return,
And overwhelm their war; the race elect
Safe towards Canaan, from the shore, advance   215
Through the wild desert – not the readiest way,
Lest, entering on the Canaanite alarmed,
War terrify them inexpert, and fear
Return them back to Egypt, choosing rather
Inglorious life with servitude; for life   220
To noble and ignoble is more sweet
Untrained in arms, where rashness leads not on.
This also shall they gain by their delay
In the wide wilderness: there they shall found
Their government, and their great senate choose   225
Through the twelve tribes, to rule by laws ordained;
God, from the mount of Sinai, whose grey top
Shall tremble, he descending, will himself,
In thunder, lightning, and loud trumpets' sound,
Ordain them laws – part, such as appertain   230
To civil justice; part, religious rites

200-4] Exod. xiii. 21-2.
207 defends] repels.
210 craze] shatter (cf. I 311).
214 war] army.
214-20] Exod. xiii. 17-18. On 'race elect' see ll. 111-13n.
224-6] Exod. xxiv. 1-11; Num. xi. 16-25.
225 Senate] See Acts v. 21; the Greek word which is there translated 'senate' (γερουσία) is sometimes used in the LXX to mean 'Sanhedrin' (συνέδριον), which is the word translated as 'council' in the same passage. It therefore seems likely that Milton saw this senate as the beginning of the Sanhedrin.
227-30] Exod. xix. 16-20.

Of sacrifice, informing them, by types
And shadows, of that destined seed to bruise
The serpent, by what means he shall achieve
Mankind's deliverance. But the voice of God   235
To mortal ear is dreadful: they beseech
That Moses might report to them his will,
And terror cease; he grants what they besought,
Instructed that to God is no access
Without mediator, whose high office now   240
Moses in figure bears, to introduce
One greater, of whose day he shall foretell,
And all the prophets, in their age, the times
Of great Messiah shall sing. Thus laws and rites
Established, such delight hath God in men   245
Obedient to his will that he vouchsafes
Among them to set up his tabernacle –
The holy one with mortal men to dwell;
By his prescript a sanctuary is framed
Of cedar, overlaid with gold; therein   250
An ark, and in the ark his testimony,
The records of his covenant; over these
A mercy-seat of gold, between the wings
Of two bright cherubim; before him burn
Seven lamps, as in a zodiac representing   255
The heavenly fires; over the tent a cloud
Shall rest by day, a fiery gleam by night,
Save when they journey; and at length they come,
Conducted by his angel, to the land
Promised to Abraham and his seed; the rest   260
Were long to tell – how many battles fought,
How many kings destroyed, and kingdoms won;
Or how the sun shall in mid-heaven stand still
A day entire, and night's due course adjourn,
Man's voice commanding, "Sun, in Gibeon stand,   265
And thou, Moon, in the vale of Aialon,
Till Israel overcome" – so call the third
From Abraham, son of Isaac, and from him
His whole descent, who thus shall Canaan win.'
    Here Adam interposed: 'O sent from heaven,   270
Enlightener of my darkness, gracious things

232-4] Heb. viii. 3-5.
235-8] Exod. xx. 18-20.
238-44] Deut. xviii. 15-19; Acts iii. 22, vii. 37.
245-56] Exod. xxv, xxvi, xxxvii; Heb. ix.
256-8] Exod. xl. 34-8.
263-7] Joshua x. 12-13. 'Israel' is Jacob (Gen. xxxii. 28).

Thou hast revealed, those chiefly which concern
Just Abraham and his seed; now first I find
Mine eyes true opening, and my heart much eased,
Erewhile perplexed with thoughts what would become 275
Of me and all mankind; but now I see
His day, in whom all nations shall be blest –
Favour unmerited by me, who sought
Forbidden knowledge by forbidden means.
This yet I apprehend not – why to those 280
Among whom God will deign to dwell on earth
So many and so various laws are given;
So many laws argue so many sins
Among them; how can God with such reside?'
　　To whom thus Michael: 'Doubt not but that sin 285
Will reign among them, as of thee begot;
And therefore was law given them, to evince
Their natural pravity, by stirring up
Sin against law to fight, that when they see
Law can discover sin, but not remove, 290
Save by those shadowy expiations weak,
The blood of bulls and goats, they may conclude
Some blood more precious must be paid for man,
Just for unjust, that in such righteousness,
To them by faith imputed, they may find 295
Justification towards God, and peace
Of conscience, which the law by ceremonies
Cannot appease, nor man the moral part
Perform, and not performing cannot live.
So law appears imperfect, and but given 300
With purpose to resign them, in full time,
Up to a better covenant, disciplined
From shadowy types to truth, from flesh to spirit,
From imposition of strict laws to free
Acceptance of large grace, from servile fear 305
To filial, works of law to works of faith.
And therefore shall not Moses, though of God
Highly beloved, being but the minister
Of law, his people into Canaan lead;

276-7 see/His day] John viii. 56.
285-306] A characteristically Protestant statement of the relation of the
　　Mosaic law of the O.T. covenant to the 'better covenant' of 'righteousness
　　... by faith imputed'. The doctrine is broadly based on the epistles to the
　　Romans, Hebrews, and Galatians.
288 pravity] depravity.
294-5 See III 290-1n.
307-9] Deut. xxxiv.

But Joshua, whom the Gentiles Jesus call,   310
His name and office bearing who shall quell
The adversary serpent, and bring back
Through the world's wilderness long-wandered man
Safe to eternal paradise of rest.
Meanwhile they, in their earthly Canaan placed,   315
Long time shall dwell and prosper, but when sins
National interrupt their public peace,
Provoking God to raise them enemies –
From whom as oft he saves them penitent,
By judges first, then under kings; of whom   320
The second, both for piety renowned
And puissant deeds, a promise shall receive
Irrevocable, that his regal throne
For ever shall endure; the like shall sing
All prophecy – that of the royal stock   325
Of David (so I name this king) shall rise
A son, the woman's seed to thee foretold,
Foretold to Abraham as in whom shall trust
All nations, and to kings foretold of kings
The last, for of his reign shall be no end.   330
But first a long succession must ensue;
And his next son, for wealth and wisdom famed,
The clouded ark of God, till then in tents
Wandering, shall in a glorious temple enshrine.
Such follow him as shall be registered   335
Part good, part bad; of bad the longer scroll:
Whose foul idolatries and other faults,
Heaped to the popular sum, will so incense
God, as to leave them, and expose their land,
Their city, his temple, and his holy ark,   340
With all his sacred things, a scorn and prey
To that proud city whose high walls thou saw'st
Left in confusion, Babylon thence called.

310] 'Jesus' is the Greek form of the Hebrew 'Joshua', who is so called in the
    LXX and N.T. (e.g. Heb. iv. 8).
321-4] On the promise which David ('The second') received see II Sam. vii. 16.
325-7] A common O.T. prophecy (e.g. Psalm lxxxix. 36-7), applied to Jesus in
    the N.T. (c.g. Luke i. 32).
330] a characteristic theme of Messianic prophecies (e.g. Dan. vii. 14, Luke i.
    33).
332-4] On the Temple of Solomon ('next son') see I Kings v.-ix. 9, II Chronicles
    ii-v.
343] See l. 62n.

There in captivity he lets them dwell
The space of seventy years; then brings them back,   345
Remembering mercy, and his covenant sworn
To David, stablished as the days of heaven.
Returned from Babylon by leave of kings,
Their lords, whom God disposed, the house of God
They first re-edify, and for a while   350
In mean estate live moderate, till grown
In wealth and multitude, factious they grow;
But first among the priests dissension springs –
Men who attend the altar, and should most
Endeavour peace: their strife pollution brings   355
Upon the temple itself; at last they seize
The sceptre, and regard not David's sons;
Then lose it to a stranger, that the true
Anointed king Messiah might be born
Barred of his right; yet at his birth a star   360
Unseen before in heaven proclaims him come,
And guides the eastern sages, who enquire
His place, to offer incense, myrrh, and gold:
His place of birth a solemn angel tells
To simple shepherds, keeping watch by night;   365
They gladly thither haste, and by a choir
Of squadroned angels hear his carol sung.
A virgin is his mother, but his sire
The power of the most high; he shall ascend
The throne hereditary, and bound his reign   370
With earth's wide bounds, his glory with the heavens.'
   He ceased, discerning Adam with such joy
Surcharged as had like grief been dewed in tears,
Without the vent of words; which these he breathed:
   'O prophet of glad tidings, finisher   375

344-7] Refers to the Babylonian Captivity. Under Nebuchadnezzar Jews were
deported to Babylon in 597 and 586 BC (II Kings xxiv. 14 16; xxv. 11);
they were allowed to return after the Persian King Cyrus captured Babylon
in 538 BC (Ezra ii). On the estimate of 'seventy years' see Jer. xxv. 12.

348-50] Ezra, Neh. i–vi. The kings are Cyrus, Artaxerxes, and Darius.

353-8] See the apocryphal II Macc. iii–vi. 'They' (l. 356) are the Hasmonaean
dynasty, one of whom, Aristobulus I, seized civil power and became the
first person to assume the title 'King of the Jews'. The 'stranger' is
Antipater, who in 47 BC was appointed by Julius Caesar procurator of
Judea, as a reward for services rendered against Pompey; he was the father
of Herod the Great.

360-9] Matt. ii, Luke ii.

369-71] Psalm ii. 8; *Aeneid* i 278-9, 287.

373 Surcharged] overwhelmed.

Of utmost hope! Now clear I understand
What oft my steadiest thoughts have searched in vain –
Why our great expectation should be called
The seed of woman; virgin mother, hail;
High in the love of heaven, yet from my loins   380
Thou shalt proceed, and from thy womb the Son
Of God most high; so God with man unites.
Needs must the serpent now his capital bruise
Expect with mortal pain; say where and when
Their fight, what stroke shall bruise the victor's heel.'   385
    To whom thus Michael: 'Dream not of their fight
As of a duel, or the local wounds
Of head or heel; not therefore joins the Son
Manhood to Godhead, with more strength to foil
Thy enemy; nor so is overcome   390
Satan, whose fall from heaven, a deadlier bruise,
Disabled not to give thee thy death's wound;
Which he who comes thy saviour shall recure,
Not by destroying Satan, but his works
In thee and in thy seed; nor can this be,   395
But by fulfilling that which thou didst want,
Obedience to the law of God, imposed
On penalty of death, and suffering death,
The penalty to thy transgression due,
And due to theirs which out of thine will grow: 400
So only can high justice rest appaid.
The law of God exact he shall fulfil
Both by obedience and by love, though love
Alone fulfil the law; thy punishment
He shall endure, by coming in the flesh   405
To a reproachful life and cursed death,
Proclaiming life to all who shall believe
In his redemption, and that his obedience
Imputed becomes theirs by faith – his merits
To save them, not their own, though legal, works.   410
For this he shall live hated, be blasphemed,

379–82] Luke i. 28–35.
383 capital] means both 'on the head' and 'fatal'.
393 recure] heal, make whole.
394–5] I John iii. 8.
396 want] lack.
401 appaid] satisfied.
403–4] Rom. xiii. 10.
408–9] See III 290–1n.
410 legal] in accordance with the Mosaic law.

Seized on by force, judged, and to death condemned
A shameful and accursed, nailed to the cross
By his own nation, slain for bringing life;
But to the cross he nails thy enemies –   415
The law that is against thee, and the sins
Of all mankind, with him there crucified,
Never to hurt them more who rightly trust
In this his satisfaction; so he dies,
But soon revives; Death over him no power   420
Shall long usurp; ere the third dawning light
Return, the stars of morn shall see him rise
Out of his grave, fresh as the dawning light,
Thy ransom paid, which man from Death redeems –
His death for man, as many as offered life   425
Neglect not, and the benefit embrace
By faith not void of works; this godlike act
Annuls thy doom, the death thou shouldst have died,
In sin for ever lost from life; this act
Shall bruise the head of Satan, crush his strength,   430
Defeating Sin and Death, his two main arms,
And fix far deeper in his head their stings
Than temporal death shall bruise the victor's heel,
Or theirs whom he redeems – a death like sleep,
A gentle wafting to immortal life.   435
Nor after resurrection shall he stay
Longer on earth than certain times to appear
To his disciples – men who in his life
Still followed him; to them shall leave in charge
To teach all nations what of him they learned   440
And his salvation, them who shall believe
Baptizing in the profluent stream – the sign
Of washing them from guilt of sin to life
Pure, and in mind prepared, if so befall,
For death like that which the redeemer died.   445
All nations they shall teach; for from that day
Not only to the sons of Abraham's loins
Salvation shall be preached, but to the sons

415-17] Col. ii. 14.
419 satisfaction] See X 803-4n.
441-5] Milton concurred with many Protestants in asserting that baptism was
    for 'them who shall believe' rather than for infants, in asserting that one
    should be baptized in running ('profluent') water rather than in a font, and
    in emphasizing that baptism is a 'sign' in the face of Counter-Reformation
    assertions (at the Council of Trent) that it is more than a sign. 'Washing'
    renders the original meaning (in Greek) of the word 'baptize'.

Of Abraham's faith wherever through the world;
So in his seed all nations shall be blest.   450
Then to the heaven of heavens he shall ascend
With victory, triumphing through the air
Over his foes and thine; there shall surprise
The serpent, prince of air, and drag in chains
Through all his realm, and there confounded leave;   455
Then enter into glory, and resume
His seat at God's right hand, exalted high
Above all names in heaven; and thence shall come,
When this world's dissolution shall be ripe,
With glory and power, to judge both quick and dead – 460
To judge the unfaithful dead, but to reward
His faithful, and receive them into bliss,
Whether in heaven or earth; for then the earth
Shall all be paradise, far happier place
Than this of Eden, and far happier days.'   465
   So spake the archangel Michaël; then paused,
As at the world's great period; and our sire,
Replete with joy and wonder, thus replied:
   'O goodness infinite, goodness immense,
That all this good of evil shall produce,   470
And evil turn to good – more wonderful
Than that which by creation first brought forth
Light out of darkness! Full of doubt I stand,
Whether I should repent me now of sin
By me done and occasioned, or rejoice   475
Much more that much more good thereof shall spring –
To God more glory, more good-will to men
From God – and over wrath grace shall abound.
But say, if our deliverer up to heaven
Must reascend, what will betide the few,   480
His faithful, left among the unfaithful herd,
The enemies of truth? Who then shall guide
His people, who defend? Will they not deal
Worse with his followers than with him they dealt?'
   'Be sure they will,' said the angel; 'but from heaven 485

<hr>

453–5] Rev. xx. 1–3, Eph. ii. 2.
460 judge ... dead] this common N.T. phrase (e.g. II Tim. iv. 1) also occurs in
   the Apostles' Creed.
469–78] Adam recapitulates the traditional paradox of the 'fortunate fall' (*felix
   culpa*) and the traditional assertion that man's salvation is 'more wonder-
   ful' than God's act of creation.
478] Rom. v. 20.

He to his own a Comforter will send,
The promise of the Father, who shall dwell,
His Spirit within them, and the law of faith
Working through love upon their hearts shall write,
To guide them in all truth, and also arm   490
With spiritual armour, able to resist
Satan's assaults, and quench his fiery darts –
What man can do against them not afraid,
Though to the death; against such cruelties
With inward consolations recompensed,   495
And oft supported so as shall amaze
Their proudest persecutors; for the Spirit,
Poured first on his apostles, whom he sends
To evangelize the nations, then on all
Baptized, shall them with wondrous gifts endue   500
To speak all tongues, and do all miracles,
As did their Lord before them. Thus they win
Great numbers of each nation to receive
With joy the tidings brought from heaven: at length,
Their ministry performed, and race well run,   505
Their doctrine and their story written left,
They die: but in their room, as they forewarn,
Wolves shall succeed for teachers, grievous wolves,
Who all the sacred mysteries of heaven
To their own vile advantages shall turn   510
Of lucre and ambition, and the truth
With superstitions and traditions taint,
Left only in those written records pure,
Though not but by the Spirit understood.
Then shall they seek to avail themselves of names,   515
Places, and titles, and with these to join
Secular power, though feigning still to act
By spiritual; to themselves appropriating
The Spirit of God, promised alike and given
To all believers; and from that pretence,   520

486 Comforter] The Holy Spirit (John xv. 26).
488-9] Gal. v. 6, Hebrews viii. 10.
491-2] Eph. vi. 11-17.
493] Psalm lvi. 11.
497-502] Acts ii.
505 race well run] a N.T. metaphor (e.g. Hebrews xii. 1).
508] Cf. Acts xx. 29, *Sonnet* XVI 14, *Lycidas* 113-31.
511-14] a characteristically Protestant assertion of the right of the believer to
    interpret Scripture guided solely by the Holy Spirit without reference to
    any authority or tradition.

Spiritual laws by carnal power shall force
On every conscience – laws which none shall find
Left them enrolled, or what the Spirit within
Shall on the heart engrave. What will they then
But force the spirit of grace itself, and bind   525
His consort, liberty? What but unbuild
His living temples, built by faith to stand –
Their own faith, not another's? For on earth
Who against faith and conscience can be heard
Infallible? Yet many will presume: 530
Whence heavy persecution shall arise
On all who in the worship persevere
Of spirit and truth; the rest, far greater part,
Will deem in outward rites and specious forms
Religion satisfied; truth shall retire   535
Bestuck with slanderous darts, and works of faith
Rarely be found; so shall the world go on,
To good malignant, to bad men benign,
Under her own weight groaning, till the day
Appear of respiration to the just   540
And vengeance to the wicked, at return
Of him so lately promised to thy aid,
The woman's seed – obscurely then foretold,
Now amplier known thy Saviour and thy Lord;
Last in the clouds from heaven to be revealed   545
In glory of the Father, to dissolve
Satan with his perverted world; then raise
From the conflagrant mass, purged and refined,
New heavens, new earth, ages of endless date
Founded in righteousness and peace and love,   550
To bring forth fruits, joy and eternal bliss.'
     He ended; and thus Adam last replied:
'How soon hath thy prediction, seer blest,
Measured this transient world, the race of time,
Till time stand fixed; beyond is all abyss –   555
Eternity, whose end no eye can reach.
Greatly instructed I shall hence depart,

525-6] II Cor. iii. 17.
527] I Cor. iii. 17.
532-3] John iv. 23-4.
539] Rom. viii. 22.
540] See Acts iii. 19, where the phrase καιροὶ ἀναψύξεως, translated quite
     correctly as 'times of refreshing' in the A.V., could also be translated 'times
     of respiration' (i.e. respite).
545-6] Matt. xxiv. 30.

Greatly in peace of thought, and have my fill
Of knowledge, what this vessel can contain;
Beyond which was my folly to aspire.   560
Henceforth I learn that to obey is best,
And love with fear the only God, to walk
As in his presence, ever to observe
His providence, and on him sole depend,
Merciful over all his works, with good   565
Still overcoming evil, and by small
Accomplishing great things – by things deemed weak
Subverting worldly-strong, and wordly-wise
By simply meek; that suffering for truth's sake
Is fortitude to highest victory,   570
And to the faithful death the gate of life –
Taught this by his example whom I now
Acknowledge my Redeemer ever blest.'
    To whom thus also the angel last replied:
'This having learned, thou hast attained the sum   575
Of wisdom; hope no higher, though all the stars
Thou knew'st by name, and all the ethereal powers,
All secrets of the deep, all nature's works,
Or works of God in heaven, air, earth, or sea;
And all the riches of this world enjoy'dst,   580
And all the rule, one empire; only add
Deeds to thy knowledge answerable, add faith,
Add virtue, patience, temperance, add love,
By name to come called Charity, the soul
Of all the rest: then wilt thou not be loath   585
To leave this Paradise, but shalt possess
A paradise within thee, happier far.
Let us descend now, therefore, from this top
Of speculation; for the hour precise
Exacts our parting hence; and see, the guards,   590
By me encamped on yonder hill, expect
Their motion, at whose front a flaming sword,
In signal of remove, waves fiercely round;
We may no longer stay; go, waken Eve;

565] Psalm cxlv. 9.
566] Rom. xii. 21.
567-8] I Cor. i. 27.
581-7] II Pet. i. 5-7, I Cor. xiii, *PL* III 216n.
588-9 top/Of speculation] The primary meaning is 'place which affords
    an extensive view', and the secondary sense is 'limit of theological
    speculation'.
591-2 expect/Their motion] await their order to move.
593 remove] departure.

Her also I with gentle dreams have calmed,   595
Portending good, and all her spirits composed
To meek submission: thou at season fit
Let her with thee partake what thou hast heard –
Chiefly what may concern her faith to know,
The great deliverance by her seed to come   600
(For by the woman's seed) on all mankind –
That ye may live, which will be many days,
Both in one faith unanimous; though sad
With cause for evils past, yet much more cheered
With meditation on the happy end.'   605
    He ended, and they both descend the hill;
Descended, Adam to the bower where Eve
Lay sleeping ran before, but found her waked;
And thus with words not sad she him received:
    'Whence thou return'st and whither went'st I know;
For God is also in sleep, and dreams advise,   611
Which he hath sent propitious, some great good
Presaging, since, with sorrow and heart's distress
Wearied, I fell asleep; but now lead on;
In me is no delay; with thee to go   615
Is to stay here; without thee here to stay
Is to go hence unwilling; thou to me
Art all things under heaven, all places thou,
Who for my wilful crime art banished hence.
This further consolation yet secure   620
I carry hence: though all by me is lost,
Such favour I unworthy am vouchsafed,
By me the promised seed shall all restore.'
    So spake our mother Eve, and Adam heard
Well pleased, but answered not; for now too nigh   625
The archangel stood, and from the other hill
To their fixed station, all in bright array,
The cherubim descended, on the ground
Gliding meteorous, as evening mist
Risen from a river o'er the marish glides,   630
And gathers ground fast at the labourer's heel
Homeward returning. High in front advanced,
The brandished sword of God before them blazed,
Fierce as a comet; which with torrid heat,

602] Gen. v. 5.
630 marish] marsh.
634-6] According to an ancient tradition the 'flaming sword' of Gen. iii. 24 was
    the heat of the tropics (hence 'Libyan'). On 'adust' see VI 514n.

And vapour as the Libyan air adust,   635
Began to parch that temperate clime; whereat
In either hand the hastening angel caught
Our lingering parents, and to the eastern gate
Led them direct, and down the cliff as fast
To the subjected plain – then disappeared.   640
They looking back, all the eastern side beheld
Of Paradise, so late their happy seat,
Waved over by that flaming brand; the gate
With dreadful faces thronged and fiery arms;   644
Some natural tears they dropped, but wiped them soon,
The world was all before them, where to choose
Their place of rest, and providence their guide;
They hand in hand with wandering steps and slow,
Through Eden took their solitary way.

THE END OF THE TWELFTH BOOK

640 subjected] subjacent, situated at a lower level.
648] Cf. **IV** 321n.

PARADISE REGAIN'D.

A
POEM

In IV *BOOKS*.

The Author
John Milton.

PARADISE REGAINED

BOOK I

I who erewhile the happy garden sung,
By one man's disobedience lost, now sing
Recovered Paradise to all mankind,
By one man's firm obedience fully tried
Through all temptation, and the tempter foiled   5
In all his wiles, defeated and repulsed,
And Eden raised in the waste wilderness.

    Thou spirit, who led'st this glorious eremite
Into the desert, his victorious field
Against the spiritual foe, and brought'st him thence   10
By proof the undoubted Son of God, inspire,
As thou art wont, my prompted song, else mute,
And bear through height or depth of nature's bounds,
With prosperous wing full summed, to tell of deeds
Above heroic, though in secret done,   15
And unrecorded left through many an age,
Worthy to have not remained so long unsung.

    Now had the great proclaimer, with a voice
More awful than the sound of trumpet, cried
Repentance, and heaven's kingdom nigh at hand   20
To all baptised; to his great baptism flocked
With awe the regions round, and with them came
From Nazareth the son of Joseph deemed
To the flood Jordan – came as then obscure,
Unmarked, unknown; but him the Baptist soon   25
Descried, divinely warned, and witness bore

Paradise Regained. The poem was written between 1665 and 1670, but the
    precise period of composition is not known. In the notes which follow there
    is no attempt to list allusions to the two Biblical accounts of the temptation
    in Matthew iv. 1–11 and Luke iv. 1–13.
1–2 Cf. *Aeneid* i 1–4.
2–4] Rom. v. 19.
7] Isa. li. 3.
8 eremite] used in the Greek sense of 'desert-dweller' (ἐημίτης).
14] See *PL* VII 421n.
18–32] See Matt. iii, Mark i. 2–11, Luke iii. 1–22, John i. 6–34.
19] Isa. lviii. 1.

As to his worthier, and would have resigned
To him his heavenly office, nor was long
His witness unconfirmed; on him baptised
Heaven opened, and in likeness of a dove   30
The Spirit descended, while the Father's voice
From heaven pronounced him his beloved Son.
That heard the Adversary, who roving still
About the world, at that assembly famed
Would not be last, and with the voice divine   35
Nigh thunder-struck, the exalted man to whom
Such high attest was given, a while surveyed
With wonder; then, with envy fraught and rage,
Flies to his place, nor rests, but in mid air
To council summons all his mighty peers,   40
Within thick clouds and dark tenfold involved,
A gloomy consistory; and them amidst,
With looks aghast and sad, he thus bespake:
    'O ancient powers of air and this wide world
(For much more willingly I mention air,   45
This our old conquest, than remember hell,
Our hated habitation), well ye know
How many ages, as the years of men,
This universe we have possessed, and ruled
In manner at our will the affairs of earth,   50
Since Adam and his facile consort Eve
Lost Paradise, deceived by me, though since
With dread attending when that fatal wound
Shall be inflicted by the seed of Eve
Upon my head; long the decrees of heaven   55
Delay, for longest time to him is short;
And now, too soon for us, the circling hours
This dreaded time have compassed, wherein we
Must bide the stroke of that long-threatened wound
(At least, if so we can, and by the head   60
Broken be not intended all our power

33 Adversary] Satan. See *PL* I 82n.
33–4] Job i. 7.
39 mid air] See *Fair Infant* 16n.
42 consistory] means 'council', and is here used with ironic reference to the
    ecclesiastical sense of an assembly of cardinals convoked by the Pope and,
    in the Anglican church, a bishop's court.
44–5] Eph. ii. 2.
48 as] i.e. as reckoned according to.
51 facile] easily led.
53 attending when] awaiting (me) until.
53–5] Gen. iii. 15.

To be infringèd, our freedom and our being
In this fair empire won of earth and air)
For this ill news I bring: the woman's seed,
Destined to this, is late of woman born;   65
His birth to our just fear gave no small cause,
But his growth now to youth's full flower, displaying
All virtue, grace and wisdom to achieve
Things highest, greatest, multiplies my fear.
Before him a great prophet, to proclaim   70
His coming, is sent harbinger, who all
Invites, and in the consecrated stream
Pretends to wash off sin, and fit them so
Purified to receive him pure, or rather
To do him honour as their king; all come,   75
And he himself among them was baptised –
Not thence to be more pure, but to receive
The testimony of heaven, that who he is
Thenceforth the nations may not doubt; I saw
The prophet do him reverence; on him, rising   80
Out of the water, heaven above the clouds
Unfold her crystal doors; thence on his head
A perfect dove descend (whate'er it meant),
And out of heaven the sovereign voice I heard,
"This is my Son beloved, in him am pleased."   85
His mother, then, is mortal, but his sire
He who obtains the monarchy of heaven;
And what will he not do to advance his Son?
His first-begot we know, and sore have felt,
When his fierce thunder drove us to the deep;   90
Who this is we must learn, for man he seems
In all his lineaments, though in his face
The glimpses of his Father's glory shine.
Ye see our danger on the utmost edge
Of hazard, which admits no long debate,   95
But must with something sudden be opposed
(Not force, but well-couched fraud, well-woven snares),
Ere in the head of nations he appear,
Their king, their leader, and supreme on earth.
I, when no other durst, sole undertook   100
The dismal expedition to find out

62 infringèd] shattered, broken.
73 Pretends] professes.
74] I John iii. 3.
87 obtains] used in the Latin sense of 'holds'.
97 couched] means both 'hidden' and 'expressed in words'.

And ruin Adam, and the exploit performed
Successfully: a calmer voyage now
Will waft me; and the way found prosperous once
Induces best to hope of like success.'   105
    He ended, and his words impression left
Of much amazement to the infernal crew,
Distracted and surprised with deep dismay
At these sad tidings; but no time was then
For long indulgence to their fears or grief: 110
Unanimous they all commit the care
And management of this main enterprise
To him, their great dictator, whose attempt
At first against mankind so well had thrived
In Adam's overthrow, and led their march   115
From hell's deep-vaulted den to dwell in light,
Regents, and potentates, and kings, yea gods,
Of many a pleasant realm and province wide.
So to the coast of Jordan he directs
His easy steps, girded with snaky wiles,   120
Where he might likeliest find this new-declared,
This man of men, attested Son of God,
Temptation and all guile on him to try;
So to subvert whom he suspected raised
To end his reign on earth so long enjoyed: 125
But, contrary, unweeting he fulfilled
The purposed counsel, pre-ordained and fixed,
Of the Most High, who in full frequence bright
Of angels, thus to Gabriel smiling spake:
    'Gabriel, this day by proof thou shalt behold,   130
Thou and all angels conversant on earth
With man or men's affairs, how I begin
To verify that solemn message late,
On which I sent thee to the virgin pure
In Galilee, that she should bear a son,   135
Great in renown, and called the Son of God;
Then told'st her, doubting how these things could be

---

112 main] highly important.
113 dictator] In the seventeenth century the word was used with reference to
    the institution of the dictatorship in early Republican Rome, when a
    'dictator' was a magistrate invested with absolute but temporary power in
    times of military (and later domestic) crisis.
117 gods] According to a patristic tradition (embodied in *PL* I 356–522) the
    fallen angels became pagan gods.
128 frequence] assembly.
129–40] Gabriel (on whom see *PL* IV 549n.) here appears as the angel of the
    annunciation. See Luke i. 26–55.

To her a virgin, that on her should come
The Holy Ghost, and the power of the Highest
O'ershadow her; this man, born and now upgrown,   140
To show him worthy of his birth divine
And high prediction, henceforth I expose
To Satan; let him tempt, and now assay
His utmost subtlety, because he boasts
And vaunts of his great cunning to the throng   145
Of his apostasy; he might have learnt
Less overweening, since he failed in Job,
Whose constant perseverance overcame
Whate'er his cruel malice could invent.
He now shall know I can produce a man,   150
Of female seed, far abler to resist
All his solicitations, and at length
All his vast force, and drive him back to hell –
Winning by conquest what the first man lost
By fallacy surprised. But first I mean   155
To exercise him in the wilderness;
There he shall first lay down the rudiments
Of his great warfare, ere I send him forth
To conquer Sin and Death, the two grand foes,
By humiliation and strong sufferance: 160
His weakness shall o'ercome Satanic strength,
And all the world, and mass of sinful flesh;
That all the angels and ethereal powers –
They now, and men hereafter – may discern
From what consummate virtue I have chose   165
This perfect man, by merit called my Son,
To earn salvation for the sons of men.'
   So spake the eternal Father, and all heaven
Admiring stood a space; then into hymns
Burst forth, and in celestial measures moved,   170
Circling the throne and singing, while the hand
Sung with the voice, and this the argument:
   'Victory and triumph to the Son of God,
Now entering his great duel, not of arms,
But to vanquish by wisdom hellish wiles!   175
The Father knows the Son; therefore secure

147–9] Job i–ii. Cf. I 368–70, 424–6, III 64–8, 95. The comparison of Jesus to
   Job can be traced to Gregory's *Moralia in Job*.
157–8] Cf. *Aeneid* xi 156–7.
161] I Cor. i. 27.
171 hand] i.e. the hand which plays a musical instrument.
176] John x. 15.

Ventures his filial virtue, though untried,
Against whate'er may tempt, whate'er seduce,
Allure, or terrify, or undermine.
Be frustrate, all ye stratagems of hell,   180
And, devilish machinations, come to nought!'
    So they in heaven their odes and vigils tuned;
Meanwhile the Son of God, who yet some days
Lodged in Bethabara, where John baptised,
Musing and much revolving in his breast   185
How best the mighty work he might begin
Of Saviour to mankind, and which way first
Publish his godlike office now mature,
One day forth walked alone, the Spirit leading
And his deep thoughts, the better to converse   190
With solitude, till, far from track of men,
Thought following thought, and step by step led on,
He entered now the bordering desert wild,
And, with dark shades and rocks environed round,
His holy meditations thus pursued: 195
    'O what a multitude of thoughts at once
Awakened in me swarm, while I consider
What from within I feel myself, and hear
What from without comes often to my ears,
Ill sorting with my present state compared.   200
When I was yet a child, no childish play
To me was pleasing; all my mind was set
Serious to learn and know, and thence to do,
What might be public good; myself I thought
Born to that end, born to promote all truth,   205
All righteous things; therefore, above my years,
The Law of God I read, and found it sweet;
Made it my whole delight, and in it grew
To such perfection that, ere yet my age
Had measured twice six years, at our great feast   210
I went into the Temple, there to hear
The teachers of our Law, and to propose
What might improve my knowledge or their own;
And was admired by all, yet this not all
To which my spirit aspired; victorious deeds   215

182 vigils] prayers sung at a nocturnal service.
184 Bethabara] John i. 28.
204–5] John xviii. 37.
206–7] Cf. *Aeneid* ix 311.
207–8] Cf. Milton's translation of Psalm i. 2 (l.5).
209–14] Luke ii. 46–50. The 'feast' is Passover; 'admired' means 'marvelled at'.

Flamed in my heart, heroic acts – one while
To rescue Israel from the Roman yoke,
Then to subdue and quell, o'er all the earth,
Brute violence and proud tyrannic power,
Till truth were freed, and equity restored: 220
Yet held it more humane, more heavenly, first
By winning words to conquer willing hearts,
And make persuasion do the work of fear;
At least to try, and teach the erring soul,
Not wilfully misdoing, but unaware   225
Misled; the stubborn only to subdue.
These growing thoughts my mother soon perceiving,
By words at times cast forth, inly rejoiced,
And said to me apart, "High are thy thoughts,
O Son, but nourish them, and let them soar   230
To what height sacred virtue and true worth
Can raise them, though above example high;
By matchless deeds express thy matchless sire.
For know, thou art no son of mortal man;
Though men esteem thee low of parentage,   235
Thy Father is the eternal King who rules
All heaven and earth, angels and sons of men;
A messenger from God foretold thy birth
Conceived in me a virgin; he foretold
Thou shouldst be great, and sit on David's throne,   240
And of thy kingdom there should be no end.
At thy nativity a glorious choir
Of angels, in the fields of Bethlehem, sung
To shepherds watching at their folds by night,
And told them the Messiah now was born,   245
Where they might see him; and to thee they came,
Directed to the manger where thou lay'st,
For in the inn was left no better room;
A star, not seen before, in heaven appearing,
Guided the wise men thither from the east,   250
To honour thee with incense, myrrh, and gold;
By whose bright course led on they found the place,
Affirming it thy star, new-graven in heaven,
By which they knew thee King of Israel born.
Just Simeon and prophetic Anna, warned   255
By vision, found thee in the Temple, and spake,
Before the altar and the vested priest,
Like things of thee to all that present stood."

238–54] Matt. i–ii, Luke i–ii.
255–8] Luke ii. 25–38.

This having heard, straight I again revolved
The Law and Prophets, searching what was writ   260
Concerning the Messiah, to our scribes
Known partly, and soon found of whom they spake
I am – this chiefly, that my way must lie
Through many a hard assay, even to the death,
Ere I the promised kingdom can attain,   265
Or work redemption for mankind, whose sins'
Full weight must be transferred upon my head.
Yet, neither thus disheartened or dismayed,
The time prefixed I waited; when behold
The Baptist (of whose birth I oft had heard,   270
Not knew by sight) now come, who was to come
Before Messiah, and his way prepare.
I, as all others, to his baptism came,
Which I believed was from above; but he
Straight knew me, and with loudest voice proclaimed   275
Me him (for it was shown him so from heaven)
Me him whose harbinger he was; and first
Refused on me his baptism to confer,
As much his greater, and was hardly won;
But as I rose out of the laving stream,   280
Heaven opened her eternal doors, from whence
The Spirit descended on me like a dove;
And last, the sum of all, my Father's voice,
Audibly heard from heaven, pronounced me his,
Me his beloved Son, in whom alone   285
He was well pleased; by which I knew the time
Now full, that I no more should live obscure,
But openly begin, as best becomes
The authority which I derived from heaven.
And now by some strong motion I am led   290
Into this wilderness; to what intent
I learn not yet, perhaps I need not know;
For what concerns my knowledge God reveals.'
    So spake our morning star, then in his rise,
And, looking round, on every side beheld   295
A pathless desert, dusk with horrid shades;

259 revolved] searched through, studied.
266–7] Isa. iii. 6.
270–89] See ll. 18–32n.
279 hardly won] with difficulty persuaded.
281 eternal doors] Psalm xxiv. 7 (*portae aeternales* Vulgate).
286–7] Gal. iv. 4.
290 motion] See *PL* XI 91n.
294 morning star] Rev. xxii. 16.
296 horrid] bristling.

The way he came not having marked, return
Was difficult, by human steps untrod;
And he still on was led, but with such thoughts
Accompanied of things past and to come   300
Lodged in his breast, as well might recommend
Such solitude before choicest society.
   Full forty days he passed – whether on hill
Sometimes, anon in shady vale, each night
Under the covert of some ancient oak   305
Or cedar, to defend him from the dew,
Or harboured in one cave, is not revealed;
Nor tasted human food, nor hunger felt,
Till those days ended, hungered then at last
Among wild beasts; they at his sight grew mild,   310
Nor sleeping him nor waking harmed; his walk
The fiery serpent fled and noxious worm;
The lion and fierce tiger glared aloof.
But now an aged man in rural weeds,
Following, as seemed, the quest of some stray ewe,   315
Or withered sticks to gather, which might serve
Against a winter's day, when winds blow keen,
To warm him wet returned from field at eve,
He saw approach; who first with curious eye
Perused him, then with words thus uttered spake: 320
   'Sir, what ill chance hath brought thee to this place,
So far from path or road of men, who pass
In troop or caravan? For single none
Durst ever, who returned, and dropped not here
His carcass, pined with hunger and with drouth.   325
I ask the rather, and the more admire,
For that to me thou seem'st the man whom late
Our new baptising prophet at the ford
Of Jordan honoured so, and called thee Son
Of God; I saw and heard, for we sometimes   330
Who dwell this wild, constrained by want, come forth
To town or village nigh (nighest is far),
Where aught we hear, and curious are to hear,
What happens new; fame also finds us out.'

301–2] See *PL* VIII 427–8n.
310–13] Mark i. 13. The docility of the animals derives from various O.T.
   prophecies (e.g. Isa. xi. 6–9). One of the eight Hebrew words used for
   'serpent' in the Old Testament is *saraph*, 'fiery serpent' (e.g. Num. xxi. 6–
   8). 'Worm' is used in a general sense: in Micah vii. 17, on which l. 312 is
   based, the A.V. marginal note to 'worms' is 'creeping things'.
334 fame ... out] i.e. news (Latin *fama*, report) also reaches us.

　　To whom the Son of God: 'Who brought me hither　335
Will bring me hence; no other guide I seek.'
　　'By miracle he may,' replied the swain;
'What other way I see not; for we here
Live on tough roots and stubs, to thirst inured
More than the camel, and to drink go far –　340
Men to much misery and hardship born;
But, if thou be the Son of God, command
That out of these hard stones be made thee bread;
So shalt thou save thyself, and us relieve
With food, whereof we wretched seldom taste.'　345
　　He ended, and the Son of God replied:
'Think'st thou such force in bread? Is it not written
(For I discern thee other than thou seem'st)
Man lives not by bread only, but each word
Proceeding from the mouth of God, who fed　350
Our fathers here with manna? In the mount
Moses was forty days, nor eat nor drank;
And forty days Elijah without food
Wandered this barren waste; the same I now.
Why dost thou, then, suggest to me distrust,　355
Knowing who I am, as I know who thou art?'
　　Whom thus answered the arch-fiend, now undisguised:
' 'Tis true, I am that spirit unfortunate
Who, leagued with millions more in rash revolt,
Kept not my happy station, but was driven　360
With them from bliss to the bottomless deep –
Yet to that hideous place not so confined
By rigour unconniving but that oft,
Leaving my dolorous prison, I enjoy
Large liberty to round this globe of earth,　365
Or range in the air; nor from the heaven of heavens
Hath he excluded my resort sometimes.
I came, among the sons of God, when he
Gave up into my hands Uzzean Job,
To prove him, and illustrate his high worth;　370
And when to all his angels he proposed

339 stubs] stumps.
349–50] Jesus' answer (Matt. iv. 4, Luke iv. 4) is a quotation from Deut. viii. 3.
351–2] Exod. xxiv. 18, xxxiv. 28, Deut. ix. 9.
353–4] I Kings xix. 8.
363 unconniving] refers to God's eye, which never closes (cf. Latin *inconivus*).
371–6] I Kings xxii. 20–38; II Chron. xviii. 19–34. The identification of this
　　'lying spirit' with Satan is suggested in the cross-reference to Job i. 6 in the
　　A.V. marginal note to II Chronicles xviii. 20. On 'fraud' see *PL* VII 143n.

To draw the proud king Ahab into fraud,
That he might fall in Ramoth, they demurring,
I undertook that office, and the tongues
Of all his flattering prophets glibbed with lies   375
To his destruction, as I had in charge:
For what he bids I do; though I have lost
Much lustre to my native brightness, lost
To be beloved of God, I have not lost
To love, at least contemplate and admire,   380
What I see excellent in good, or fair,
Or virtuous; I should so have lost all sense.
What can be then less in me than desire
To see thee and approach thee, whom I know
Declared the Son of God, to hear attent   385
Thy wisdom, and behold thy godlike deeds?
Men generally think me much a foe
To all mankind: why should I? They to me
Never did wrong or violence; by them
I lost not what I lost, rather by them   390
I gained what I have gained, and with them dwell
Copartner in these regions of the world,
If not disposer – lend them oft my aid,
Oft my advice by presages and signs,
And answers, oracles, portents and dreams,   395
Whereby they may direct their future life.
Envy, they say, excites me, thus to gain
Companions of my misery and woe.
At first it may be; but, long since with woe
Nearer acquainted, now I feel by proof   400
That fellowship in pain divides not smart,
Nor lightens aught each man's peculiar load.
Small consolation, then, were man adjoined;
This wounds me most (what can it less?) that man,
Man fallen, shall be restored, I never more.'   405
     To whom our Saviour sternly thus replied:
'Deservedly thou griev'st, composed of lies
From the beginning, and in lies wilt end;
Who boast'st release from hell, and leave to come
Into the heaven of heavens; thou com'st indeed,   410
As a poor miserable captive thrall
Comes to the place where he before had sat
Among the prime in splendour, now deposed,
Ejected, emptied, gazed, unpitied, shunned,

393–6] According to a patristic tradition fallen angels were responsible for the
     oracular pronouncements of classical antiquity.
414 emptied] See *Circumcision* 20n.

A spectacle of ruin, or of scorn,   415
To all the host of heaven; the happy place
Imparts to thee no happiness, no joy –
Rather inflames thy torment, representing
Lost bliss, to thee no more communicable;
So never more in hell than when in heaven.   420
But thou art serviceable to heaven's King.
Wilt thou impute to obedience what thy fear
Extorts, or pleasure to do ill excites?
What but thy malice moved thee to misdeem
Of righteous Job, then cruelly to afflict him   425
With all inflictions? But his patience won.
The other service was thy chosen task,
To be a liar in four hundred mouths;
For lying is thy sustenance, thy food.
Yet thou pretend'st to truth; all oracles   430
By thee are given, and what confessed more true
Among the nations? That hath been thy craft,
By mixing somewhat true to vent more lies.
But what have been thy answers, what but dark,
Ambiguous, and with double sense deluding,   435
Which they who asked have seldom understood,
And, not well understood, as good not known?
Who ever by consulting at thy shrine,
Returned the wiser, or the more instruct
To fly or follow what concerned him most,   440
And run not sooner to his fatal snare?
For God hath justly given the nations up
To thy delusions; justly, since they fell
Idolatrous; but, when his purpose is
Among them to declare his providence,   445
To thee not known, whence hast thou then thy truth,
But from him, or his angels president
In every province, who, themselves disdaining
To approach thy temples, give thee in command
What, to the smallest tittle, thou shalt say   450
To thy adorers? Thou, with trembling fear,
Or like a fawning parasite, obey'st;
Then to thyself ascrib'st the truth foretold.
But this thy glory shall be soon retrenched;
Nor more shalt thou by oracling abuse   455
The Gentiles; henceforth oracles are ceased,

428] I Kings xxii. 6.
447 president] presiding.
454 retrenched] cut short.
456] Cf. *Nativity* 173; Micah v. 12.

And thou no more with pomp and sacrifice
Shall be enquired at Delphos or elsewhere –
At least in vain, for they shall find thee mute.
God hath now sent his living oracle   460
Into the world, to teach his final will,
And sends his spirit of truth henceforth to dwell
In pious hearts, an inward oracle
To all truth requisite for men to know.'
   So spake our Saviour; but the subtle fiend,   465
Though inly stung with anger and disdain,
Dissembled, and this answer smooth returned:
   'Sharply thou hast insisted on rebuke,
And urged me hard with doings which not will,
But misery, hath wrested from me; where   470
Easily canst thou find one miserable,
And not enforced oft-times to part from truth,
If it may stand him more in stead to lie,
Say and unsay, feign, flatter, or abure?
But thou art placed above me, thou art Lord;   475
From thee I can and must submiss, endure
Check or reproof, and glad to scape so quit.
Hard are the ways of truth, and rough to walk,
Smooth on the tongue discoursed, pleasing to the ear,
And tunable as sylvan pipe or song;   480
What wonder, then, if I delight to hear
Her dictates from thy mouth? Most men admire
Virtue who follow not her lore: permit me
To hear thee when I come (since no man comes),
And talk at least, though I despair to attain.   485
Thy Father, who is holy, wise, and pure,
Suffers the hypocrite or atheous priest
To tread his sacred courts, and minister
About his altar, handling holy things,
Praying or vowing, and vouchsafed his voice   490
To Balaam reprobate, a prophet yet
Inspired; disdain not such access to me.'
   To whom our Saviour, with unaltered brow:
'Thy coming hither, though I know thy scope,
I bid not, or forbid; do as thou find'st   495

462] John xvi. 13.
477 quit] discharged.
486–90] Satan assumes with Scholastic and Counter-Reformation theologians
    that the sacraments confer grace *ex opere operato*, through the act per-
    formed, regardless of the subjective attitude of the minister (or the
    recipient).

Permission from above; thou canst not more.'
  He added not; and Satan, bowing low
His grey dissimulation, disappeared,
Into thin air diffused: for now began
Night with her sullen wing to double-shade   500
The desert; fowls in their clay nests were couched;
And now wild beasts came forth the woods to roam.

THE END OF THE FIRST BOOK

500 sullen] of a dark and dull colour.

BOOK II

Meanwhile the new-baptised, who yet remained
At Jordan with the Baptist, and had seen
Him whom they heard so late expressly called
Jesus Messiah, Son of God declared,
And on that high authority had believed,   5
And with him talked, and with him lodged – I mean
Andrew and Simon, famous after known,
With others, though in Holy Writ not named –
Now missing him, their joy so lately found,
So lately found and so abruptly gone,   10
Began to doubt, and doubted many days,
And, as the days increased, increased their doubt;
Sometimes they thought he might be only shown,
And for a time caught up to God, as once
Moses was in the mount and missing long;   15
And the great Thisbite, who on fiery wheels
Rode up to heaven, yet once again to come.
Therefore, as those young prophets then with care
Sought lost Elijah, so in each place these
Nigh to Bethabara – in Jericho   20
The city of palms, Aenon, and Salem old,
Machaerus, and each town or city walled
On this side the broad lake Genezaret,

1–7] John i. 35–41. *Messiah* is the Hebrew term which was translated into the Greek of the LXX and the New Testatment as χριστός, Christ. Both words mean 'the anointed one'.

15] Exod. xxxii. 1.

16–17] Elijah is called 'the Tishbite' in I Kings xvii. 1; the precise meaning of the term is not known, but see ll. 312–14n. On his second coming see Mal. iv. 5. See *PL* III 522n.

18–19] II Kings ii. 15–17.

20–4] On Bethabara see John i. 28; on Jericho as 'city of palms' see Deut. xxxiv. 3. On Aenon and Salem see John iii. 23; Salem is 'old' in deference to a patristic tradition which identified the 'Salim' of John the Baptist with the Salem of Melchizedek (Gen. xiv. 18, Heb. vii. 1–2). Machaerus was a fortress overlooking the Dead Sea from the east; John the Baptist was imprisoned and executed there. Genezaret is the name of the Sea of Galilee in I Macc. xi. 67, Luke v. 1, and in Josephus. Perea is the name given by Josephus to the district described in rabbinical literature and the N.T. as 'beyond Jordan' (see Matt. xi. 1).

Or in Perea – but returned in vain.
Then on the bank of Jordan, by a creek,   25
Where winds with reeds and osiers whispering play,
Plain fishermen (no greater men them call)
Close in a cottage low together got,
Their unexpected loss and plaints outbreathed:
    'Alas, from what high hope to what relapse   30
Unlooked-for are we fallen! Our eyes beheld
Messiah certainly now come, so long
Expected of our fathers; we have heard
His words, his wisdom full of grace and truth:
"Now, now, for sure, deliverance is at hand;   35
The kingdom shall to Israel be restored":
Thus we rejoiced, but soon our joy is turned
Into perplexity and new amaze:
For whither is he gone, what accident
Hath rapt him from us? Will he now retire   40
After appearance, and again prolong
Our expectation? God of Israel,
Send thy Messiah forth, the time is come;
Behold the kings of the earth, how they oppress
Thy chosen, to what height their power unjust   45
They have exalted, and behind them cast
All fear of thee; arise, and vindicate
Thy glory; free thy people from their yoke!
But let us wait; thus far he hath performed –
Sent his Anointed, and to us revealed him,   50
By his great prophet pointed at and shown
In public, and with him we have conversed;
Let us be glad of this, and all our fears
Lay on his providence; he will not fail,
Nor will withdraw him now, nor will recall –   55
Mock us with his blest sight, then snatch him hence:
Soon we shall see our hope, our joy, return.'
    Thus they out of their plaints new hope resume
To find whom at the first they found unsought;
But to his mother Mary, when she saw   60
Others returned from baptism, not her son,
Nor left at Jordan, tidings of him none;
Within her breast though calm, her breast though pure,

34] John i. 14.
36] Acts i. 6.
40 rapt] carried away.
44] Psalm ii. 2.
50 Anointed] See ll. 1–7n.

Motherly cares and fears got head, and raised
Some troubled thoughts, which she in sighs thus clad: 65
    'Oh, what avails me now that honour high,
To have conceived of God, or that salute,
"Hail, highly favoured, among women blest!"
While I to sorrows am no less advanced,
And fears as eminent above the lot   70
Of other women, by the birth I bore;
In such a season born, when scarce a shed
Could be obtained to shelter him or me
From the bleak air; a stable was our warmth,
A manger his; yet soon enforced to fly   75
Thence into Egypt, till the murderous king
Were dead, who sought his life, and missing filled
With infant blood the streets of Bethlehem;
From Egypt home returned, in Nazareth
Hath been our dwelling many years; his life   80
Private, unactive, calm, contemplative,
Little suspicious to any king; but now,
Full grown to man, acknowledged, as I hear,
By John the Baptist, and in public shown,
Son owned from heaven by his Father's voice,   85
I looked for some great change. To honour? No,
But trouble, as old Simeon plain foretold,
That to the fall and rising he should be
Of many in Israel, and to a sign
Spoken against – that through my very soul   90
A sword shall pierce; this is my favoured lot,
My exaltation to afflictions high;
Afflicted I may be, it seems, and blest;
I will not argue that, nor will repine.
But where delays he now? Some great intent   95
Conceals him; when twelve years he scarce had seen,
I lost him, but so found, as well I saw
He could not lose himself, but went about
His Father's business; what he meant I mused –
Since understand; much more his absence now   100
Thus long to some great purpose he obscures.
But I to wait with patience am inured;
My heart hath been a storehouse long of things

67–8] Cf. *PL* V 385–7n.
87–91] Luke ii. 34–5; cf. I 255–8.
92 exaltation] Miriam, the Hebrew form of Mary, is of uncertain etymology,
    but was sometimes believed to mean 'exaltation'.
96–9] Luke ii. 42–51.
103–4] Luke ii. 19.

And sayings laid up, portending strange events.'
  Thus Mary, pondering oft, and oft to mind   105
Recalling what remarkably had passed
Since first her salutation heard, with thoughts
Meekly composed awaited the fulfilling:
The while her son, tracing the desert wild,
Sole, but with holiest meditations fed,   110
Into himself descended, and at once
All his great work to come before him set –
How to begin, how to accomplish best
His end of being on earth, and mission high:
For Satan, with sly preface to return,   115
Had left him vacant, and with speed was gone
Up to the middle region of thick air,
Where all his potentates in council sat.
There, without sign of boast, or sign of joy,
Solicitous and blank, he thus began: 120
  'Prince, heaven's ancient sons, ethereal thrones –
Demonian spirits now, from the element
Each of his reign allotted, rightlier called,
Powers of fire, air, water, and earth beneath
(So may we hold our place and these mild seats   125
Without new trouble!) – such an enemy
Is risen to invade us, who no less
Threatens than our expulsion down to hell.
I, as I undertook, and with the vote
Consenting in full frequence was empowered,   130
Have found him, viewed him, tasted him; but find
Far other labour to be undergone
Than when I dealt with Adam, first of men,
Though Adam by his wife's allurement fell
However to this man inferior far –   135
If he be man by mother's side at least,
With more than human gifts from heaven adorned,
Perfections absolute, graces divine,
And amplitude of mind to greatest deeds;
Therefore I am returned, lest confidence   140

115 preface] used in the etymological sense of 'something said before', with
    reference to I 483–5.
116 vacant] unoccupied.
117] See *Fair Infant* 16n.
120 blank] disconcerted, resourceless.
130 frequence] assembly.
131 tasted] experienced, examined.
139 amplitude of mind] magnanimity; see *PL* VII 511n.

Of my success with Eve in Paradise
Deceive ye to persuasion over-sure
Of like succeeding here; I summon all
Rather to be in readiness with hand
Or counsel to assist, lest I, who erst   145
Thought none my equal, now be overmatched.'
   So spake the old serpent, doubting, and from all
With clamour was assured their utmost aid
At his command; when from amidst them rose
Belial, the dissolutest spirit that fell,   150
The sensualest, and after Asmodai
The fleshliest incubus, and thus advised:
   'Set women in his eye and in his walk,
Among daughters of men the fairest found;
Many are in each region passing fair   155
As the noon sky; more like to goddesses
Than mortal creatures, graceful and discreet,
Expert in amorous arts, enchanting tongues
Persuasive, virgin majesty with mild
And sweet allayed, yet terrible to approach,   160
Skilled to retire, and in retiring draw
Hearts after them tangled in amorous nets.
Such object hath the power to soften and tame
Severest temper, smooth the rugged'st brow,
Enerve, and with voluptuous hope dissolve,   165
Draw out with credulous desire, and lead
At will the manliest, resolutest breast,
As the magnetic hardest iron draws.
Women, when nothing else, beguiled the heart
Of wisest Solomon, and made him build,   170
And made him bow, to the gods of his wives.'
   To whom quick answer Satan thus returned:
'Belial, in much uneven scale thou weigh'st
All others by thyself; because of old
Thou thyself dot'st on womankind, admiring   175
Their shape, their colour, and attractive grace,
None are, thou think'st, but taken with such toys.
Before the flood, thou, with thy lusty crew,
False titled sons of God, roaming the earth,

147 old serpent] Rev. xii. 9, xx. 2.
150 Belial] Cf. *PL* I 490–505, II 109–17, and I 490n.
151 Asmodai] See *PL* VI 166–71n.
152 incubus] an evil spirit that had sexual intercourse with women while they
    slept.
169–71] I Kings xi. 1–8.

Cast wanton eyes on the daughters of men, 180
And coupled with them, and begot a race.
Have we not seen, or by relation heard,
In courts and regal chambers how thou lurk'st,
In wood or grove, by mossy fountain-side,
In valley or green meadow, to waylay 185
Some beauty rare, Callisto, Clymene,
Daphne, or Semele, Antiopa,
Or Amymone, Syrinx, many more,
Too long – then lay'st thy scapes on names adored,
Apollo, Neptune, Jupiter, or Pan, 190
Satyr, or Faun, or Sylvan? But these haunts
Delight not all; among the sons of men
How many have with a smile made small account
Of beauty and her lures, easily scorned
All her assaults, on worthier things intent! 195
Remember that Pellean conqueror,
A youth, how all the beauties of the East
He slightly viewed, and slightly overpassed;
How he surnamed of Africa dismissed,
In his prime youth, the fair Iberian maid. 200
For Solomon, he lived at east, and, full
Of honour, wealth, high fare, aimed not beyond
Higher design than to enjoy his state;
Thence to the bait of women lay exposed.
But he whom we attempt is wiser far 205
Than Solomon, of more exalted mind,
Made and set wholly on the accomplishment
Of greatest things; what woman will you find,
Though of this age the wonder and the fame,
On whom his leisure will vouchsafe an eye 210

178–81] Gen. vi. 1–4. Cf. *PL* III 463–5, V 447–8, XI 574–627.

186–8] Callisto, one of the 'nymphs of Diana's train' (l. 355), was the mother by Zeus of Arcas (see *Comus* 341n.); Clymene, an oceanid, was the mother by Helius of Phaethon; on Daphne see *PL* IV 272–4n.; Semele was consumed by the fire of Jove, by whom she was the mother of Bacchus, who was born posthumously from the thigh of Jove; Antiopa was the mother by Zeus of Amphion and Zethus; Amymone was the mother by Poseidon of Nauphius; Syrinx was pursued by Pan and changed into a reed.

191 haunts] habits.

196–8] The 'Pellean conqueror' is Alexander the Great (born at Pella, in Macedonia), who in 333 BC (at the age of twenty-three) captured and treated honourably the wife and daughters of Darius.

199–200] In 210 BC Scipio Africanus, aged twenty-four, restored a beautiful Spanish captive to her lover after the fall of New Carthage.

205–6] Matt. xii. 42.

Of fond desire? Or should she, confident,
As sitting queen adored on beauty's throne,
Descend with all her winning charms begirt
To enamour, as the zone of Venus once
Wrought that effect on Jove, so fables tell;   215
How would one look from his majestic brow,
Seated as on the top of virtue's hill,
Discountenance her despised, and put to rout
All her array; her female pride deject,
Or turn to reverent awe! For beauty stands   220
In the admiration only of weak minds
Led captive; cease to admire, and all her plumes
Fall flat, and shrink into a trivial toy,
At every sudden slighting quite abashed;
Therefore with manlier objects we must try   225
His constancy – with such as have more show
Of worth, of honour, glory, and popular praise
(Rocks whereon greatest men have oftest wrecked);
Or that which only seems to satisfy
Lawful desires of nature, not beyond;   230
And now I know he hungers, where no food
Is to be found, in the wide wilderness;
The rest commit to me; I shall let pass
No advantage, and his strength as oft assay.'
     He ceased, and heard their grant in loud acclaim;   235
Then forthwith to him takes a chosen band
Of spirits likest to himself in guile,
To be at hand and at his beck appear,.
If cause were to unfold some active scene
Of various persons, each to know his part;   240
Then to the desert takes with these his flight;
Where still, from shade to shade, the Son of God,
After forty days' fasting, had remained,
Now hungering first, and to himself thus said: 244
     'Where will this end? Four times ten days I have passed
Wandering this woody maze, and human food
Nor tasted, nor had appetite; that fast
To virtue I impute not, or count part
Of what I suffer here; if nature need not,
Or God support nature without repast,   250
Though needing, what praise is it to endure?
But now I feel I hunger, which declares

214–15] *Iliad* xiv 214 ff.
223–3] Alludes to Ovid's remark about the peacock (*Ars Amatoria* i. 627–8).
236–7] Matt. xii. 45.

Nature hath need of what she asks; yet God
Can satisfy that need some other way,
Though hunger still remain: so it remain　　255
Without this body's wasting, I content me,
And from the sting of famine fear no harm,
Nor mind it, fed with better thoughts, that feed
Me hungering more to do my Father's will.'
　　It was the hour of night, when thus the Son　　260
Communed in silent walk, then laid him down
Under the hospitable cover nigh
Of trees thick interwoven; there he slept,
And dreamed, as appetite is wont to dream,
Of meats and drinks, nature's refreshment sweet;　　265
Him thought he by the brook of Cherith stood,
And saw the ravens with their horny beaks
Food to Elijah bringing even and morn –
Though ravenous, taught to abstain from what they
　　　brought;
He saw the prophet also, how he fled　　270
Into the desert, and how there he slept
Under a juniper – then how, awaked,
He found his supper on the coals prepared,
And by the angel was bid rise and eat,
And eat the second time after repose,　　275
The strength whereof sufficed him forty days;
Sometimes that with Elijah he partook,
Or as a guest with Daniel at his pulse.
Thus wore out night; and now the herald lark
Left his ground-nest, high towering to descry　　280
The Morn's approach, and greet her with his song;
As lightly from his grassy couch up rose
Our Saviour, and found all was but a dream;
Fasting he went to sleep, and fasting waked.
Up to a hill anon his steps he reared,　　285
From whose high top to ken the prospect round,
If cottage were in view, sheep-cote, or herd;
But cottage, herd, or sheep-cote, none he saw –
Only in a bottom saw a pleasant grove,
With chant of tuneful birds resounding loud;　　290
Thither he bent his way, determined there
To rest at noon, and entered soon the shade,

259] John iv. 34.
266–9] I Kings xvii. 3–7; 'ravenous' is a pun.
270–6] I Kings xix. 3–8.
278] Dan. i. 8–19.

High-roofed, and walks beneath, and alleys brown,
That opened in the midst a woody scene;
Nature's own work it seemed (Nature taught Art),   295
And, to a superstitious eye, the haunt
Of wood-gods and wood-nymphs; he viewed it round,
When suddenly a man before him stood,
Not rustic as before, but seemlier clad,
As one in city, or court, or palace bred,   300
And with fair speech these words to him addressed:
     'With granted leave officious I return,
But much more wonder that the Son of God
In this wild solitude so long should bide,
Of all things destitute, and, well I know   305
Not without hunger. Others of some note,
As story tells, have trod this wilderness:
The fugitive bond-woman, with her son,
Outcast Nebaioth, yet found he relief
By a providing angel; all the race   310
Of Israel here had famished, had not God
Rained from heaven manna; and that prophet bold,
Native of Thebez, wandering here was fed
Twice by a voice inviting him to eat.
Of thee these forty days none hath regard,   315
Forty and more deserted here indeed.'
To whom thus Jesus: 'What conclud'st thou hence?
They all had need; I, as thou seest, have none.'
     'How hath thou hunger then?' Satan replied;
'Tell me, if food were now before thee set,   320
Wouldst thou not eat?' 'Thereafter as I like
The giver,' answered Jesus. 'Why should that
Cause thy refusal?' said the subtle fiend.
'Hast thou not right to all created things?
Owe not all creatures, by just right, to thee   325
Duty and service, nor to stay till bid,
But tender all their power? Nor mention I
Meats by the law unclean, or offered first

---

302 officious] Satan uses the word in the sense 'eager to serve or please' (cf.
   Latin *officiosus*), but by the seventeenth century the word had also come to
   mean 'unduly forward in proffering services'.
308–10] Gen. xxi. 9–21. Ismael is here called by the name of his eldest son
   Nebaioth (Gen. xxv. 13).
310–12] Exod. xvi. 35.
312–14] I Kings xix. 3–8. Thebez is Milton's conjectural identification of the
   place signified by the word 'Thisbite' (l. 16).
327–8 nor . . . unclean] a falsehood. See l. 345n.
328–9 or . . . idols] Acts xv. 29, I Cor. viii. 4–13, x. 25–31.

To idols – those young Daniel could refuse;
Nor proffered by an enemy – though who   330
Would scruple that, with want oppressed? Behold
Nature ashamed, or, better to express,
Troubled, that thou shouldst hunger, hath purveyed
From all the elements her choicest store,
To treat thee as beseems, and as her Lord   335
With honour; only deign to sit and eat.'
   He spake no dream; for as his words had end,
Our Saviour, lifting up his eyes, beheld
In ample space under the broadest shade,
A table richly spread in regal mode,   340
With dishes piled and meats of noblest sort
And savour – beasts of chase, or fowl of game,
In pastry built, or from the spit, or boiled,
Grisamber-steamed; all fish, from sea or shore,
Freshet or purling brook, of shell or fin,   345
And exquisitest name, for which was drained
Pontus, and Lucrine bay, and Afric coast,
Alas how simple, to these cates compared,
Was that crude apple that diverted Eve!
And at a stately sideboard, by the wine   350
That fragrant smell diffused, in order stood
Tall stripling youths rich-clad, of fairer hue
Than Ganymede or Hylas; distant more,
Under the trees now tripped, now solemn stood,
Nymphs of Diana's train, and Naiades   355
With fruits and flowers from Amalthea's horn,
And ladies of the Hesperides, that seemed
Fairer than feigned of old, or fabled since
Of fairy damsels met in forest wide

---

329 those . . . refuse] Dan. i. 8.
344 Grisamber] ambergris, a morbid secretion in the intestines of the sperm-
   whale, used in cookery to impart a sweet odour to food.
345 shell] The Mosaic dietary laws forbid as 'an abomination' all fish without
   fins or scales (Lev. xi. 9–12).
347] Pontus, i.e. Pontus Euxinus, the Black Sea, was famous in antiquity for its
   fish; Lucrine bay, a salt-water lagoon in Campania, for its shellfish.
353] Ganymede was the cupbearer of Jove, and Hylas was the page of Hercules.
355 Naiades] river and fountain nymphs.
356] 'Amalthea's horn' is the Greek phrase (κέρας Ἀμαλθείας) equivalent to the
   Latin cornu copiae, the horn of plenty. Milton seems to allude specifically to
   the horn of Achelous, which the Naiades filled with fruit and flowers
   (Metamorphoses ix 87–8.
357] See Comus 393–5n.

By knights of Logres, or of Lyonesse,   360
Lancelot, or Pelleas, or Pellenore;
And all the while harmonious airs were heard
Of chiming strings or charming pipes; and winds
Of gentlest gale Arabian odours fanned
From their soft wings, and Flora's earliest smells.   365
Such was the splendour; and the tempter now
His invitation earnestly renewed:
   'What doubts the Son of God to sit and eat?
These are not fruits forbidden; no interdict
Defends the touching of these viands pure;   370
Their taste no knowledge works, at least of evil,
But life preserves, destroys life's enemy,
Hunger, with sweet restorative delight.
All these are spirits of air, and woods, and springs,
Thy gentle ministers, who come to pay   375
Thee homage, and acknowledge thee their Lord;
What doubt'st thou, Son of God? Sit down and eat.'
   To whom thus Jesus temperately replied:
'Said'st thou not that to all things I had right?
And who withholds my power that right to use?   380
Shall I receive by gift what of my own,
When and where likes me best, I can command?
I can at will, doubt not, as soon as thou,
Command a table in this wilderness,
And call swift flights of angels ministrant,   385
Arrayed in glory, on my cup to attend:
Why shouldst thou, then, obtrude this diligence
In vain, where no acceptance it can find?
And with my hunger what hast thou to do?
Thy pompous delicacies I contemn,   390
And count thy specious gifts no gifts, but guiles.'
   To whom thus answered Satan, malcontent:
'That I have also power to give thou seest;
If of that power I bring thee voluntary

360] Logres is the area of England east of the Severn and south of the Humber.
   Lyonesse is a mythical country (associated with Arthur), once located
   between Land's End and the Scilly Isles, and now covered by the sea.
361] In Malory both Lancelot and Pelleas have amorous adventures. Pellenore
   may be an allusion to Pellenore's son Percival, whose experience of a
   banquet and sexual temptation bears some resemblance to that of Milton's
   Jesus (Morte d'Arthur xiv. 9).
365 Flora] Roman goddess of flowers.
368 What doubts] Why hesitates.
370 Defends] forbids.
384] Psalm lxxviii. 19.

What I might have bestowed on whom I pleased,   395
And rather opportunely in this place
Chose to impart to thy apparent need,
Why shouldst thou not accept it? But I see
What I can do or offer is suspect;
Of these things others quickly will dispose,   400
Whose pains have earned the far-fet spoil.' With that
Both table and provision vanished quite,
With sound of harpies' wings and talons heard,
Only the importune tempter still remained,
And with these words his temptation pursued: 405
    'By hunger, that each other creature tames,
Thou art not to be harmed, therefore not moved;
Thy temperance, invincible besides,
For no allurement yields to appetite;
And all thy heart is set on high designs,   410
High actions. But wherewith to be achieved?
Great acts require great means of enterprise;
Thou art unknown, unfriended, low of birth,
A carpenter thy father known, thyself
Bred up in poverty and straits at home,   415
Lost in a desert here and hunger-bit;
Which way, or from what hope, dost thou aspire
To greatness? Whence authority deriv'st?
What followers, what retínue canst thou gain,
Or at thy heels the dizzy multitude,   420
Longer than thou canst feed them on thy cost?
Money brings honour, friends, conquest, and realms;
What raised Antipater the Edomite,
And his son Herod placed on Judah's throne
(Thy throne) but gold, that got him puissant friends?   425
Therefore, if at great things thou wouldst arrive,
Get riches first, get wealth, and treasure heap –
Not difficult, if thou hearken to me,
Riches are mine, fortune is in my hand;
They whom I favour thrive in wealth amain,   430
While virtue, valour, wisdom, sit in want.'
    To whom thus Jesus patiently replied:
'Yet wealth without these three is impotent
To gain dominion, or to keep it gained.

401 fet] fetched.
403 harpies] See *Comus* 605n.
414] Matt. xiii. 55.
423–5] See *PL* XII 353–8n.
429] Hag. ii. 8.

Witness those ancient empires of the earth,   435
In height of all their flowing wealth dissolved;
But men endued with these have oft attained,
In lowest poverty, to highest deeds –
Gideon, and Jephtha, and the shepherd lad
Whose offspring on the throne of Judah sat   440
So many ages, and shall yet regain
That seat, and reign in Israel without end.
Among the heathen (for throughout the world
To me is not unknown what hath been done
Worthy of memorial) canst thou not remember   445
Quintius, Fabricius, Curius, Regulus?
For I esteem those names of men so poor,
Who could do mighty things, and could contemn
Riches, though offered from the hand of kings.
And what in me seems wanting but that I   450
May also in this poverty as soon
Accomplish what they did, perhaps and more?
Extol not riches, then, the toil of fools,
The wise man's cumbrance, if not snare; more apt
To slacken virtue and abate her edge   455
Than prompt her to do aught may merit praise.
What if with like aversion I reject
Riches and realms! Yet not for that a crown,
Golden in show, is but a wreath of thorns,
Brings dangers, troubles, cares, and sleepless nights,   460
To him who wears the regal diadem,
When on his shoulders each man's burden lies;
For therein stands the office of a king,
His honour, virtue, merit, and chief praise,
That for the public all this weight he bears.   465
Yet he who reigns within himself, and rules
Passions, desires, and fears, is more a king –

439] On Gideon see Judges vi–viii; on Jephtha see Judges xi–xii; on David, 'the shepherd lad', see Psalm lxxviii. 70–1, Ezek. xxxiv. 23–4.
441–2] Luke i. 32–3.
446] Lucius Quinctius Cincinnatus was a farmer who in 458 BC was appointed dictator and defeated the Aequi. Gaius Fabricius Luscinus, consul in 282 and 278 BC, was famous for his poverty, austerity, and incorruptibility. Manius Curius Dentatus was a Roman plebeian hero, famous for his humble birth, incorruptibility, and frugality. Marcus Atilius Regulus, a hero of the First Punic War (255 BC), was according to legend tortured to death in Carthage (see Horace, *Odes* III. v).
453 toil] trap, snare.
458 for that] because.
466–7] Prov. xvi. 32.

Which every wise and virtuous man attains;
And who attains not, ill aspires to rule
Cities of men, or headstrong multitudes,   470
Subject himself to anarchy within,
Or lawless passions in him, which he serves.
But to guide nations in the way of truth
By saving doctrine, and from error lead
To know, and, knowing, worship God aright,   475
Is yet more kingly; this attracts the soul,
Governs the inner man, the nobler part;
That other o'er the body only reigns,
And oft by force – which to a generous mind
So reigning can be no sincere delight.   480
Besides, to give a kingdom hath been thought
Greater and nobler done, and to lay down
Far more magnanimous, than to assume.
Riches are needless, then, both for themselves,
And for thy reason why they should be sought   485
To gain a sceptre, oftest better missed.'

THE END OF THE SECOND BOOK

481–3] Seneca, *Thyestes* 529. Milton may have in mind the abdications of
   Diocletian (in AD 305), the Emperor Charles V (1555), and Christina of
   Sweden (1654). On 'magnanimous' see *PL* VII 511n.

BOOK III

So spake the Son of God; and Satan stood
A while as mute, confounded what to say,
What to reply, confuted and convinced
Of his weak arguing and fallacious drift;
At length, collecting all his serpent wiles,   5
With soothing words renewed, him thus accosts:
  'I see thou know'st what is of use to know,
What best to say canst say, to do canst do;
Thy actions to thy words accord; thy words
To thy large heart give utterance due; thy heart   10
Contains of good, wise, just, the perfect shape.
Should kings and nations from thy mouth consult,
Thy counsel would be as the oracle
Urim and Thummim, those oraculous gems
On Aaron's breast, or tongue of seers old   15
Infallible; or wert thou sought to deeds
That might require the array of war, thy skill
Of conduct would be such that all the world
Could not sustain thy prowess, or subsist
In battle, though against thy few in arms.   20
These godlike virtues wherefore dost thou hide?
Affecting private life, or more obscure
In savage wilderness, wherefore deprive
All earth her wonder at thy acts, thyself
The fame and glory – glory, the reward   25
That sole excites to high attempts the flame
Of most erected spirits, most tempered pure
Ethereal, who all pleasures else despise,
All treasures and all gain esteem as dross,
And dignities and powers, all but the highest?   30

13–15] The precise meaning of Urim and Thummim is not known. The
vocalization of the words indicates that Massoretic scholars connected
Urim with light, and Thummim with perfection, or innocence. The plural
form is probably not intended to indicate plurality (as the R.V. marginal
note to Exod. xxviii. 30 would have it) but is rather an intensive plural.
Urim and Thummim are associated with the breastplate of Aaron in Exod.
xxviii. 30 and Lev. viii. 8. They are most clearly oracular in the LXX text
of I Sam. xiv. 41–2, part of which may be translated 'And Saul said, "if the
guilt be in me or in Jonathan my son, give Urim, O Lord God of Israel; but
if you say it is in my people Israel, give Thummin"'.
22 Affecting] seeking.
27 erected] exalted.

Thy years are ripe, and over-ripe: the son
Of Macedonian Philip had ere these
Won Asia, and the throne of Cyrus held
At his dispose; young Scipio had brought down
The Carthaginian pride; young Pompey quelled   35
The Pontic king, and in tríumph had rode.
Yet years, and to ripe years judgement mature,
Quench not the thirst of glory, but augment.
Great Julius, whom now all the world admires,
The more he grew in years, the more inflamed   40
With glory, wept that he had lived so long
Inglorious: but thou yet are not too late.'
   To whom our Saviour calmly thus replied:
'Thou neither dost persuade me to seek wealth
For empire's sake, nor empire to affect   45
For glory's sake, by all thy argument.
For what is glory but the blaze of fame,
The people's praise, if always praise unmixed?
And what the people but a herd confused,
A miscellaneous rabble, who extol   50
Things vulgar, and well weighed, scarce worth the praise?
They praise and they admire they know not what,
And know not whom, but as one leads the other;
And what delight to be by such extolled,
To live upon their tongues, and be their talk?   55
Of whom to be dispraised were no small praise –
His lot who dares be singularly good.
The intelligent among them and the wise
Are few, and glory scarce of few is raised.
This is true glory and renown – when God,   60
Looking on the earth, with approbation marks

31–4] Jesus was 'about thirty' at his baptism (Luke iii. 23). Philip of Macedon's
    son was Alexander the Great, who in 334 BC (aged twenty-two) crossed the
    Hellespont and 'won Asia', and in 330 assumed the throne of the empire
    which Cyrus had founded.
34–5] Scipio was sent to Spain as proconsul in 210 BC, aged twenty-four, and
    eight years later defeated the Carthaginians in the battle of Zama, thus
    ending the Second Punic War.
35–6] Pompey defeated Mithridates VI, King of Pontus, in 66 BC (when he was
    forty) and in 61 BC returned to Italy to celebrate the most magnificent
    triumph that Rome had ever witnessed. Pompey had been granted a
    triumph in 81 BC (though he was merely an *eques*, and not legally qualified
    for one) and another in 71 BC. Even if Satan is referring to this earliest
    triumph, he certainly misrepresents Pompey's age during the Mithridatic
    War.
39–42] According to Plutarch, in 68 BC Caesar (aged thirty) read the history of
    Alexander's campaigns, and wept because Alexander, at his age, was the
    king of so many people, whereas Caesar had yet to achieve a brilliant
    success (*Life of Caesar* xi. 3).

The just man, and divulges him through heaven
To all his angels, who with true applause
Recount his praises; thus he did to Job,
When, to extend his fame through heaven and earth,   65
As thou to thy reproach may'st well remember,
He asked thee, "Hast thou seen my servant Job?"
Famous he was in heaven; on earth less known,
Where glory is false glory, attributed
To things not glorious, men not worthy of fame.   70
They err who count it glorious to subdue
By conquest far and wide, to overrun
Large countries, and in field great battles win,
Great cities by assault; what do these worthies
But rob and spoil, burn, slaughter, and enslave   75
Peaceable nations, neighbouring or remote,
Made captive, yet deserving freedom more
Than those their conquerors, who leave behind
Nothing but ruin wheresoe'er they rove,
And all the flourishing works of peace destroy,   80
Then swell with pride, and must be titled gods,
Great benefactors of mankind, deliverers,
Worshipped with temple, priest, and sacrifice?
One is the son of Jove, of Mars the other;
Till conqueror Death discover them scarce men,   85
Rolling in brutish vices, and deformed,
Violent or shameful death their due reward.
But if there be in glory aught of good,
It may by means far different be attained,
Without ambition, war, or violence –   90
By deeds of peace, by wisdom eminent,

62 divulges] publicly proclaims.
64–8] Cf. I 147–9n.
81 titled gods] The title *divus* was accorded to deceased Roman emperors, and
from the time of Domitian emperors were regarded as gods during their
lifetime. Antiochus II of Syria had assumed the title ὁ θεός (a god). Cf. Acts
ii. 22, where the voice of Herod Agrippa I is said to be that of a god.
82 benefactors] The title εὐεργέτης (benefactor) was conferred on various
persons by the Greeks, and was enjoyed by two of the Macedonian kings of
Egypt, Ptolemy III and Ptolemy VIII. Cf. Luke xxii. 25, which refers to
the title.
  deliverers] The title Σωτήρ (deliverer, saviour) was anciently used of deities,
and in Hellenistic times it was used of kings to imply deification. The most
famous holder of the title was probably Ptolemy I. In the LXX the word is
used of various warriors, and of God; in the N.T. it is often applied to Jesus.
84] The 'son of Jove' is Alexander (see *PL* IX 507–9n.); the son of Mars is
Romulus, first king of Rome and (after his translation to heaven) the god
Quirinus.
91–2] II Pet. i. 6.

By patience, temperance; I mention still
Him whom thy wrongs, with saintly patience borne,
Made famous in a land and times obscure;
Who names not now with honour patient Job?   95
Poor Socrates (who next more memorable?),
By what he taught and suffered for so doing,
For truth's sake suffering death unjust, lives now
Equal in fame to proudest conquerors.
Yet, if for fame and glory aught be done,   100
Aught suffered – if young African for fame
His wasted country freed from Punic rage –
The deed becomes unpraised, the man at least,
And loses, though but verbal, his reward.
Shall I seek glory, then, as vain men seek,   105
Oft not deserved? I seek not mine, but his
Who sent me, and thereby witness whence I am.'
     To whom the tempter, murmuring, thus replied:
'Think not so slight of glory, therein least
Resembling thy great Father: he seeks glory,   110
And for his glory all things made, all things
Orders and governs; nor content in heaven,
By all his angels glorified, requires
Glory from men, from all men, good or bad,
Wise or unwise, no difference, no exemption;   115
Above all sacrifice, or hallowed gift,
Glory he requires, and glory he receives,
Promiscuous from all nations, Jew, or Greek,
Or barbarous, nor exception hath declared;
From us, his foes pronounced, glory he exacts.'   120
     To whom our Saviour fervently replied:
'And reason; since his word all things produced,
Though chiefly not for glory as prime end,
But to show forth his goodness, and impart
His good communicable to every soul   125
Freely; of whom what could he less expect
Than glory and benediction – that is, thanks –
The slightest, easiest, readiest recompense
From them who could return him nothing else,
And, not returning that, would likeliest render   130
Contempt instead, dishonour, obloquy?
Hard recompense, unsuitable return

96–9] According to an ancient tradition the teaching and death of Socrates
     foreshadowed that of Jesus.
101–2] See ll. 34–5n.
106–7] John v. 31–2, vii. 18, viii. 50.
119 barbarous] non-Hellenic.

For so much good, so much beneficence!
But why should man seek glory, who of his own
Hath nothing, and to whom nothing belongs   135
But condemnation, ignominy, and shame –
Who, for so many benefits received,
Turned recreant to God, ingrate and false,
And so of all true good himself despoiled;
Yet, sacrilegious, to himself would take   140
That which to God alone of right belongs?
Yet so much bounty is in God, such grace,
That who advance his glory, not their own,
Them he himself to glory will advance.'

So spake the Son of God; and here again   145
Satan had not to answer, but stood struck
With guilt of his own sin – for he himself,
Insatiable of glory, had lost all;
Yet of another plea bethought him soon –
'Of glory, as thou wilt,' said he, 'so deem;   150
Worth or not worth the seeking, let it pass;
But to a kingdom thou art born – ordained
To sit upon thy father David's throne,
By mother's side thy father, though thy right
Be now in powerful hands, that will not part   155
Easily from possession won with arms;
Judea now and all the promised land,
Reduced a province under Roman yoke,
Obeys Tiberius, nor is always ruled
With temperate sway: oft have they violated   160
The Temple, oft the Law, with foul affronts,
Abominations rather, as did once

138 recreant] false, apostate.
146 not] nothing.
153] Luke i. 32.
154] The gospels are silent about the ancestry of Mary, but according to
    patristic tradition she was descended from David.
157–60] In AD 6 Judea was annexed to the province of Syria, and was thereafter
    ruled by procurators. Tiberius was Roman emperor from AD 14–37. From
    AD 26–36 the procurator of Judea was Pontius Pilate; Josephus and Philo
    both testify to the intemperance of his rule (*Antiquities* xviii. 3, *Jewish War*
    ii. 8 ff.; *Legatio ad Gaium* xxxviii).
160–3] In 169 BC Antiochus IV had pillaged the temple, and had forced the
    Jews to offer swine on the altar; he later rededicated the temple to
    Olympian Zeus, thus precipitating the Maccabean revolt. In 63 BC Pompey
    had entered the Holy of Holies with several of his officers. When Pontius
    Pilate had arrived in Judea in AD 26 he had offended the Jews by bringing
    images of the emperor into Jerusalem.

Antiochus: and think'st thou to regain
Thy right in sitting still, or thus retiring?
So did not Maccabeus: he indeed   165
Retired unto the desert, but with arms;
And o'er a mighty king so oft prevailed
That by strong hand his family obtained,
Though priests, the crown, and David's throne usurped,
With Modin and her suburbs once content.   170
If kingdom move thee not, let move thee zeal
And duty – zeal and duty are not slow,
But on Occasion's forelock watchful wait.
They themselves rather are occasion best –
Zeal of thy Father's house, duty to free   175
Thy country from her heathen servitude;
So shalt thou best fulfil, best verify,
The prophets old, who sung thy endless reign –
The happier reign the sooner it begins:
Reign then; what canst thou better do the while?'   180
    To whom our Saviour answer thus returned:
'All things are best fulfilled in their due time,
And time there is for all things, Truth hath said;
If of my reign prophetic writ hath told
That it shall never end, so, when begin   185
The Father in his purpose hath decreed –
He in whose hand all times and seasons roll.
What if he hath decreed that I shall first
Be tried in humble state, and things adverse,
By tribulations, injuries, insults,   190
Contempts, and scorns, and snares, and violence
Suffering, abstaining, quietly expecting
Without distrust or doubt, that he may know
What I can suffer, how obey? Who best
Can suffer, best can do; best reign who first   195
Well hath obeyed – just trial ere I merit
My exaltation without change or end.
But what concerns it thee when I begin
My everlasting kingdom, why are thou

165–70] The revolt led by Mattathias and his son Judas Maccabeus began in
    Modin, the location of which has not been established with certainty. See I
    Macc. ii–ix.
173 Occasion] opportunity, the forelock of which was proverbial.
175] Psalm lxix. 9, John ii. 17.
182–3] Eccles. iii. 1.
187] Acts i. 7.
194–6] A classical commonplace, a version of which occurs in Matt. xx. 26–7.

Solicitous, what moves thy inquisition?   200
Know'st thou not that my rising is thy fall,
And my promotion will be thy destruction?'
      To whom the tempter, inly racked, replied:
'Let that come when it comes; all hope is lost
Of my reception into grace; what worse?   205
For where no hope is left is left no fear;
If there be worse, the expectation more
Of worse torments me than the feeling can.
I would be at the worst; worst is my port,
My harbour, and my ultimate repose,   210
The end I would attain, my final good.
My error was my error, and my crime
My crime; whatever, for itself condemned,
And will alike be punished, whether thou
Reign or reign not – though to that gentle brow   215
Willingly I could fly, and hope thy reign,
From that placid aspéct and meek regard,
Rather than aggravate my evil state,
Would stand between me and thy Father's ire
(Whose ire I dread more than the fire of hell)   220
A shelter and a kind of shading cool
Interposition, as a summer's cloud.
If I then to the worst that can be haste,
Why move thy feet so slow to what is best,
Happiest, both to thyself and all the world,   225
That thou, who worthiest art, shouldst be their king?
Perhaps thou linger'st in deep thoughts detained
Of the enterprise so hazardous and high;
No wonder, for though in thee be united
What of perfection can in man be found,   230
Or human nature can receive, consider
Thy life hath yet been private, most part spent
At home, scarce viewed the Galilean towns,
And once a year Jerusalem few days'
Short sojourn; and what thence couldst thou observe?   235
The world thou hast not seen, much less her glory,
Empires, and monarchs, and their radiant courts –
Best school of best experience, quickest in sight
In all things that to greatest actions lead.
The wisest, unexperienced, will be ever   240
Timorous and loath, with novice modesty
(As he who, seeking asses, found a kingdom)

221–2] Isa. xxv. 4–5.
234] Luke ii. 41.
242 he] Saul; I Sam. ix–x. 1.

Irresolute, unhardy, unadventurous;
But I will bring thee where thou soon shalt quit
Those rudiments, and see before thine eyes   245
The monarchies of the earth, their pomp and state –
Sufficient introduction to inform
Thee, of thyself so apt, in regal arts,
And regal mysteries; that thou may'st know
How best their opposition to withstand.'   250
    With that (such power was given him then), he took
The Son of God up to a mountain high.
It was a mountain at whose verdant feet
A spacious plain outstretched in circuit wide
Lay pleasant; from his side two rivers flowed,   255
The one winding, the other straight, and left between
Fair champaign, with less rivers interveined,
Then meeting joined their tribute to the sea;
Fertile of corn the glebe, of oil, and wine,
With herds the pasture thronged, with flocks the hills; 260
Huge cities and high-towered, that well might seem
The seats of mightiest monarchs; and so large
The prospect was that here and there was room
For barren desert, fountainless and dry.
To this high mountain-top the tempter brought   265
Our Saviour, and new train of words began:
    'Well have we speeded, and o'er hill and dale,
Forest and field and flood, temples and towers,
Cut shorter many a league; here thou behold'st
Assyria, and her empire's ancient bounds,   270
Araxes and the Caspian lake; thence on
As far as Indus east, Euphrates west,
And oft beyond; to south the Persian bay,
And, inaccessible, the Arabian drouth;

247 inform] train.
249 mysteries] In Milton's time the word 'mystery' retained the senses of two
    different Latin roots, and meant both 'skill, occupation' (from *ministerium*)
    and 'secret' (from *mysterium*).
255–6] The 'two rivers' are the Euphrates and the Tigris. The Greek word
    Tigris was known in antiquity to derive from the Persian word *tigra*, 'an
    arrow', hence Milton's 'straight'.
257 champaign] Mesopotamia.
271 Araxes] now Aras, a river which rises in eastern Turkey, and forms the
    Soviet–Iranian border as it flows to the Caspian.
274 drouth] desert.

Here, Nineveh, of length within her wall 275
Several days' journey, built by Ninus old,
Of that first golden monarchy the seat,
And seat of Salmanassar, whose success
Israel in long captivity still mourns;
There Babylon, the wonder of all tongues, 280
As ancient, but rebuilt by him who twice
Judah and all thy father David's house
Led captive, and Jerusalem laid waste,
Till Cyrus set them free; Persepolis,
His city, there thou seest, and Bactra there; 285
Ecbatana her structure vast there shows,
And Hecatompylos her hundred gates;
There Susa by Choaspes, amber stream,
The drink of none but kings; of later fame
Built by Emathian or by Parthian hands, 290
The great Seleucia, Nisibis, and there
Artaxata, Teredon, Ctesiphon,
Turning with easy eye, thou may'st behold.
All these the Parthian (now some ages past
By great Arsaces led, who founded first 295
That empire) under his dominion holds,
From the luxurious kings of Antioch won.

275–9] Ninus was the legendary eponymous founder of Nineveh, the Assyrian capital on the Tigris. On the 'several days' journey' requisite to walk around it see Jonah iii. 3. Shalmaneser (or Salmanasar in II Esdras xiii. 40), King of Assyria from 727–722 BC, made Hoshea of Samaria (King of Israel) 'his servant' (II Kings xvii. 3), and later besieged Samaria, and 'carried Israel away into Assyria' (II Kings xvii. 4–6).

280–4] PL XII 344–7n.; 'wonder of all tongues' refers to such wonders as the temple of Bel and the hanging gardens, but also glances at the confusion of tongues (PL XII 38–62).

284–9] Persepolis was the summer capital of Persia, and Susa (see PL X 306–11n.) the winter residence of the kings on the banks of the Choaspes, which according to an ancient tradition was 'the drink of none but kings'. Bactra (now Balkh, in Afghanistan) was the capital of the Persian province of Bactria (cf. PL X 433n.). On Ecbatana see PL XI 393n. Hecatompylos ('hundred-gated') was a royal residence of Parthian kings; its location is not known.

290–2] Emathian refers to the Macedonian successors of Alexander, the Seleucids. On Seleucia see PL IV 212n. Nisibis is modern Nusaybin, in Turkey. Artaxata was the ancient capital of Armenia. Teredon was an ancient Babylonian city near the confluence of the Tigris and Euphrates. Ctesiphon, on the Tigris near Seleucia, was the winter capital of Parthia.

294–7] The Parthian Empire was founded by Arsaces in 247 BC in the Seleucid satrapy of Parthia, south of the Caspian Sea. The Seleucid capital was Antioch.

And just in time thou com'st to have a view
Of his great power; for now the Parthian king
In Ctesiphon hath gathered all his host   300
Against the Scythian, whose incursions wild
Have wasted Sogdiana; to her aid
He marches now in haste: see, though from far,
His thousands, in what martial equipage
They issue forth, steel bows and shafts their arms,   305
Of equal dread in flight or in pursuit –
All horsemen, in which fight they most excel;
See how in warlike muster they appear,
In rhombs, and wedges, and half-moons, and wings.'
 He looked, and saw what numbers numberless   310
The city gates outpoured, light-armed troops
In coats of mail and military pride.
In mail their horses clad, yet fleet and strong,
Prancing their riders bore, the flower and choice
Of many provinces from bound to bound –   315
From Arachosia, from Candaor east,
And Margiana, to the Hyrcanian cliffs
Of Caucasus, and dark Iberian dales;
From Atropatia, and the neighbouring plains
Of Adiabene, Media, and the south   320
Of Susiana, to Balsara's haven.
He saw them in their forms of battle ranged,
How quick they wheeled, and flying behind them shot

298–336] Milton's account of a war between the Scythians (an ancient tribe of
 south Russia) and the Parthians does not refer to any specific historical
 event.
302 Sogdiana] an ancient province of the Achaemenian Empire, and the north-
 eastern limit of Alexander's empire. At the time of Jesus it was not a
 Parthian province, but was occupied by the Scythians.
306] Many classical authors testify that Parthian horsemen often shot their
 arrows backwards while in real or pretended flight.
316–21] Arachosia, called White India by the Parthians, was their easternmost
 province: it occupied an area that straddles modern Afghanistan and
 Pakistan. Candaor (now Kendahar, in Afghanistan) was the frontier city of
 the Parthian Empire. Margiana was a province centred on the ancient town
 of Merv (now Mary, Turkmanistan). Hyrcania was a province south-east of
 the Caspian Sea. Iberia (modern Georgia) was a vassal state rather than a
 province, as were Atropatia (now Azerbaijan) and Adiabene (the ancient
 Assyria). Ancient Media was divided into four provinces by the Parthians.
 Susiana (modern Ilam, in south-west Iran) was a rebellious vassal state.
 Balsara (modern Basra) was not founded until AD 636; it was built on the
 joint stream that unites the Tigris and the Euphrates, and at the time of
 Jesus the site was probably part of the Persian Gulf. Jesus has viewed the
 Parthian Empire in a huge semi-circle from east to north to west.

Sharp sleet of arrowy showers against the face
Of their pursuers, and overcame by flight;   325
The field all iron cast a gleaming brown.
Nor wanted clouds of foot, nor, on each horn,
Cuirassiers all in steel for standing fight.
Chariots, or elephants endorsed with towers
Of archers; nor of labouring pioneers   330
A multitude, with spades and axes armed,
To lay hills plain, fell woods, or valleys fill,
Or where plain was raise hill, or overlay
With bridges rivers proud, as with a yoke;
Mules after these, camels and dromedaries,   335
And waggons fraught with útensils of war.
Such forces met not, nor so wide a camp,
When Agrican, with all his northern powers,
Besieged Albracca, as romances tell,
The city of Gallaphrone, from thence to win   340
The fairest of her sex, Angelica,
His daughter, sought by many prowest knights,
Both paynim and the peers of Charlemagne.
Such and so numerous was their chivalry;
At sight whereof the fiend yet more presumed,   345
And to our Saviour thus his words renewed:
   'That thou may'st know I seek not to engage
Thy virtue, and not every way secure
On no slight grounds thy safety, near and mark
To what end I have brought thee hither, and show   350
All this fair sight: thy kingdom, though foretold
By prophet or by angel, unless thou
Endeavour, as thy father David did,
Thou never shalt obtain; prediction still
In all things, and all men, supposes means;   355
Without means used, what it predicts revokes.
But say thou wert possessed of David's throne

328 Cuirassiers] horse soldiers wearing cuirasses, i.e. body armour consisting of
       a breastplate and a backplate.
329 endorscd] used in the etymological sense of 'carrying on the back'.
337–43] In Boiardo's *Orlando Innamorato* I. x–xiv, Agrican, the Tartar king,
       besieges with 2,200,000 men Albracca, a city of Gallaphrone, King of
       Cathay, in order to win the latter's daughter, the fair Angelica. At the
       beginning of the poem Angelica had won the heart of the *douzepers* (thc
       twelve 'peers of Charlemagne'), including Orlando, and of the pagan
       (paynim) knights. 'Prowest' means 'most gallant'.
353] David's struggle ('endeavour') for the throne is described in I Sam. xvi–II
       Sam. v.

By free consent of all, none opposite,
Samaritan or Jew; how couldst thou hope
Long to enjoy it quiet and secure   360
Between two such enclosing enemies,
Roman and Parthian? Therefore one of these
Thou must make sure thy own: the Parthian first,
By my advice, as nearer, and of late
Found able by invasion to annoy   365
Thy country, and captive lead away her kings,
Antigonus and old Hyrcanus, bound,
Maugre the Roman; it shall be my task
To render thee the Parthian at dispose:
Choose which thou wilt, by conquest or by league.   370
By him thou shalt regain, without him not,
That which alone can truly reinstall thee
In David's royal seat, his true successor –
Deliverance of thy brethren, those ten tribes
Whose offspring in his territory yet serve   375
In Habor, and among the Medes dispersed:
Ten sons of Jacob, two of Joseph, lost
Thus long from Israel, serving, as of old
Their fathers in the land of Egypt served,
This offer sets before thee to deliver.   380
These if from servitude thou shalt restore
To their inheritance, then, nor till then,
Thou on the throne of David in full glory,

358 opposite] opposed.
359] The hostility of the Jews to the Samaritans was proverbial (John iv. 9,
     vii. 48).
361–2] Although the peace between Rome and Parthia established by Augustus
     lasted until AD 58, the Romans had periodically prepared for war during
     the time of Jesus, and enmity between Rome and Parthia had previously
     been well established by the invasions of Sulla, Pompey, Crassus, and
     Antony.
364–8] 'Of late' is an exaggeration, and the captivity of Antigonus is a
     fabrication. Antigonus, the last member of the cadet branch of the
     Hasmonaean dynasty (see *PL* XII 353–8n.), supported the Parthian
     invasion of Judea in 40 BC and was made king. He then mutilated his uncle
     Hyrcanus II (whom Caesar had appointed ethnarch) to render him inelig-
     ible for priestly office, and gave him to the Parthians as a prisoner. Herod
     fled to Rome, where he was appointed King of Judea, and three years later
     re-captured Jerusalem, and deposed and crucified Antigonus. 'Maugre'
     means 'in spite of'.
373–8] David ruled all twelve tribes. After the death of Solomon in 933 BC the
     tribes of Judah and Benjamin attached themselves to Rehoboam, and the
     other ten tribes, including the 'two of Joseph' (Manasseh and Ephraim),
     followed Jeroboam, and in 721 BC were carried away to Assyria, and placed
     'in Halah and in Habor ... and in the cities of the Medes' (II Kings
     xviii. 11).

From Egypt to Euphrates and beyond,
Shalt reign, and Rome or Caesar not need fear.'   385
    To whom our Saviour answered thus, unmoved:
'Much ostentation vain of fleshly arm
And fragile arms, much instrument of war,
Long in preparing, soon to nothing brought,
Before mine eyes thou hast set; and in my ear   390
Vented much policy, and projects deep
Of enemies, of aids, battles, and leagues,
Plausible to the world, to me worth naught.
Means I must use, thou say'st; prediction else
Will unpredict, and fail me of the throne!   395
My time, I told thee (and that time for thee
Were better farthest off), is not yet come;
When that comes, think not thou to find me slack
On my part aught endeavouring, or to need
Thy politic maxims, or that cumbersome   400
Luggage of war there shown me – argument
Of human weakness rather than of strength.
My brethren, as thou call'st them, those ten tribes,
I must deliver, if I mean to reign
David's true heir, and his full sceptre sway   405
To just extent over all Israel's sons!
But whence to thee this zeal? Where was it then
For Israel, or for David, or his throne,
When thou stood'st up his tempter to the pride
Of numbering Israel – which cost the lives   410
Of threescore and ten thousand Israelites
By three days' pestilence? Such was thy zeal
To Israel then, the same that now to me.
As for those captive tribes, themselves were they
Who wrought their own captivity, fell off   415
From God to worship calves, the deities
Of Egypt, Baal next and Ashtaroth,
And all the idolatries of heathen round,
Besides their other worse than heathenish crimes;
Nor in the land of their captivity   420
Humbled themselves, or penitent besought

384] See I Kings iv. 21, where 'the river' is the Euphrates.
396–7] John vii. 6.
409–12] I Chron. xxi. 1–14.
414–19] The 'captive tribes' are the ten tribes in Assyria. Jeroboam erected
    calves of gold at Bethel and Dan in imitation of the gods of Egypt (I Kings
    xii. 28; cf. *PL* I 482–5 and notes). On Baal and Ashtaroth see *Nativity* 197–
    200 and notes, and cf. *PL* I 421–3.

The God of their forefathers, but so died
Impenitent, and left a race behind
Like to themselves, distinguishable scarce
From Gentiles, but by circumcision vain,   425
And God with idols in their worship joined.
Should I of these the liberty regard,
Who, freed, as to their ancient patrimony,
Unhumbled, unrepentant, unreformed,
Headlong would follow, and to their gods perhaps   430
Of Bethel and of Dan? No, let them serve
Their enemies who serve idols with God.
Yet he at length, time to himself best known,
Remembering Abraham, by some wondrous call
May bring them back, repentant and sincere,   435
And at their passing cleave the Assyrian flood,
While to their native land with joy they haste,
As the Red Sea and Jordan once he cleft,
When to the promised land their fathers passed.
To his due time and providence I leave them.'   440
   So spake Israel's true King, and to the fiend
Made answer meet, that made void all his wiles.
So fares it when with truth falsehood contends.

THE END OF THE THIRD BOOK

425] Rom. ii. 25.
431–2] Jer. v. 19.
436 Assyrian flood] Euphrates; see Isa. xi. 15–16.
438] Exod. xiv. 21–2, Joshua iii. 14–17.

BOOK IV

Perplexed and troubled at his bad success
The tempter stood, nor had what to reply,
Discovered in his fraud, thrown from his hope
So oft, and the persuasive rhetoric
That sleeked his tongue, and won so much on Eve,   5
So little here, nay lost; but Eve was Eve,
This far his over-match, who, self-deceived
And rash, beforehand had no better weighed
The strength he was to cope with, or his own.
But – as a man who had been matchless held   10
In cunning, over-reached where least he thought,
To salve his credit, and for very spite,
Still will be tempting him who foils him still,
And never cease, though to his shame the more;
Or as a swarm of flies in vintage-time,   15
About the wine-press where sweet must is poured,
Beat off, returns as oft with humming sound;
Or surging waves against a solid rock,
Though all to shivers dashed, the assault renew,
Vain battery, and in froth or bubbles end –   20
So Satan, whom repulse upon repulse
Met ever, and to shameful silence brought,
Yet gives not o'er, though desperate of success,
And his vain importunity pursues.
He brought our Saviour to the western side   25
Of that high mountain, whence he might behold
Another plain, long, but in breadth not wide,
Washed by the southern sea, and on the north
To equal length backed with a ridge of hills
That screened the fruits of the earth and seats of men   30
From cold Septentrion blasts; thence in the midst
Divided by a river, of whose banks

1 Perplexed] distressed.
  success] result.
15–17] *Iliad* ii 469–71, xvi 641–3, xvii 570–2.
18–20] *Iliad* xv 618–21, *Aeneid* vii 586–90.
27–33] The long and narrow plain of Lazio (Latium) lies south-west of the
    Apennines ('a ridge of hills'), which protect it from the north wind
    (Septentrion). The river is the Tiber, and the 'imperial city' Rome.

On each side an imperial city stood,
With towers and temples proudly elevate
On seven small hills, with palaces adorned,   35
Porches and theatres, baths, aqueducts,
Statues and trophies, and triumphal arcs,
Gardens and groves, presented to his eyes,
Above the height of mountains interposed –
By what strange parallax, or optic skill   40
Of vision, multiplied through air, or glass
Of telescope, were curious to enquire.
And now the tempter thus his silence broke:
  'The city which thou seest no other deem
Than great and glorious Rome, queen of the earth   45
So far renowned, and with the spoils enriched
Of nations; there the Capitol thou seest,
Above the rest lifting his stately head
On the Tarpeian rock, her citadel
Impregnable; and there Mount Palatine,   50
The imperial palace, compass huge, and high
The structure, skill of noblest architects,
With gilded battlements, conspicuous far,
Turrets and terraces, and glittering spires.
Many a fair edifice besides, more like   55
Houses of gods (so well I have disposed
My airy microscope) thou may'st behold
Outside and inside both, pillars and roofs,
Carved work, the hand of famed artificers
In cedar, marble, ivory, or gold.   60
Thence to the gates cast round thine eye, and see
What conflux issuing forth, or entering in:
Praetors, proconsuls to their provinces

40 parallax] difference of the apparent position of an object caused by an actual
      change of position of the point of observation.
47 Capitol] one of the 'seven small hills'.
49] The 'Tarpeian rock' is the steep cliff that surrounds much of the Capitoline
      hill. The citadel (*arx*) was on the northern summit of the hill, and the
      Temple of Jupiter on the southern summit.
50–4] The Palatine is another of Rome's seven hills. Milton's description of the
      'imperial palace' (presumably the Domus Tiberiana, on the west corner of
      the hill) is speculative: its location makes terraces possible, but Roman
      buildings did not have turrets and spires.
59 hand] handiwork.
63] Under Tiberius the election of the praetors (who then numbered about 14)
      was transferred to the Senate, who appointed them as civil magistrates.
      They sometimes acted as provincial governors. Under the emperors a
      proconsul was the governor of a senatorial province.

Hasting, or on return, in robes of state;
Lictors and rods, the ensigns of their power;   65
Legions and cohorts, turms of horse and wings;
Or embassies from regions far remote,
In various habits, on the Appian road,
Or on the Aemilian – some from farthest south,
Syene, and where the shadow both way falls,   70
Meroë, Nilotic isle, and, more to west,
The realm of Bocchus to the Blackmoor sea;
From the Asian kings (and Parthian among these),
From India and the golden Chersoness,
And utmost Indian isle Taprobane,   75
Dusk faces with white silken turbans wreathed;
From Gallia, Gades, and the British west;
Germans, and Scythians, and Sarmatians north
Beyond Danubius to the Tauric pool.
All nations now to Rome obedience pay –   80
To Rome's great emperor, whose wide domain,
In ample territory, wealth and power,
Civility of manners, arts and arms,
And long renown, thou justly may'st prefer
Before the Parthian; these two thrones except,   85

65] Lictors were officers attending upon magistrates; they carried bundles of
rods (*fasces*) before the magistrates as an emblem of their power.
66] There were ten cohorts in a legion, and a legion under the Empire numbered
about six thousand men. 'Turms' were troops of about thirty horsemen.
68–9] The chief Roman road to south Italy was the Via Appia, which ended at
Brindisi. The Via Aemelia ran from Rimini to Piacenza.
69–79] Syene (modern Aswan, in Egypt) was the southernmost limit of the
Roman Empire. The Island of Meroë is the region bounded on three sides
by the Nile, the Atbara, and the Blue Nile; as it lies between the Tropic of
Cancer and the Equator, shadows fall to the south in summer and the north
in winter. Bocchus was the king of ancient Mauretania (modern Morocco
and coastal Algeria, not modern Mauritania) at the time of the Jugurthine
War (111–106 BC); the 'Blackmoor sea' is the portion of the Mediterranean
off the coast of Mauretania. On 'golden Chersoness' see *PL* XI 392n. The
Taprobane described by ancient writers was identified in Milton's time with
either Ceylon or Sumatra. Gallia (Gaul) encompassed modern France and
Belgium, and parts of Holland, Germany, and Switzerland. Gades was the
Latin name for Cadiz. As Britain had not yet been conquered in the reign of
Tiberius, 'the British West' is probably Brittany, which was part of the
imperial province of Lugudunensis. The Scythians were a south Russian
tribe who by the time of Tiberius had been displaced by the Sarmatians, a
related tribe. Until Dacia was invaded in AD 101, the Danube (Danubius)
was the north-east frontier of the Empire. The Tauric pool is the Sea of
Azov, on the shores of which was the Bosporan Kingdom, the ruler of
which had been given his royal title by Tiberius.

The rest are barbarous, and scarce worth the sight,
Shared among petty kings too far removed;
These having shown thee, I have shown thee all
The kingdoms of the world, and all their glory.
This emperor hath no son, and now is old,   90
Old and lascivious, and from Rome retired
To Capreae, an island small but strong
On the Campanian shore, with purpose there
His horrid lusts in private to enjoy;
Committing to a wicked favourite   95
All public cares, and yet of him suspicious;
Hated of all, and hating; with what ease,
Endued with regal virtues as thou art,
Appearing, and beginning noble deeds,
Might'st thou expel this monster from his throne,   100
Now made a sty, and, in his place ascending,
A victor-people free from servile yoke!
And with my help thou may'st; to me the power
Is given, and by that right I give it thee.
Aim therefore at no less than all the world;   105
Aim at the highest; without the highest attained,
Will be for thee no sitting, or not long,
On David's throne, be prophesied what will.'
    To whom the Son of God, unmoved, replied:
'Nor doth this grandeur and majestic show   110
Of luxury, though called magnificence,
More than of arms before, allure mine eye,
Much less my mind; though thou should'st add to tell
Their sumptuous gluttonies, and gorgeous feasts
On citron tables or Atlantic stone   115
(For I have also heard, perhaps have read),
Their wines of Setia, Cales, and Falerne,
Chios and Crete, and how they quaff in gold,
Crystal, and myrrhine cups, embossed with gems

90–7] The emperor is Tiberius (42 BC–AD 37), whose sons – Drusus, Germanius
    (an adopted son), and an infant – were all dead by AD 23. He returned to
    Capri (Capreae) in AD 26. His 'wicked favourite' was Sejanus, who after
    being denounced by Tiberius was executed in AD 31. Stories of Tiberius'
    vice on Capri (recounted by Seutonius and Tacitus) lack serious evidence.
    He was indeed hated by the Romans, who welcomed the news of his death.
103–4] Luke iv. 6.
115] Citron is the wood of the highly-prized citrus tree; Atlantic means 'from
    the Atlas mountains'.
117–18] Wines from these three Italian districts (all south of Rome) and two
    Greek islands were all mentioned by Roman writers.
119] Ancient writers describe 'myrrhine cups' and bowls (*murrina vasa*), but
    the identity and provenance of myrrha were (and are) disputed.

And studs of pearl – to me should'st tell, who thirst   120
And hunger still; then embassies thou show'st
From nations far and nigh; what honour that,
But tedious waste of time, to sit and hear
So many hollow compliments and lies,
Outlandish flatteries! Then proceed'st to talk   125
Of the emperor, how easily subdued,
How gloriously; I shall, thou say'st, expel
A brutish monster: what if I withal
Expel a devil who first made him such?
Let his tormentor, Conscience, find him out;   130
For him I was not sent, nor yet to free
That people, victor once, now vile and base,
Deservedly made vassal – who, once just,
Frugal, and mild, and temperate, conquered well,
But govern ill the nations under yoke,   135
Peeling their provinces, exhausted all
By lust and rapine; first ambitious grown
Of triumph, that insulting vanity;
Then cruel, by their sports to blood inured
Of fighting beasts, and men to beasts exposed;   140
Luxurious by their wealth, and greedier still,
And from the daily scene effeminate.
What wise and valiant man would seek to free
These, thus degenerate, by themselves enslaved,
Or could of inward slaves make outward free?   145
Know therefore when my season comes to sit
On David's throne, it shall be like a tree
Spreading and overshadowing all the earth,
Or as a stone that shall to pieces dash
All monarchies besides throughout the world –   150
And of my kingdom there shall be no end;
Means there shall be to this, but what the means
Is not for thee to know, nor me to tell.'
     To whom the tempter, impudent, replied:
'I see all offers made by me how slight   155
Thou valuest, because offered, and reject'st;
Nothing will please the difficult and nice,
Or nothing more than still to contradict;

136 Peeling] plundering.
142 scene] stage performance, play.
147–8] Dan. iv. 10–12.
149–50] Dan. ii. 31–5.
151] Luke i. 33.
157 nice] fastidious, difficult to please.

On the other side I know also thou that I
On what I offer set as high esteem,   160
Nor what I part with mean to give for naught;
All these, which in a moment thou behold'st,
The kingdoms of the world, to thee I give –
For, given to me, I give to whom I please –
No trifle; yet with this reserve, not else,   165
On this condition, if thou wilt fall down,
And worship me as thy superior lord –
Easily done – and hold them all of me;
For what can less so great a gift deserve?'
    Whom thus our Saviour answered with disdain: 170
'I never liked thy talk, thy offers less,
Now both abhor, since thou hast dared to utter
The abominable terms, impious condition;
But I endure the time, till which expired
Thou hast permission on me. It is written,   175
The first of all commandments, "Thou shalt worship
The Lord thy God, and only him shalt serve";
And dar'st thou to the Son of God propound
To worship thee, accursed, now more accursed
For this attempt, bolder than that on Eve,   180
And more blasphémous? Which expect to rue.
The kingdoms of the world to thee were given,
Permitted rather, and by thee usurped;
Other donation none thou canst produce;
If given, by whom but by the King of kings,   185
God over all supreme? If given to thee,
By thee how fairly is the giver now
Repaid! But gratitude in thee is lost
Long since. Wert thou so void of fear or shame
As offer them to me, the Son of God –   190
To me my own, on such abhorred pact,
That I fall down and worship thee as God?
Get thee behind me; plain thou now appear'st
That Evil One, Satan for ever damned.'
    To whom the fiend with fear abashed replied: 195
'Be not so sore offended, Son of God –
Though sons of God both angels are and men –
If I to try whether in higher sort
Than these thou bear'st that title, have proposed
What both from men and angels I receive,   200
Tetrarchs of fire, air, flood, and on the earth,

201 Tetrarchs] Rulers of fourth parts (like Herod Antipas and his brother
    Philip, Luke iii. 1).

Nations besides from all the quartered winds –
God of this world invoked, and world beneath.
Who then thou art, whose coming is foretold
To me most fatal, me it most concerns.   205
The trial hath endamaged thee no way,
Rather more honour left and more esteem;
Me naught advantaged, missing what I aimed.
Therefore let pass, as they are transitory,
The kingdoms of this world; I shall no more   210
Advise thee; gain them as thou canst, or not.
And thou thyself seem'st otherwise inclined
Than to a worldly crown, addicted more
To contemplation and profound dispute;
As by that early action may be judged,   215
When, slipping from thy mother's eye, thou went'st
Alone into the Temple, there wast found
Among the gravest rabbis disputant
On points and questions fitting Moses' chair,
Teaching, not taught; the childhood shows the man,   220
As morning shows the day. Be famous, then,
By wisdom; as thy empire must extend,
So let extend thy mind o'er all the world
In knowledge: all things in it comprehend;
All knowledge is not couched in Moses' law,   225
The Pentateuch, or what the prophets wrote;
The Gentiles also know, and write, and teach
To admiration, led by nature's light;
And with the Gentiles much thou must converse,
Ruling them by persuasion, as thou mean'st;   230
Without their learning, how wilt thou with them,
Or they with thee, hold conversation meet?
How wilt thou reason with them, how refute
Their idolisms, traditions, paradoxes?
Error by his own arms is best evinced.   235
Look once more, ere we leave this specular mount,
Westward, much nearer by south-west; behold
Where on the Aegean shore a city stands,
Built nobly, pure the air and light the soil –

203] II Cor. iv. 4.
215–20] Luke ii. 41–50. On 'Moses' chair', from which the Law was expounded,
    see Exod. xviii. 13–16 and Matt. xxiii. 2.
226 Pentateuch] the first five books of the O.T.
228 To admiration] admirably.
235 evinced] overcome.
236 specular] cf. PL XII 588–9n.

Athens, the eye of Greece, mother of arts   240
And eloquence, native to famous wits
Or hospitable, in her sweet recess,
City or suburban, studious walks and shades;
See there the olive-grove of Academe,
Plato's retirement, where the Attic bird   245
Trills her thick-warbled notes the summer long;
There, flowery hill, Hymettus, with the sound
Of bees' industrious murmur, oft invites
To studious musing; there Ilissus rolls
His whispering stream; within the walls then view   250
The schools of ancient sages – his who bred
Great Alexander to subdue the world,
Lyceum there; and painted Stoa next:
There thou shalt hear and learn the secret power
Of harmony, in tones and numbers hit   255
By voice or hand, and various-measured verse,
Aeolian charms and Dorian lyric odes,
And his who gave them breath, but higher sung,
Blind Melesigenes, thence Homer called,
Whose poem Phoebus challenged for his own.   260
Thence what the lofty grave tragedians taught

240] Athens and Sparta had been described in antiquity as the eyes of Greece; here 'eye' means 'the seat of intelligence or light'.

244–6] Plato established his school in the Academy, a wooded park in a suburb of Athens. Nearby was Colonus, which according to Sophocles, who was born there, was the home of many nightingales (*Oedipus at Colonus* 671).

247–50] Hymettus is a range of hills south-east of Athens; Hymettus honey was famed for its pale colour and sweet flavour. Bees were said to have fed the infant Plato with honey. Plato's *Phaedrus* is set beside the Ilissus, a small river which rises in Hymettus.

250–3] Alexander's tutor was Aristotle, who founded his school, the Lyceum, in a park north-east of Athens (not 'within the walls'). The *Stoa Poikile* ('painted Stoa') was a covered colonnade on the north side of the Athenian market-place; Zeno and his followers taught in this stoa, and so were called Stoics.

257] The lyric poems of Sappho and Alcaeus are written in the Aeolian dialect (Lesbos, where both were born, belonged to the Aeolians), and are here called 'charms' in imitation of Latin *carmen* (song). Pindar wrote in the Dorian dialect.

259] Melesigenes is an Homeric epithet commonly used in the ancient lives of Homer; it affirms that he was born near the river Meles (near Smyrna, modern Izmir); 'thence' refers to 'Blind', for according to an ancient popular etymology Homer (ὅμηρος) was the Cumean word for 'blind'.

260] See the epigram in *Greek Anthology* ix. 455, in which Apollo/Phoebus claims authorship of Homer's poems.

In chorus or iambic, teachers best
Of moral prudence, with delight received
In brief sententious precepts, while they treat
Of fate, and chance, and change in human life, 265
High actions and high passions best describing;
Thence to the famous orators repair,
Those ancient whose resistless eloquence
Wielded at will that fierce democraty,
Shook the Arsenal, and fulmined over Greece 270
To Macedon and Artaxerxes' throne;
To sage philosophy next lend thine ear,
From heaven descended to the low-roofed house
Of Socrates – see there his tenement –
Whom, well inspired, the oracle pronounced 275
Wisest of men; from whose mouth issued forth
Mellifluous streams that watered all the schools
Of Academics old and new, with those
Surnamed Peripatetics, and the sect
Epicurean, and the Stoic severe; 280

262] Iambic refers to the metre of the dialogue in Greek tragedy (iambic trimeter acatalectic); the chorus is written in various metres. Cf. Milton's preface to SA.

264] Probably refers specifically to the style of Euripides, which was said by Quintilian (X. i. 68) to be *sententiis densus* (dense with philosophical aphorisms).

270] The naval dockyard at Pireus was called the Arsenal, which Demosthenes could be said to have shaken when on his advice public funds were directed from its construction to the war against Philip of Macedon; there was a large explosion at the *Arsenale* in Venice on 15 September 1569; 'fulmined' means 'sent forth lightning and thunder' (cf. Aristophanes' comment on Pericles in *Archarnians* 530–1).

273–4] According to Cicero, Socrates was the first to call philosophy down from heaven (*Tusculan Disputations* V. iv. 10). He is said to have a small house (οἰκίδιον) in Aristophanes, *Clouds* 92.

275–6] Plato, *Apology* 21.

276–7] On Socrates as the fountain of philosophy see Quintilian I. x. 13.

278] According to an ancient distinction Academic philosophy had three phases: Plato founded the Old Academy, Arcesilias the Middle Academy, and Carneades the New Academy.

279–80] Peripatetics were Aristotelians, so called from the covered walk (περίπατος) in the buildings which Theophrastus provided for the school. The 'sect Epicurean' descended from Socrates through his friend Aristippus, whose grandson (also Aristippus) founded the Cyrenaics, the intellectual pioneers of Epicureanism. Similarly, the Stoics descended from Socrates through his friend Aristhenes, whose Cynic sect influenced Stoic doctrine. See *Comus* 707–8n.

These here revolve, or, as thou likest, at home,
Till time mature thee to a kingdom's weight;
These rules will render thee a king complete
Within thyself, much more with empire joined.'
    To whom our Saviour sagely thus replied: 285
'Think not but that I know these things; or, think
I know them not, not therefore am I short
Of knowing what I ought: he who receives
Light from above, from the fountain of light,
No other doctrine needs, though granted true;   290
But these are false, or little else but dreams,
Conjectures, fancies, built on nothing firm.
The first and wisest of them all professed
To know this only, that he nothing knew;
The next to fabling fell and smooth conceits;   295
A third sort doubted all things, though plain sense;
Others in virtue placed felicity,
But virtue joined with riches and long life;
In corporal pleasure he, and careless ease;
The Stoic last in philosophic pride,   300
By him called virtue; and his virtuous man,
Wise, perfect in himself, and all possessing,
Equal to God, oft shames not to prefer,
As fearing God nor man, contemning all
Wealth, pleasure, pain or torment, death and life –   305
Which, when he lists, he leaves, or boasts he can;
For all his tedious talk is but vain boast,
Or subtle shifts conviction to evade.
Alas, what can they teach, and not mislead,
Ignorant of themselves, of God much more,   310
And how the world began, and how man fell,
Degraded by himself, on grace depending?
Much of the soul they talk, but all awry,
And in themselves seek virtue, and to themselves
All glory arrogate, to God give none;   315
Rather accuse him under usual names,

293–4 first] Socrates. See Plato, *Apology* 21–3.
295 next] Plato.
296 third sort] the Sceptics, founded by Pyrrhon. A form of scepticism was also
    espoused by Arcesilias and Carneades (l. 278n.).
297–8 Others] Aristotle and the Peripatetics.
299 he] Epicurus, who was reviled by patristic writers because he taught that
    man is mortal, that the cosmos is a result of accident, that there is no
    providential god, and that the criterion of the good life is pleasure.
300–9] Cf. *PL* II 564n.

Fortune and Fate, as one regardless quite
Of mortal things. Who, therefore, seeks in these
True wisdom finds her not, or, by delusion
Far worse, her false resemblance only meets,   320
An empty cloud. However, many books,
Wise men have said, are wearisome; who reads
Incessantly, and to his reading brings not
A spirit and judgement equal or superior,
(And what he brings what needs he elsewhere seek?)   325
Uncertain and unsettled still remains,
Deep-versed in books and shallow in himself,
Crude or intoxicate, collecting toys
And trifles for choice matters, worth a sponge,
As children gathering pebbles on the shore.   330
Or, if I would delight my private hours
With music or with poem, where so soon
As in our native language can I find
That solace? All our Law and story strewed
With hymns, our Psalms with artful terms inscribed,   335
Our Hebrew songs and harps, in Babylon
That pleased so well our victor's ear, declare
That rather Greece from us these arts derived –
Ill imitated while they loudest sing
The vices of their deities, and their own,   340
In fable, hymn, or song, so personating
Their gods ridiculous, and themselves past shame.
Remove their swelling epithets, thick-laid
As varnish on a harlot's cheek, the rest,
Thin-sown with aught of profit or delight,   345
Will far be found unworthy to compare
With Zion's songs, to all true tastes excelling,
Where God is praised aright and godlike men,
The Holiest of Holies and his saints –

319–21] Cf. *Passion* 56n.

321–2] Eccles. xii. 12.

328 Crude] unable to digest.

329 worth a sponge] means both 'worth very little' and 'worthy to be
obliterated'.

334 story] the historical books of the O.T.

335 artful terms] probably refers to the rubrics in the Massoretic and LXX
texts of the Psalms.

336–7] Psalm cxxxvii. 1–3.

338] The idea that the arts were original to the Jews, who while in bondage had
passed them on to the Egyptians, who in turn bequeathed them to the
Greeks, was a Patristic and Renaissance commonplace.

347] Cf. *PL* III 30n.

Such are from God inspired, not such from thee –   350
Unless where moral virtue is expressed
By light of nature, not in all quite lost.
Their orators thou then extoll'st as those
The top of eloquence – statists indeed,
And lovers of their country, as may seem;   355
But herein to our prophets far beneath,
As men divinely taught, and better teaching
The solid rules of civil government,
In their majestic, unaffected style,
Than all the oratory of Greece and Rome.   360
In them is plainest taught, and easiest learnt,
What makes a nation happy, and keeps it so,
What ruins kingdoms, and lays cities flat;
These only, with our Law, best form a king.'
    So spake the Son of God; but Satan, now   365
Quite at a loss, for all his darts were spent,
Thus to our Saviour, with stern brow, replied:
    'Since neither wealth nor honour, arms nor arts,
Kingdom nor empire, pleases thee, nor aught
By me proposed in life contemplative   370
Or active, tended on by glory or fame,
What dost thou in this world? The wilderness
For thee is fittest place: I found thee there,
And thither will return thee; yet remember
What I foretell thee: soon thou shalt have cause   375
To wish thou never hadst rejected, thus
Nicely or cautiously, my offered aid,
Which would have set thee in short time with ease
On David's throne, or throne of all the world,
Now at full age, fulness of time, thy season,   380
When prophecies of thee are best fulfilled.
Now, contrary – if I read aught in heaven,
Or heaven write aught of fate – by what the stars
Voluminous, or single characters
In their conjunction met, give me to spell,   385
Sorrows and labours, opposition, hate,
Attends thee; scorns, reproaches, injuries,

---

351 Unless] refers back to 'unworthy' (l. 346).
354 statists] statesmen.
384] an analogy to a large book ('voluminous') and to single letters ('characters') in the book.
385] Conjunction, the apparent proximity of two heavenly bodies, is an unfavourable sign in astrology. Cf. *PL* X 661n. 'Spell' means 'interpret' (cf. *Penseroso* 170–1).

Violence and stripes, and, lastly, cruel death;
A kingdom they portend thee, but what kingdom,
Real or allegoric, I discern not;   390
Nor when, eternal sure – as without end,
Without beginning; for no date prefixed
Directs me in the starry rubric set.'
      So saying, he took (for still he knew his power
Not yet expired), and to the wilderness   395
Brought back the Son of God, and left him there,
Feigning to disappear. Darkness now rose,
As daylight sunk, and brought in louring Night,
Her shadowy offspring, unsubstantial both,
Privation mere of light and absent day.   400
Our Saviour, meek, and with untroubled mind
After his airy jaunt, though hurried sore,
Hungry and cold, betook him to his rest,
Wherever, under some concourse of shades,
Whose branching arms thick-intertwined might shield 405
From dews and damps of night his sheltered head;
But, sheltered, slept in vain; for at his head
The tempter watched, and soon with ugly dreams
Disturbed his sleep; and either tropic now
Gan thunder, and both ends of heaven; the clouds   410
From many a horrid rift abortive poured
Fierce rain with lightning mixed, water with fire
In ruin reconciled; nor slept the winds
Within their stony caves, but rushed abroad
From the four hinges of the world, and fell   415
On the vexed wilderness, whose tallest pines,
Though rooted deep as high, and sturdiest oaks,
Bowed their stiff necks, loaden with stormy blasts,
Or torn up sheer; ill wast thou shrouded then,
O patient Son of God, yet only stood'st   420
Unshaken; nor yet stayed the terror there:
Infernal ghosts and hellish furies round
Environed thee; some howled, some yelled, some shrieked,

---

393 rubric] a title or caption written in red letters.
402 jaunt] fatiguing journey.
409–10] 'Either tropic' means north (Cancer) and south (Capricorn); the 'ends
    of heaven' are presumably east and west.
411 abortive] probably means 'unnaturally premature'.
412–13] Cf. Aeschylus, *Agamemnon* 650–1; 'ruin' means both 'falling' and
    'destruction'.
415 hinges] cardinal points (Latin *cardo*, hinge).
419 shrouded] sheltered.

Some bent at thee their fiery darts, while thou
Sat'st unappalled in calm and sinless peace.   425
Thus passed the night so foul, till Morning fair
Came forth with pilgrim steps, in amice grey;
Who with her radiant finger stilled the roar
Of thunder, chased the clouds, and laid the winds,
And grisly spectres, which the fiend had raised   430
To tempt the Son of God with terrors dire.
And now the sun with more effectual beams
Had cheered the face of earth, and dried the wet
From drooping plant, or dropping tree; the birds,
Who all things now behold more fresh and green,   435
After a night of storm so ruinous,
Cleared up their choicest notes in bush and spray,
To gratulate the sweet return of morn;
Nor yet, amidst this joy and brightest morn,
Was absent, after all his mischief done,   440
The prince of darkness; glad would also seem
Of this fair change, and to our Saviour came;
Yet with no new device – they all were spent –
Rather by this his last affront resolved,
Desperate of better course, to vent his rage   445
And mad despite to be so oft repelled,
Him walking on a sunny hill he found,
Backed on the north and west by a thick wood;
Out of the wood he starts in wonted shape,
And in a careless mood thus to him said: 450
    'Fair morning yet betides thee, Son of God,
After a dismal night; I heard the rack,
As earth and sky would mingle; but myself
Was distant; and these flaws, though mortals fear them,
As dangerous to the pillared frame of heaven,   455
Or to the earth's dark basis underneath,
Are to the main as inconsiderable
And harmless, if not wholesome, as a sneeze
To man's less universe, and soon are gone;
Yet, as being ofttimes noxious where they light   460
On man, beast, plant, wasteful and turbulent,

427 amice] an article of costume (variously a cap, hood, or cape) made of, or
    lined with, grey fur.
452 rack] destruction (as in 'rack and ruin').
453] *Aeneid* i 133–4.
454 flaws] squalls.
455] Cf. *Comus* 598n.
457 main] universe.

Like turbulencies in the affairs of men,
Over whose heads they roar, and seem to point,
They oft fore-signify and threaten ill:
This tempest at this desert most was bent;   465
Of men at thee, for only thou here dwell'st.
Did I not tell thee, if thou didst reject
The perfect season offered with my aid
To win thy destined seat, but wilt prolong
All to the push of fate, pursue thy way   470
Of gaining David's throne no man knows when –
For both the when and how is nowhere told –
Thou shalt be what thou art ordained, no doubt;
For angels have proclaimed it, but concealing
The time and means: each act is rightliest done   475
Not when it must, but when it may be best.
If thou observe not this, be sure to find
What I foretold thee – many a hard assay
Of dangers, and adversities, and pains,
Ere thou of Israel's sceptre get fast hold;   480
Whereof the ominous night that closed thee round,
So many terrors, voices, prodigies,
May warn thee, as a sure foregoing sign.'
    So talked he, while the Son of God went on,
And stayed not, but in brief him answered thus: 485
    'Me worse than wet thou find'st not; other harm
Those terrors which thou speak'st of did me none;
I never feared they could, though noising loud
And threatening nigh; what they can do as signs
Betokening or ill-boding I contemn   490
As false portents, not sent from God, but thee;
Who, knowing I shall reign past thy preventing,
Obtrud'st thy offered aid, that I, accepting,
At least might seem to hold all power of thee,
Ambitious Spirit, and would'st be thought my god;   495
And storm'st, refused, thinking to terrify
Me to thy will; desist – thou art discerned,
And toil'st in vain – nor me in vain molest.'
    To whom the fiend, now swoll'n with rage, replied:
'Then hear, O Son of David, virgin-born,   500
For Son of God to me is yet in doubt;
Of the Messiah I have heard foretold
By all the prophets; of thy birth, at length
Announced by Gabriel, with the first I knew,
And of the angelic song in Bethlehem field,   505
On thy birth-night, that sung thee Saviour born.
From that time seldom have I ceased to eye

Thy infancy, thy childhood, and thy youth,
Thy manhood last, though yet in private bred;
Till, at the ford of Jordan, whither all   510
Flocked to the Baptist, I among the rest –
Though not to be baptised – by voice from heaven
Heard thee pronounced the Son of God beloved.
Thenceforth I thought thee worth my nearer view
And narrower scrutiny, that I might learn   515
In what degree or meaning thou art called
The Son of God, which bears no single sense;
The son of God I also am, or was;
And, if I was, I am; relation stands:
All men are sons of God; yet thee I thought   520
In some respect far higher so declared.
Therefore I watched thy footsteps from that hour,
And followed thee still on to this waste wild,
Where, by all best conjectures, I collect
Thou art to be my fatal enemy.   525
Good reason, then, if I beforehand seek
To understand my adversary, who
And what he is; his wisdom, power, intent;
By parle or composition, truce or league,
To win him, or win from him what I can.   530
And opportunity I here have had
To try thee, sift thee, and confess have found thee
Proof against all temptation, as a rock
Of adamant and as a centre, firm
To the utmost of mere man both wise and good,   535
Not more; for honours, riches, kingdoms, glory,
Have been before contemned, and may again:
Therefore, to know what more thou art than man,
Worth naming Son of God by voice from heaven,
Another method I must now begin.'   540
   So saying, he caught him up, and, without wing
Of hippogrif, bore through the air sublime,
Over the wilderness and o'er the plain,
Till underneath them fair Jerusalem,
The holy city, lifted high her towers,   545
And higher yet the glorious Temple reared

518–20] See Job i. 6, and Milton's translation of Psalm lxxxii. 6.
524 collect] infer.
529 composition] truce.
542 hippogrif] a fabulous creature, half horse ('hippo' means 'horse'), half
   griffin. Ariosto's *ippogrifo* carries his heroes on their journeys.
546–8] Milton draws on Josephus (*Jewish War* V. v. 6) for his description of the
   temple that Herod the Great built.

Her pile, far off appearing like a mount
Of alabaster, topped with golden spires:
There, on the highest pinnacle, he set
The Son of God, and added thus in scorn: 550
     'There stand, if thou wilt stand; to stand upright
Will ask thee skill; I to thy Father's house
Have brought thee, and highest placed: highest is best;
Now show thy progeny; if not to stand,
Cast thyself down; safely, if Son of God;   555
For it is written, "He will give command
Concerning thee to his angels; in their hands
They shall uplift thee, lest at any time
Thou chance to dash thy foot against a stone." '
     To whom thus Jesus: 'Also it is written,   560
"Tempt not the Lord thy God";' he said, and stood.
But Satan, smitten with amazement, fell;
As when Earth's son, Antaeus (to compare
Small things with greatest), in Irassa strove
With Jove's Alcides, and, oft foiled, still rose,   565
Receiving from his mother earth new strength,
Fresh from his fall, and fiercer grapple joined,
Throttled at length in the air expired and fell,
So, after many a foil, the Tempter proud,
Renewing fresh assaults, amidst his pride   570
Fell whence he stood to see his victor fall.
And as that Theban monster that proposed
Her riddle, and him, who solved it not, devoured,
That once found out and solved, for grief and spite
Cast herself headlong from the Ismenian steep,   575
So, struck with dread and anguish, fell the fiend,
And to his crew, that sat consulting, brought
Joyless triumphals of his hoped success,
Ruin, and desperation, and dismay,
Who durst so proudly tempt the Son of God.   580

549] The meaning of 'pinnacle' (πτερύγιον, Vulgate *pinnaculum* and *pinna*) in
   Matt. iv. 5 and Luke iv. 9 was (and is) disputed; in Milton's time it was
   variously identified as a parapet, the ridge of the roof, the flat roof, a spire,
   etc.

563–8] Antacus was a giant who when wrestling renewed his strength by
   touching his mother Gaea (the earth). Hercules was the son of Zeus and
   Alceme (hence 'Jove's'), whose husband Amphitryon was the son of
   Alceaeus (hence 'Alcides'). At Irassa, in Libya, Hercules lifted Antaeus off
   the ground and strangled him.

572–5] The Theban monster is the Sphinx, who leapt to her death from the
   acropolis at Thebes ('Ismenian steep', so called from the river Ismenus)
   after Oedipus answered her riddle.

578 triumphals] tokens of success.

So Satan fell; and straight a fiery globe
Of angels on full sail of wing flew nigh,
Who on their plumy vans received him soft
From his uneasy station, and upbore,
As on a floating couch, through the blithe air;   585
Then, in a flowery valley, set him down
On a green bank, and set before him spread
A table of celestial food, divine
Ambrosial fruits fetched from the tree of life,
And from the fount of life ambrosial drink,   590
That soon refreshed him wearied, and repaired
What hunger, if aught hunger, had impaired,
Or thirst; and, as he fed, angelic choirs
Sung heavenly anthems of his victory
Over temptation and the tempter proud: 595
　'True image of the Father, whether throned
In the bosom of bliss, and light of light
Conceiving, or, remote from heaven, enshrined
In fleshy tabernacle and human form,
Wandering the wilderness – whatever place,   600
Habit, or state, or motion, still expressing
The Son of God, with godlike force endued
Against the attempter of thy Father's throne
And thief of Paradise; him long of old
Thou didst debel, and down from heaven cast   605
With all his army; now thou hast avenged
Supplanted Adam, and, by vanquishing
Temptation, has regained lost Paradise,
And frustrated the conquest fraudulent;
He never more henceforth will dare set foot   610
In Paradise to tempt; his snares are broke:
For, though that seat of earthly bliss be failed,
A fairer Paradise is founded now
For Adam and his chosen sons, whom thou,
A Saviour, art come down to reinstall;   615
Where they shall dwell secure, when time shall be,
Of tempter and temptation without fear.
But thou, infernal serpent, shalt not long
Rule in the clouds; like an autumnal star,

581 globe] used in the Latin sense of a throng.
583 vans] fans, i.e. wings.
589] Gen. ii. 9, Rev. xxii. 2, 14. 'Ambrosial' here means 'heavenly' and
　'fragrant'.
605 debel] vanquish, expel by force of arms.
611] Psalm cxxiv. 7.
619 autumnal star] a meteor or comet. Cf. *PL* II 708–11.

Or lightning, thou shalt fall from heaven, trod down   620
Under his feet; for proof, ere this thou feel'st
Thy wound – yet not thy last and deadliest wound –
By this repulse received, and hold'st in hell
No triumph; in all her gates Abaddon rues
Thy bold attempt; hereafter learn with awe   625
To dread the Son of God: he, all unarmed,
Shall chase thee, with the terror of his voice,
From thy demoniac holds, possession foul –
Thee and thy legions; yelling they shall fly,
And beg to hide them in a herd of swine,   630
Lest he command them down into the deep,
Bound, and to torment sent before their time.
Hail, Son of the Most High, heir of both worlds,
Queller of Satan; on thy glorious work
Now enter, and begin to save mankind.'   635
     Thus they the Son of God, our Saviour meek,
Sung victor, and, from heavenly feast refreshed,
Brought on his way with joy; he, unobserved,
Home to his mother's house private returned.

620–1] Gen. iii. 15, Mal. iv. 3, Luke x. 18, and Rom. xvi. 20 (on which see *PL* X 189–90n.).

624 Abaddon] In his translation of Psalm lxxxviii. l. 47 Milton translates this Hebrew word as 'perdition'. Elsewhere it refers to the destruction associated with Sheol (Job xxvi. 6, Prov. xv. 11, xxvii. 20) and with death (Job xxxviii. 22). Cf. Rev. ix. 11.

628] Rev. xviii. 2.

630–2] Matt. viii. 28–33.

636] Matt. xi. 29.